Cambridge Studies in Early Modern British History

CENTRAL GOVERNMENT AND THE LOCALITIES: HAMPSHIRE 1649–1689

Cambridge Studies in Early Modern British History

Series editors

ANTHONY FLETCHER
Professor of Modern History, University of Durham

JOHN GUY
Reader in British History, University of Bristol

and JOHN MORRILL
*Lecturer in History, University of Cambridge, and
Fellow and Tutor of Selwyn College*

This is a new series of monography and studies covering many aspects of the history of the British Isles between the late fifteenth century and the early eighteenth century. It will include the work of established scholars and pioneering work by a new generation of scholars. It will include both reviews and revisions of major topics and books which open up new historical terrain or which reveal startling new perspectives on familiar subjects. It is envisaged that all the volumes will set detailed research into broader perspectives and the books are intended for the use of students as well as of their teachers.

Titles in the series

CENTRAL GOVERNMENT AND THE LOCALITIES: HAMPSHIRE 1649–1689

ANDREW M. COLEBY

University of Sheffield

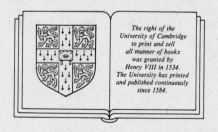

The right of the
University of Cambridge
to print and sell
all manner of books
was granted by
Henry VIII in 1534.
The University has printed
and published continuously
since 1584.

CAMBRIDGE UNIVERSITY PRESS

Cambridge

New York   New Rochelle   Melbourne   Sydney

Published by the Press Syndicate of the University of Cambridge
The Pitt Building, Trumpington Street, Cambridge CB2 1RP
32 East 57th Street, New York, NY 10022, USA
10 Stamford Road, Oakleigh, Melbourne 3166, Australia

First published 1987

Printed in Great Britain at the University Press, Cambridge

British Library cataloguing in publication data

Coleby, Andrew M.
Central government and the localities:
Hampshire 1649–1689. – (Cambridge studies
in early modern British history).
1. Local government – England – Hampshire
– History – 17th century 2. Hampshire –
Politics and government
I. Title
352.0422'7   JS3325.H35

Library of Congress cataloguing in publication data

Coleby, Andrew M.
Central government and the localities.
(Cambridge studies in early modern British history)
Bibliography.
Includes index.
1. Hampshire – Politics and government.
2. Central-local government relations – England – Hampshire
– History – 17th century. 3. Local government – England –
Hampshire – History – 17th century. 4. County government –
England – History – 17th century. 5. Great Britain –
Politics and government – 1649–1660. 6. Great Britain –
Politics and government – 1660–1688. I. Title.
II. Series.
JS3325.H355C65   1987   320.9422'7   87–18270

ISBN 0 521 32979 5

For my mother and father

CONTENTS

MAPS

ACKNOWLEDGEMENTS

The research upon which this book is based has received support and encouragement from numerous quarters. On a material level, I am grateful to the Department of Education and Science for granting me a major state studentship while I was working for my doctorate at Oxford. The Rector and Fellows of Lincoln College, Oxford and the Board of Management of the Amy Mary Preston Read Scholarship elected me to various senior scholarships for parts of this period. Finally the thesis was completed and presented during my tenure of the De Velling Willis Research Fellowship in the Faculty of Arts in the University of Sheffield. I am grateful to all these bodies for their generosity.

I am also indebted to the owners and custodians of the various manuscript collections, upon which I have drawn for my research. Quotations from the Coventry papers at Longleat House are made with the permission of the Marquess of Bath. I am grateful to Lady Anne Bentinck, Major Ralph B. Verney, Mr J. L. Jervoise, the Warden and Fellows of All Souls College, Oxford, Test Valley Borough Council, the Trustees of Carisbrooke Castle Museum in the Isle of Wight and Mr James Hoyle, the Borough Solicitor of Christchurch (now in Dorset) for the use of manuscripts belonging to them.

I would also like to thank Mr Norman Barber, Mr David Carter and Drs P. J. Challinor, E. Davies, J. D. Eames, P. G. I. Gaunt, W. N. Hammond, Jack Jones, H. M. Reece, A. B. Rosen, John Taylor, Anne Whiteman and J. R. Williams for permission to refer to their theses and dissertations in print, and the libraries of the Universities of London and Southampton for permission to cite theses in their custody.

My doctoral research was supervised by Dr Anne Whiteman. One is hard put to devise an original prefatory tribute to her, as she has deservedly received so many over the years. But let me simply state that Anne has been a marvellously sympathetic, encouraging and business-like supervisor over several years. My debt to her is immeasurable.

I have many other debts of a scholarly nature, some of which I shall attempt to list here. At Oxford, I am grateful to Dr Blair Worden for pointing me in the direction of Anne as a possible supervisor, and for the kind interest he has shown in my research over the years. I also gained greatly from the informal research seminar which he and Anne jointly ran and from the contributions of my fellow students at its meetings. Through it I got to know Dr Ronald Hutton of Bristol University, who has been very encouraging and helpful to me in my research. The examiners of my Oxford thesis, Dr Gerald Aylmer and Dr John Morrill first recommended that it should be published and made several useful suggestions as to how it might be improved. I would like to thank them both very warmly.

I have also been extremely fortunate in my colleagues in the Department of History at Sheffield University, who have made me very welcome. Anthony Fletcher has taken a particular interest in my work and has read this book at several stages in its production and has made some valuable criticisms. My fellow research students at Sheffield have also been stimulating company at seminars and elsewhere. Cheryl Keen in particular has helped to shake some of my more facile assumptions about party identity in the later seventeenth century.

Outside the world of professional historians, I would like to thank Mr Norman Barber and Mr Derek Hall, who helped with innumerable points relating chiefly to Cromwellian Hampshire and its notables. With their wide learning and professionalism, they belie the traditional and now fortunately fading image of the local historian. Needless to say, the interpretations and imperfections contained in this book remain distinctly and obstinately my own.

I have been helped by the kind co-operation of the staff of the Bodleian Library, the British Library, the Carisbrooke Castle Museum, the Hampshire County Library and County Record Office, the Isle of Wight County Record Office, the Public Record Office, the Southampton Record Office, the Staffordshire County Record Office and of Dr Williams' Library.

I have received much hospitality in the course of my research. Amongst those who deserve particular mention are Dr Steve Gunn, of Merton College, Oxford, Brian Lyndon of Southampton, my brother and sister-in-law and my sister. Their generosity has been much appreciated. I completed my research while living in the house of Peter Burt in Sheffield. His forbearance and reluctance to take this historian or his subject too seriously have been most welcome.

The dedication to my parents which this book carries is no empty filial piety or traditional formality. In typing and proof-reading both my Oxford thesis and the typescript of this book my mother and father have gone way beyond the normal call of parental duty. I am very grateful to them for their labours and their encouragement and support. The present work would never have appeared without their cheerful efforts.

DATING AND STYLE

Dating is in Old Style, except that the year is taken to begin on 1 January. In quotations from original sources, the spelling has largely been left unchanged.

ABBREVIATIONS

Repositories

Bodl.	Bodleian Library, Oxford
Brit. Lib.	British Library
H.C.R.O.	Hampshire County Record Office
H.L.R.O.	House of Lords Record Office
I.W.C.R.O.	Isle of Wight County Record Office
P.R.O.	Public Record Office
S.C.R.O.	Southampton City Record Office

Works cited

B.I.H.R.	*Bulletin of the Institute of Historical Research*
Cal.Clar.S.P.	*Calendar of the Clarendon State Papers*
C.J.	*House of Commons Journal*
Cal.S.P.Dom.	*Calendar of the State Papers Domestic*
Cal.Treas.Bks.	*Calendar of the Treasury Books*
D.N.B.	*Dictionary of National Biography*
E.H.R.	*English Historical Review*
F. & R.	C. H. Firth and R. S. Rait (eds.), *Acts and Ordinances of the Interregnum 1642–60* (3 vols., London, 1911)
H.C.	B. D. Henning (ed.), *The House of Commons 1660–1690* (3 vols., History of Parliament Trust, 1983)
H.J.	*Historical Journal*
Hist. MSS Comm.	*Historical Manuscripts Commission*
L.J.	*House of Lords Journal*
S.R.	*Statutes of the Realm*
Th.S.P.	*Thurloe State Papers*
T.R.H.S.	*Transactions of the Royal Historical Society*

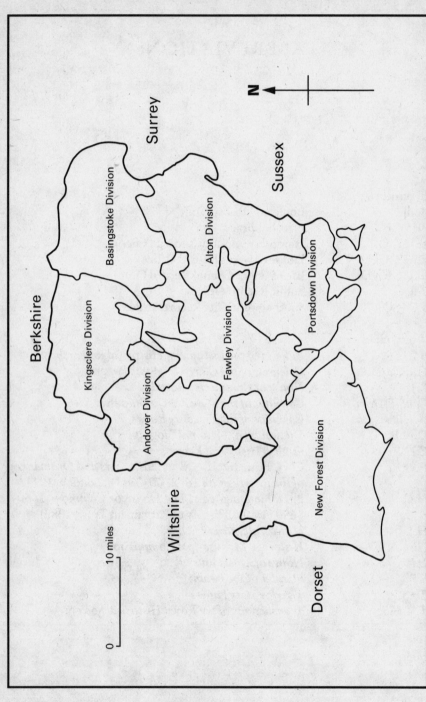

Map 1. The administrative structure of mainland Hampshire in the seventeenth century, showing divisions.

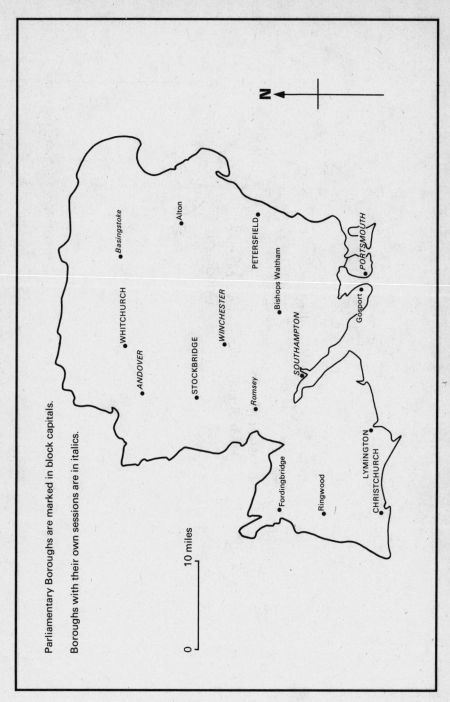

Parliamentary Boroughs are marked in block capitals.

Boroughs with their own sessions are in italics.

N

Basingstoke

Alton

WHITCHURCH

PETERSFIELD

ANDOVER

WINCHESTER

Bishops Waltham

STOCKBRIDGE

PORTSMOUTH

Romsey

SOUTHAMPTON

Gosport

Fordingbridge

LYMINGTON

Ringwood

CHRISTCHURCH

0   10 miles

Map 2. Parliamentary boroughs (on the mainland) and other places mentioned in the text.

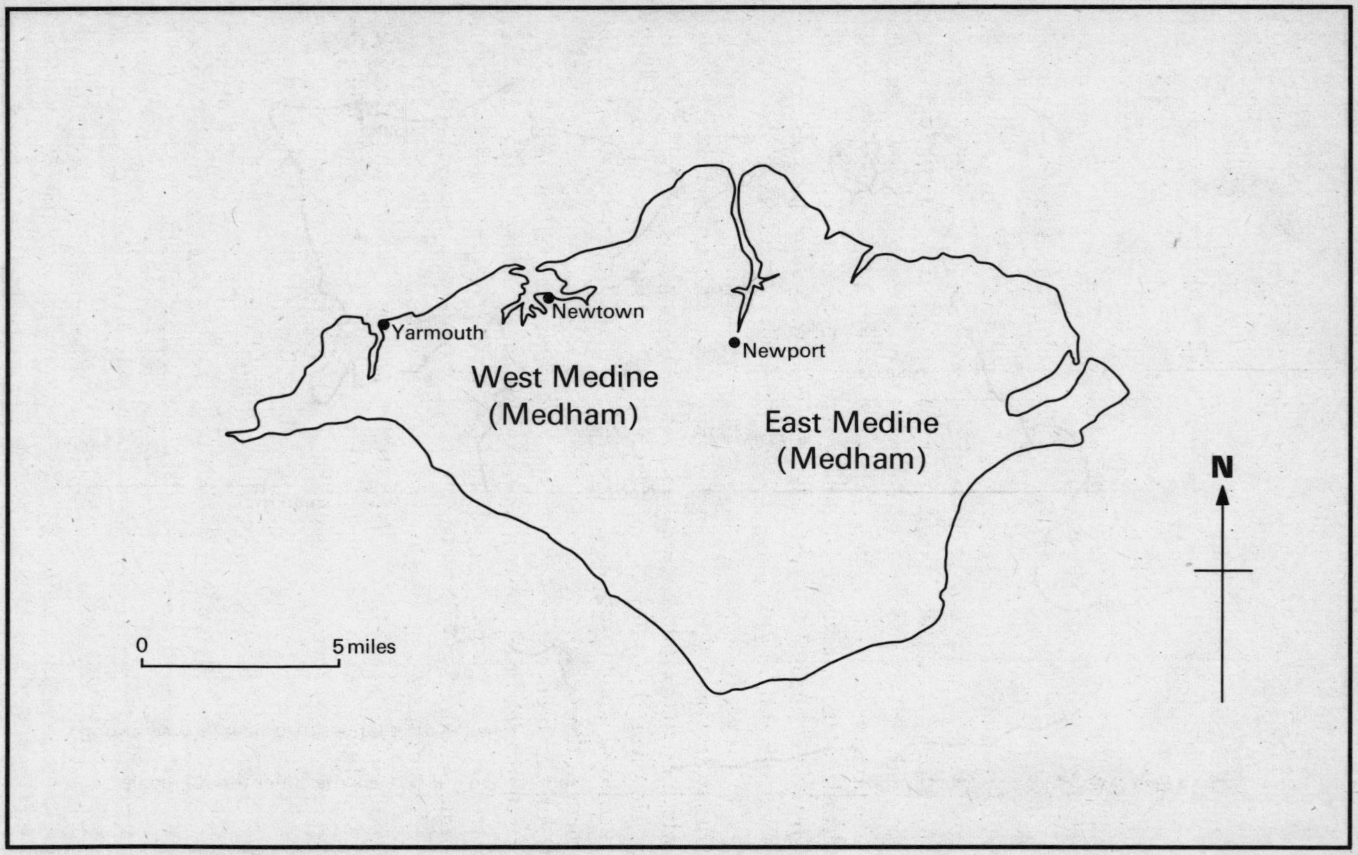

Map 3. Parliamentary boroughs and administrative divisions in the Isle of Wight.

INTRODUCTION AND PROLOGUE

Historians of early modern England no longer need to apologize for devoting considerable attention to the localities. In recent decades, local studies have provided vital insights into the origins and course of the Reformation of the sixteenth century and the Civil Wars of the seventeenth. However, for some obscure reason, until recently this approach has not been extended to the decades of the seventeenth century after the restoration of Charles II in 1660. Historians already established in the field of Restoration politics have acknowledged the significance of the local dimension, but have done little to follow this up with local research.[1] Other scholars have not been so coy and the last few years have seen the appearance of several important local studies which extend beyond the previously hallowed watershed of 1660.[2]

However, this is the first such study to make centre–local relations rather than local administration and society its principal theme. Central involvement in the localities after the mid-century and especially after the Restoration has been widely ignored and underestimated by historians, with a resultant distortion in current views of the Restoration regime. Local reactions to central government and its policies have fared little better for the same period. The intention of this present study is to go some way towards redressing the historiographical balance.

But even while shifting to a slightly later period, it is difficult to throw off the influence of the local historians of the early Stuart period. When the research on which this book is based was begun, the debate over the concept

---

[1] J. Miller, *James II, a Study in Kingship* (Hove, 1977), chapter 3, pp. 28–30; Dr Miller's article, 'The Crown and the Borough Charters in the reign of Charles II', *E.H.R.*, c (1985), 53–84, as he freely admits, is not based on detailed local research; Professor J. R. Jones called for research to be undertaken on the boroughs in his *The Revolution of 1688 in England* (London, first published 1972, reprint 1984), pp. 142–3.

[2] P. Jenkins, *The Making of a Ruling Class: The Glamorgan Gentry 1640–1790* (Cambridge, 1982); S. K. Roberts, *Recovery and Restoration in an English County: Devon Local Administration 1646–1670* (Exeter, 1985).

of 'county communities' in the pre-Civil-War period was in full swing.[3] Scholars like Dr Clive Holmes and Dr Ann Hughes questioned the utility of the 'county community' model for understanding early Stuart England, outside exceptional counties such as Kent or Cheshire.[4] The concept is widely seen to have obscured more than it clarified about English politics in the 1640s and beyond. Some scholars have simply abandoned it, but even its original proponents have since moved on to embrace a more sophisticated view of local identities and of centre–local relationships in the early modern period as a whole.[5] So a fresh assault on the old misconceptions associated with the 'county community', now so widely abandoned, would be totally redundant. It would also divert attention from the immense debt which historians of the seventeenth century owe the scholars who first focused attention on the localities. They were absolutely right to put centre–local relations in the forefront of discussion about seventeenth-century politics and government. My own research would never have been begun without their pioneering efforts.

It is admittedly somewhat artificial to talk of 'central government' in this period. As Dr Stephen Roberts has pointed out, there was no clear distinction in the minds of contemporaries between central and local government.[6] Dr Colin Brooks has aptly written of the localities 'merging with the central government of the nation' after 1688.[7] The forty years before 1688 saw numerous and rapid changes in the structure and role of central institutions of government, as well as in the personnel who manned them. However, despite these qualifications, there was throughout the period a national government residing principally at Whitehall, where policies were formulated, which then had to be enforced at local level. There was a relationship between those who wielded power at the centre and those who governed the

---

[3] A. M. Everitt, *The Community of Kent and the Great Rebellion* (Leicester, 1966); J. S. Morrill, *Cheshire 1630–1660: County Government and Society during the English Revolution* (Oxford, 1974); *The Revolt of the Provinces: Conservatives and Radicals in the English Civil War, 1630–1650* (London, 1976); A. J. Fletcher, *A County Community in Peace and War: Sussex 1600–1660* (London and New York, 1975).

[4] C. Holmes, 'The county community in Stuart historiography', *Journal of British Studies*, xix, no. 2 (1980), 54–73; A. L. Hughes, 'Warwickshire on the eve of the Civil War: a county community?', *Midland History*, 7 (1982), 42–72.

[5] E.g. A. M. Everitt, 'Country, county and town: patterns of regional evolution in England', *T.R.H.S. Fifth Series*, 29 (1979), 79–106; A. Fletcher, 'National and local awareness in the county communities', *Before the English Civil War*, ed. H. C. Tomlinson (London, 1983), pp. 151–74.

[6] S. K. Roberts, 'Local government reform in England and Wales during the Interregnum: a survey', *'Into Another Mould': Aspects of the Interregnum*, ed. I. Roots (Exeter, 1981), p. 26.

[7] C. Brooks, 'Public finance and political stability: the administration of the Land Tax 1688–1720', *H.J.*, 17 (1974), 300.

localities on their behalf, and through them with the wider local community. This present study is an attempt to examine that relationship and to explore centre–local interaction at various levels, in the context of one particular county.

Before proceeding, something should be said about the structure of this book. For the structure is very much part of the argument. The main concerns of central government in the localities are dealt with in each chronological section under the heading of 'The Enforcement of Policy'. It is not possible to cover everything that central authorities attempted to do, but I would suggest that in each case I have presented a representative picture of the concerns and activity of central government, and have attempted to account for changes in these priorities, when they took place. However, it should rapidly become clear, indeed it is one of the main themes of this book, that there was a considerable degree of continuity in central involvement in the localities running through the whole period.

Hampshire of course was not a typical county; which is? It contained the strategically vital Solent area and the naval base at Portsmouth, which no government could afford to ignore, and yet for this very reason Hampshire is an ideal testing ground for the effectiveness of successive regimes, and their relationship with people in the provinces. If governments failed here and were despised here, it boded ill for their performance and popularity elsewhere. And the general policies of government had to be enforced in Hampshire as they were in any other county.

Seventeenth-century Hampshire contained within its boundaries several different regions and innumerable neighbourhoods. As Professor Everitt has observed 'contrasting types of countryside are rarely delimited by county boundaries'.[8] So in Hampshire, the chalk downlands of the north, with their large sheep flocks had more in common with the comparable terrain over the Wiltshire border than with the still wooded areas in the south of the county. Social structures were different. The downland farmers of Hampshire had for some time been involved in large-scale farming, which could only be undertaken with the aid of a large number of wage-labourers.[9] Manorial control remained strong and, according to John Aubrey, the old festive customs were more resilient in this region than elsewhere.[10] But in the New Forest, which dominated the south-western corner of the county, there emerged a rural

---

[8] Everitt, 'Country, county and town', p. 82.
[9] *The Agrarian History of England and Wales*: vol. 4: *1500–1640*, ed. J. Thirsk (Cambridge, 1967), pp. 65, 70.
[10] Cited in D. Underdown, *Revel, Riot and Rebellion: Popular Politics and Culture in England 1603–1660* (Oxford, 1985), p. 88.

economy characterized by a large number of independent or semi-independent small-holders, relying on stock-keeping for their livelihood.[11]

Urban Hampshire also presents a varied picture in the early modern period. On the one hand there were the large long-established urban centres of Winchester and Southampton, which were in a state of economic decline before 1640.[12] On the other hand, there were the numerous small market towns, which prospered by catering for the neighbouring rural communities or the travellers on the trunk routes, notably the Great West Road, which crossed the county. They, along with the naval towns of Portsmouth and Gosport, provided the really dynamic element in Hampshire's demography in the early modern period.[13]

Socially and economically, the county consisted of a patchwork of communities, localities and neighbourhoods, often very different from each other. The Isle of Wight, to take an extreme example, though technically part of the county, was a distinct community on its own. Here there was a clearly defined group of gentry families, closely intermarried and enjoying a very individual, not to say insular, social life, based on festive gatherings and the rites of passage of members of the community. Nevertheless, this situation should not be sentimentalized. Gentry society in the Isle of Wight was riven by feuds and disputes over precedence, and Sir John Oglandet detected a lack of genuine friendship amongst his neighbours.[14]

But however diverse its social and economic components may have been, Hampshire did represent a single administrative unit. Compared with many other shires, it was administratively centralized and unified. Almost the whole county was subject to the assizes held at Winchester twice a year, and to the quarter sessions, which in contrast to neighbouring Sussex and Wiltshire, virtually never moved from the county capital. Ecclesiastically the whole county was contained within the same diocese and archdeaconry of Winchester.

But the administrative dominance of county institutions was by no means total or unchallenged. The county contained a maze of municipal privileges. Southampton was a county in its own right, with sheriff, justices and its own quarter sessions, exempt from the jurisdiction of county assizes. Apart from

---

[11] C. R. Tubbs, 'The development of the small-holding and cottage stock-keeping economy of the New Forest', *Agricultural History Review*, xiii (1965), 23–39.

[12] A. Rosen, 'Winchester in transition 1580–1700', *Country Towns in Pre-Industrial England*, ed. P. Clark (Leicester, 1981), pp. 148–62.

[13] J. R. Taylor, 'Population, disease and family structure in early modern Hampshire, with special reference to the towns' (Southampton Univ., Ph.D. thesis, 1980), pp. iii, 55–68, 222–31.

[14] J. D. Jones, 'The Isle of Wight, 1558–1642' (Southampton Univ., Ph.D. thesis, 1978), pp. 66–8, 87–8, 108–13.

this, Portsmouth, Winchester, Basingstoke, Andover, Romsey and Newport in the Isle of Wight had their own justices and sessions, and enjoyed a lesser degree of independence. There were serious disputes between the county and the boroughs of Portsmouth and Andover during the reign of Charles I. The county justices looked for external support, notably from the assize judges, to win their case, though as the successive endorsement of Andover's privileges in 1637 and 1652 showed, the judges did not necessarily side with the county.[15] No central government thought to deal with such anomalies until the Tory reaction of the 1680s.

There was also a degree of decentralization in the administrative structure of the rest of the county. Back in 1561, the people of the Isle of Wight had obtained a warrant from Queen Elizabeth exempting them from jury service and attendance at mainland assizes and quarter sessions, except in such matters as concerned the island.[16] The Isle of Wight had its own house of correction, and did not contribute to the county one; it collected its own rates for maimed soldiers and had its own treasurer for that fund, and was only once rated for the repair of a mainland bridge during the early Stuart period.[17] But justices from the island did attend and participate in the decisions of the county quarter sessions. The island had its own military structure, subject to a Crown appointed captain or governor, with two regiments of militia foot and parochial artillery.[18] Since the reign of Elizabeth, mainland Hampshire had also been divided into seven divisions.[19] But despite its internal complexity, Hampshire for the purposes of this study will be treated as an administrative unit.

THE COUNTY AND THE CIVIL WARS 1640–8

Hampshire's gentry were well placed to air their county's grievances against the royal government when Charles I at last resorted to Parliament in 1640. With twenty-four borough seats as well as two county ones, Hampshire was in fact somewhat over-represented.[20] Despite a tradition of court and aristocratic influence in several of the boroughs, the majority of seats usually went to native gentry or their close relatives, a tendency which was enhanced in

---

[15] B. J. Richmond, 'The work of the justices of the peace in Hampshire, 1603–1642' (Southampton Univ., M.Phil. thesis, 1969), pp. 16–24; J. S. Furley, *Quarter Sessions Government in Hampshire in the Seventeenth Century* (Winchester, 1937), pp. 53–5; H.C.R.O., QO 3, p. 145.
[16] Furley, *Quarter Sessions Government in Hampshire*, p. 17.
[17] Richmond, 'The work of the justices of the peace in Hampshire', pp. 42–4.
[18] Jones, 'The Isle of Wight', pp. 46, 241–2.
[19] Alton, Andover, Basingstoke, Kingsclere, New Forest, Fawley, Portsdown, see map 1.
[20] Under the Instrument of Government the county's representation was nearly halved to fourteen MPs.

1640 by a reduction in external influence. Most of those elected to the Long Parliament were also associated with opposition to the royal government.[21]

John Pym's rhetoric about a Catholic conspiracy to subvert both church and state made sense to Hampshire's native MPs as the county contained a comparatively large and apparently growing Roman Catholic community.[22] The county's leading Catholic layman, John Paulet, fifth marquis of Winchester, had been prominent in his support for the king in the first Bishops' War, in contrast with several of the parliamentary gentry.[23] Their fears were exacerbated in the summer of 1641 by the discovery of a huge stock of arms at Winchester's formidable mansion of Basing House. By the autumn of 1641, Pym was using the supposed movements of Catholics in Hampshire to arouse concern at Westminster. In the following spring, the framers of an assize petition from Hampshire, endorsing Pym's programme, drew attention to an alarming influx of Catholics into the county. It called for all Catholics to be secured and for Catholic peers to be excluded from the House of Lords.[24]

In the ensuing crisis, a substantial majority of Hampshire's MPs sided with Parliament against the king and local government was brought into line behind them.[25] Already by the spring of 1642, the sheriff and assize grand jury were clearly on their side.[26] The Militia Ordinance enabled Hampshire's parliamentarians to take over the lieutenancy. By 21 June, the parliamentary deputy-lieutenants were able to muster the county's militia numbering 5,000 men along with several contingents of volunteers, who all subscribed a declaration in support of the Militia Ordinance, despite the attempts of the 'Malignant Party' to invalidate it with a royal proclamation.[27] The king's counter strategy of purging sixteen avowed parliamentarians including seven of the county's MPs from the commission of the peace was less effective than

[21] J. K. Gruenfelder, *Influence in Early Stuart Elections 1604–1640* (Columbus, 1981), pp. 194, 207–8, n. 24, appendix 6, 232; M. F. Keeler, *The Long Parliament, 1640–1* (Philadelphia, 1954), pp. 48–50.

[22] W. H. Mildon, 'Puritanism in Hampshire and the Isle of Wight from the reign of Elizabeth to the Restoration' (London Univ., Ph.D. thesis, 1934), p. 56.

[23] C. Hibbard, *Charles I and the Popish Plot* (Chapel Hill, 1983), p. 101; Keeler, *The Long Parliament*, pp. 234, 237, 377, 400; *C.J.*, ii. 263.

[24] *The Journal of Sir Simonds D'Ewes*, ed. W. H. Coate (New Haven, 1942), pp. 58, 68, 102, 172; *The Petition of the County of Southampton* (that the votes of the popish lords may be taken away, and all papists confined) (London, 1642).

[25] Out of twenty-six sitting MPs in 1642, sixteen sided with Parliament, two others who had shown signs of supporting Parliament died on the eve of war, Keeler, *The Long Parliament*, *passim*.

[26] John Fielder of Borough Court, a future Rumper, had been made sheriff for 1641–2.

[27] Seven MPs and Richard Norton of Southwick reported the progress which had been made to the earl of Pembroke, who had been appointed lord lieutenant of the county under the Militia Ordinance, *L.J.*, v. 156, 172.

it might have been, as quarter sessions had already ceased to sit, and would not meet again until Easter 1646.[28]

The parliamentarians used their control of the militia and the shrievalty in 1642 to crush opposition within the shire, making Hampshire appear more parliamentarian than it actually was. Bands of royalists seeking to execute the Commission of Array within the county were treated as common criminals, their endeavours nipped in the bud and their would-be local accomplices deterred.[29] When George Goring declared for the king at Portsmouth in August, he was rapidly blockaded by local forces with naval support and a garrison which might otherwise have been a focus for the undeclared royalists of west Sussex, and eastern Hampshire was surrendered early in September.[30]

Hampshire's parliamentarians were able to manipulate the understandable local dread of civil war to their own advantage. They promoted an assize grand jury petition in July 1642, which purported to call for an accommodation. But it was far from being a neutralist document: it protested at the recent purge of the commission of the peace and called upon the king to be reconciled to Parliament.[31] The desire to keep the war out of their locality turned the largely neutral gentry of the Isle of Wight, with a few exceptions, into moderate parliamentarians, who proved surprisingly generous in providing the mainland war effort with provisions and reinforcements.[32] On the mainland, true neutralism failed to find a county focus in the summer of 1642. County solidarity was not apparent. However, when Parliament's hold on the county gave way in the face of the royalist advance of 1643, several borough oligarchies were quick to come to terms with the ascendant party.[33]

The turning of the military tide in 1643 also enabled some of Hampshire's latent royalism to become apparent. By November of that year, the royalists were convening meetings of gentry at Winchester to approve a contribution to support Basing House, which the marquis of Winchester had garrisoned for the king the year before. By that time, it was possible to appoint a council of war of fifty-two members, consisting mostly of native peers and gentry of

[28] P.R.O., Crown Office Docquet Book, C231/5.fol. 528.
[29] *A Letter sent from one Mr Parker a Gentleman, dwelling at Upper Wallop in Hampshire, to his friend a Gentleman in London, wherein is related some remarkable passages there, as of a Battell fought between the Inhabitants of the County, and of the Cavaliers about the settlement of the Militia and Commission of Array* (London, 1642).
[30] J. Webb, *The Siege of Portsmouth in the Civil War* (The Portsmouth Papers, 1967, revised 1977); Fletcher, *Sussex*, p. 261.
[31] *Cal.S.P.Dom.*, 1641–3, pp. 356–7.
[32] Jones, 'Isle of Wight', pp. 255–71; A. Fletcher, *The Outbreak of the English Civil War* (London, 1981), p. 385.
[33] Rosen, 'Winchester in transition', in Clark, *Country Towns in Pre-Industrial England*, p. 163; H.C.R.O. Lymington borough records, 27M74A DBC/2, fol. 41; Christchurch Civic Offices, borough archives, council minute book 1615–1857, fol. 567.

whom thirty-one would later be sequestered for active royalism. Hampshire produced at least twenty royalist field officers during the course of the Civil Wars and Interregnum, the same as neighbouring Wiltshire.[34]

Yet in terms of actual fighting men, popular royalism in Hampshire seems to have been a comparatively insignificant phenomenon. The sources are problematical and retrospective, but for what the figures are worth, 185 individuals were listed as suspects in 1655 and 140 indigent royalist soldiers or their dependents were dealt with by the county quarter sessions between the Restoration and 1672, a much lower number than for neighbouring Wiltshire or Dorset.[35]

But the royalists too learnt how to manipulate local dislike of the war in their favour. In April 1644, a petition which claimed to speak for 8,677 of the county's inhabitants was promoted which called upon Parliament to respond to the king's gracious promises in order to end the war. If Parliament did not make peace they were ready to rise 'all as one man' to save 'our deare Country'. Defeated at Cheriton a few weeks before, local royalists were now waging the war by other means. The royalist press gleefully took up the petition, and the king adopted the 'all as one man' formula in a subsequent propaganda campaign.[36] However, at this stage, Parliament was sufficiently strong locally to stamp out this 'peace' movement.

The clubmen risings of 1645 were rather more formidable, though in most of Hampshire no less royalist in motivation. There was a high degree of collusion between the clubmen in neighbouring shires, and royalist clergy were prominent amongst them.[37] One local parliamentarian observer saw these crypto-royalists for what they were and attributed this to their origins

[34] Brit. Lib., Addit. MS 26781 (Hampshire correspondence of the lord lieutenant, militia affairs, etc. 1630–43), fol. 115; *Calendar of the Committee for the Advance of Money, 1642–1656*, ed. M. A. E. Green (3 vols., London, 1888) and *Calendar of the Committee for Compounding, 1643–1660*, ed. M. A. E. Green (5 vols., London, 1889), *passim*; P. R. Newman, 'The Royalist Officer Corps 1642–1660: Army command as a reflection of social structure', *H.J.*, 26 (1983), 952.

[35] For a discussion of the sources and the problems with them, see Underdown, *Revel, Riot and Rebellion*, pp. 192–207; Professor Underdown found 327 individual indigent royalists from identifiable places in Wiltshire in the county records and 815 from Dorset, and there were 384 and 1,507 suspects respectively listed in 1655; the disparity between the latter figures and that for Hampshire is only partly explained by the fact that Major-General Goffe did not take bonds for good behaviour from royalists on whom he was levying the decimation tax; see n. 11, p. 34 below; H.C.R.O., QO4 *passim*.

[36] The petition was not a narrowly localist document, but began by reminding the Commons that they had been elected to represent the petitioners 'and other our Countrymen of this Kingdome'. *Mercurius Aulicus*, sixteenth week, 20 April 1644, pp. 940–2; R. Hutton, 'The royalist war effort', *Reactions to the English Civil War 1642–9*, ed. J. S. Morrill (London, 1982), pp. 60–1.

[37] D. Underdown, 'The chalk and the cheese: contrasts among the English clubmen', *Past and Present*, 85 (1979), 41.

in the east of the county where Papists and episcopal tenants were concentrated.[38] Far from desiring an end to hostilities on any terms, the bulk of Hampshire's clubmen actually impeded peace by obstructing the forces which were besieging Winchester in September 1645. They had to be militarily crushed at Petersfield and Bishops Waltham (a former royalist garrison).[39] Finally, in October 1645, Winchester surrendered and Basing House with its exclusively Catholic garrison was bloodily stormed by forces under Cromwell's command, completing the military defeat of royalism in the shire.[40]

Victory in the Civil War at last enabled Hampshire's parliamentarians to establish a proper administrative infrastructure in the county, which had been lacking since 1642. For much of the war, the county committee had not had a settled existence or place of residence, fluctuating between Portsmouth and Basingstoke with the fortunes of war, and liable to be overthrown by a sudden royalist incursion. Now with the war virtually over, it was given a fixed membership of fifty and full powers except over the Isle of Wight.[41] It contained fifteen of the living MPs who had remained loyal to Parliament, and four of the nine men shortly to be 'recruited' to the Long Parliament in by-elections, but apart from these notables, only two had been in the commission of the peace by 1642. The rest were mostly minor gentry who had worked their way up through parliamentarian administration during the war.[42] In this way it reflected very clearly the uneven support for Parliament among the gentry in different parts of the county. The New Forest division accounted for ten members of the county committee whilst the north-western Kingsclere division was represented by only one member. This imbalance would later be incorporated into Interregnum commissions of the peace, which were to a large extent composed of the committeemen of the 1640s.[43]

The county committee in Hampshire did not become the preserve of a faction and posed no serious threat to the normal institutions of county government, such as quarter sessions, which were revived at Easter 1646. The latter were soon dealing not only with problems such as bridge repair and unlicensed alehouses, but also with such matters as invigorating local tax collection and adjudicating rating disputes. By April 1648, according to John Woodman, a local sequestration official, the county committee was seldom

---

[38] Brit. Lib., Addit. MS 24860 (Maijor papers), fol. 137.
[39] G. N. Godwin, *The Civil War in Hampshire* (2nd edn), (Southampton and London, 1904), pp. 321–2.
[40] Godwin, *The Civil War in Hampshire*, pp. 335–48.
[41] P.R.O., Papers of the Committee of Compounding with Delinquents, S.P.23/257/75; *F. & R.*, i. 694–6.
[42] *F. & R.*, i. 696; H.C.R.O., 5M53, no. 964; P.R.O., C231/5, fol. 528.
[43] See below, p. 20.

sitting, despite a backlog of sequestration business which had not been dealt with.[44]

In the wake of the Civil War, the parliamentarians pushed through the religious changes which had been held up by the fighting. They had long perceived that a majority of the county's clergy were unsympathetic to their cause. The assize petition of March 1642 had complained that less than one fifth of the county's parishes were 'furnished with conscionable, constant Preaching Ministers'. An earlier draft of that petition had accused hostile clergy of trying 'to exasperate the people against Parliament's proceedings'.[45] Since then the royalism of many of the clergy had become overt, and several of them had been involved in organizing the clubmen. These clergy were now at the mercy of the parliamentarians, and the bulk of the ejections of 'scandalous ministers' in Hampshire took place in 1645 and 1646. Altogether, taking the 1640s and 1650s as a whole, more than ninety parochial clergy may have been affected and at least seventy-two livings (28 per cent of the county's total of 253) were sequestered.[46] In 1646–7, there was also a campaign against Catholic recusancy which resulted in 625 presentments to quarter sessions.[47]

As M. G. Finlayson has stressed, the religious views of many MPs in the 1640s are obscure.[48] However, this does not imply that the views they had were not strongly held. Of Hampshire's sitting MPs in 1648, Professor Underdown was able to classify only seven unambiguously, with four Presbyterians and three Independents. Of these, their views varied from the intolerant Presbyterianism of Sir William Lewis (MP for Petersfield) to the tolerant Independency of Richard Norton ('recruiter' MP for the county). The views of the majority of the other MPs were probably ranged somewhere between these two extremes. Their religious differences did not spill over into open conflict at local level, but they may explain why, after a few initial

---

[44] H.C.R.O., QO2, fols. 216–77; P.R.O., S.P.23/118, pp. 1013, 1015; in the relative ineffectiveness of its county committee, Hampshire resembles Devon, but differs markedly from Somerset and other counties, Roberts, *Recovery and Restoration in an English County*, pp. 13–14; D. Underdown, *Somerset in the Civil War and Interregnum* (Newton Abbot, 1973), pp. 121–37.

[45] *The Petition of the County of Southampton* [that the votes of the popish lords may be taken away, and all papists confined] (London, 1642); Brit. Lib. Addit. MS 29975 (Pitt papers), fol. 129.

[46] A. G. Matthews, *Walker Revised* (Oxford, 1948), p. xiv; I. M. Green, 'The persecution of "scandalous" and "malignant" parish clergy during the English Civil War', *E.H.R.*, xciv (1979), 523; the earliest estimate of the number of clergy ejected in Hampshire dates from 1662 and occurs in *A List of the Clergy of Hampshire* by T.C., which is reproduced in W. Kennett, *A Register and Chronicle Ecclesiastical and Civil* (London, 1728), pp. 821–2, the figure there given is ninety-five; I am grateful to Dr I. M. Green for advice about the number of sequestered livings as a proportion of the total number of livings in the county.

[47] H.C.R.O., QI, fols. 9–26, 27–36, 38.

[48] M. G. Finlayson, *Historians, Puritanism and the English Revolution: the Religious Factor in English Politics before and after the Interregnum* (Toronto, 1983), p. 6.

consultations, the county committee seems to have failed to establish the full Presbyterian system locally.[49]

The 'recruiter' elections brought to light some differences between the local parliamentarians, but they were hardly ideological in nature. Most of Hampshire's nine 'recruiter' MPs were resident gentlemen, and most seem to have been elected without contests. But at Newport, in the Isle of Wight, William Stephens resorted to sharp practice to secure his return in a bitter contest.[50] John Lisle obtained the writ of the Christchurch 'recruiter' election and tried to use the opportunity to keep John Kemp, a former mayor of the borough, from being elected for one of the seats there. Kemp wrote an indignant letter to the mayor against this manoeuvre, in which he unashamedly described Lisle as 'my professed ennimy' and harked back to slights received from him at the beginning of the Civil War.[51] Kemp was duly elected. There appears to have been no significant ideological difference between Lisle and Kemp, and although both Lisle and Sir William Lewis were involved in partisan electioneering elsewhere, they do not seem to have indulged in it in Hampshire.[52] Several of the newly elected MPs were soon being called upon by their constituents to secure mitigations of the excise and other favours to their localities.[53]

However, the crisis of 1647 seriously disrupted Hampshire's representation at Westminster. Two MPs, Sir William Lewis and Sir William Waller (MP for Andover) were amongst the eleven members against whom the army brought charges during the summer, and were forced to withdraw from the Commons. William Jephson (MP for Stockbridge) seems to have supported the excluded members. But four or five others sided with the army early in August.[54] However, the response of the majority was simply to keep their heads down and hope that the crisis would blow over, and their absenteeism

[49] D. Underdown, *Pride's Purge: Politics in the Puritan Revolution* (Oxford, 1971), pp. 369, 378, 379, 381, 385, 388, 389; G. Yule, *Puritans in Politics: Religious Legislation of the Long Parliament 1640–1647* (Sutton Courtenay Press, 1981), appendix 1, pp. 260–2; Brit. Lib., Addit. MS 24860, fols. 145, 149.

[50] E. B. James, *Letters Archaeological and Historical Relating to the Isle of Wight* (2 vols., London, 1896), ii. 187.

[51] Christchurch Civic Offices, borough archives, volume of sixteenth- and seventeenth-century correspondence relating to elections, p. 46: John Kemp to the mayor and corporation, 6 Dec. 1645.

[52] D. Underdown, 'Party management in the recruiter elections 1645–8', *E.H.R.* lxxxiii (1968), 254, 256, 258–60.

[53] E.g. Nicholas Love, MP for Winchester, who was approached by his old college at Winchester to obtain concessions over the excise, *Winchester College Muniments: a descriptive list* compiled by S. Himsworth (3 vols., Chichester, 1976–84), i. 40; John Kemp and Richard Edwards, MPs for Christchurch were contacted by the mayor and corporation with a similar end in view, Christchurch Civic Offices, volume of correspondence relating to elections, p. 40; John Kemp to the Mayor, 29 Jan. 1645/6.

[54] Underdown, *Pride's Purge*, pp. 377, 378, 379, 385, 386, 388.

continued into the autumn. When the House was called on 9 October, nine of Hampshire's MPs were absent without excuse apart from the two excluded members.[55] In the case of Richard Whitehead (knight of the shire) and John Bulkeley ('recruiter' MP for Newtown) this simply reflected their failure to hurry back to London after the Michaelmas quarter sessions which began on 5 October. But in the case of at least three others their absence seems to have represented a withdrawal from active politics which would subsequently be confirmed by their abstention at the time of Pride's Purge.[56]

But if Hampshire's parliamentarian MPs and gentry wished to stay clear of national issues, they were in for a nasty shock in the winter of 1647–8. The flight of Charles I to the Isle of Wight in November 1647 brought the central political crisis straight into that locality. The bungled attempt by Captain Burley (a former fort commander on the island) to raise the island on the king's behalf, to secure his release from custody, further confronted the local community with the issue of his detention. It also gave hardline opponents of the king a chance to use Burley's subsequent trial for propaganda purposes. There were several MPs amongst the commissioners of oyer and terminer appointed to try him at Winchester. Ironically, Burley was condemned for treason, and a carefully chosen Hampshire grand jury issued a declaration in support of Parliament's recent vote of no addresses, urging Parliament to settle the kingdom unilaterally, which was part of a wider campaign to obtain provincial endorsement for this policy.[57] In Hampshire, some of the same grand jurymen would serve again later in the year as an assize jury at the trial of Major Rolfe for allegedly plotting to kill the king at Carisbrooke. After a character reference for Rolfe from the recently victorious Oliver Cromwell, he was rapidly acquitted.[58]

With both the king and the mouthpiece of county opinion in the hands of hardline parliamentarians, local royalists had good reason to feel frustrated. The growing unpopularity of Parliament's rule with local people was very clear. The county committee had tried to shield the local community from free quarter, but an attempt by some people near Alton to enforce the committee's ban against some of Ireton's horse in August 1646 resulted in fighting between them and the soldiery.[59] High and novel taxation was also unpopular. Rioters who attacked excisemen at Chippenham at the end of 1647 were

---

[55] *C.J.*, v. 330; for a similar rate of absenteeism in the case of Devon, see Roberts, *Recovery and Restoration in an English County*, pp. 9–10.

[56] H.C.R.O., QO 2, fol. 250; Underdown, *Pride's Purge*, pp. 373, 377, 390.

[57] *C.J.*, v. 429, 441–2; *The Humble and Thankful Acknowledgement and Declaration of the County of Southampton* (London, 1648); the seventeen-man grand jury contained two members of the county committee and two others who would obtain local office under the Commonwealth; for the wider campaign see Underdown, *Revel, Riot and Rebellion*, p. 230.

[58] G. F. T. Jones, *Saw-Pit Wharton* (Sydney, 1967), pp. 126, 282.

[59] *The Moderate Intelligencer*, no. 76, 14 Aug. 1646, pp. 601–2.

said to have expected help from Hampshire (amongst other counties) where meetings had been held to promote common action.[60] Puritan church reforms were also unpopular in some places. The hasty introduction of closed communion at Dibden in 1645 provoked violence against the 'intruded' incumbent and petitions to the county committee. Elsewhere some ejected ministers were re-instated and continued to use the prayer book with parochial connivance.[61]

Local royalists in Hampshire saw the opportunity to turn these discontents to their own advantage and give them an ideological slant. As in 1644, they planned a petition to Parliament, this time following the example of Kent, Essex, Sussex, Surrey and other counties. But the county committee intervened to stop the agitation, and, sitting at Winchester on 9 June 1648, issued a declaration to be read in every parish church in the county banning tumultuous meetings and the gathering of signatures to a petition, which it claimed had already begun to take place in Hampshire.[62] The promoters of the Hampshire petition, deterred by the suppression of the Surrey petitioners, had their petition published in the name of the lords, knights, gentlemen, ministers and freeholders of the county.

The petition attacked the continued restraint of the king, heavy taxation, lack of accountability for it, 'Arbitrary power' and 'those that thinke they have monopolized all truth and would therefore square our Religion according to their own confused Modeles'. It called for the restoration of the king to 'all his indutible Right', the re-establishment of 'the true reformed Protestant religion profest in the reigns of Q. Elizabeth, and K. James of blessed memory', the thankful acceptance of the king's offer of 'ease to tender consciences', the disbandment of the army and the auditing of money raised. This was an Anglican royalist manifesto which was designed to have wide appeal, though it had no specifically local content.[63]

But after the battle of Preston in August, it was not royalists, but the army which would decide the nation's political future. As a confrontation once again loomed between the army and Parliament, Hampshire's MPs were again divided. William Jephson, MP for Stockbridge, defected from the parliamentarian cause altogether in Ireland.[64] John Bulkeley, MP for Newtown, was one of the commissioners sent to negotiate with the king at

[60] Underdown, *Revel, Riot and Rebellion*, p. 216.
[61] Brit. Lib., Addit. MS 24860, fols. 117–20; Mildon, 'Puritanism in Hampshire', pp. 181–2, 191–4; for such phenomena nationally see J. S. Morrill, 'The Church in England, 1642–9', in Morrill, *Reactions to the English Civil War*, pp. 100–3, 108–12.
[62] *A Declaration of the Committee for the Safety of the County of Southampton sitting at Winton, 9 June 1648* (London, 1648).
[63] *The Declaration: together with the petition and Remonstrance of the Lords, Knights, Gentlemen, Ministers and Freeholders of the County of Hampshire* (London, 1648).
[64] *D.N.B.*, William Jephson (1615?–1659?).

Newport and co-chaired the committee on the new militia ordinance designed to undermine the position of the army.[65] But Richard Norton warned his fellow MPs against offending the army on the day this ordinance passed, 'for they are resolved to have a free Parliament to debate the king's Answer, if we refuse'.[66] In fact, of course, the army resorted to Pride's Purge.

Between 1642 and 1648, Hampshire had been turned into a battleground between nationwide parties. True county consciousness or solidarity never showed itself. Instead county institutions were ruthlessly taken over for partisan purposes and declarations and petitions issued in the county's name which tended simply to endorse one side or the other in the national contests of the moment, with decreasing local content. Political fragmentation amongst the county's gentry elite continued throughout the decade, leaving it in turmoil by the time the king was executed.

[65] J. D. Jones, *The Royal Prisoner* (2nd edn., Trustees of the Carisbrooke Castle Museum, 1974), pp. 106, 117; L. G. Schwoerer, *'No Standing Armies!' The Anti-Army Ideology in Seventeenth-Century England* (Baltimore and London, 1974), pp. 56, 58–9.

[66] W. Cobbett, *Parliamentary History from the Norman Conquest in 1066 to the Year 1803* (36 vols., London, 1806–20), iii. column 1147.

Part I

THE INTERREGNUM

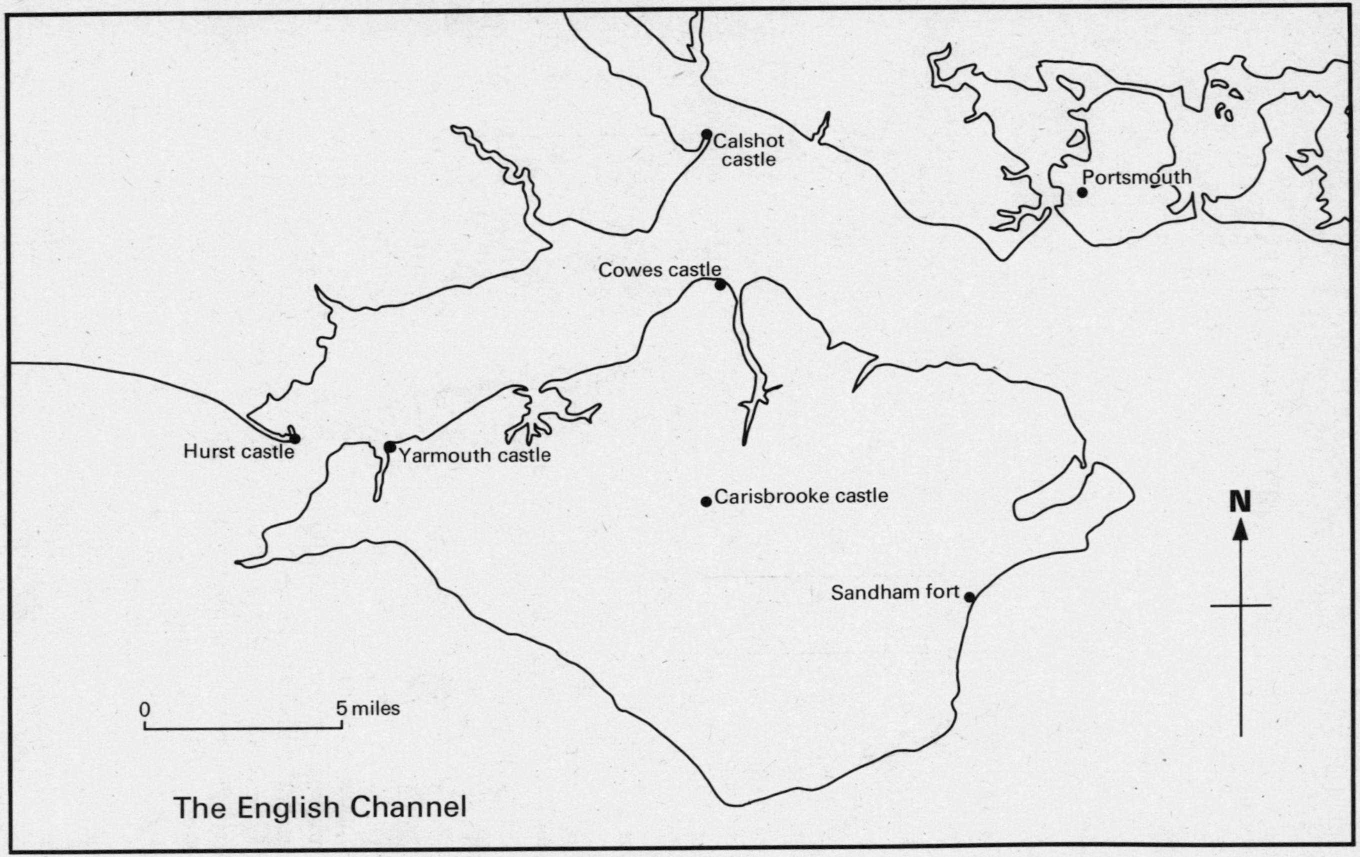

Map 4. The Solent garrisons.

The English Channel

Portsmouth

Calshot castle

Cowes castle

Carisbrooke castle

Sandham fort

Yarmouth castle

Hurst castle

5 miles

0

1

Local office-holding 1649–60

Local office-holding was clearly vital to the relationship between central government and the localities. Nomination to office at county level lay with central government, but it was up to those named to decide whether to serve the state in the office to which they had been appointed. The Civil Wars, Pride's Purge and the establishment of the republic rendered the situation one of unprecedented complexity, with ambivalent and ambiguous motivations existing side by side within both Whitehall and local society. Yet the evidence of appointments in local government has been used to assess the commitment of members of central government in this period to the conciliation of their erstwhile opponents and the creation of a lasting political settlement; and a willingness on the part of these opponents to serve at the local level has been seen as signifying a wider acceptance of the permanence of Interregnum regimes.[1] Conversely, the new resources of the state, notably in the military and revenue establishments brought into existence by the Civil Wars, may be seen as providing central government with unpopular but effective levers in local administration, overcoming entrenched elites and interests.

Paradoxically, Hampshire seems to conform neither to the conciliation nor the centralization model. As will be demonstrated below, the impact of Interregnum governments upon office-holding in the county was far from clear-cut. There is evidence of conciliatory appointments of former opponents by successive regimes at various points during the 1650s, but no marked increase of such appointments in the period with which they are generally associated, the last years of the Protectorate (1657–9). But any potential for centralization in local government by the locally stationed military and revenue establishments went largely unrealized in Hampshire in these years, as local government remained firmly in the hands of local elites.

Before proceeding further, something needs to be said about the influences

---

[1] D. Underdown, 'Settlement in the counties 1653–8', *The Interregnum*, ed. G. E. Aylmer (London, 1972), pp. 165–82 remains one of the very few general surveys of the localities in the 1650s to have appeared in print.

which were exerted on the appointment of office-holders. Several bodies had influence on the composition of the local commissions, in whose hands so much administration lay during the Interregnum. On 8 February 1649, the Rump appointed a committee to review local commissions of the peace, which included the two Winchester MPs, John Lisle and Nicholas Love. Lisle, as one of the Lords Commissioners of the Great Seal, would subsequently be in a good position to exercise influence in this area, though it is not clear to what extent he did so. The Lords Commissioners received nominations for the Hampshire commission of the peace from the Council of State, though it is clear on at least one occasion that it was simply passing on names which had been put forward by others.[2] The Admiralty Committee was also in independent contact with the Lords Commissioners of the Great Seal, to ensure that the Navy Commissioners were appointed as JPs in the maritime shires, and in particular William Willoughby, resident commissioner at Portsmouth, to the Hampshire commission.[3] Thereafter however, the origin of particular appointments is hard to trace. But radical pressure in 1649 and 1659 for far-reaching changes in the Hampshire commission, from the Solent garrisons and local Quakers respectively, appears to have been resisted.[4]

But it would be wrong to assume from silence that all appointments were centrally made, without local consultation, as is clearly demonstrated by reference to the nomination of assessment and militia commissioners. In December 1650, the existing assessment commissioners at Southampton nominated four men, including the local garrison commander, to be added to their number.[5] In 1655, eleven militia commissioners were added to the sixteen already nominated by the Council of State, at the request of several men in the latter category. Central government relied heavily on well-informed agents, based in the localities, for suitable recommendations. It was Colonel William Sydenham, the governor of the Isle of Wight, who recommended men to be militia commissioners there in August 1650.[6]

There was a mixture of central and local patronage too in the appointment of militia officers. Under the Commonwealth, officers recommended by local commissioners were commissioned by the Council of State, which had a clear veto over all such appointments.[7] In practice, though, local nominees were automatically commissioned, and it was left to the militia commissioners in the localities to weed out the undesirables. However, during the Protectorate,

---

[2] C.J., vi. 134; *Cal.S.P.Dom.*, 1650, p. 143.
[3] *Cal.S.P.Dom.*, 1650, p. 162.
[4] *To the Honourable the Commons House of England, the Humble Petition and Representation of the Officers and Souldiers of the Garrisons of Portsmouth* [etc.] (London, 1649); *Cal.S.P.Dom.*, 1658–9, p. 360.
[5] S.C.R.O., SC 14/2/18: 12 December 1650.
[6] Bodl., MS Rawl. A 33, p. 738; *Cal.S.P.Dom.*, 1650, p. 270.
[7] F. & R., ii. 398; *Cal.S.P.Dom.*, 1651, p. 11.

and subsequently during the rule of the restored Rump, militia officers were appointed directly from the centre, because militia commissioners had not yet begun to act.[8]

Every regime insisted that those who bore arms on its behalf in the localities should be politically loyal and reliable. Under the Commonwealth, not only officers but militiamen as well were ordered to be drawn from the well-affected and to take the Engagement of loyalty to the Commonwealth. The rank and file of the Cromwellian militia troops were to be men of 'good life and conversation' who had to promise to be faithful to the protector, before being listed. When the Rump returned to power it purged Cromwellian officers, wisely as it turned out, for in Hampshire several subsequently became involved in a conspiracy against it.[9]

However, with offices that did not involve bearing arms, members of central government thought they could afford to be more relaxed. For example, the office of sheriff, which was a dubious privilege, was bestowed on a very diverse set of gentlemen in Hampshire during the Interregnum. Those appointed included John Stewkeley (1649–50), a staunch Anglican royalist, and Bartholemew Smith (1654–5), formerly a sequestered recusant. John Hildesley, appointed in 1656, was perhaps the first politically reliable one since 1649.[10] Similarly diverse appointments were made in other counties.[11] Through its relaxed, or ill-informed, policy of appointments, central government had seriously compromised its control over local juries, whose nomination lay with the sheriff. In July 1656, Major-General Goffe was shocked to discover that the assize grand jury in Hampshire included some decimated royalists, but he did nothing to rectify the situation, and could only hope that it was not politically influential. The grand jury was staunchly loyal to the Protectorate by 1659, however.[12]

Some counties saw far-reaching purges in their commissions of the peace, soon after the beginning of the Commonwealth period.[13] But members of the Rump showed a marked reluctance to undertake a far-reaching alteration of the Hampshire commission. Royalists had largely disappeared from it in the wake of the Civil War, and the Rump did not remove many of the MPs alienated by Pride's Purge. Out of fourteen living resident MPs who had been imprisoned, secluded or who had abstained at that time, eight continued to be

---

[8] *Calendar of the Committee for Compounding*, ed. Green, i. 383; P.R.O., S.P. 46/97, fol. 164; *Cal.S.P.Dom.*, 1659–60, p. 24.

[9] *Cal.S.P.Dom.*, 1650, p. 471; *F. & R.*, ii, 398; P.R.O., Additional State Papers, S.P. 46/97, fol. 164; *Cal.Clar.S.P.*, iv. 316–17, 369.

[10] P.R.O., *Lists and Indexes No. ix Sheriffs of England and Wales to 1831* (1898), p. 56; *Hampshire Registers I*, ed. R. E. Scantlebury (Catholic Record Society, XLII, 1948), p. 2n.

[11] Roberts, 'Local government reform in England and Wales' in Roots, *'Into Another Mould'*, p. 31.

[12] *Th.S.P.*, v. 215; see below, p. 78.   [13] Underdown, *Pride's Purge*, p. 311.

named to the commission of the peace throughout the Commonwealth period.[14] Several neuters like Sir Richard Kingsmill and Sir William Uvedale survived, perhaps because of their being resident in the thinly represented Kingsclere and Portsdown divisions which made them administratively indispensable, as the Commonwealth commission of the peace had inherited the divisional imbalance of the county committee. By the summer of 1654, Sir Richard Kingsmill was the only active JP in the Kingsclere division and was exempted from being treasurer for maimed soldiers on that account. In the Kingsclere division, even the sequestered royalist, Sir William Kingsmill, survived until at least October 1653.[15]

Both the Commonwealth and Protectorate regimes continued to hold out an olive branch to moderate parliamentarians who had ceased to be active, especially those with titles, like Charles, Lord De la Warr and Sir John Compton, who continued to be named to the commission of the peace, though they never acted. At last, the Cromwellian government gave up with Lord De la Warr, omitting him from the commission by September 1656. In Hampshire, there was no surge of re-admissions of men from old families to the bench in 1655–6, as there was in Sussex, nor in 1657–8 as there was in other counties. In fact, the size of the Hampshire commission declined markedly during the Protectorate from ninety-five in 1653 to seventy-two in 1658.[16] This may have been because there was no pressure for it at local level, or such pressure as there was may have been blocked by men with influence at the centre, like John Lisle and Richard Maijor. Richard Cromwell, who had married Maijor's daughter in 1649 and became active in local government in Hampshire, does not seem to have enjoyed much influence at the centre before he became protector.[17] But there was no large-scale politically inspired purges of the Hampshire commission of the peace during the 1650s which, as a result, remained very stable in its composition.

Local gentlemen were usually included in all the various commissions to which local government and tax collection were entrusted. The membership of the commission of the peace in 1650 was virtually identical with that of the local assessment commission, except for representatives of Winchester and

---

[14] Of the forty men left in the commission of the peace in July 1642, fifteen were subsequently sequestered for royalism, of whom all but one were removed from the commission by Parliament, H.C.R.O., 5M53, no. 964; Underdown, *Pride's Purge*, pp. 367, 369, 372, 373, 374, 377, 378, 381, 388–90; Brit. Lib. MS Stowe 577 (Liber Pacis 1652), fols. 46–7; P.R.O., C193/13/3, fols. 56–7; C193/13/4, fols. 85–9.

[15] For the imbalance in the county committee see p. 9, above; H.C.RO., QO 3, p. 224; P.R.O., C193/13/4, fol. 86.

[16] P.R.O., C193/13/4; C193/13/5, fols. 77–9; Cambridge University Library, Dd. 8. 1, fols. 91–5; Fletcher, *Sussex*, p. 311; Underdown, 'Settlement in the counties' in Aylmer, *The Interregnum*, pp. 177–8.

[17] See below, p. 77.

Newport corporations who appeared in the latter but not in the former. The same men were named in the county commission of sewers in 1651, and it was apparently from the same cadre that the twenty-seven active members of the militia commission were drawn.[18]

It is important not to exaggerate the political significance of appointments and even activity in local offices during the Interregnum. However well-meant, not every appointment which government made was well received by the appointee. The shrievalty was of course particularly unpopular. John Hooke of Bramshott hid when Francis Tylney sent the Rump's order for him to serve as sheriff to his house, and his wife refused to receive it.[19] More remarkable was the ingratitude of John Bulkeley, a secluded MP, who, though nominated as an 'ejector' in the ordinance of 28 August 1654, voted for its suspension on 6 November in the first Protectorate Parliament. Not even a personal appeal from his old friend Oliver Cromwell could induce Richard Norton to act as a militia commissioner in 1655.[20]

However, in the case of traditional and prestigious offices like justice of the peace, the ambition, even the force of habit, of the gentry led them to accept the honour even from a regime whose origins were repugnant. Sir John Oglander (d. 1655) had warned his descendants 'we are not born only to ourselves but for the public . . . if thou hast not some command in the country, thou wilt not be esteemed by the common sort of people'.[21] But those who accepted office for such reasons were not necessarily loyal to the regime which had appointed them. Sir William Uvedale acted as a justice in the early Commonwealth period, yet at the same time his house at Wickham was being used as a posting station for royalist correspondence. In the same period, Sir William Kingsmill was active as a JP, yet his private poetry reveals how heartily he detested the regime and everything it stood for.[22] Not too much therefore should be read into the willingness of some to serve as justices. Conciliation could be more apparent than real.

Even so, the proportion of justices who were active under the Commonwealth was not spectacular. Out of seventy-two non-honorific appointees in

---

[18] *The Names of the Justices of the Peace As they stand in Commission of their several Counties this Michaelmas Terme 1650* (London, 1650); *F. & R.*, ii. 42–3, 308–9; *C.J.*, vi. 241, 268, 357, 367; Brit. Lib., Addit. MS 24863, fol. 60; P.R.O., Hampshire militia accounts 1651–4, S.P. 28/154; S.P. 28/230.

[19] H. Cary, *Memorials of the Great Civil War in England 1646–52* (2 vols., London, 1842), ii. 115.

[20] *F. & R.*, ii. 975; *C.J.*, vii. 382; *The Writings and Speeches of Oliver Cromwell*, ed. W. C. Abbott (4 vols., Cambridge, Mass., 1937–47), iv. 25; *Th.S.P.*, iv. 238–9.

[21] F. Bamford, *A Royalist's Notebook* (London, 1936), p. 246.

[22] *Cal.Clar.S.P.*, ii. 75; *Calendar of the Committee for Compounding*, ed. Green, ii. 883; J. D. Eames, 'The poems of Sir William Kingsmill (1613–1661): a critical edition' (Birmingham Univ., Ph.D. thesis, 1982), ii. 36–47.

the commission of the peace in 1652, only thirty-six (50 per cent) left evidence of having acted, either by attending quarter sessions, having reference made to them by that court or performing some out of sessions duty. But this was higher both numerically and proportionately than the twenty-four out of fifty-six JPs (just under 43 per cent) who served under the Protectorate in 1657.[23]

Former members of the Rump adopted a variety of attitudes to serving under the Protectorate. Richard Norton was willing to act as JP, and six other members of the Rump, who were resident in the county, also acted, though Robert Reynolds, the ousted solicitor-general, later made much of the fact that he absented himself from sessions 'during all Cromwell's Usurped Rule'.[24] Dr William Stephens, by contrast, not only attended, but acted as chairman of the justices at their Epiphany sessions in 1656, in the presence of Major-General Goffe, 'and in all things expresseth himselfe very cordially for his highness and the present affaires'. Nicholas Love was also compliant, but Goffe found him hard to fathom.[25] Nicholas Love and Robert Reynolds would be prominent in the opposition to the Protectorate in 1659.[26]

But the new machinery of the state in the 1650s, notably in the locally stationed military and revenue establishments seemed to offer central government a means of controlling or at least influencing local administration, through its paid dependants. Dr Reece has drawn attention to the number of army officers who were appointed to local offices in the 1650s, suggesting that this development counteracted any attempt to conciliate local gentry elites. In Hampshire, with its substantial military presence spread out through the several castles and garrisons, there was certainly the potential for a significant number of officers to become involved in local government and large numbers of them were appointed. The local military establishment did decline from more than 1,200 in 1651 to just under 550 in 1655, but Portsmouth, Calshot and Hurst castles in the mainland remained as garrisons and the several forts and castles in the Isle of Wight continued to be manned by regular troops (see Table 1).[27] Sydenham was one of the militia commissioners in the Isle of Wight under the Commonwealth, and Peter Murford, governor of Southampton, was one on the mainland. Murford was named again as a militia commissioner in 1655, this time at Portsmouth, where he

[23] Brit. Lib., Stowe MS 577, fols. 46–7; P.R.O. C193/13/6, fols. 92–5; E372 (Pipe Rolls) 496 (1651–2); 501 (1656–7); H.C.R.O., QO3, pp. 107–46, 306–29; I.W.C.R.O., Car/PR/1.

[24] P.R.O., Exchequer K.R., Bills and Answers of (Interregnum) Accountants, E113, Box 14 (Hampshire): The Answer of Sir Robert Reynolds.

[25] *Th.S.P.*, iv. 408; v. 215.

[26] See below, pp. 78–9.

[27] H. M. Reece, 'The military presence in England, 1649–1660' (Oxford Univ., D.Phil. thesis, 1981), pp. 4, 177–200, appendix 2, 292–3.

Table 1. *Garrison establishments in Hampshire during the Interregnum*

	1651	1655	1660
Calshot castle	18	18	18
Hurst castle	36	36	36
Isle of Wight	500	240	280
Portsmouth	440	247	240
Southampton	220 disbanded		

was now stationed.[28] In that year too, Major-General Goffe and at least five other serving military officers were named as militia commissioners for the county.[29] Colonel Nathaniel Whetham, who had been commissioned to command a regiment of militia foot back in 1651, was made a militia commissioner of the county in July 1659, and Sydenham and Thomas Bowreman, a fort commander, were then appointed for the Isle of Wight.[30] Colonel Okey, a temporary area commander, was added to the Hampshire commission in August.[31]

Before then, military officers had been equally evident amongst those appointed as assessment commissioners. Several were nominated in the early years of the Commonwealth, and there were four named (apart from Oliver Cromwell) in the commission of 1652. This military presence was subsequently maintained under the Protectorate, and even increased to six in 1657, in accordance with an upward trend observed by Dr Reece.[32]

The military had an even more substantial presence on the commission of the peace. In 1650, there were five serving army officers in the Hampshire commission (apart from Oliver Cromwell whose appointment was honorific), a figure mirrored in the county commission of sewers the next year. By March 1652, it had risen to seven serving officers, and military representation would remain at about the same level for the rest of the Interregnum. Naval representation, which was merely a token one in the early years of the

[28] *Cal.S.P.Dom.*, 1650, p. 486; Brit. Lib., Addit. MS 29319 (Sydenham papers), fols. 67–8; Addit. MS 19516 (Letter book of major-generals' registry), fols. 17, 84; P.R.O., S.P. 28/154 (documents relating to Hampshire).

[29] Bodl., MS Rawl. A 33, p. 738.

[30] *Cal.S.P.Dom.*, 1651, p. 513; *F. & R.*, ii. 1332–3.

[31] *Cal.S.P.Dom.*, 1659–60, p. 79.

[32] *F. & R.*, ii. 42–3, 308–9, 477–8, 674–5, 1080; *C.J.*, vi. 268; *Cal.S.P.Dom.*, 1655–6, p. 40; Reece, 'The military presence in England', p. 208.

Commonwealth, rose spectacularly to six at the outbreak of the Dutch War in 1652, but declined rapidly on the conclusion of peace.[33]

But despite the large number of military appointees in the various commissions, their impact upon local administration in Hampshire was distinctly muted. For one thing, by no means all garrison commanders were outsiders to the communities in which they were stationed. During the 1640s, local parliamentarian gentry had taken it in turns to command the Solent garrisons, and they were by no means totally ousted in the 1650s. Peter Bettsworth, son of a local gentry family, commanded Calshot castle throughout the Interregnum.[34] Thomas Bowreman and John Basket, two of the fort commanders in the Isle of Wight, were both local men, the former coming from an established gentry family, though according to Sir John Oglander, one 'in no repute' before 1642.[35] And Richard Norton, who had held commands in Portsmouth off and on since 1636, was made governor of the garrison in 1655.[36] Those few officers who were consistently active in local administration in the 1650s were mostly of this type, local gentry, who simply happened to hold garrison commands.

It was much rarer for true outsiders to be regularly involved in local government. Though recommended to be appointed as an assessment commissioner in Southampton in December 1650, the governor Major Peter Murford never seems to have acted.[37] Colonel Nathaniel Whetham, governor of Portsmouth, though appointed as a colonel in the Hampshire militia in 1651, left no evidence of having acted in that capacity.[38] Goffe was active as a militia commissioner when he was appointed major-general in Hampshire in 1655–6, but Colonel Okey appointed to a similar post in 1659 does not seem to have been so.[39]

Though the military presence was more substantial in Hampshire than in many other counties in the 1650s, it failed to have a significant impact upon local administration there, which remained firmly under the control of the local gentry though the majority of office-holders were now drawn from the lower levels of that class.

[33] *The Names of the Justices of the Peace As they stand in Commission in their several Counties this Michaelmas Terme 1650*; Brit. Lib., Addit. MA 24863, fol. 60; P.R.O., C193/13/4, fols. 85–8; C193/13/6, fols. 92–5; Cambridge University Library, Dd. 8. 1, fols. 91–5.
[34] P.R.O., E101/67/11B (Treasurers at War, Second Account), fol. 82; S.P. 28/154, Thomas Gallet's Account.
[35] Bamford, *A Royalist's Notebook*, p. 110.
[36] H.C.R.O., Borthwick–Norton MSS, 4M53, i. 17. I am very grateful to Messrs Hall and Barber for this reference; *Cal.S.P.Dom.*, 1655–6, p. 106.
[37] S.C.R.O., SC14/2/18.
[38] C. D. & W. C. D. Whetham, *A History of the Life of Colonel Nathaniel Whetham* (London, 1907), provides no evidence that he did and I have found none.
[39] Bodl., MS Rawl. C 179, pp. 181–2, 209–10.

The new revenue establishments were another professional arm stretching down into the localities. They represented another structure of patronage, another cadre of office-holders who might have an impact upon local administration. The 1640s had witnessed a massive inflation in such offices, chiefly arising from the excise and the sequestration and administration of confiscated lands. The latter were contracting under the Commonwealth as lands were sold off and sequestration machinery rationalized. But there remained in the 1650s, a substantial body of officials scattered through the counties, dedicated to raising state revenue in one way or another. In Hampshire there were about thirty salaried officials employed in the customs and excise, who employed their own staff, quite apart from the excise farmers and their staffs; and for much of the decade the inland commodities excise in Hampshire, outside Southampton, Portsmouth and the Isle of Wight, was out to farm.[40]

But many of these revenue officials were recruited from the ruling elites of the communities in which they served, with the full connivance of the central authorities. Thomas Mason was an alderman of Southampton before he became an excise sub-commissioner there under the Commonwealth.[41] Edward Marsh, another sub-commissioner, was already a free burgess, as was Jacob Le Gay, who became collector of customs there in 1650. William Burrard, a free burgess at Lymington, became customs waiter there. Francis Guidott, also a long-standing member of that corporation and mayor for four years successively (1656–9) had a share in the farm of the salt excise at Lymington, Pennington, Milford and Keyhaven for much of the decade.[42] Some may have taken up these posts out of a desire to protect their local community rather than any dedication to the interests of the state. Three months before his appointment as customs collector at Southampton, Jacob Le Gay had been delegated by the corporation to represent it over the issue of the special customs levy which was supposed to be raised in other ports according to an Elizabethan grant, to help Southampton keep its town wall in repair.[43]

But central government did not try to keep revenue offices out of the hands of members of local elites, quite the opposite. In December 1652, the Rump approved a plan that counties be allowed to farm their own excise, which would put the nomination of collectors totally into local hands. But a plan by

[40] P.R.O., E351/1296 (Excise Declared Account 1650–3); E364/129 (Customs Declared Account 1656–7).

[41] *Cal.S.P.Dom.*, 1652–3, pp. 252.

[42] *Cal.S.P.Dom.*, 1651–2, p. 413; P.R.O., E112 (Exchequer Bills and Answers) 564 no. 362; E351/650 (Customs Declared Account 1650–1); S.C.R.O., SC3/1/1 (Burgess admissions book), fol. 217; I.W.C.R.O., 45/16a (Newport convocation book), p. 556; Bodl., MS Rawl. C 386, fols. 9, 56; C. St Barbe (ed.), *Records of the Corporation of New Lymington* (1848), pp. 8, 17.

[43] S.C.R.O., SC2/1/8, fol. 57.

JPs at Hampshire quarter sessions to launch such a scheme in the county early in the following year does not seem to have borne fruit, so direct collection was resumed.[44]

But many revenue offices remained in local hands, and remarkably few local hands at that, because pluralism was widely practised as officials sought to maximize their profits through the accumulation of salaries. John Woodman, a previously rather humble citizen of Winchester, who had risen through the sequestration service during the 1640s, in a case in point. Under the Commonwealth he became receiver of dean and chapter revenues in Winchester and Chichester dioceses, and at the same time served as steward of St Cross hospital near Winchester.[45] Thomas Muspratt, another local man, became one of the three sub-commissioners for sequestrations in 1650 through co-option by John Champion and Edward Hooker, who were already sub-commissioners and were also local men. Between 1651 and 1654, Muspratt was also treasurer of the local militia and again in 1655–6 and thereafter became the local agent of the Trustees for the Maintenance of Ministers, while continuing as the sole sub-commissioner of sequestrations.[46]

Such men often pursued their own interests rather than those of the state. John Woodman was guilty of serious embezzlement and forgery and performed none of his offices efficiently to the irritation of the local justices and gentry.[47] Thomas Muspratt, though not dishonest was not totally reliable either; in 1659 he failed to pass his account in spite of an order from the Trustees for the Maintenance of Ministers to do so.[48] And outsiders were no better. Armiger Warner, a Londoner by origin, acted as the Army Committee's agent in Hampshire under the Commonwealth. Up until the summer of 1651, he was also treasurer of the local militia, and thereafter acted as its muster-master. In that year, he also became a sub-commissioner of excise at Portsmouth and was involved in supplying victuals to the army in Ireland. Perhaps he was overstretched, but he failed to perform his tasks as the Army Committee's agent with any great efficiency.[49]

Some men who were politically disaffected managed to obtain posts in the

44 *C.J.*, vii. 225; H.C.R.O., QO 3, p. 151; *Cal.S.P.Dom.*, 1652–3, p. 251.
45 *Calendar of the Committee for Compounding*, ed. Green, i. 236, 385; P.R.O., S.P. 28/258, pt 2, fol. 204; H.C.R.O., QO 3, p. 135.
46 P.R.O., S.P. 28/129, pt 9; E113/14; Answers of Thomas Muspratt; S.P. 28/230 (Hampshire).
47 H.C.R.O., QO 3, p. 135; 44M69 (Jervoise of Herriard MSS) E77, John Belchamber to Sir Thomas Jervoise 18 June 1649; see below, p. 50.
48 Mildon, 'Puritanism in Hampshire', p. 332.
49 *Cal.S.P.Dom.*, 1651–2, pp. 413, 552, 589, 596, 614; P.R.O., E101/67/11B; S.P. 28/230 (Hampshire); E113/14; Answer of A. Warner; H.C.R.O., QO 3, p. 89; S.C.R.O., S.C. 14/2/18 (Southampton assessment book), fol. 1 and *passim*; Warner took seven weeks to deliver the Rump's letter of 27 April 1649 about the assessment to commissioners at Southampton and the period of the six months assessment of 1651 had virtually elapsed before he delivered the act and instructions to the commissioners.

revenue establishments, and they were not all weeded out. In the summer of 1651, four employees of Launcelot Faulkner of London, farmer of the inland commodities excise in Hampshire, were provoking disorders in the county through their misconduct. Upon investigation, two of them were found to be 'scandalous and ill affected to the present Government'. The Commissioners of Excise ordered that they be dismissed.[50] But William Cole of Southampton, a Leveller involved in circulating anti-government propaganda under the Protectorate, retained his post as a customs officer at Cowes. And George Embree (or Every), a Quaker with similar views, retained his post in the excise department at Southampton, despite protests from John Dunch, a local militia commander.[51] At least in Hampshire, the new revenue establishments seem to have been a mixed blessing as far as central government was concerned. Indeed, it was almost as difficult to control them as to control amateur officials in county and borough.

Before leaving the subject of local office-holding, it is necessary to say something about the impact of the Interregnum regimes upon the boroughs. These semi-autonomous bodies with their ruling oligarchies represented a serious encumbrance to central government and the enforcement of its policies. As Dr Williams' study of the west country has shown, Interregnum regimes are remarkable for the lack of impact which they had upon the personnel of borough corporations, and the evidence from Hampshire seems to confirm this assessment.[52]

Victory in the Civil War enabled the parliamentarians to remove active royalists from borough government and obtain offices for themselves, but in none of Hampshire's boroughs with the exception of Winchester, were these changes very far-reaching before 1649. Local committeemen were appointed to the corporations of Portsmouth and Lymington in the latter stages of the Civil War. In October 1644, Nicholas Love displaced the royalist Thomas Willys as recorder of Basingstoke.[53] In November 1645, after the reduction of the royalist garrison, Robert Wallop replaced the earl of Southampton as high steward of Winchester, and royalist gentry were replaced by parliamentarians on the corporation. The royalist Ferdinando Bye's bid to obtain the

---

[50] Bodl., MS Rawl. C 386 (Copy book of orders of the Committee of Parliament for the Excise 1649–52), fols. 51, 57.

[51] P.R.O., E351/649 (Customs Declared Account 1648–9); E364/129 (Customs Declared Account 1656–7); P.R.O., E351/1299 (Excise Declared Account 1659); *Th.S.P.*, v. 287, 396; Bodl., MS Rawl. A 56, fol. 360.

[52] J. R. Williams, 'County and municipal government in Cornwall, Devon, Dorset and Somerset 1649–1660' (Bristol Univ., Ph.D. thesis, 1981), ch. 2, pp. 65–119.

[53] St Barbe, *Lymington*, p. 8; R. East (ed.), *Extracts from Records in the Possession of the Municipal Corporation of the Borough of Portsmouth and from other documents relating thereto* (2nd edn, Portsmouth, 1891), p. 353; H.C.R.O., 148M71 1/3 (Basingstoke Town Council Minutes 1641–1700).

town clerkship with royal support in 1647 was thwarted by John Lisle, the recorder, and the county committee, acting under the recent ordinance of 9 September excluding royalists from appointments to office. Next year, there was a parliamentary intervention in the borough, when one alderman was removed and another re-instated by order of the House of Commons.[54]

But royalism flared up in several boroughs in 1648 and disaffection in this quarter was one of the most serious problems facing the newly established Commonwealth in 1649. Sir John Oglander was elected mayor of Yarmouth in the Isle of Wight in 1647–8, and members of Lymington corporation collaborated with the royalist ships.[55] In December 1648, as Charles I passed by Winchester on his way to his trial, the mayor and aldermen of Winchester came out to meet him and presented him with the mace of the city until the army guard intervened.[56] John Ashe was travelling towards London from the west in Parliament's service in September 1649 and was beaten up by some royalists on Salisbury Plain, two of whom he managed to apprehend and bring to Andover. Joseph Hinxman, bailiff of Andover, not only failed to arrest them, but imprisoned Ashe instead for several days with the connivance of Roger Sherfield, the sub-steward or town clerk.[57]

How then did the Commonwealth regime deal with open disaffection amongst borough office-holders? In the case of Winchester, influenced by the city's two MPs, John Lisle and Nicholas Love, the Rump resorted to a completely new charter imposed by act of Parliament in September 1649, nominating a new mayor, three aldermen, seven new benchers and ten new members of the Twenty-Four (a select body of senior freemen), several of the new men being officials and dependants.[58] But the new charter envisaged no purge of the existing corporation, though Joseph Butler, the mayor of 1648, had disappeared from it by December 1649, and it contained no mechanism to give central government greater control over office-holding in the city. John Lisle continued to exercise patronage in appointments to the corporation, but it was left to the Engagement to purge the disaffected from Winchester's corporation, eight members of it being removed in September 1650.[59]

Elsewhere the enforcement of the Engagement proved problematical. At Southampton, James Capelin, mayor in 1649, was a strong supporter of the

[54] Godwin, *The Civil War in Hampshire*, p. 318; H.C.R.O., W/B1/5, fols. 1, 146–7; C.J., v. 535.
[55] List of Mayors, Yarmouth Town Hall; Godwin, *The Civil War in Hampshire*, p. 383.
[56] H.L.R.O., Main Papers, 15 June 1660, fol. 24.
[57] P.R.O., S.P. 24 (Papers of the Committee for Indemnity) /31, J. Ashe's petition; Andover's bailiff was the equivalent of the mayor in other corporations.
[58] H.L.R.O., Main Papers, 13 June 1660, fol. 22: copy of Winchester charter of 13 September 1649.
[59] H.C.R.O., W/B1/5, fols. 23, 28.

Rump and a patron of local Independent ministers.[60] But very few of his colleagues on the corporation shared his sentiments. Several of them tried to avoid taking the Engagement at all or supplied unacceptable glosses of their own. The Council of State tried to deal with the problem by corresponding with successive mayors and bringing the influence of the governor of the garrison, Major Peter Murford, to bear upon recalcitrant members of the corporation. At one point the Council of State became so impatient with the conduct of the mayor, Christopher Walleston, that it ordered his deposition, but apparently thought better of it. In the end no magistrate seems to have been removed from the corporation as a result of the affair. Murford remained a valued watch-dog for the regime there, becoming an active member of the corporation in 1651, and was a JP the next year.[61] Thomas Bowreman, performed a similar role at Yarmouth, which had proved a centre of royalism in 1648. Bowreman was mayor there in 1650.[62] There was no apparent disaffection within the corporation of Portsmouth, but Colonel Nathaniel Whetham, the governor, was ordered to report back on its enforcement of government orders. Strangely though, Whetham never participated in the government of the borough. Indeed, he did not even become a burgess until 1655, the year he left for Scotland.[63]

In other places, the hold of the regime proved weaker. Though summoned to appear before the Indemnity Committee in December 1649, to answer for their conduct in the Ashe affair, neither Hinxman nor Sherfield appeared. But no action was taken against them.[64] The Indemnity Committee though charged since October 1647 with policing the personnel of the boroughs to root out delinquency, apparently lacked the means to enforce its will at local level. Under the Commonwealth, the membership of Hampshire's corporations seems to have remained remarkably stable.

It is true that in several boroughs supporters or dependents of the regime might exercise an influence on its behalf. John Hildesley succeeded John Lisle as recorder of Winchester in 1650; he was also a long-standing member of Christchurch and Lymington corporations, and in December 1651, he wrote to Southampton corporation suggesting that they might replace their neuter-royalist recorder, Thomas Levingstone, with John Lisle, a suggestion which

[60] J. S. Davies, *A History of Southampton* (Southampton, 1883), p. 495.
[61] *Cal.S.P.Dom.*, 1649–50, pp. 285, 310, 323–4, 337, 366; *Cal.S.P.Dom.*, 1650, pp. 137, 159; S.C.R.O., SC2/1/8, fols. 49–50, 66–76.
[62] J. C. Hughes, 'Town account of Yarmouth 1646–7', *Proceedings of the Isle of Wight Natural History and Archaeological Society*, i. (1928), 581.
[63] *Cal.S.P.Dom.*, 1651, p. 299; East, *Portsmouth*, p. 355.
[64] P.R.O., S.P. 24/5, fols. 75, 109; S.P. 24/6, fol. 39; the corporation had clearly supported their bailiff and town clerk in the affair, resolving on 8 October to cover their costs in the case out of borough funds, H.C.R.O. (Andover Archives), 37M84, 4/MI/1, Bundle of Town Council Minutes 1641–54.

they followed, having gained Levingstone's consent.[65] Hildesley who himself rose to government office under the Protectorate, also became a justice in Andover.[66] In July 1654, Richard Cromwell became high steward of the town.[67] As the 1650s progressed, the mayoralty and corporation of Portsmouth came to be dominated by men with close links with the local naval establishment.[68]

But the significance of the presence of some government official on the roll of the corporation should not be exaggerated. Those who were active politicians like John Lisle, Nicholas Love or William Stephens (recorder of Newport) rarely, if ever, performed their duties personally, relying instead upon deputies. And the 1650s saw a retreat of such men from borough office. John Lisle resigned his recordership at Southampton in December 1658, when Thomas Levingstone, who had been accused of royalism, obtained a writ of restitution in Upper Bench.[69]

The Protectorate government, like its Commonwealth predecessor, showed itself capable of removing only active royalists from municipal government. At the time of Penruddock's Rising some of the crypto-royalism of Southampton's rulers showed itself when they supported the rebels and discountenanced local people who were prepared to fight them. A committee of Hampshire JPs was ordered to investigate by the protector's Council and on consideration of their findings, and further investigations, the Council ordered that the mayor, sheriff and an alderman be removed and replacements elected, which duly took place.[70] But one of the replacements, William Horne, was probably the Southampton merchant of that name who had tried to arrange Charles II's passage out of the kingdom in 1651, so the crypto-royalists remained.[71]

Interregnum governments also left the charters of most of Hampshire's boroughs untouched. Apart from the new charter for Winchester and the exemplification of Newport's charter from Edward VI made in February 1656, no alterations were made to the status quo, though Newport's more recent charters had been called in under the Rump.[72] With the complete dis-

[65] St Barbe, *Lymington*, p. 7; H.C.R.O., W/B1/5, fol. 28; S.C.R.O., SC 2/1/8, fol. 77–8.
[66] A. Woolrych, *Commonwealth to Protectorate* (Oxford 1982), p. 384; H.C.R.O., 37M84, 2/JC/2.
[67] H.C.R.O., 37M84, 4/MI/1.
[68] East, *Portsmouth*, pp. 314–15, 328, 354–5.
[69] S.C.R.O., SC 2/1/8, fols. 142, 145; the simultaneous admission of several Cromwellian courtiers as free burgesses was of no administrative significance, SC 3/1/1, fol. 222.
[70] *Cal.S.P.Dom.*, 1655, pp. 98, 222, 243, 257, 590; *Hist. MSS Comm. Eleventh Report App. pt III Southampton MSS*, p. 30.
[71] *Charles II's Escape from Worcester: A Collection of Narratives Assembled by Samuel Pepys*, ed. W. Matthews (London, 1967), p. 140.
[72] B. L. K. Henderson, 'The Commonwealth charters', *T.R.H.S. Third Series*, vi. (1912), 131; I.W.C.R.O., 45/16a, p. 592.

enfranchisement of so many smaller boroughs (including eight in Hampshire) under the Instrument of Government, there was little political incentive for the Cromwellian government to undertake a nationwide remodelling of borough charters. But on the administrative level, it must at least put a question mark over the zeal in Whitehall for centralization, when so many boroughs remained almost untouched in their autonomy, simply by offering tacit acquiescence to governmental authority. There was no systematic policy towards the boroughs, only a haphazard series of reactions to particular circumstances. The local parliamentarian gentry were a resource, who, as the Southampton case showed, could be deployed to reduce municipal independence, but it was a resource which Interregnum governments seemed strangely reluctant to use.

When the Protectorate was overthrown and the Rump was restored in 1659, local republicans were acutely aware of the strength of entrenched conservatism in the boroughs. Some of the 'well affected' of the Portsmouth area in an address of June 1659 urged the Rump that 'at your leisure, you will please to take Inspection into the state of Corporations, Constitutions whereof we humbly conceive are contrary to, and Inconsistent with a Free State'.[73] But nothing was done.

Interregnum regimes had by and large failed to break the mould in local government. They continued to rely upon office-holders drawn from the local gentry and borough elites to govern the localities. The military and revenue establishments in Hampshire failed to have a significant impact upon local administration, which is hardly surprising in the light of the fact that several of the garrison commanders and revenue officers were themselves recruited from the traditional rulers of the localities. Generally, central government was prepared to accept the most grudging acquiescence from local office-holders, rather than any positive loyalty as a condition of their service. But in Hampshire at any rate, the reconciliation of former enemies through their involvement in local government did not greatly accelerate as the 1650s drew to a close. In fact, office-holding remained remarkably stable in Hampshire throughout the decade.

[73] To the Supream Authority The Parliament of the Commonwealth of England The humble Petition of divers well affected Persons Inhabitants of the Town of Portsmouth and Places Adjacent (London, 1659).

2

The enforcement of policy 1649–60

DEFENCE AND INTERNAL SECURITY

In accounting for the Rump's failure to develop imaginative domestic policies, Professor Underdown has succinctly summarized its main casues:

Defence against the Commonwealth's enemies, internal and external, was necessarily their first priority; this meant dealing with Ireland, Scotland, the French, Royalists in and outside the country, and finally, overwhelmingly, the Dutch war. It meant the militia, the navy, and foreign policy.[1]

Much of the government's involvement in the provinces was now concerned with defence and security. Even when the Council of State turned its attention to poverty, it is not hard to detect a concern for internal security motivating the initiatives it took. In July 1651, the Council of State wrote to the mayor and aldermen of Portsmouth, ordering them to relieve and find employment for the growing number of poor in the town. But this was not part of a coherent social policy. The Council made no attempt to conceal the fact that its concern arose solely from the potential threat which growing poverty posed to the security of the garrison.[2]

Though its enemies changed slightly, the government's main concerns did not greatly alter under the Protectorate. Even spectacular initiatives, like the major-generals' experiment, were primarily concerned with internal security. The major-generals' militia was part of a retrenchment scheme designed to sustain the reduction of the tax burden on at least those members of the land-owning classes who had not fought against Parliament.[3] If one follows Gardiner's interpretation of the formulation of the major-generals' instructions, those concerned with moral reformation were a personal addition by Oliver Cromwell to a scheme which had already been worked out with the

---

[1] Underdown, *Pride's Purge*, pp. 294–5.
[2] *Cal.S.P.Dom.*, 1651, p. 298.
[3] P. G. I. Gaunt, 'The Councils of the Protectorate from December 1653 to September 1658' (Exeter Univ., Ph.D. thesis, 1983), pp. 169–70.

intention of preserving peace in the provinces at as low a cost as possible.[4] In the case of the restored Rump of 1659, internal security became the 'be all and end all' of government.

Superficially the governments of the Interregnum appear to have been successful in the areas of defence and security at least. No rebellion which seriously endangered the existence of the regime broke out in England in this period; Ireland and Scotland were pacified, and apart from the Worcester campaign, no foreign invasion took place. But these bare facts conceal a catalogue of failure and mismanagement in relation to the provinces, which left central government vulnerable in several important respects, and which represent a real lack of control over the localities in an area where strong central leadership might have been expected.

For much of the decade, central government was not particularly well informed about the state of security even in a strategically vital area like the Solent. The reputation of the central intelligence system built up by Interregnum governments stands high today, partly thanks to the researches of Professor Underdown.[5] He showed (more than a quarter of a century ago) how the government was able to penetrate the conspiracies of royalists at home and abroad, thus gaining timely warning of any possible outbreak. Whether the system of the 1650s was innately superior to the networks controlled by the executive committees of Parliament in the 1640s, or the secretaries of state after 1660, is open to question.[6] Furthermore, the system of the 1650s seems to have lacked a regular local dimension even in the Solent area, leaving central government strangely purblind. On 8 March 1658, Colonel Richard Norton wrote to Thurloe from Portsmouth about a royalist conspiracy brewing locally. But even though, as governor of Portsmouth, he might have been expected to provide the government with regular bulletins, his opening sentence makes it clear that he did not do so: 'I do not love to trouble you nor my selfe with frivolous reports, wherefore you have not heard much of me.' Norton knew that his was not a frivolous report because some royalists had approached him personally in an attempt to draw him into the conspiracy, but he did not reveal this to Thurloe.[7]

Local supporters of central government, like Richard Norton, only bothered to inform Whitehall when an actual rebellion seemed to be imminent. The well affected of Southampton reported the dubious activities

[4] S. R. Gardiner, *The History of the Commonwealth and Protectorate* (4 vols., London, 1903), iii. 318–40.
[5] D. Underdown, *Royalist Conspiracy in England 1646–1660* (New Haven, 1960).
[6] J. D. Jones, *Royal Prisoner*, p. 90; P. M. Fraser, *The Intelligence of the Secretaries of State 1660–1688* (Cambridge, 1956).
[7] Bodl., MS Rawl. A 58 fol. 58; Underdown, *Royalist Conspiracy*, p. 223.

of certain members of the corporation at the time of Penruddock's Rising.[8] Towards the end of 1657, John Dunch, commander of one of the county's two militia troops, in response to a circular letter from the protector, entered into correspondence with John Thurloe alerting him to local conspiracies, allegedly involving Catholics, royalists and Quakers.[9] Some of the servants of the West family deserted them to join the local republican militia rather than be a party to Lord De la Warr's conspiracy in 1659, which they thus made known to the government. At the same time, John Barkstead, who had become a local landowner, sent a report to Thomas Scot from Eling about the wider aspects of the conspiracy. This enabled the Rump to nip the rising in the bud and initiate a thorough investigation, carried out under the auspices of locally based politicians like Nicholas Love. The depositions which he and others collected provided the central government with a unique insight into the mood and the activities of its opponents in the locality.[10]

The only regular reports which Whitehall received about more routine matters of government and politics were dispatched by William Goffe, the major-general, during the comparatively short period he was in the county, between November 1655 and September 1656. Also during this period, the names of 185 suspects who had given bond for their good behaviour reached the central register from Hampshire.[11] This was certainly a great improvement in the knowledge of central government about local security, though the value of Goffe's reports was reduced by his previous ignorance of the county, his naivety and his many other concerns. Apart from these exceptional periods, the government's information about what was going on in the localities was patchy and irregular.

For much of the 1650s, Whitehall relied on fairly traditional forms of authority to safeguard the security of the localities. JPs in Hampshire were appealed to collectively or in small groups to help slight fortifications, to be vigilant, keep up the local watch, and to secure suspicious persons and suppress their meetings. To a large extent, Interregnum governments depended on ordinary justices, just as any Tudor or Stuart monarch might have done. The governor and fort captains of the Isle of Wight, to whom the care of the island's security devolved during the 1650s had also been a Tudor development.[12]

There were of course more novel agencies to which appeal could be made,

8 *Cal.S.P.Dom.*, 1655, p. 98.
9 Bodl., MS Rawl. A 56, fol. 360.
10 *Cal.Clar.S.P.*, iv. 274, 313, 316–17, 321, 323–4, 370–1.
11 *Th.S.P.*, iv., v. *passim*; Brit. Lib., Addit. MS 34013 (Major-generals' register) fols. 2–5, 8–9, 11–13, 15–16, 18–22, 24–25, 27–28, 30–41, 44–7, 50–2, 54.
12 *Cal.S.P.Dom.*, 1649–50, p. 320; *Cal.S.P.Dom.*, 1651, p. 293; *Cal.S.P.Dom.*, 1655, pp. 93–4; Brit. Lib., Addit. MS 24861, fol. 32; Jones, 'Isle of Wight', pp. 41–6.

though these tended to be manned by the same people. The Council of State continued to look to the county committee in Hampshire during 1649.[13] The transition to militia commissioners during the Rump's rule was not as significant as Dr Clive Holmes seems to think.[14] Commissioners for musters had been employed by the Tudors before the centralizing measure of the lieutenancy had taken shape. On the level of personnel, most of the active militia commissioners of 1651 and after in Hampshire, had been active committeemen and were also mostly JPs. Nor were the militia commissioners of the 1650s by the nature of their office more dependent on central government than any other local officials, or the servants of previous or subsequent regimes. Indeed, the limitations of the government's hold over them is well expressed in the Rump's militia act of 12 August 1651, which stipulated that the commissioners, militia officials and soldiers were to do their duty with diligence and faithfulness, 'upon pain of being Censured and Adjudged Enemies of their Countrey, and to undergo such penalties as in that behalf shall be by the Parliament thought fit to be inflicted upon them'.[15] Doubtless such punishments would be the 'terrors of the earth'! Despite the lack of serious sanctions against them however, the amateur officials who were prepared to act in Hampshire showed themselves willing to do the government's bidding, both in 1651 and 1655.[16]

Successive Interregnum regimes in fact fell foul of two potentially conflicting urges, one to exert more control over local defence and security arrangements and the other to involve local people more in their own defence and policing their own areas. As a result, in Hampshire, they failed to do either adequately. Attempts to enhance central control over local security continued throughout the Interregnum. In the early years of the Commonwealth, the governor and fort commanders of the Isle of Wight were included in the local militia commission and on the mainland garrison commanders like Nathaniel Whetham were encouraged to help in mustering and commanding the militia.[17] The Rump also tried to use MPs and civilian members of the government to encourage local militia commissioners to greater efforts. In 1650, Nicholas Love, MP for Winchester, was sent down to Hampshire to supervise the enforcement of the militia act and to report back to the Council of State.[18] In August 1651, Robert Wallop and Richard Cromwell were ordered to ensure that a rendezvous of the county's forces took place, to

---

[13] *Cal.S.P.Dom.*, 1649–50, pp. 86, 294.
[14] C. Holmes, *Seventeenth-Century Lincolnshire* (Lincoln, 1980), p. 206.
[15] *F. & R.*, ii. 552.
[16] Brit. Lib., Addit. MS 24861, fol. 56; Bodl., MS Rawl. A 32, pp. 809, 935; *Th.S.P.*, iv. 238, 257.
[17] P.R.O., S.P. 25 (State Papers Interregnum) vol. 9, p. 5; S.P. 25/15, p. 15.
[18] *C.J.*, vi. 458.

report the numbers mustered and expect the future order of the Council. And the next day, on 22 August, Nicholas Love and Bulstrode Whitelocke were delegated to speak to Robert Reynolds, the solicitor-general (who had purchased episcopal land in the county), on going into Hampshire to tell him to 'stir up the rest of the commissioners to promote and hasten that worke with what expedition they can', for 'the forces of that county are not in that forwardnesse that the present state of affaire doe require'.[19] The Protectorate government appointed the major-generals to supervise the militia, and there were similar schemes in 1659.[20] However, these initiatives were either short-lived or ineffective, or both.

But successive regimes also sought to involve as many people as possible in the defence and security of their localities. In this they sought to reverse a tendency which had been apparent in the Solent area at least since 1648, when garrison soldiers had increasingly been relied upon to defend the coast, while field units policed the places further inland.[21] The regular army was expensive and over-stretched and the Rump's militia legislation is clear testimony of its desire to devolve more duties to local amateur forces. Even when this legislation did not apply, as in the Isle of Wight, persistent efforts were made to raise the traditional militia, and these were renewed by Cromwellian and republican governments in 1656 and 1658–9.[22] On the mainland, units were regularly commissioned, either to be standing militia forces or to serve part-time, in 1651, 1655–6 and 1659.[23] The Rump regime also sought to involve local people in the building up of some fortifications and the slighting of others, as the work was 'conducing to their own security'.[24]

Despite all the efforts that were made, however, militia units often existed only on paper in Hampshire during the Interregnum. Before September 1649, a county troop and foot company were being kept up in the county. But by December the horse troop was on the point of disbandment as a result of lack of funds. In December 1650, the Council of State ordered the militia commissioners to put one of their horse troops on stand-by to secure the peace of the county.[25] Between then and May 1651, Captain John Gale's (or Geale's) troop was active, being quartered mostly at Winchester, but also for a short

---

[19] P.R.O., S.P. 25/21, pp. 52, 64.
[20] The schemes of 1659 only seem to have existed on paper. Bodl., MS Rawl. C 179, pp. 181–2, 297, 300–1; *C.J.*, vii. 759.
[21] *Cal.S.P.Dom.*, 1648–9, pp. 57, 212; Brit. Lib. Addit. MS 24861, fol. 73.
[22] *C.J.*, vi. 556; *C.J.*, vii, 341, 757–8; *Th.S.P.*, v. 397–8; *Cal.S.P.Dom.*, 1658–9, pp. 48, 98.
[23] *Cal.S.P.Dom.*, 1650, p. 511; *Cal.S.P.Dom.*, 1651, pp. 513, 516; *Cal.S.P.Dom.*, 1659–60, pp. 24, 64; *C.J.*, vii. 759, 772.
[24] *Cal.S.P.Dom.*, 1649–50, p. 320; *Cal.S.P.Dom.*, 1651, pp. 81, 125–6; *Cal.S.P.Dom.*, 1651–2, p. 174; Brit. Lib. Addit. MS 29319, fols. 77, 101.
[25] *Calendar of the Committee for Compounding*, ed. Green, i. 155; *Cal.S.P.Dom.*, 1649–50, pp. 449–50; *Cal.S.P.Dom.*, 1650, p. 471.

time at Portsmouth. The quartermaster of a troop of dragoons was paid for twenty-one days' service during the same period at the rate of three days per fortnight. Steven Worlidge was employed as marshal for the same period. A contingent under Gale participated in the standing horse militia of the summer of 1651. In August 1651, Charles Terry's troop was mustered to a strength of 117 officers and men, and dispatched to join Cromwell at Worcester, but it does not seem to have got there in time for the battle, and the county's foot regiment was not completed before the crisis had passed.[26] Thereafter, Hampshire's militia lapsed entirely for nearly four years until in 1655 two horse troops were listed.[27] Initially numbering a hundred men, they had to be reduced to eighty as an economy. Because of shortage of funds from the decimation tax, no muster was possible before 22 March 1656, and this was the only recorded occasion on which they were mustered, though they were supposed to be so quarterly.[28] Then the second Protectorate Parliament abolished even this inadequate funding by refusing to renew the decimation tax. Again Hampshire was without an operational militia, this time until the summer of 1659, when two horse troops did see service, one of them helping to disperse De la Warr's confederates.[29] But it is generally true to say of Hampshire as of the west country that 'on the whole, attempts to create an efficient militia capable of replacing the army were not a success'.[30] Neither was there much community involvement in the building or demolition of fortifications.

Failure to involve many people in the county in their own defence and security arose from a number of factors, not least of which was the political isolation of Interregnum regimes. People simply did not care enough to want to defend them. They did not come flocking in to help to slight Winchester castle or to help to build up the fortifications of the Isle of Wight. They did not volunteer in large numbers for the militia; rather they laughed at those who did in 1655, telling them they would never get any pay.[31]

Shortage of funds was indeed a serious problem. The whole object of raising militia forces was to cut down on expensive regular troops, thus

[26] *Cal.S.P.Dom.*, 1651, p. 406; P.R.O., S.P. 28/230 (Hampshire militia accounts); E101/67/11B (Treasurers at war, second account), fols. 73–4.

[27] The Hampshire militia accounts show that though the militia commissioners of 1651 continued to be active until 1654, no payment was made for militia activity after the battle of Worcester; a scheme to raise a county troop of seventy horse to assist JPs in their internal security duties which was decided on at a meeting of the commissioners on 14 August 1651 does not seem to have come to anything, Brit. Lib., Addit. MS 24861, fol. 56; P.R.O., S.P. 28/129, pt 9; S.P. 28/230 (Hampshire).

[28] *Th.S.P.*, iv. 643; *Th.S.P.*, v. 365; Gaunt, 'The Councils of the Protectorate', p. 170.

[29] *The Clarke Papers*, ed. C. H. Firth (Camden Society, New Series, 4 vols., 1891–1901), iv. 37.

[30] Williams, 'County and municipal government in Cornwall, Devon, Dorset and Somerset', p. 288.

[31] *Th.S.P.*, iv. 238.

lowering the huge tax burden. But if the cost of the militia was passed back
to the tax-payer, the whole exercise would have been futile. Successive
regimes grappled with this problem, but none came to a satisfactory solution.
Initially, the Rump promised central funding for the militia, but having no
funds to spare resorted at first to taxing 'persons most disafected to the
present Government', to provide for the standing horse of 1651, but was
finally reduced to raising an assessment to re-imburse those who provided
arms and pay during the Worcester crisis.[32] This, at a time when taxation was
already at unprecedented levels, must have been most unpopular. To avoid
similar opprobrium the Cromwellian government resorted once again to
punitive taxation of its known enemies. But the decimation tax in Hampshire
produced little more than £1,000, barely half of what was actually required
to pay the militia troops. Goffe spent much of his time begging for funds from
elsewhere, but to no avail. By November 1656, there was an arrear of
£1,268 7s 5d owing to Goffe's association of Sussex, Hampshire and
Berkshire, and it was proposed that it be met out of the profits of the Spanish
prize plate, a precarious and over-estimated source.[33] After the decimation
was abolished in 1657, the protector promised to provide John Dunch's
troop of horse with pay, but amidst the growing financial difficulties of the
government, nothing came of this.[34] The restored Rump spent money it could
ill afford, paying the militia troops in Hampshire and elsewhere for their
services in the summer of 1659, out of the local assessment.[35]

The failure to involve many local people in the work of defending and
policing the localities had serious repercussions, leading to deficiencies in
these crucial areas of government policy. Responsibility for defending the
coastline and preventing conspiracy and insurrection by the disaffected
devolved to the regular forces, who by the mid-1650s were already over-
stretched. Portsmouth garrison was bolstered to meet the crisis of 1655,
enabling the deputy-governor to send a company to pacify Southampton. At
the same time, the arrival of a troop of horse at Winchester deterred a royalist
attempt on the city, and regular soldiers arrested royalist suspects in the wake
of Penruddock's Rising.[36] A relatively small number of men could control
access to the Isle of Wight.[37] But on the mainland, it proved impossible to con-

[32] Brit. Lib., Addit. MS 29319, fol. 81; *F. & R.*, ii. 401, 555–6.
[33] The decimation raised £1,308 5s 8d in its second year, see below, pp. 46–7, *Th.S.P.*, iv, 238,
     497–8, 643; *Cal.S.P.Dom.*, 1656–7, pp. 172–3.
[34] Bodl., MS Rawl. A 56, fol. 360.
[35] Bodl., MS Rawl. C 179, pp. 276–7; P.R.O., S.P. 28/154, Thomas Gallet's Account.
[36] *The Nicholas Papers*, ed. G. F. Warner (Camden Society, New Series, 3 vols. 1887–97), ii.
     231–2, 238; A. Woolrych, *Penruddock's Rising 1655* (Historical Association, 1973), p. 17;
     H.C.R.O., QO 3, p. 253; Brit. Lib., Addit. MS 24861, fol. 113.
[37] 'Early Quaker letters from the Swarthmore MSS to 1660', ed. G. F. Nuttall (Typescript
     Calendar, 1952), no. 404 (copy in Bodleian Library).

trol the movement of the disaffected. The military failed to prevent twenty-five gentlemen and others from Hampshire going to join Penruddock in March 1655, though the rising was known about in advance.[38] Soldiers failed to prevent Sir William Kingsmill and Dowse Fuller, two former royalists, from holding a horse race in July 1656 despite the national ban. Indeed, there is no evidence that the local military or the central government knew anything about it.[39] More seriously in 1659, soldiers failed to track down Lord De la Warr between mid-July when his conspiracy first became known, and early August when the revolt broke out and sixty horse-men were able to assemble and had to be dispersed by force. Gentry from the borders of Hampshire were able to ride north and join Booth's rising.[40] But in the securing of dangerous opponents, the nadir was undoubtedly reached under the military government which ruled from October to December 1659. Displaced members of the Rump were allowed to roam the countryside quite unhindered, which enabled a group of them to seize control of Portsmouth garrison, and bring in supporters from their estates, launching a rebellion which played no small part in the overthrow of the government which then ruled at Whitehall.[41] This incident also highlighted the dangers, apparent since 1653, of relying on the army to police the provinces. Governments were impotent in the face of military revolts. The defence of the coast was also left largely in military hands. Central efforts to involve people in coastal defence were apparently to no avail.[42] The inhabitants of Southampton and Portsmouth were quite happy to leave defence to local garrisons.[43] Garrison commanders for their part, starved of central funds, had a choice of seeing the fortifications fall down around them, or dipping into their own pockets. Not surprisingly, little was achieved.[44] It was just as well for Interregnum governments that the sea-borne wars of the 1650s generally went in their favour; if they had not, the coasts would have been very exposed to attack.

Dr Miller has recently depicted the demands of war in the period 1642–60 as factors for centralization and even absolutism.[45] It is true that in some very limited areas the needs of the war effort in the 1650s inspired centralizing initiatives. For example, naval administration was brought under stricter central control during the Commonwealth, with a navy commissioner per-

[38] *Cal.S.P.Dom.*, 1655, p. 80; *Th.S.P.*, iii, 306–8.
[39] H.C.R.O., Kingsmill MSS 19M61, no. 1290; *Clarke Papers*, ed. Firth, iv. 37.
[40] *Ludlow's Memoirs 1625–1672*, ed. C. H. Firth (2 vols., Oxford, 1894), ii. 108.
[41] Reece, 'The military presence in England', p. 265.
[42] Bodl., MS Carte 74, fol. 294.
[43] Bodl., MS Carte 74, fol. 472; P.R.O., Privy Council Register, P.C. 2/55, p. 254.
[44] *Cal.S.P.Dom.*, 1651, pp. 175–6; Bodl., MS Rawl. A 184, fol. 383.
[45] J. Miller, 'The potential for "absolutism" in later Stuart England', *History*, 69 (June 1984), 197–8.

manently resident in Portsmouth to oversee every aspect of naval affairs in the locality.[46] During the crisis of the first Dutch War, the newly streamlined Admiralty Commission visited Portsmouth to discover for themselves how things stood locally, and were able to give appropriate orders.[47] But this initiative was shortlived, and in general the needs of naval warfare, with its unprecedented call on manpower, made the central state more dependent on the co-operation of amateur officials in the localities. This is clear from the Commonwealth's legislation on naval impressment.[48] Seamen were impressed in the coastal parts of Hampshire during the naval wars of the Interregnum.[49] The task was made more difficult by the fact that the towns of Christchurch and Southampton were separate from the vice-admiralty of Hampshire, an anomalous situation which no government did anything to rectify. The magistrates and merchants of Southampton were particularly uncooperative, partly because the town's declining trade made it hard for them to be anything else. They sought to spare their own ships from impressment, and the numbers of men whom they supplied regularly fell short of the quotas demanded. The anger of the naval authorities arose from their impotence in the face of such an attitude, which was by no means unique to Southampton. Even when the net was spread wider under the major-generals to include a search for runaway seamen in the whole county, it still depended for success on the co-operation of JPs and constables, and though JPs did their best, results were disappointing and there was little that the Cromwellian government could do about it.[50]

The government depended on borough magistrates to perform other ancillary tasks in the naval war effort, such as accommodating sick or wounded seamen, and foreign prisoners of war. An effort was made to spread the burden as widely as possible: some Dutch sailors were billeted as far inland as Andover during the Dutch War. But the whole policy was undermined through lack of funds.[51] In 1653, the Admiralty Commission complained to Colonel Nathaniel Whetham of the 'great neglect and remissenesse of the magistrates in Portsmo[uth]', over the accommodation of sick and

---

[46] W. N. Hammond, 'The administration of the English navy 1649–1660' (British Columbia Univ., Ph.D. thesis, 1974), p. 119; the practice was resumed after the Restoration in 1664.

[47] Bodl., MS Rawl. A 227, fols. 48–9.

[48] Hammond, 'The administration of the English navy', pp. 168–73.

[49] Against the Dutch 1652–4, against Spain 1655–9; *Cal.S.P.Dom.*, 1652–3, pp. 28, 497; *Cal.S.P.Dom.*, 1655–6, p. 463; *Cal.S.P.Dom.*, 1658–9, p. 531; Bodl., MS Rawl. A 227, fol. 14.

[50] R. G. Marsden, 'The vice-admirals of the Coast', *E.H.R.*, xxii. (1907), 742–3; *Cal.S.P.Dom.*, 1652–3, pp. 197, 249, 527; *Cal.S.P.Dom.*, 1655–6, p. 475; *Th.S.P.*, v. 150; Bodl., MS Rawl. A 35, fol. 163.

[51] *Cal.S.P.Dom.*, 1650, p. 291; *Cal.S.P.Dom.*, 1651, p. 253; *Cal.S.P.Dom.*, 1652–3, pp. 196, 228, 233, 253, 280, 544; *Cal.S.P.Dom.*, 1653–4, pp. 238–9; *Cal.S.P.Dom.*, 1654, pp. 36, 68, 121; *Cal.S.P.Dom.*, 1656–7, pp. 449, 455; *Cal.S.P.Dom.*, 1659–60, p. 275.

wounded seamen.[52] But with the failure of a scheme to take over Porchester castle as a hospital, the naval authorities had to depend on the magistrates to deal with the desperate situation.[53] In this, as in so many other aspects of defence and security, the central government depended on the co-operation of amateur officials in the locality.

The record of Interregnum governments in defence and security policy was disappointing. They continued to depend heavily on amateur officials in county and borough to meet basic needs, as previous regimes had done, whilst failing to exert strong or sustained central control over them. They generally failed to involve local people in their own defence and the security of their own locality, leaving an excessive burden on the shoulders of the regular forces, which had serious political repercussions. Further reductions in the army were rendered impossible and the government's dependence on its good-will increased. Far from being a period of effective centralizing government in this vital area of policy, the Interregnum saw a series of failures, which partly arose from and certainly contributed to the political isolation of the ruling regimes.

FINANCE

The raising of taxation, always a major concern of the rulers of England, inevitably necessitated their involvement in the localities. The 1640s had seen the development of much more effective means of tapping the nation's wealth, notably the assessment and the much hated excise, as well as punitive and selective taxation such as sequestration. But levying every kind of tax involved a good deal of administrative effort. In this section, the main problems facing central government in relation to finance after 1649 will be examined, along with the means by which it sought to overcome them. How successfully did the central authorities exert their control over the sums of money levied in their name in Hampshire and over those delegated to raise them? Were centralization and accountability successfully imposed in this area?

Before going further, a brief outline of the structure of revenue collection in the provinces is desirable. The assessment was a general property tax, based originally on the ship money ratings and raised like ship money on the basis of a fixed quota imposed on each county. It was administered by the later 1640s, through bodies of commissioners in each county, who appointed local assessors and collectors, who were usually changed with each new assessment

---

[52] Bodl., MS Rawl. A 227, fol. 50.
[53] *Letters and Papers relating to the First Dutch War 1652–4*, ed. S. R. Gardiner and C. T. Atkinson (Navy Record Society, 6 vols. 1899–1930), iv. 114, 220–1, 240–1, 256, 296.

ordinance, or even each new instalment of the same assessment. Central control and standardization were therefore hard to enforce, and professionalism, except on the part of the county receiver-general and his staff, a rarity. The excise, a tax on a variety of commodities levied on the vendor, had a separate administration of its own, headed by central commissioners in London, with sub-commissioners in each locality. This tax was sometimes farmed on a localised basis, so that entrepreneurs contracted to collect it in a particular area for their own profit. Finally, sequestration revenue was collected from property seized from 'delinquents' (royalists and Catholics) until it was compounded for under certain restrictions, by the payment of a fine by the owner. The local administration of this tax was under the control of the county committees which employed sequestrators to collect money from sequestered estates.

The most obvious problem with all taxes in the 1640s was the slow rate of their payment, and this continued to be a problem even after the end of hostilities in England. For example, the Irish assessment to support Parliament's troops in Ireland was appallingly badly paid in Hampshire. Initiated by an ordinance of 18 October 1644, by which Hampshire and the Isle of Wight were rated at £125 per week, no steps were taken to levy the sum there before April 1647.[54] Even then payment was very slow. JPs at Michaelmas quarter sessions in 1647 in Hampshire declared that tithingmen had been 'remisse, carelesse & negligent in the levying and collecting of the said assessment'[55] (the collection of this assessment was still in their hands). The first instalment was not paid in until 22 October 1647, and the money was still coming in very slowly in December 1649, by which time the collection of the next Irish assessment, due by an ordinance of February 1648, had not been started. Payments of this assessment into the centre did not apparently begin until October 1650.[56]

Apart from the laxity of lesser officials, another reason for delay was dissatisfaction with the rating of particular places or individuals. This bred a host of disputes which came before the county quarter sessions in 1647 and afterwards. As the ratings were based on the same assessment as the poor rate, and people did not differentiate between the two, this is not a very surprising situation.[57] But it merely accentuated another problem of the assessment, namely its dependence on the activity of unaccountable amateur

---

[54] *F. & R.*, i. 533; Bodl., MS Rawl. D 666, fol. 118.

[55] H.C.R.O., QO 2, fol. 252.

[56] P.R.O., Lay Subsidy Rolls, E179/175/552; S.P. 28/154: Account Book of Richard Webb; S.P. 28/293, pt 2, fol. 248; *Cal.S.P.Dom.*, 1649–50, p. 434.

[57] H.C.R.O., QO 2, fols. 250, 252, 253–5, 257–8, 260, 263–7; *Western Circuit Assize Orders 1629–1648: A Calendar*, ed. J. S. Cockburn (Camden Society, Fourth Series, 17, 1976), pp. 284–5.

officials, the assessment commissioners. Under the Commonwealth, it proved difficult getting sufficient numbers of assessment commissioners to act. In Southampton, where only a dozen had been named by December 1650, the inactivity of a substantial proportion of them greatly impeded the assessment and collection of revenue. Several times between April 1649 and October 1651, none of the commissioners turned up to a meeting so it had to be postponed.[58] Even after the Hampshire and Southampton commissions had been amalgamated into a single county one, the turn out was not massive, with only seven (out of eighty-two possible) commissioners attending a meeting in January 1654.[59] Controlling the conscripted lesser officials, the assessors and collectors, whom the commissioners appointed, proved even more difficult. When they actually did meet, the Southampton commissioners spent much of their time dealing with errors or partiality committed by the assessors.[60]

In general the accountability of revenue collectors was difficult to enforce. Local sequestration machinery in Hampshire was in chaos before 1649, and excise collection was on a loose rein. In Hampshire, as in other counties, the local accounts sub-committee made a vigorous start towards bringing such officials to account. But they were ordered to desist from taking the accounts of local excise officers at the behest of the central Commissioners for Excise, and an act of 1649 brought a premature end to their other activities.[61]

The means which Interregnum governments possessed to control or invigorate local tax collection were surprisingly limited. There was legislation: under the Commonwealth an attempt was made to rationalize and standardize the assessment system.[62] But customary practices persisted in the northern shires, and even the assessment act of December 1649 recognized that central government could not enforce standardization on the provinces, and commissioners were allowed to use the most just and usual assessment.[63]

The Army Committee, the executive agency concerned with the collection of the assessment, did its best to hasten payment either by corresponding with local commissioners and receivers-general, or by employing local agents. Both these means were employed in Hampshire under the Commonwealth. Armiger Warner was the agent of the Army Committee in Hampshire during

---

58 S.C.R.O., SC14/2/18; *F. & R.*, ii. 43, 477.
59 H.C.R.O., 44M69 (Jervoise of Herriard MSS) 027, XLV 11A.
60 S.C.R.O., SC14/2/18.
61 P.R.O., S.P. 28/253A, fol. 45; S.P. 28/260, fol. 235; Exchequer K.R. Bills and Answers of (Interregnum) Accountants, E114/14 (Hampshire); *F. & R.*, ii. 277–81; provision was made for the revival of the sub-committees in June 1653, *Cal.S.P.Dom.*, 1652–3, pp. 429–32, but this does not seem to have been carried out in Hampshire.
62 J. S. Morrill, *The Revolt of the Provinces* (2nd edn, London, 1980), p. 59.
63 J. V. Beckett, 'Local custom and the "new taxation" in the seventeenth and eighteenth centuries', *Northern History*, 12 (1976), 113; *F. & R.*, ii. 318–19.

this period. In March 1649, he was ordered to report the names of those whose negligence was obstructing the payment of the Irish assessment. On 12 December, the Council of State ordered him to hasten the collection of this tax, and to prevent it being diverted to local uses. He delivered letters to local commissioners and helped with collection. But he had other concerns, and was not as assiduous in the government's behalf as he might have been.[64]

The government rarely resorted to direct military support to raise or hasten payment of taxes in Hampshire. Fairfax wrote to Hampshire's committee along with nineteen other counties on 2 January 1649 urging them to pay arrears of assessment and holding out an end to free quarter as an inducement for rapid payment.[65] The threat of a resumption of free quarter continued to be deployed throughout the Interregnum.[66] The assessment act of 7 December 1649 ordered soldiers to co-operate in the collection of tax if called upon to do so. Governor Peter Murford duly put himself at the disposal of the Southampton commissioners.[67] However, soldiers were seldom involved in the collection anywhere in the county for much of the Interregnum. On one rare occasion where they did intervene, to distrain Somborne Park from Richard Giffard Esq., they did so at the behest of the inhabitants of Houghton parish, who were involved in a dispute over rating with neighbouring King's Somborne parish.[68] There were not enough soldiers to enforce the payment of taxes in the county at large, and as the military presence contracted during the 1650s, even the sanction of free quarter would have applied to a relatively small section of the population. Only after the army coup of October 1659, did the central government resort to naked force to bring assessments in, by which time organized resistance to taxes was taking place in Hampshire. Fleetwood deputed Colonel Packer to send a contingent of twelve horsemen from his regiment to collect £500 from the hands of Mr Reeve, high collector of the Basingstoke division, which was duly done on 16 December 1659.[69]

Even in the early days of the Commonwealth, it would have been problematical to use troops to raise some of the more controversial taxes. There was strong opposition to the excise amongst Hampshire's garrison officers. A petition subscribed by nearly forty of them in January 1649 called, amongst other things, for the excise to be removed from all except imported com-

---

[64] S.C.R.O., SC14/2/18; Brit. Lib., Addit. MS 24861, fols. 37–8; P.R.O., E101/67/11B; *Cal.S.P.Dom.*, 1649–50, pp. 50, 434; P.R.O., S.P. 28/335, pt 2, fol. 468; for his unreliability, see above, p. 26 n. 49.

[65] J. Rushworth (ed.), *Historical Collections* (2nd edn, London, 7 vols., 1721), vii. 1383.

[66] E.g. S.C.R.O., SC14/2/18; Brit. Lib., Addit. MS 24861, fol. 37.

[67] *F. & R.*, ii. 316; S.C.R.O., SC14/2/18; 31 January 1650.

[68] H.C.R.O., QO 3, p. 69.

[69] P.R.O., S.P. 28/230: Bundle of orders and acquittances relating to assessment, autumn–winter 1659.

modities, and ultimately to be abolished altogether, along with all other new taxes.[70] In these circumstances, it is hardly surprising that the impact of the Commonwealth regime upon revenue collection was distinctly muted. It imposed unprecedentedly large taxes on the provinces, without giving them a breathing space in which arrears might have been gathered. In 1651, £41,594 16s 0d was demanded from Hampshire in assessment alone, nearly seven times as much as the ship money levy. On top of this £1,689 2s 3d was actually raised as a militia assessment to pay off those who had provided a month's pay for the soldiers of the militia.[71] Besides this several thousand pounds would have been expected from the excise.

As a result of the huge tax burden, arrears continued to mount. Attempts to bring in arrears met with some initial success. £108 1s 5d of taxes due in 1648 from the Basingstoke division came in in April 1649. But in 1653, £109 5s 11d was still due from the Basingstoke division of the assessment from March 1649 to June 1650.[72] Robert Richbell did not pay in Southampton's assessment for the first three months of 1648 to the Treasurers at War until 3 March 1651. In fact, whole quotas due from the town of Southampton under the Commonwealth were not paid until later years of the Protectorate. Collection got hopelessly behind, and arrears which built up in this way could not be collected until after the Protectorate tax cuts had reduced the burden of the assessment. More than £3,600 worth of arrears due from Hampshire from the beginning of 1648 to the end of 1651 were only paid in November 1655 or afterwards.[73] And £4,143 15s 0d of the assessment due between 25 March 1649 and 25 December 1651 was still unaccounted for as late as 1682.[74]

Soaring levels of taxation under the Commonwealth made the problems of rating and assessment with the resultant delays in collection far worse. Between Michaelmas 1648 and Epiphany 1653, thirty-one rating disputes involving assessments for national taxation came before the quarter sessions court in Hampshire. Cases concerned exclusively with the demands of national taxation were sometimes referred to the assessment commissioners, not all of whom were JPs. Otherwise they were referred to local JPs and orders made upon the basis of their reports, but some cases came back to the court again and again.[75]

The high taxation brought out all the worst excesses of district localism,

[70] *To the Honourable the Commons House of England; the Humble Petition and Represen-tation of the Officers and Souldiers of the Garrisons of Portsmouth* [etc.] (London, 1649).
[71] F. & R., ii. 459, 511–13; iii. lxxxii, lxxxvi; P.R.O., S.P. 28/129, pt 9.
[72] H.C.R.O., 148M71, 1/1/2; 44M69 013, Arrears of Taxes in the Basingstoke Division 1653.
[73] P.R.O., E113/14 Hampshire: Answer of Robert Richbell; S.P. 28/260; pt 1, fols. 49–67.
[74] *Cal.Treas.Bks.*, vii. 525.
[75] H.C.R.O., QO 2, fols. 271, 279, 282, 285; QO 3, pp. 1, 3, 15, 32, 59, 60, 61, 65, 67, 69–76, 79, 82–3, 89–90, 102, 104, 107, 121, 125, 149.

with people using a variety of means and dubious pretexts to reduce the tax burden for their hundred, neighbourhood or village. Absentee landlords, even those who were members of the central government, tried to reduce their share of the tax burden. Augustine Garland, who was actually a member of the Army Committee, tried to claim a total exemption for the close at Winchester which he had purchased. But the commissioners stuck to the letter of the legislation and would not connive in this way any more than in the selfish ruses of local people. But Richard Maijor, writing to the Army Committee on behalf of the assessment commissioners, did concede that there were gross inequalities in the distribution of taxation within the county, and he looked for some central initiative to rectify this. But the system was so hand to mouth in its operation that only ad hoc alterations to the distribution of the assessment proved possible. By March 1654, a pound rate was being levied throughout the shire, but new surveys which had been drawn up to make assessment fairer had to be laid aside for lack of time.[76]

It is indicative of governmental impotence that the only way in which it could alleviate the acute problems of collection was by cutting taxes, as initiated under the Protectorate. In 1655, rating disputes coming before quarter sessions declined dramatically. By 1656, the assessment was apparently being paid in its entirety, though it is not clear how long it was taking to come in.[77] But no serious opposition was encountered thereafter until November 1659, when in response to the army's coup of the previous month, some tax payers in Wiltshire, Berkshire and Hampshire inspired by local Rumpers banded together to pay no more taxes except by act of Parliament 'except it be forced from them'. As a result there was a shortfall of £127 3s 6d in the receipt of the assessment, the first for more than three years.[78]

But in order to reduce taxation, the Protectorate government was obliged to resort to fiscal expedients which were just as awkward and divisive at local level as the high assessments of the Commonwealth had been. The most famous of such expedients was the decimation tax by which government sought to off-load the burden of the new militia onto implacable royalists. Men who had supported the king more than a decade before were now singled out to pay a punitive tax, but worse than that, those who could prove a genuine change of heart would be freed from it. In Hampshire, Parkinson Odber and Lord Henry Paulet successfully deployed the sympathy or friendship of local parliamentarians to escape the tax and Thomas Offley of Winchester also got out of it by petitioning the protector, protesting his conversion. Sir William

---

[76] Brit. Lib., Addit. MS 24861, fol. 53; H.C.R.O., 44M69 027, XLV 11A.
[77] P.R.O., S.P. 28/154 Thomas Gallet's Account.
[78] Bodl., MS Clarendon 67, fol. 42; R. Hutton, *The Restoration* (Oxford, 1985), p. 78; P.R.O., S.P. 28/154 Thomas Gallet's Account.

Kingsmill of Sydmonton narrowly failed to get an exemption.[79] He and thirty-six other substantial local royalists were charged with the tax. Even in its second and last year of operation, it produced the quite inadequate sum of £1,308 5s 8d, but it had also revived bitter memories of the Civil War.[80]

The only way the Interregnum revenue system could be made to work at all was on a highly decentralized basis, not so much because of the localism of provincial officials, as the failure of central government to develop means to exert control over it. Professor Underdown seems to suggest that decentralized control of revenue represented part of the reconciliation of the provinces in 1657.[81] But he overlooks the fact that this was a constant element in the centre–local relations of the 1650s. It partly arose from the lack of centralization within government itself, which had been inherited from the 1640s. Government credit being as bad as it was, there was little point in bringing money in only to send it down into the provinces again to repay its chief creditors, members of the armed services.

Under the Commonwealth, a system of assignments developed, by which garrisons and field units were usually paid out of the assessment of the county where they were quartered, under the distant supervision of the Army Committee and Treasurers at War.[82] Hampshire's assessment went to pay the garrison forces, as also those of the Channel Islands, and payments were also made to the navy and passing field units. It was expected that money raised in the county would be employed in the county. £105 which had originally been assigned to pay Colonel Ireton's men when they were working in the county was subsequently diverted by the militia commissioners to help cover the cost of demolishing Winchester castle's defences, Ireton's men having moved on elsewhere.[83] So deeply ingrained was the habit of sending money to Portsmouth, that the rebels of 1659 had no difficulty in persuading the receiver-general of the county and the high collector of the Basingstoke division to provide them with substantial sums on demand.[84] At the same time, one local constable was offering £14 of assessment money to help a royalist conspiracy.[85]

In the case of the Rump's militia assessment of 1651, decentralization was total, though it had been raised like other assessments through the structure of high collectors in the divisions.[86] The militia commissioners themselves

[79] *Cal.S.P.Dom.*, 1655–6, pp. 89, 172, 338; *Calendar of the Committee for Compounding*, ed. Green, iii. 1658–9; H.C.R.O., 19M61, no. 1375.
[80] P.R.O., E179/176/554.
[81] Underdown, 'Settlement in the counties', in Aylmer, *The Interregnum*, p. 178.
[82] Reece, 'The military presence in England', pp. 39–49.
[83] P.R.O., S.P. 28/154 Thomas Gallet's Account, and loose order 1651.
[84] Thomas Gallet, receiver-general, provided £260, Bernard Reeve, high collector, £234, P.R.O., S.P. 28/154; S.P. 28/230 (Hampshire).
[85] *Cal.Clar.S.P.*, iv. 370.   [86] P.R.O., S.P. 28/129, pt 9.

used the money freely, for example to pay off the debts incurred in demolishing Winchester and Christchurch castles. Account was rendered not to the central government but to the local quarter sessions, which proceeded to treat the surplus as an ordinary county fund, spending £32 of it on a variety of local causes, such as compensating fire victims. Central government had no knowledge of this, and the money was not centrally accounted for until after the Restoration.[87]

It proved difficult to get money raised by local excise officials paid into the centre, despite the appointment of a Commission for Arrears of Excise in 1653, and other parliamentary initiatives.[88] In 1654, there was £5,447 5s 11½d awaiting settlement by farmers and sub-commissioners in Hampshire.[89] Under the later Protectorate some centralization was achieved with £4,050 being paid directly into the Exchequer by the farmers of Berkshire, Hampshire and the Isle of Wight, and by the end of September 1659, the amount due from local sub-commissioners and farmers was down to £4,441 7s 5½d.[90] But the Committee of Safety abandoned this policy and resorted to the decentralized use of excise money, in a desperate attempt to find funds for the garrisons of the Isle of Wight.[91]

But excise administration was subjected to the scrutiny of local courts, long before JPs were given wide powers to regulate the excise by the act of 1657. Hampshire's JPs upheld the law against the excesses of the employees of the local excise farmers in 1651 and 1653. They sought to shield the impoverished local feltmakers and the keeper of the county gaol from demands of the excisemen. But it would be wrong to present these matters crudely in terms of a confrontation between central demands and local interests. The JPs always behaved responsibly and in accordance with the excise legislation. They recommended the cause of the feltmakers to the Committee for Regulating the Excise, while granting them an interim immunity from the tax. The decision about the beer brewed in the county gaol was in accordance with the view of a parliamentary committee upheld by the House in December 1651, that only beer or ale brewed by common brewers or sold by innkeepers should be excisable.[92] They strove to keep the enforcement of the excise separate from county administration, ordering constables to return goods which they had confiscated on behalf of the excise, as it was up to the excise officers to distrain goods.[93] For their part the central

[87] P.R.O., S.P. 29/129, pt 9; S.P. 28/230 (Hampshire): note on the back of accounts, by T. Bettsworth; H.C.R.O., QO 3, pp. 89, 205, 218–19, 223, 225.
[88] F. & R., ii. 828–9; C.J., vii. 634–5, 637.
[89] P.R.O., E351/1297 (Excise Declared Account 1653–4).
[90] P.R.O., E401 (Receipt Book) 1931, fols. 177, 251; E401/1932, fols. 18, 20, 33, 50, 67, 79; E351/1299 (Excise Declared Account 1659).
[91] Brit. Lib., Addit. MS 29319, fols. 119, 120, 122.
[92] H.C.R.O., QO 3, pp. 100, 132, 185, 266.   [93] H.C.R.O., QO 3, p. 294.

authorities did not discourage the JPs from adjudicating cases concerned with the excise, but rather relied on them to keep local excise officers under control.[94]

There was only one branch of revenue for which administrative centralization was undertaken during the Commonwealth, and that was in the comparatively narrow field of sequestration. In Hampshire, as in the rest of the country, responsibility for it was taken away from the county committees, and given to more dependent sub-commissioners, Edward Hooker, John Champion and Thomas Muspratt, who were answerable directly to the central Commissioners for Compounding. This development met with some resistance from the sequestrators of Southampton, who refused to recognize the authority of the sub-commissioners.[95] Serious efforts were made, though they were not totally successful, to suppress the diversion of sequestration money to local ends.[96] The bulk of sequestration money was undoubtedly paid to the Commissioners for Compounding, and subsequently residual sums were paid into the Exchequer by Thomas Muspratt (the treasurer and, from 1654, sole sub-commissioner), amounting to £1,435 8s 11d in 1655 and 1657.[97] But the protector's experiment with punitive taxation, the decimation, was assessed, levied and deployed on a rigidly, even cripplingly, decentralized basis. Despite Goffe's plea for centralization, it was not possible even to top up the shortfall of the tax in one county with the surplus of another. Initially the only central control lay in the fact that Goffe signed all the warrants for payments. The central supervision by the Army Committee, which was belatedly introduced, was being put into effect in Hampshire by mid-July 1656, but this was rather too late to have an impact.[98]

The problem, which no Interregnum government adequately overcame, was to make revenue officials fully accountable to central authority. The eclipse of the Exchequer on the one hand and the abolition of the accounts sub-committees for political reasons in 1649 on the other, made the Commonwealth curiously impotent in this regard, and the Protectorate was only slightly more effective. As was seen above, large sums like the 1651 militia assessment could be raised and spent in the localities without coming under the scrutiny of central government, not so much as a result of localism, as of the simple failure of central bodies to investigate.[99]

Again only in the somewhat specialized area of sequestration was much headway made, and this was at the initiative of the Commissioners for Compounding. The sub-commissioners appointed in 1650 were detailed to call

[94] Bodl., MS Rawl. C 386, fols. 51, 57.
[95] *Calendar of the Committee for Compounding*, ed. Green, i. 236.
[96] *Calendar of the Committee for Compounding*, ed. Green, i. 155, 193–4, 253, 348.
[97] P.R.O., E401/1930, fols. 73, 76, 107; E401/1931, fol. 41.
[98] *Th.S.P.*, iv. 497–8; v. 215.   [99] See above, pp. 47–8.

former sequestration officers to account. However, their investigations were thwarted by the loss of vital documents during the 1640s, and attempts by the central Commissioners to fine members of the county committee £20 each for their default were resisted not only by the committeemen themselves, but also by the sub-commissioners on the grounds that this was unfair and unreasonable.[100] Other accounts and documents were in the custody of former accounts sub-committee at Southampton until at least the end of March 1650. However, the sub-commissioners were able to bring some former sequestration officials to account between March 1650 and May 1653.[101] In the case of John Woodman, the former solicitor for sequestrations, they uncovered serious fraud, forgery and embezzlement. £873 7s 10d which he had received was unaccounted for.[102] There were hearings before the Commissioners for Compounding, but little seems to have come of them; Thomas Muspratt, one of the sub-commissioners, later claimed never to have heard the outcome. Further action in the matter was referred to the old county committee which apparently discharged Woodman on 23 March 1654. But only in the case of the dean and chapter of Winchester's library was the misappropriated property ever recovered. Another attempt to call Woodman to account for sequestration money initiated by Goffe, as part of a wider campaign by the major-generals to chase up arrears of taxes, achieved nothing.[103] From 1655 onwards, the Protectorate government came to rely increasingly on traditional Exchequer procedures in the management and investigation of sequestration in Hampshire.[104]

In the later years of the Protectorate, the central Committee for Accounts again began to investigate former revenue officials in Hampshire. They called John Woodman to account, in 1657, and gor further than they had done in 1650, when Woodman had protested he was too busy to appear. But it is not exactly clear how far they got with him this time.[105] Most of the committee's energy in relation to Hampshire during 1658 was devoted to the case of a

[100] *Calendar of the Committee for Compounding*, ed. Green, i. 339–40, 550, 552–3; P.R.O., S.P. 23/257/75.
[101] P.R.O., S.P. 28/258, pt 4, fol. 463; *Calendar of the Committee for Compounding*, ed. Green, i. 406; P.R.O., E113/14 (Hampshire), Answers of accountants; these answers drawn up after the Restoration often describe former efforts to bring the accountants to book.
[102] *Calendar of the Committee for Compounding*, ed. Green, i. 282–3, 383, 385–6, 405, 406, 424, 447, 448, 453, 523, 524, 530, 532, 533.
[103] *C.J.*, vii. 136; P.R.O., S.P. 46 (Additional State Papers) 97, fol. 160; E134, 13 Chas. II Mich. 1. Deposition of Arthur Lipscomb; E134, 13 & 14 Chas. II, Hil. 16: Depositions of John Champion, Thomas Muspratt and Ellis Mew; S.P. 28/230 (Hampshire); *Cal.S.P.Dom.*, 1655–6, p. 370.
[104] *Th.S.P.*, iv. 240; P.R.O., E178 (Special Commissions) 6456: Inquisitions as to delinquents' estates sequestered in Hants (1657); E351/442 (1655); E113/14 (Hampshire) Answers of T. Muspratt, J. Champion, E. Hooker; E112/564, no. 345.
[105] P.R.O., S.P. 28/253A, pp. 477–8, 481, 498; S.P. 28/258, pt 2, fol. 204.

single revenue official, Malachi Dudeney of Upton Grey, former joint commissary-general, treasurer and muster-master-general to Sir William Waller's South Eastern Association army in the Civil War. He was called before the committee and ordered to explain a gap of £1,000 between what he had received and what he could present warrants and acquittances for having paid out. But Dudeney managed to prevaricate and delay proceedings from the beginning of February until the middle of August 1658, before stunning the committee with the news that the matter was now the subject of a suit in Upper Bench and was therefore *sub judice*, and he refused to give them any further answer. Little more was achieved in the case before the committee became moribund.[106]

The garrison officers of 1649 had wanted to see the establishment of a more effective system for bringing revenue officers to account.[107] But by abolishing local sub-committees of accounts and vesting power in central bodies whilst failing to re-establish the Exchequer fully, the government of the Commonwealth had reduced its ability to investigate local tax-collectors. Some improvement is discernable in the later Protectorate period, but effective accountability for a wide range of taxes would not be restored until after the Restoration.

Central control over the money which was raised in the localities was inadequate during the 1650s and little was achieved in the way of centralization.

COUNTY GOVERNMENT AND MORAL REFORMATION

The mid seventeenth century saw a dramatic transformation in the involvement of central government in the localities. Its most striking manifestation lay in the fact that after the collapse of the personal rule of Charles I, government largely ceased to involve itself in the supervision of poor law administration at local level, the quality of which came to depend entirely on the vigour and enthusiasm of local magistrates.

This change was less the result of provincial pressure than shifting priorities at Whitehall. There is evidence that in the absence of royal initiatives to cope with the economic crisis of the early 1640s, many in the provinces were looking for parliamentary action. Ten counties (including Hampshire) and six boroughs petitioned the Long Parliament about the decay of trade in the first three months of 1642.[108] But Parliament was soon embroiled in fighting the

[106] P.R.O., S.P. 28/253A, pp. 504, 505, 514, 524, 528, 531, 533, 534, 536, 537–8, 553–4, 567.
[107] *To the Honourable the Commons House of England: the Humble Petition and Representation of the Officers and Souldiers of the Garrisons of Portsmouth* [etc.] (London, 1649).
[108] Fletcher, *Outbreak*, Map 3, p. 224.

Civil War, and quite unable to frame or enforce a social policy. The Civil War itself had the effect of finalizing the shift of central government away from this sort of involvement in the localities, for although it increased poverty in the provinces and was followed by a serious economic crisis, the poor had shown themselves to be less formidable a threat to stability than central government's ideologically motivated enemies. It was quite natural, therefore, for government's main concern to shift to coping with the latter, leaving local authorities to deal with the problem of poverty.[109]

The Rump did make some gestures in the direction of dealing with poverty, issuing orders to JPs in 1649 to enforce the laws against vagrancy.[110] But such measures were dwarfed by its obsession with internal security and the politically motivated threats to stability in the provinces. Moral reformation was not systematically enforced in the localities by central government either, at least until the major-generals' experiment, and the latter was shortlived, and in many areas unimpressive in its impact, especially when compared with the continuing endeavours of local magistrates.

Former channels of central supervision of poor law administration declined. The contribution of the assize judges decreased dramatically, so that between Lent assizes 1654 and Lent assizes 1656, only three orders relating to local administration in Hampshire were issued.[111] But JPs were quite ready to follow the lead of the assize judges when given. At Michaelmas 1655, the Hampshire JPs of their own volition decided to revive a general western circuit assize order for the return of 'sufficient jurors', by the keeping up of lists of suitable freeholders, thus neatly anticipating part of the brief of the major-generals.[112]

This decline in central supervision was not initially justified by any amelioration of social problems within the shire. Poverty in some areas was certainly a threat to order. In the Basingstoke area, in the early years of the Commonwealth, extreme privation was driving many people to attack carts carrying grain to market, and spoil the woods on the marquis of Winchester's sequestered estate. It was left to JPs in the divisions 'to take care in these hard times for suppressinge of Idleness and setting the poore people of every p[ar]ish within this countie to worke for their better maintenance and subsistence'. But vagrancy was still a serious problem in 1656.[113]

---

[109] Local authorities were quite capable of rising to the challenge: working on Norfolk sources, Tim Wales has argued that the crisis years 1647–50 saw an upward shift in the maximum level of parish relief payments, T. Wales, 'Poverty, poor relief and the life-cycle: some evidence from seventeenth-century Norfolk', *Land, kinship and life-cycle*, ed. R. M. Smith (Cambridge, 1985), pp. 354–5.

[110] M. James, *Social Problems and Policy in the Puritan Revolution* (London, 1930), p. 286.

[111] P.R.O., ASSI 24/22, fols. 25, 31, 37, 39, 43.

[112] H.C.R.O., QO 3, pp. 263–4; the order dated from 1648.

[113] [B. Whitelocke] *Memorials of the English Affairs* (London, 1682), p. 424 (the attack on grain

Interregnum governments preferred to deal with the symptoms rather than the causes of poverty. Under the Commonwealth, the Council of State issued proclamations for the punishment of vagrants, and launched a campaign against the crime wave, with the help of military officers.[114] Such modest measures met with a positive response from Hampshire justices, and even from some hundred constables, though the Council did not follow them up.[115]

Numerous local studies have demonstrated that JPs during the 1650s were quite up to the task of administering their counties without the supervision of Whitehall, and this is equally true of Hampshire's justices.[116] They met a certain amount of opposition, and abuse, as they went about their work.[117] Their insistence on the administrative primacy of the county was a threat to lesser jurisdictions.[118] The shift of business away from petty sessions to quarter sessions, which was a feature of the period in Hampshire, as in other counties, with the extra expense and travelling for those obliged to attend, was resented locally and protested against.[119] But it was not reversed until after the Restoration.

Central involvement in moral reformation was distinctly spasmodic before 1655.[120] But, whatever people in Whitehall may have thought, the commitment of Hampshire's JPs to moral reformation was fairly constant, and was not in need of a major-general to mobilize it. Even if the dating of quarter sessions according to the feasts of Epiphany, Easter, the translation of St Thomas the Martyr and Michaelmas does not exactly resonate with puritan zeal, the desire of most active JPs to enforce order and sobriety is not in doubt.[121] A campaign against unlicensed alehouses which had begun with the resumption of quarter sessions after the Civil War, continued under the Commonwealth and Protectorate, a general order for the purpose being issued to JPs in the divisions at Epiphany sessions 1649. The Council of State's order

carts occurred in 1650); *Calendar of the Committee for Compounding*, ed. Green, i. 253; H.C.R.O., QO 2, fols. 275, 283; QO 3, pp. 22, 27; Brit. Lib., Addit. MS 24861, fol. 115.
[114] Brit. Lib., Addit. MS 24861, fol. 32; H.C.R.O., QO 3, p. 13; *Cal.S.P.Dom.*, 1649–50, pp. 400, 453, 503.
[115] H.C.R.O., QO 3, pp. 40, 207, 251; QI, fols. 68–9, 71, 87.
[116] A. L. Beier, 'Poor relief in Warwickshire, 1630–1660', *Past and Present*, 35 (1966), 77–100; Morrill, *Cheshire 1630–1660*, ch. 6, pp. 223–54; G. C. F. Forster, 'County government in Yorkshire during the Interregnum', *Northern History*, 12 (1976), 84–104.
[117] H.C.R.O., QO 2, fol. 281; QO 3, p. 296.
[118] E.g. Andover, which was said to be a haven for criminals in 1650, but the assize judges upheld Andover's independence, H.C.R.O., QO 3, pp. 29, 145.
[119] H.C.R.O., QO 3, p. 101; Brit. Lib., Addit. MS 24861, fol. 115.
[120] The Rump passed a series of measures to placate Presbyterian opinion, but no systematic attempt was made to enforce them: K. V. Thomas, 'The Puritans and adultery: the Act of 1650 Reconsidered', *Puritans and Revolutionaries*, ed. D. H. Pennington and K. V. Thomas (Oxford, 1978), p. 276.
[121] H.C.R.O., QO 3, QO 4, *passim*.

of November 1649 on the same subject, as so often with such initiatives during the Interregnum, came after the situation had been taken in hand anyway at local level.[122] The Council's interest in such alehouses seems to have been largely motivated by a concern for internal security. Unlicensed or disorderly alehouse-keepers continued to be prosecuted during the 1650s, with the help and support of local ministers, constables and leading inhabitants who made up the parish elites.[123] According to the quarter sessions order books, between Michaelmas sessions 1649 and Epiphany sessions 1660, twenty-nine people were ordered by name to desist from running disorderly or unlicensed alehouses, another two were investigated, and general orders issued for the suppression of unlicensed alehouses in Bishops Waltham and the liberty of Beaulieu. A few had to be suppressed more than once, but this was not generally necessary. Several more were presented or indicted, and may well have been suppressed too, though no reference to that suppression occurs in the order books.[124]

There was a steady stream of presentments, indictments and imprisonments for fornication and bastardy during the 1650s in Hampshire. Sabbath-breaking too was regularly presented though it is hard to determine how often people were convicted.[125] Enforcement was uneven because of the variable quality of local constables. The constables of Andover petitioned the Epiphany quarter sessions in 1651 against breaches of the Sabbath which occurred through the laxity of constables in neighbouring villages, who were duly ordered to keep watch and ward against Sunday travellers.[126]

Enforcement of moral reformation was patchy in the boroughs for the same reason; borough officers were a very diverse group. Some were themselves guilty of moral lapses. Three members of Portsmouth corporation were guilty of breaches of fast or Sabbath days in 1656.[127] In 1657, the mayor and some members of Newport corporation refused to remove a scandalous parish clerk at the request of the local minister. The mayor also refused to allow the recent parliamentary act for the better keeping of the Sabbath to be read in church as it had to be. In desperation, Robert Tutchin the minister, appealed to the protector's Council and eventually the mayor was forced to submit.[128]

---

122 H.C.R.O., QO 2, fol. 275; Brit. Lib., Addit. MS 24861, fol. 32.
123 E.g. H.C.R.O., QO 2, fols. 277, 281; QO 3, pp. 53, 73.
124 H.C.R.O., QO 2, QO 3, QO 4 *passim*; Furley, *Quarter Sessions Government*, p. 106, has a figure of 1284 derived from H.C.R.O., QI, which includes presentments and indictments and which does not allow for recurring cases.
125 H.C.R.O., Q1 *passim*; QO 3, pp. 192, 264; QO 4, p, 8; P.R.O., ASSI 24/1 (Western Circuit Bail Book) *passim*.
126 H.C.R.O., QO 3, p. 73.
127 Mildon, 'Puritanism in Hampshire', p. 358.
128 *Cal.S.P.Dom.*, 1657–8, pp. 36–7, 159, 162.

Under the Protectorate, the central government got involved in the systematic enforcement of moral reformation, during the rule of the major-generals. Expectations were high at Whitehall. Cromwell recommended the moral reformation side of Goffe's work to Richard Norton as 'part of the return we owe God'.[129] Norton knew a good deal more about the practicalities of moral reformation than Cromwell did since he had been involved in it as a justice at quarter sessions since leaving active military service a decade before, while Cromwell had been playing politics at the centre.

As it turned out, Goffe's achievement was insignificant, when set in the context of the work of active local justices in this area throughout the decade. They, of course, were quite prepared to co-operate with Goffe. Writing from the Lent assizes in March 1656, Goffe reported 'Coll. Norton seemeth to be zealous in the business, and the justices doe all seeme desirous to indeavoure after the reformation of open profanes'.[130] JPs were also active in the divisions, apprehending and punishing vagrants. But Goffe's visit, and his attendance at assizes and quarter sessions made no appreciable impact on moral reformation in the county. There was no sudden increase in the prosecution of unlicensed alehouses, which continued at the same rate after his departure. He can be credited with the closure of only one alehouse, and that one was in a suburb of Winchester.[131] This is not very surprising, as he was only in the county a short time, and one would only have expected him to have a dramatic impact if one assumed, like the Cromwellian government, that moral reformation was being obstructed by magisterial indolence at county level. So it may have been elsewhere, but not in Hampshire, and one suspects in many other counties as well. If there was a problem of inadequate enforcement it lay at a lower administrative level, with the hundred and parish constables, but the rule of the major-generals did nothing to rectify this. At the summer sessions of 1656, the last of which Goffe attended, an order was passed for the suppression of 'Help ales', drinking parties held at private houses on Saturdays, which lasted into Sunday mornings, leaving many people hopelessly drunk. The order was to be distributed and read in every market town in the county, but its enforcement lay with the traditional agents, hundred constables and tithingmen. Nothing appears to have come of it.[132]

The difficulties confronting moral reformation in the 1650s in many ways reflect the wider problems of Interregnum governments in relation to the localities. At the lowest level of administration, in the boroughs and rural

[129] *The Writings and Speeches of Oliver Cromwell*, ed. Abbott, iv. 25.
[130] *Th.S.P.*, iv. 582.
[131] Bodl., MS Rawl. A. 35, fol. 163; H.C.R.O., QI, fols. 105, 106, 108, 109, 110, 111; H.C.R.O., QO 3, pp. 274, 301.
[132] H.C.R.O., QO 3, pp. 292–3.

parishes of England, they depended upon an amorphous mass of minor officials recruited locally, with no necessary commitment to the regime or its objectives, many of them holding their posts for only a year.[133] The governments of the period were unable to change this situation. The new military resources of the state seemed to offer a means of overcoming it, but in practice they made little impact on the lowest level of government, and as these resources contracted during the 1650s under fiscal and political pressure, the opportunities for effective intervention declined.

RELIGIOUS POLICY

In the area of local religious life, the 1640s had seen two significant and related phenomena. One was the rise of sectarianism and the other ecclesiastical decentralization: both took place on an unprecedented scale even before Pride's Purge and the establishment of the republic, which merely confirmed them.

The sects did not make spectacular headway in Hampshire in the 1640s. Baptist missionaries crossed and recrossed the county in the wake of the Civil War, and a group was established at Portsmouth and probably at other places in the south of the county.[134] The Baptists were sufficiently strong in the north of the shire by 1649 to hold a disputation with orthodox puritan divines at Basingstoke in that year.[135] There were also groups of radical Independents at Alton and Southampton, which seem to have dated from the 1640s.[136] Nevertheless, it appears that the vast majority of people probably continued to attend their parish churches. This was certainly the assumption of the county committee which ordered its ban on the petitioning agitation in June 1648 to be read in parish churches.[137]

But central control over what went on in these parish churches had never been weaker. Parliament abolished episcopal administration in the localities before the Presbyterian system had been properly established to take its

---

[133] For a wider discussion of this problem and an attempt to rectify it in Lancashire after the Civil War, see K. Wrightson, 'Two concepts of order: justices, constables and jurymen in seventeenth-century England', *An Ungovernable People: The English and their Law in the Seventeenth and Eighteenth Centuries*, ed. J. Brewer and J. Styles (New Brunswick, 1980), pp. 20–46.

[134] W. T. Whitley, 'Early Baptists in Hampshire', *Baptist Quarterly, New Series*, i. (1923), 223; F. Ridoutt, *The Early Baptist History of Portsmouth* (n.pl., 1888), pp. 8–9.

[135] H. Ellis, *Pseudochristus: or A true and faithful Relation of the Grand Imposters, Abominable Practices, Horrid Blasphemies, Gross Deceits; lately spread abroad and acted in the County of Southampton, by William Franklin and Mary Gadbury and their Companions* (London, 1650), p. 60.

[136] Brit. Lib., Addit. MS 24861, fol. 67; Mildon, 'Puritanism in Hampshire', pp. 153–6.

[137] *A Declaration of the Committee for the Safety of the County of Southampton* (1648).

place.[138] That system does not seem to have been fully operational in Hampshire.[139] The county committee purged the ministry of royalists and Laudians, and this task was performed thoroughly.[140] Over-sight of parochial life in county and towns devolved to JPs and borough magistrates.[141]

Especially in the boroughs, such devolution gave the initiative to some men with very conservative views in religious matters. They did what they could to halt the rise of sects, sometimes with excessive zeal. William Newland, a member of Newport corporation, tried to prevent a group of people meeting for spiritual exercises outside the time of divine service in 1645, and Richard Maijor remonstrated with him for his intolerance. Local authorities in the Isle of Wight combined to prevent Baptists preaching there in 1646 and 1647. In 1647, the corporation of Southampton tried to prevent Nathaniel Robinson from preaching on the grounds that he was not ordained.[142] At Andover, a ban on lay preaching was still in force as late as November 1649. Conservative borough magistrates remained in office under the Commonwealth. William Newland rose to be mayor of Newport in 1651. The mayor and some aldermen of Southampton chose the autumn of 1653, of all times, to interrupt the combination lecture in the town, established under the auspices of the Committee for Plundered Ministers, replacing Nathaniel Robinson and other Independent ministers with one Mr Bernard, a more conservative clergyman, who would conform after the Restoration.[143]

Under the Rump there was *de facto* toleration, which did not even have statutory basis until the Toleration Act of September 1650. No central attempt was made to define the outer limit of toleration until the passing of the Blasphemy Act in August 1650. So when William Franklin proclaimed himself as Christ in and around Andover in the closing months of 1649, it was left to 'diverse godly and well affected ministers and others' to protest to the JPs at their Epiphany quarter sessions in 1650.[144] Franklin, despite his local origins (he came originally from nearby Overton, though he had been working as a rope-maker in London for some time) and apparently bigamous

---

[138] Morrill, 'The Church in England 1642–9', in Morrill, *Reactions to the English Civil War*, esp. pp. 95–8.

[139] Shaw's claim that 'Hampshire probably possessed a complete classical organization' seems highly implausible, especially as the only two items of evidence he cites derive from the 1659–60 period, W. A. Shaw, *A History of the English Church during the Civil Wars and under the Commonwealth* (2 vols., London, 1900), ii. 30.

[140] See above, p. 10.

[141] Morrill, 'The Church in England 1642–9', in Morrill, *Reactions to the English Civil War*, pp. 97–8.

[142] Mildon, 'Puritanism in Hampshire', pp. 265–9.

[143] Ellis, *Pseudochristus*, p. 17; I.W.C.R.O., 45/16a, p. 586; *Cal.S.P.Dom.*, 1653–4, pp. 216–17; Mildon, 'Puritanism in Hampshire', pp. 201–2.

[144] This and what follows is derived from Humphrey Ellis' *Pseudochristus*.

relationship with his companion, Mary Gadbury, had quite an impact in the area. He even won over Mr Woodward, minister of Crux Easton and his wife, who gave him shelter. The county justices acted swiftly to suppress the sect, issuing warrants to local constables to round up the ringleaders. Two JPs, sitting at Winchester, used the existing vagrancy laws against Franklin and Gadbury; they sent the latter to the house of correction as a rogue. They managed to threaten Franklin into a recantation and he was bound over to the assizes, along with his principal followers. At the assizes on 8 March, Chief Justice Rolle ordered them to find security for their good behaviour, which all managed to do except Franklin himself, as no one would stand surety for him. Gadbury was discharged from the house of correction at the Easter quarter sessions. She and Franklin's other followers were disillusioned by his repeated recantation, and the sect melted away. Without any clear guidelines from the centre, the local magistracy had had to take the initiative using the existing law to stifle what they regarded as an unacceptable sect. The relatively mild treatment which Franklin received reflected less the leniency of JPs (Richard Cromwell who attended the Epiphany sessions would later favour the death sentence for that more notorious 'messiah' James Nayler) than the deficiencies of the existing law.[145] Humphrey Ellis, who was one of the ministers installed to preach at Winchester cathedral in the wake of the Civil War and the abolition of the chapter, gave a full written account of the Franklin affair. He clearly hoped to influence central policy-makers against the 'boundless Toleration', as he described the existing situation, but the role of his pamphlet in the formulation of the Blasphemy Act later that summer is debatable. Dr McGregor believes that it probably had an influence, but Dr Smith argues that Ranter activity in London rather than events in the provinces prompted the Rump to take action.[146]

Under the Rump, central government had little impact on the quality of the local ministry. Parochial surveys were carried out in 1650–1, but not acted upon immediately; the augmentations policy begun in the 1640s continued. But it is clear that bodies like the Council of State were far more interested in the political loyalty of ministers than anything else. On 9 November 1650, the Council of State wrote to Colonel Sydenham and the militia commissioners in the Isle of Wight ordering them to report all those ministers who failed to keep the day of thanksgiving, who disturbed the peace or depraved

---

[145] Dr Hill does not mention this factor in the situation, C. Hill, *The World Turned Upside Down* (London, 1972), p. 200; for Richard Cromwell's role, H.C.R.O., QO 3, p. 25; *The Diary of Thomas Burton Esq.*, ed. J. T. Rutt (4 vols., London, 1828), i. 126.

[146] Ellis, *Pseudochristus*, esp. pp. 2, 54–62; J. F. McGregor, 'Seekers and Ranters', *Radical Religion in the English Revolution*, ed. J. F. McGregor and B. Reay (Oxford, 1984), p. 133. *A Collection of Ranter Writings from the 17th Century*, ed. N. Smith (London, 1983), p. 13.

the government. It wrote to them again on 28 December to tender the Engagement to two local clergy and to remove them from the island if they refused.[147]

The decentralized nature of the church meant that central authorities were largely ignorant of practices in the parishes, and the knowledge of local magistrates was also circumscribed. In these circumstances, the ban on traditional Anglicanism proved impossible to enforce, and it is clear that the traditional sacramental cycle survived in several parishes in Hampshire as it did elsewhere.[148]

It is impossible to tell how widely the prayer book was still being used in the parishes, but our ignorance merely reflects that of central government, which lacked the machinery to find out. A draft Hampshire assize petition of uncertain authorship which was canvassed but not adopted in 1653 called for the 'due execution' of 'those Acts and ordinances against the usage of those former ceremonies and superstitious vanities prescribed in the booke called the booke of Common Prayer, which have been often inhibited and yet in many places retained'.[149] But before the law could be executed more detailed information was needed about exactly where and by whom the old liturgy was being used. This was rarely forthcoming. Thomas Wither, churchwarden of Newtown parish on the Berkshire border, petitioned the summer quarter sessions in Hampshire in 1654, alleging that the minister Francis Edwards had turned the communion table 'altar-wise' and usually read the prayer book, but Wither's denunciation was clearly a last resort to force the parishioners to pay him the seventeen shillings they owed him to pay for recent repair work to the interior of the church.[150] The puritan ministers who had been settled at Winchester eventually petitioned Oliver Cromwell personally in November 1655 about the activities of Thomas Preston, a sequestered minister, who since the early days of the Commonwealth had been holding prayer book services at St Michael's, Kingsgate Street, an abandoned church in the suburbs of the city, which attracted wide support from local royalists.[151] William Goffe, arriving in the county at this very time, was hopeful of being able to silence ejected ministers and to deal with the Anglican chaplains of royalists in accordance with the recent proclamation, but there is no evidence that he did so.[152]

The central government's initiatives of 1655 against Catholics and Anglicans were in fact little more than security measures, arising from their

---

[147] Brit. Lib., Addit. MS 29319, fols. 65–67.
[148] E.g. at Chawton, Easton, North Waltham and Soberton, H.C.R.O., 1M70 PW1; 72M70 PW1; 41M64 PW1; 50M73 PW1; for this phenomenon elsewhere see Morrill, 'The Church in England 1642–9', in Morrill, *Reactions to the English Civil War*, pp. 105–6.
[149] Brit. Lib., Addit. MS 24861, fol. 72.
[150] H.C.R.O., QO 3, pp. 225–6.
[151] Brit. Lib., Addit. MS 24861, fols. 113–14.   [152] *Th.S.P.*, IV. 239.

supposed involvement in Penruddock's Rising. Such religious minorities posed a security problem rather than a theological one to central regimes after the Civil War. Men might believe what they liked, and the Rump had specifically eschewed the idea of coercing even Catholics to attend services which they found abhorrent.[153]

But the Protectorate did see some reduction in the decentralization which had characterized the church under the Commonwealth. In accordance with widespread conservative prejudices, a central procedure for examining candidates for the ministry was established by the ordinance of August 1654, appointing the 'triers'. But coupled with this was the virtual re-establishment of the power of the county committees in the commissions of local 'ejectors'. However, the system does seem to have had an impact on the parochial ministry in Hampshire during the later Protectorate, with at least thirteen new ejections in the 1656–8 period and at least one formerly sequestered clergyman being kept out of a living.[154] A parallel commission for implementing changes in the parochial structure in Hampshire recommended in the 1650–1 surveys, was not operative before the arrival of Major-General Goffe. Subsequently some changes were made in 1657–8.[155] But fundamentally what William Lamont has called 'a *deliberate* vacuum at the centre' in the area of religious policy characterized the Protectorate as it had the Commonwealth before it.[156]

Central to Cromwell's laissez-faire religious policy was the broad toleration laid down in the Instrument of Government, which excluded only Papists, Prelatists and the licentious. Blair Worden has convincingly argued that Cromwell's central, even exclusive concern was for the liberty of the 'godly' to practise their religion in peace, though his government contained men of a more generous disposition.[157] But the pressure for limiting toleration generally came from the localities, especially through Parliament. In 1657, after the Nayler debate, and the disquiet expressed from several counties, Cromwell allowed the Quakers to be effectively outlawed in the Humble Petition and Advice, and other measures.[158] At the same time, despite pledges to Cardinal Mazarin, Cromwell agreed to the act against Catholics produced by the same Parliament. This is not to say that Cromwell abandoned toleration altogether. He vetoed the intolerant Catechism bill passed by Parlia-

[153] Underdown, *Pride's Purge*, p. 275.
[154] I am grateful to Dr I. M. Green for his advice about the dating of ejections in Hampshire; H.C.R.O., 19M61, nos. 1382, 1383, 1385.
[155] Mildon, 'Puritanism in Hampshire', pp. 318–19.
[156] W. M. Lamont, *Godly Rule: Politics and Religion 1603–1660* (London, 1969), p. 143.
[157] B. Worden, 'Toleration and the Cromwellian Protectorate,' *Persecution and Toleration: Studies in Church History*, 21, ed. W. Shiels (Oxford, 1984), pp. 199–233.
[158] B. Reay, *The Quakers and the English Revolution* (London, 1985), p. 56.

ment, and his Council made various attempts to alleviate the lot of Quakers at local level.[159]

But the counsels of the Protectorate were divided over religious liberty and several leading supporters of the regime in Hampshire were unhappy with even the more limited toleration of 1657. John Hildesley, by now a member of the Army Committee as well as sheriff of Hampshire, acted as a teller against the clause encapsulating the limited toleration which the Humble Petition and Advice contained in March 1657.[160] In December of that year, John Dunch, another prominent Cromwellian in Hampshire, wrote to Thurloe, attempting to convince him of the insurrectionary intentions of local Quakers. He tried to suggest that they were in league with the Catholics in a common design.[161] No action was taken.

Like his Stuart successors, Cromwell could exert restraint over the persecuting zeal of his local supporters, if he bothered to do so. He gave Parliament its head in 1656–7, and cannot be exonerated from the consequences. 'The Papists in England . . . ' he told it in his opening speech, 'they have been accounted ever since I was born Spaniolized'. In other words, they were a potential fifth column: an open invitation to persecution. Parliament obliged with the act against Catholics, which was enforced in the counties with large Catholic communities like Staffordshire and Sussex.[162] Vigorous enforcement also took place in Hampshire, where 639 Catholic recusants were convicted and their convictions certified to the Exchequer, to add to the 1657 recusant roll, the very bulk of which is testimony to the execution of the act in many places.[163]

The vague terms of Cromwellian toleration left much room for provincial interpretation. The law or government directives might be twisted by intolerant local magistrates. In Hampshire, such tactics were used to thwart Quaker evangelism. Edmund Pitman, a justice at Basingstoke, used it to break up a Quaker conventicle in the borough in July 1655 and commit its leaders to prison. William Knight, who had hosted the meetings, was cross-examined about his attitude to the local ministry and the national church in general, and on his refusal to answer was also imprisoned.[164] The law against vagrancy,

---

[159] C. H. Firth, *The Last Years of the Protectorate* (2 vols., London, 1909), i. 75–9; I. Roots, 'Law making in the second Protectorate parliament', *British Government and Administration*, ed. H. Hearder and H. R. Loyn (Cardiff, 1974), p. 136; *Cal.S.P.Dom.*, 1657–8, pp. 156–7.

[160] *C.J.*, vii. 507.   [161] Bodl., MS Rawl. A 56, fol. 360.

[162] *Writings and Speeches of Oliver Cromwell*, ed. Abbott, iv. 264; T. S. Smith, 'The persecution of Staffordshire Roman Catholic recusants 1625–60', *Journal of Ecclesiastical History*, xxx. (1979), 344; Fletcher, *Sussex*, p. 97.

[163] H.C.R.O., QI, fols. 118–31; P.R.O., E377 (Recusant roll) no. 63.

[164] J. Besse (ed.), *A Collection of the Sufferings of the People called Quakers* (2 vols., London, 1753), i. 228; H.C.R.O., 24M54/14 (Quaker Sufferings Book), fol. 3; 148M71 (Basingstoke Borough records) 2/6/1: Examination of William Knight.

strengthened in 1657, was applied to Quakers by local magistrates, again with a view to stifling their evangelism. In February 1658, John Bulkeley sent Humphrey Smith from Herefordshire, James Melledge from Poole and William Bayly from Poulnar, near Ringwood, to the county gaol at Winchester on a mittimus which omitted Bayly's place of residence and alleged that they were guilty of divers misdemeanours. They were later charged with vagrancy, though as Bayly protested he could not be a vagrant within his own parish. However, Bulkeley's committal of the three men was upheld at the assizes and they were sent to the house of correction until released by the Rump's committee in May 1659. Bulkeley later boasted of his action to Richard Cromwell's Parliament.[165]

There were other arbitrary proceedings. Philip Bence, coming to visit the Quakers imprisoned at Winchester, was imprisoned in the Gatehouse by the mayor, Thomas Muspratt, and the next day turned out of the city. William and Richard Baker were imprisoned by John Hooke, a local justice, for no more than criticizing the excessive distraint which John Corbett, the local minister, was taking for tithes. And though neither Hooke nor anybody else appeared to accuse them at sessions, they remained in prison for twenty-four weeks.[166]

But garrison officers and soldiers, over whom the government might have exercised a more direct control, were equally involved in restraining Quaker evangelism. In 1655, the guard at Portsmouth ordered Fox off his horse as he journeyed westward, and brought him before the captain of the guard who proved friendly, and allowed him to pass.[167] Quakers were barred by soldiers from the Isle of Wight in 1657 and when Thomas Murford managed to obtain entry he was violently ejected.[168]

Dr Reay has written that 'Oliver Cromwell's policy of toleration was only what the local communities would make of it.'[169] If for 'communities' one reads magistrates and garrison commanders, then there is much truth in this, as the Hampshire evidence shows. Yet it is important not to exaggerate the independence of local authorities. Most of the persecution of Quakers which took place locally was in fact clearly in line with stated government policy. From the very beginning, Cromwell had strongly opposed the Quaker habit of interrupting ministers, and his government was committed to the continuance of tithes.[170]

---

[165] H.C.R.O., 24M54/14, fol. 4; *Burton's Diary*, ed. Rutt, iv. 300; Mildon, 'Puritanism in Hampshire', p. 432.

[166] H.C.R.O., 24M54/14, fols. 2, 6.

[167] *The Journal of George Fox*, ed. J. L. Nickalls (Cambridge, 1952), pp. 230–1.

[168] Besse, *Sufferings of . . . Quakers*, i. 229; Nuttall, 'Swarthmore MSS to 1660' (typescript catalogue) no. 404.

[169] Reay, *The Quakers and the English Revolution*, p. 52.

[170] W. C. Braithwaite, *The Beginnings of Quakerism* (2nd edn, Cambridge, 1955), pp. 434–5.

Most of the Quakers to suffer in Hampshire in the Cromwellian period did so for offences connected with these two matters. Apart from itinerant preachers who suffered in the absence of any clear policy from the government, there are twenty-two imprisonments of Quakers listed in the local sufferings book for the 1650s. Seventeen of these imprisonments concerned disturbing a minister or refusal to pay tithes in the first instance. If anyone was uncertain as to official approval of such punishment, their doubts would have been dispelled by the sight of Lord Commissioner Lisle coming down to preside at Southampton quarter sessions in his position as recorder there, and handing down stiff penalties to those who had disturbed local ministers.[171]

Under Richard Cromwell there was a renewed attempt to exert central control over local persecution, with a conciliar investigation into the commitments of Quakers to provincial gaols. This produced a great deal of information about the sufferings of the Quakers, but it was left to the restored Rump in May 1659 to act upon it to the extent of freeing large numbers of them from local prisons. Six Quakers were freed in Hampshire at the direct order of the committee of Parliament.[172] Such a policy can only have antagonized further an already suspicious conservative provincial magistracy.

The governments of the Interregnum seem to have had surprisingly little impact on local religious life. For example, they came nowhere near stamping out Anglicanism, which helps to explain the relative ease with which it was re-established after 1660. Governments failed to define toleration clearly enough, leaving the way open for intolerant provincial magistrates to have their own way. But when Whitehall chose to exert control over persecution in the localities it proved quite possible to do so, though the political consequences of a tolerant policy might be far-reaching.[173]

---

[171] H.C.R.O., 24M54/14, fols. 2–6.
[172] *Cal.S.P.Dom.*, 1658–9, pp. 158–9, 199; H.C.R.O., 24M54/14, fols. 2, 4; QO 4, p. 17.
[173] B. Reay, 'The Quakers, 1659, and the restoration of the monarchy', *History*, 63 (1978), 193–213.

3

Government and county 1649–60

It is extremely difficult to measure attitudes and reactions of people in the provinces to central government during the 1650s. This is partly a problem of evidence: for many places the silence is impenetrable. But there are also problems with interpreting the evidence that there is. For Professor Underdown, 'There is no great mystery about the politics of the elite' in this period, and yet his own pioneering interpretation of the subject has been questioned in the light of recent research. Underdown concedes that there is more difficulty in gauging popular opinion.[1]

In Hampshire, as in other counties in the period, treasonable activities were the preserve of only a small minority at least before 1659. Twenty-five obscure gentlemen and others from Hampshire were taken prisoner in the west, in the wake of Penruddock's Rising in 1655.[2] Even treasonable words were rare, or at least were rarely reported. There were only six presentments or indictments for seditious or libellous words at Hampshire quarter sessions between Easter 1646 and Michaelmas 1660.

Despite the difficulties of the evidence, many historians have argued that Interregnum governments were unpopular in the provinces, and have in turn attributed this unpopularity mainly to their supposed commitment to centralization and the extensive military presence. Unfortunately there is no commonly agreed definition of centralization and detailed local studies of the military presence and military–civilian relations are still few. Professor Everitt believed that Interregnum governments were equally involved in centralization, whilst Professor Underdown has argued that it was a more sporadic phenomenon, alternating with conciliation during the Protectorate. Dr Clive Holmes regards the new local commissions of the Interregnum as

---

[1] Underdown, *Revel, Riot and Rebellion*, pp. 209, 232; Reece, 'The military presence in England', pp. 201–10; Williams, 'County and municipal government in Cornwall, Devon, Dorset and Somerset', *passim*.
[2] *Th.S.P.*, iii. 306–8.
[3] Furley, *Quarter Sessions Government*, p. 106.

inherently more dependent on the centre than traditional institutions and the men of lesser social status who staffed these and the commissions of the peace are supposed to have been more centrally minded than their social superiors whom they displaced in local office. Dr Roberts in his stimulating and sceptical exploration of the subject posits another definition, 'Centralization if it means anything in this period, means the acquisition by government of a more finely tuned awareness of the behaviour of citizens.'[4]

In fact, very few of these sorts of centralization seem to have been achieved in Hampshire, or indeed elsewhere in the 1650s. Dr Williams in his study of the west country in this period has argued convincingly that the committees and commissions of the 1640s and 1650s represented no radical innovation in local administration, and were not intrinsically more subject to central control.[5] My own study confirms his view that much was left to the discretion of local JPs. In Hampshire, the local administrative primacy of the quarter sessions court, effectively re-established in the wake of the Civil War, was never seriously questioned, by central government or any local agency. But contrary to what some historians have believed, these JPs were not inherently more responsive to central government by virtue of their inferior social rank. The JPs in Hampshire in the 1650s were certainly not militant localists, but neither were they the mere lackeys of central authority.[6] In this they were just like the men who had served before them (some of whom also acted in the Interregnum) and those who served after them. They were no more and no less centrally minded.

Where there is evidence that the office-holders of the 1650s were resented locally, it is not because they were seen as agents of centralization, but because they were social upstarts, who were thought to be acting arbitrarily. To royalists who had been removed from office, the socially inferior quality of their replacements was particularly offensive. Sir John Oglander criticized this phenomenon at national and local level.[7] The disruption of social hierarchy featured prominently in the satirical poetry of Sir William Kingsmill.[8] The wider community was bitterly resentful of what it saw as the arbitrary actions of the new men. Reminiscing about the Maijor menage at Hursley in the 1650s, Richard Morley, the local blacksmith, wrote 'we had justice right or wrong by power; for if we did offend they had power to send us a thousand

---

[4] Underdown, 'Settlement in the counties' in Aylmer, *The Interregnum*, pp. 166–7; Holmes, *Seventeenth-Century Lincolnshire*, p. 206; Roberts, 'Local government reform in England and Wales' in Roots, *'Into Another Mould'*, p. 36.

[5] Williams, 'County and municipal government in Cornwall, Devon, Dorset and Somerset', chapter 3, pp. 121–93 and pp. 302, 339–53.

[6] For example over the excise, see above, pp. 48–9.

[7] Bamford, *A Royalist's Notebook*, pp. 127, 129, 132–3.

[8] Eames, 'The poems of Sir William Kingsmill', i. 153–61.

miles off, and that they told us'.[9] Richard Maijor was certainly guilty of some arbitrary actions which alienated the local community, like evicting William Morrant from his house in Hursley and preventing Christopher Light, a former royalist soldier, from returning to his home there. Most of the substantial inhabitants of the parish would petition quarter sessions against these actions after the Restoration.[10] Other magistrates were seen as exploiting their positions for their own profit, like Thomas Muspratt, twice mayor of Winchester, who 'by his tyrannical power has ordered that no inhabitant or victualler shall brew beer or ale to sell' except at his own brewhouse. Local victuallers petitioned against him after the Restoration.[11] In April 1656, Southampton corporation petitioned the Committee for Trade and Navigation that locally based revenue officers should not be allowed to indulge in trade on their own behalf, implying that this led to corruption.[12] It is probably significant that when Sir Robert Howard, who had been resident in Hampshire during the 1650s, came to write *The Committee* soon after the Restoration, it was the social pretensions and corrupt practices of puritan officials which he singled out for satire.[13]

Other forms of centralization apart from the purely bureaucratic sort came no nearer to being realized. To follow Dr Roberts' definition cited above, there was no 'finely tuned awareness' at the centre of the behaviour of Hampshire's citizens. Government was often hopelessly in the dark, as its intelligence system was incomplete. Restoration governments would be much better equipped in this respect. With the arrival of Major-General Goffe in the county, central government came nearer than ever before to obtaining that all too elusive awareness of its subjects' behaviour, but Goffe's interpretation of the local scene could hardly be described as 'finely tuned'. As for his administrative role, he achieved as little in Hampshire as he did in Sussex, where 'military rule was more a bogey than a reality'.[14] But there is no evidence in Hampshire, or apparently in the west country either, to support the view that the mere fact of participation by military men in local government was enough to alienate the gentry, though royalists of course were alienated already. Dr Williams has argued that relations between the military and the gentry in the west country were cordial, at least before 1659.[15] Major-

[9] J. Marsh, *Memoranda of the Parishes of Hursley and North Baddesley in the County of Southampton* (Winchester, 1808). p. 12.

[10] H.C.R.O., QO 4, pp. 58, 92.

[11] *Hist. MSS Comm. Seventh Report, App. pt I*, p. 93.

[12] S.C.R.O., SC2/1/8, fol. 118.

[13] Sir Robert Howard, *The Committee or the Faithful Irishman* (University of Illinois Studies in Language and Literature, vii. February, 1921).

[14] Fletcher, *Sussex*, p. 311.

[15] Williams, 'County and municipal government in Cornwall, Devon, Dorset and Somerset', p. 293.

General Goffe 'received many outward civilities from the gentlemen in and about [Winchester]'.[16] His role of acting as a local justice was easily the least controversial part of his whole mission.

But some historians appear to believe that the mere fact of the military presence made central government unpopular in the provinces in the 1650s. Edward Carpenter, in describing the mood of the Restoration, has written of 'a fanatical hatred of the efficient but severe government of the Protector with its major generals and its standing army'.[17] Leaving aside the efficiency of the Protectorate government (which is highly debatable), this remark assumes that there was a deep popular hatred of the major-generals and the military as such. But as Dr Reece has observed, 'popular reaction to the major-generals was muted, if not negligible'.[18] Of course, abuses like free quarter and excessive billeting infuriated the local population, as they had always done in Hampshire as elsewhere, for example in 1628 and 1646. In January 1649, the inhabitants of Portsmouth petitioned Fairfax against excessive quartering. Later in the year, a county assize grand jury petitioned against the persistence of free quarter contrary to the Rump's act. The government, keen not to jeopardize its sole propaganda coup, made sure that the act was enforced.[19]

Even some garrison commanders who lacked local roots were capable of seeing things from the local point of view. Sir John Oglander seems to have been on friendly terms with Colonel William Sydenham when he was governor of the Isle of Wight, and raised with him the matter of a ban on goods being exported from the island, to which he replied 'God forbid I should do it! We have hitherto fought for our liberties, and I hope I shall not infringe them.' Oglander observed in his common-place book that Sydenham was 'Truly a very civil gentleman and one that applied himself to do all good to our Island'. Later, having been entertained by Newport corporation, he helped to get a bill for the maintenance of a minister there through the second Protectorate Parliament.[20]

But Sydenham was not the only garrison commander who attempted to look after the interests of the place where he was posted, despite having no

---

[16] *Th.S.P.*, iv. 239.
[17] E. Carpenter, *The Protestant Bishop* (London, 1956), p. 25; Professor Baxter expresses himself in similar terms, S. B. Baxter, *The Development of the Treasury 1660–1702* (London, 1957), p. 79.
[18] Reece, 'The military presence in England', p. 5.
[19] Schwoerer, *No Standing Armies!*, p. 22; L. Boynton, 'Billeting: the example of the Isle of Wight', *E.H.R.*, lxxiv (1959), 23–40; *The Moderate Intelligencer*, no. 76, 14 Aug. 1646, pp. 601–2; Brit. Lib., Addit. MS 18979 (Fairfax papers), fol. 262; Bodl., MS Nalson, XXII (Dep. C. 175), no. 119.
[20] Bamford, *A Royalist's Notebook*, p. 129; I.W.C.R.O., 45/16a, pp. 681–2; *Burton's Diary*, ed. Rutt, i. 223, 245.

previous connection with it. In September 1651, Colonel Nathaniel Whetham opposed the siting of a naval victuallers' slaughterhouse in a certain position because it was offensive to the inhabitants of Portsmouth as well as the garrison, and he got his way. In June 1653 he petitioned the Admiralty Commissioners on behalf of the mayor and aldermen that steps be taken to clean and pave the streets of the town to prevent the spread of disease.[21] Major Peter Murford, governor of Southampton, agreed in June 1651, to present a petition on behalf of the town to the Council of Trade. Subsequently, as a sub-commissioner of excise, he appealed to the Admiralty Commissioners not to send too many Dutch prisoners to the town, because there was a shortage of space and excessive numbers would spread disease. Murford looked back to the time (during the Civil War in 1644) when 1,000 men of Essex's broken army billeted in the town contributed to the outbreak of an epidemic which killed 100 citizens there.[22] A little local knowledge enabled even military commanders to appreciate the genuine problems of the localities.

Once abuses like free quarter had been rectified, local people grew quite accustomed to the military presence and indeed came to value it, as a protection against external threats. The inhabitants of Portsmouth in 1658, recognized the value of the local garrison as at least a temporary check to any foreign invasion. They protested against any plan to scale it down. Abuse or hostility by the local civilian population was very rare and certainly no more common before 1660 than afterwards.[23] At Southampton, where the tensions between soldier and civilian had been greater under the Commonwealth, there was still a recognition amongst magistrates and people of the usefulness of troops stationed locally. In June 1661, the mayor, aldermen, merchants and inhabitants of the town petitioned the Privy Council to have Hurst and Calshot castles continued as garrisons, because they acted as a check on piracy.[24]

Even royalist observers seem to have been more concerned with the army's political role than the military presence in the provinces. Sir William Kingsmill, a very hostile observer, aimed his satire against the intervention of the military in central politics, rather than its presence in the localities. The earl of Southampton, who was resident in Hampshire for much of the decade, was impressed by the 'sober and religious' quality of Cromwell's army, while

[21] *Cal.S.P.Dom.*, 1651, p. 451; *Cal.S.P.Dom.*, 1652–3, pp. 236, 432.
[22] S.C.R.O., SC2/1/8, fol. 71; *Cal.S.P.Dom.*, 1652–3, p. 196.
[23] Bodl., MS Carte 74, fol. 472; *A Calendar of Portsmouth Borough Sessions Papers 1653–1688*, ed. M. J. Hoad (Portsmouth Record Society, 1971), *passim*.
[24] S.C.R.O., T.C. Misc. Box 2, no. 87; P.R.O., P.C. 2/55, p. 254.

lamenting 'the effects of the military government'.[25] Both these men were royalists and therefore already alienated from the regime.

In fact, the centralization which alienated the gentry and urban elites in Hampshire from Interregnum governments consisted in the blocking of the usual channels for consultation through which consent might have been obtained. In normal times, Hampshire had a large representation in Parliament, which was mostly supplied from resident gentry families, or their near relations. This delegation was slashed by Pride's Purge. Nine were secluded or imprisoned. Seven abstained, of whom only two were subsequently re-admitted. In 1650, this meant that there were only nine members sitting for Hampshire seats, which had only risen to ten by 1653.[26] The purge had interrupted the careers of some of Hampshire's most active politicians, such as John Bulkeley. With Barebone's Parliament, Hampshire's representation dropped to three, who were chosen centrally anyway.

It was a shock for local communities to be deprived of representation in this way. There were now fewer people in touch with the centre to advance their interests. One of Southampton's MPs had been secluded at Pride's Purge and the other had abstained. In seeking to alleviate the town's lot, the corporation took to petitioning central bodies directly, its first petition to the Rump being delivered only a few months after the execution of the king. The stream of petitions to the Rump and lesser bodies was kept up throughout the Interregnum, but seldom achieved any success. As was seen above, even the local garrison commander, Major Murford, was called into service to represent the town's interests. After he lost his command with the disbanding of the garrison, Southampton obtained a more influential patron in the person of John Lisle, one of the Lord Commissioners of the Great Seal, who became recorder in December 1651. In July 1654, he was sent a 'shopping list' of matters which the corporation wished him to pursue on its behalf. But Lisle never seems to have achieved much for the town, and the corporation put up little resistance to his replacement in 1659.[27] Yet of all the councillors of state to be recruited locally Lisle was almost the only one to be sufficiently active to really represent local interests at the centre. Robert Wallop was extremely sporadic in his attendance as a councillor of state, so that eventually in February 1651 he lost his place. Nicholas Love and John Fielder who were elected on to the Council of State at this time were more active, but Fielder soon lost his place and Wallop was back in December, though hardly more

[25] Eames, 'The poems of Sir William Kingsmill', i. 164; ii. 46–54; G. Burnet, *History of My Own Time*, ed. O. Airy (2 vols., Oxford, 1897–1900), i. 279.
[26] Underdown, *Pride's Purge*, pp. 367, 369, 372–4, 377–8, 381, 389–90; A. B. Worden, *The Rump Parliament* (Cambridge, 1974), p. 396.
[27] Underdown, *Pride's Purge*, pp. 373, 374; S.C.R.O., SC2/1/8, fols. 44–5, 46, 57, 71, 75, 78, 83, 105, 118, 140; *Cal.S.P.Dom.*, 1652–3, p. 249.

assiduous. Only in the Rump's last four months in power in 1653 was there a substantial group of councillors from Hampshire, regularly attending the Council of State.[28] In this Hampshire was considerably better off than most counties. Under the Protectorate, Hampshire's conciliar representation slumped to one, in the person of Richard Maijor, who ceased to be active after the summer of 1654.[29]

But neither the councillors nor the members of the Rump seem to have used their power for the benefit of the wider community. Their patronage was narrow and partisan in its effects. Robert Wallop and Sir Thomas Jervoise, both sporadic attenders of the Rump, spent their time there promoting their own interests, for example an act to compensate them for Civil War losses out of the estate of the marquis of Winchester, in 1649.[30] John Lisle abused his position as Lord Commissioner of the Great Seal to help John Cole of Odiham, a former parliamentarian, get the better of George Rodney of Lyndhurst, a sequestered royalist, in a law suit between them, as later came out during the second Protectorate Parliament.[31] Richard Maijor's arbitrary actions and attitudes and their impact on the local community have already been referred to.[32] Those who benefited most from conciliar influence seem to have been the local employees of the state, past or present. Thus Colonel Whetham, through Nicholas Love's influence, managed to have the poor condition of Portsmouth's fortifications raised at the Council of State. And some former sequestration officials in Hampshire managed to get the question of their unpaid salaries resolved by the protector's Council apparently through Richard Maijor's influence.[33]

Under the Instrument of Government, Hampshire had fourteen parliamentary seats allotted to it, just over half its traditional quota, but two more than it would have had if allocation had been based strictly on the distribution of the 1649 assessment. Eight of the county's twelve boroughs were disenfranchised completely, whilst the remaining four all lost one seat, the Isle of Wight was given two seats to itself, and the number of county seats was increased to eight. Elections were to be conducted on a partisan basis with royalists debarred from voting.[34]

[28] *Cal.S.P.Dom.*, 1649–50, pp. xlviii–lxxv; *C.S.P.D.*, 1650, pp. xvi–xxxix; *Cal.S.P.Dom.*, 1651, pp. xxvi–xxxv; *1651–2*, p. xlvii; *Cal.S.P.Dom.*, 1652–3, pp. xxxiii.
[29] *Cal.S.P.Dom.*, 1654, p. xliii; Gaunt, 'The Councils of the Protectorate', p. 130.
[30] Worden, *The Rump Parliament*, pp. 99–100; *C.J.*, vi. 269, 290, 294–6; *C.J.*, vii. 177, 182, 190; P.R.O., S.P. 46/95, fols. 168–83.
[31] *Burton's Diary*, ed. Rutt, i. 19, 105–6, 135–6.
[32] See above, p. 66.
[33] Bodl., MS Rawl. A 184, fols. 381, 383; *Cal.S.P.Dom.*, 1654, pp. 242, 257.
[34] *The Constitutional Documents of the Puritan Revolution 1625–1660*, ed. S. R. Gardiner (Oxford, 3rd edn, revised reprint, 1979), pp. 408, 410; Worden, *The Rump Parliament*, p. 396.

Boroughs found it hard to adapt to their reduced importance. On 6 July 1654, Andover held an election after the traditional fashion with John Dunch and the recorder John Shuter (four times MP during the 1620s) being declared elected. John Bulkeley was also in the poll, but only obtained seven votes. Dunch was also elected for Berkshire, and Bulkeley for Hampshire. Both sat accordingly. At the by-election held in December, a traditional election for two burgesses were again held in flagrant breach of the Instrument. But there was not sufficient time for either candidate to take his seat in the House before Cromwell dissolved it in January 1655.[35]

But even worse, from the local point of view, than such restrictions on representation was the attempt in 1656 by the Protectorate government to manage elections. An attempt was made to pack Parliament with the government's supporters. This was the really unpopular aspect of the major-generals' mission. In Hampshire, it was expected by some people that the assize grand jury would be influential in the selection of county MPs, though Goffe hoped this would not be so, as Richard Norton was its foreman, John Bulkeley his second and it contained several decimated royalists. Norton had had 'scruples' about collaborating with Goffe, perhaps due to pressure from his father-in-law Lord Saye and Sele, and probably because of the decimation tax, which several of his relations were obliged to pay.[36] Goffe suspected Norton, but as opposition grew he began to look to him to save him from an electoral humiliation. Anti-court feeling developed and an opposition list of candidates was circulating which omitted Goffe, Richard Cromwell and all other relatives of the protector, whilst including several former members of the Long Parliament, all of whom were independent of, if not totally hostile to, the court. Goffe claimed that letters which he had received from the protector had been instrumental in rallying 'some honest men' to the court, but it would require more than this if it were to avoid a humiliating defeat in Hampshire. Goffe wanted Norton to co-operate with Richard Cromwell to devise a list of candidates acceptable to the court. Norton did indeed issue a list of candidates, though he thought it discreet to omit Goffe's name, as he told the anxious major-general 'better not to be named than receive a baffle'.[37]

If Goffe was defeated, Norton assured him that he would try to get him elected for Portsmouth where he was now governor. In the event, Goffe was returned, along with Richard Cromwell and two gentlemen who had acted as militia commissioners. But Captain Pitman, one of the militia troop captains was not returned despite the 'greate number of honest and resolute men that

[35] H.C.R.O., 37M84, 4/MI/1 (Andover Town Council Minutes 1641–54).
[36] *Th.S.P.*, iv. 238; v. 215; Abbott, *Writings and Speeches of Oliver Cromwell*, iv. 25.
[37] *Th.S.P.*, v. 329, 396–7.

did cleave to him'. Some open opponents and critics of the regime, notably Robert Wallop, John Bulkeley and Edward Hooper were also returned. An opposition attempt at Southampton to keep John Lisle out of the seat for that town failed by only four votes.[38]

The government compounded the unpopularity of its bungled electoral management, by failing to honour the decision of the electorate. Two of Hampshire's MPs, Bulkeley and Hooper, were amongst the hundred or so excluded from sitting by the protector's Council. Nevertheless, this Parliament was sufficiently full and sat for long enough for local matters as well as the great issues of the day to be aired. There was a spate of local bills, several of them from Hampshire, though only one, that for maintenance of ministers at Newport, reached the statute book.[39]

From the point of view of conciliating traditional elites in the provinces, Richard Cromwell's government was wise to revert to the old distribution of seats and franchise. Hampshire's representation was nearly doubled at a stroke. Electoral management was also more low key in the subsequent elections. Richard Cromwell simply appealed to leading figures in the counties to ensure that favourable men were returned. He relied upon friends and relations like John Dunch to perform this task in Hampshire.[40] Court patronage was not exerted, even where there was some traditional grounds for it. The governor of the Isle of Wight had the right to nominate to one seat in each of the island's boroughs. Yet there is no evidence that Sydenham sought to exercise this right. Indeed, Samuel Bull his deputy, though a burgess of Newtown, approached the Barringtons, who had an interest in the borough, in the hope of being elected MP, but he was unsuccessful.[41] The sheriff of Hampshire and the mayor of Petersfield were subsequently accused of gerrymandering, in the latter case with some justice, but there is no evidence that this was at the behest of the court, or that it profited from their practices. Nevertheless, more than half the delegation to Richard Cromwell's Parliament were office-holders, relations of Cromwell or supporters of the regime.[42] But the Parliament was still not free, because former royalists were excluded from voting or sitting as MPs, by governmental fiat. Parliamentary independence and unhindered representation was not achieved under the Protectorate, and as Dr Ronald Hutton has pointed out, the Parliament of

[38] *Th.S.P.*, v. 287.
[39] *C.J.*, vii. 425, 455, 473–5, 514, 536, 538.
[40] *Calendar of State Papers Venetian*, vol. 31, 1657–9, p. 255; *The Collection of Autograph Letters and Historical Documents formed by Alfred Morrison* (printed for private circulation, 3 vols., 1893–8), ii. 369.
[41] Brit. Lib., MS Egerton 2648 (Barrington papers), fol. 370.
[42] *Burton's Diary*, iii. 596; *C.J.*, vii. 595, 605, 608–9, 617; *Return . . . of Every member of the Lower House of Parliament 1213–1874* (1878), pt i, p. 509.

1659 was so concerned with high matters of state that there was not time to deal with private bills.[43]

Despite the general lack of consent for their rule, Interregnum governments imposed huge taxes on the landowning classes and the population at large, which were one of the main causes of their unpopularity in the provinces. Southampton found its tax burden crippling, and vainly appealed to the Rump to have it lightened.[44] And the Rump regime's ability to consume huge revenues provoked the bitter satire of Sir William Kingsmill.[45] The Protectorate government recognized the unpopularity of high taxation and set about its disastrous tax-cutting policy which had virtually bankrupted it by 1659. Worse, it resorted to divisive expedients like the decimation tax, which alienated many of the provincial gentry whom it was attempting to woo.[46]

The Protectorate government's inability to pay its way provoked the ridicule and anger of the local community. When Goffe arrived in Hampshire in November 1655, he found to his dismay 'the country beginns to jeare the soldiers [of the militia] telling them they are but cheated, and must never expect any pay'. But the mirth turned to anger when it was the country that was out of pocket. Goffe authorized the justices to promise that payment would be made to constables for money spent on the impressment of seamen, yet none was forthcoming.[47] Worse was to follow when the government failed to provide the money which it had promised for the supply of carts to transport prize plate from Portsmouth to London in 1657. William Rowe found that, 'the countrymen say it comes by Com[missioner] Willoughby wanting of money to clear them all'. So none was paid, and as tithings had clubbed together to provide the carts, the carters began to sue their neighbours to get redress.[48] It was not its efficiency that would have struck the average Hampshireman most about the Protectorate government, but rather its crippling insolvency, though taxation remained high. Government was caught in a vicious circle, cutting taxes to woo popularity and then alienating people through its desperate lack of funds.

But quite apart from these material grievances, there were ideological factors which alienated a majority of people in Hampshire as in other counties from central government in the 1650s. There was a cultural polarization at local level between those who were committed to the religious reforms of the 1640s and to continuing godly reformation and those who harked back to the old order.[49] The royalist nobility and gentry harboured, corresponded with

43 Hutton, *The Restoration*, p. 32.
44 S.C.R.O., SC2/1/8, fols. 75, 83.
45 Eames, 'The poems of Sir William Kingsmill', ii. 53–4, 246.
46 Reece, 'The military presence in England', pp. 42–9.
47 *Th.S.P.*, iv. 238; *Th.S.P.*, v. 150.   48 P.R.O., S.P. 18/156, fol. 126.
49 Underdown, *Revel, Riot and Rebellion*, esp. chs. 8 and 9, pp. 208–70.

and encouraged sequestered Anglican clergy and practised a sort of cultural separatism. John Stewkeley, an Anglican royalist who had not actually fought in the Civil War, made enquiries about the state of Oxford University in the 1650s and on reflection did not send his son there. Sir William Kingsmill, as his private poems show, was nostalgic for hierarchy and vitriolically anti-puritan. Anglican practices persisted in a number of places.[50]

Large sections of the population remained indifferent or hostile to the cause of godliness and moral reformation. Robert Dingley, minister of Brightstone in the Isle of Wight, in his dedicatory epistle of a tract entitled *Vox Coeli* (1658) addressed to Major Samuel Bull, wrote

O that we had many more such as yourself to countenance Religion and good men in this place. I wish that all our Gentry were such as you are; then would our lecture and conference be more frequented; Vice and Heresie be more curbed; and the hands of good Pastors and People more strengthened in the work, and way of the Lord.[51]

Next year, Bull would fall victim to a political purge and leave the island. In that year (1659) William Gearing, minister of Lymington, in dedicating his book *The Arraignment of Ignorance* to three local puritan notables (John Button, John Bulkeley and John Hildesley) observed 'what gross darkness is yet among us' though 'These are dayes that abound in the meanes of saving knowledge.'[52] The puritan experiment had left the bulk of the population unmoved.

Nevertheless, even Richard Cromwell's mild government felt obliged to adopt the rhetoric of the parliamentarian cause of the 1640s, issuing a proclamation against those who were trying to revive prayer book services, 'and other superstitious rites in the service of God'.[53] For active support in Hampshire, the regimes of the Interregnum looked to the 'godly' minority. The radical sects, the more extreme Independents, Baptists and others were not sufficiently numerous to provide much of a power base there and anyway were likely to become disillusioned with the less than radical governments which ruled after 1649. A group of radical Independents at Alton were content enough with the rule of the Rump as late as 1653.[54] But radicals from other parts of the county, with Leveller sympathies, were thoroughly dis-

[50] H.C.R.O., 19M61, nos. 1380, 1382, 1385, 1388; I.W.C.R.O., OG/19/14; *The Life of Edward, earl of Clarendon, being a Continuation of the History of the Great Rebellion from the Restoration to his banishment in 1667* (3 vols., Oxford, 1827), iii. 238; *Memoirs of the Verney Family during the Civil War, during the Commonwealth and from the Restoration to the Revolution,* ed. F. P. and M. M. Verney (4 vols., London, 1892–9), iv. 95; Eames, 'The poems of Sir William Kingsmill', ii. 38, 48; for the persistance of Anglican practices see above, p. 59.

[51] R. Dingley, *Vox Coeli* (London, 1658), epistle dedicatory.

[52] W[illiam] G[earing], *The Arraignment of Ignorance* (London, 1659), epistle dedicatory.

[53] *A Proclamation For the Better Encouragement of Godly Ministers and others and their enjoying their dues and liberty according to law* (London, 1658).

[54] Brit. Lib., Addit. MS 24861, fol. 67.

satisfied by the Rump's conservatism and supposed corruption by the time of its dissolution.[55] The more politically minded Baptists and other sectaries were liable to be alienated from the Protectorate by Fifth Monarchist propaganda, as Goffe discovered in 1655. But radicals of any sort were in a tiny minority in the local community. William Cole of Southampton, a Leveller whom Goffe interviewed in 1656, was a figure of fun locally, popularly known as 'Comon Freedome'.[56]

Radical support was too slight and uncertain to be relied upon. In these circumstances, the best that Interregnum regimes could hope for was to rally the conservative puritan and former parliamentarian element in local society to support their rule. Successive governments managed to do this to some extent by portraying themselves as the bulwark against radicalism and further revolution. The desire to prevent far-reaching charge probably motivated some of Hampshire's MPs in their conformity to the Rump. John Fielder of Borough Court, a 'recruiter' MP for St Ives, who conformed in 1649, became a very active member, in contrast to his absenteeism before Pride's Purge. He made it a personal speciality to block law reform in the Rump and rose to the Council of State in February 1651. Richard Norton of Southwick, an abstainer, took longer to be persuaded. It required strong pressure from Oliver Cromwell, and the battle of Worcester to bring him into the Rump.[57] But the rise of radicalism in the army and the expression of radical views in the press in 1652 transformed the attitude of many of Hampshire's moderate parliamentarians towards the Rump. They came to see it as the upholder of the parochial ministry and property. Inspired by Baxter's Worcester petition of December 1652, John Bulkeley and Richard Whitehead (two secluded Hampshire MPs) were co-operating with Richard Maijor early in 1653, canvassing signatures for a similar venture in Hampshire. Radical Independents were worried by its conservative implications and refused to support it, but a modified version was adopted at the assizes by the grand jury, and was said to have obtained 8,000 signatures, before being presented to the Rump on 8 April. The support which it represented for the Rump was clearly conditional, as it contained little of the flattery which appeared in the Worcestershire petition.[58] John Bulkeley, one

[55] This is clear from a petition which some of them promoted to be presented to Barebone's Parliament, Brit. Lib., Addit. MS 24861, fols. 79–80.

[56] *Th.S.P.*, iv. 445; *Th.S.P.*, v. 396.

[57] Worden, *The Rump Parliament*, pp. 48n, 116, 249; Underdown, *Pride's Purge*, pp. 289, 291.

[58] Brit. Lib., Addit. MS 24861, fols. 67, 71; Dr Williams' Library, Baxter Correspondence, vol. iii, fol. 183; *The Cryes of England to the Parliament For the Continuance of Good Entertainment to the Lord Jesus his Embassadors* (London, 1653), pp. 6–8; *The Humble Petition of Many thousands, Gentlemen, Freeholders, and others of the County of Worcester* (London, 1652), pp. 3–6.

of the promoters of the petition, had a strong dislike for much of what the Commonwealth stood for. Looking back in 1659, he would call it 'a monster'.[59] His support for the Rump in 1653 was to a large extent a tactical manoeuvre. The petition praised the work of the puritan ministry, 'contending for the faith, against Popish, Arminian and other Adversaries'. It called on the Rump to ignore radical criticism of the ministry, and to preserve it, tithes and the universities and to find some settled way to admit orthodox candidates for the ministry. But it was in vain, as the Rump was dissolved less than two weeks after the petition was presented.

Coming in the wake of the frightening experience of Barebone's Parliament, the Protectorate was even better placed to attract moderate puritan support. All three of Hampshire's representatives in that body (Richard Maijor, John Hildesley and Richard Norton) were moderates, and two of them were in central office under the Protectorate.[60] A delegation of Hampshire gentry led by Cornelius Hooker, the recorder of Winchester, presented a petition to Parliament in favour of tithes in September 1653, to counteract a radical Kentish petition. Hooker indeed was allowed to address the assembly, extolling the virtues of property and the rights of ministers. The petition itself referred to the members of Barebone's Parliament as 'the Protectors of our laws, lives, liberties and estates', but after the debacle of December 1653, that role fell to Oliver Cromwell.[61] The relief which local puritan ministers felt at this change was immense. Looking back a few months later, Robert Dingley, minister of Brightstone, declared that by the establishment of the Protectorate 'an happy Period was set to very strange designs, our Liberties and properties secured, the Universities and faithful ministers not a little encouraged; Peace concluded with the Netherlands'.[62]

Some local lay puritans were not at once so enchanted with the Protectorate. John Bulkeley later told Richard Cromwell's Parliament, 'After this we had an Instrument of Government, which had much of good in it, but in the bowels of it took away your [i.e. Parliament's] rights. That liberty was not left you which is your due: not that I would set the crown upon the heads of the people.' Bulkeley, having sought the opinion of various puritan divines about whether sitting in a new Parliament was a breach of the Covenant, took his seat in that of 1654. Here he joined the 'country' opposition in trying to redress the balance of the constitution in Parliament's favour, and failing paid

[59] *Burton's Diary*, ed. Rutt, iii. 106–7.
[60] Woolrych, *Commonwealth to Protectorate*, pp. 382, 384–5, 418–19, 422–3, 424–5.
[61] *The Humble Petition of the well affected of the County of Southampton in behalf of the ministers of the Gospel and for Continuance of their maintenance* (London, 1653).
[62] R. Dingley, *The Deputation of Angels or the Angell-Guardian* (London, 1654), epistle dedicatory.

the price by his exclusion from the next.[63] But the Protectorate had come near to winning the support of local parliamentarians such as Bulkeley and would eventually succeed in doing so. It never came near to winning the support of most local royalists.

'This new false Act that mocks us with a King' was how Sir William Kingsmill described the Instrument of Government.[64] Occasionally men who had been royalists in the Civil Wars came to think that Parliament's cause had been right. Parkinson Odber was one such. He managed to convince John Warner, minister of Christchurch and John Hildesley, a rising Cromwellian, of his conversion, and by their intercession escaped the decimation tax. In 1657, he was even named to the assessment commission for the county.[65] Richard Cromwell did his best to woo men from royalist backgrounds. He went hunting with Lord Sandys, Lord De la Warr and Sir William Kingsmill. Yet before he became protector, Richard Cromwell really lacked the influence at the centre to help his royalist friends. In February 1658, Francis Reade of Faccombe was said to have an interest with Richard Cromwell sufficient to get his cousin, Dr Reade, admitted to the living of Litchfield in Hampshire, despite their former royalism. But in the event Dr Reade's past became known to the 'triers' and it was necessary for the Kingsmills, who were the patrons of the living concerned, to find another candidate.[66] Only once he became protector was Richard able to offer patronage to men of royalist backgrounds, like Sir John Mill of Mottisfont, upon whom he bestowed a forest office.[67] Men of royalist inclinations in the locality found Richard Cromwell a sympathetic figure. According to Richard Morley 'he was a very good neighbourly man while he lived with us at Hursley'.[68] Had his reign lasted longer, he might have been instrumental in healing some of the divisions in local society as well as reconciling royalists to the government.

Even before 1658, friendly relations existed across the divide of political differences in Hampshire. The good opinion of several of his fellow gentry, who had the ear of the government, enabled Lord Henry Paulet to escape the decimation. His son was a friend of Thomas Jervoise, a former parliamentarian officer and now a JP.[69] Even the implacably royalist Sir William Kingsmill had won the 'good thoughts' of 'several gent[s] in the countrey now

[63] *Burton's Diary*, iii. 107; Dr Williams' Library, Baxter Correspondence, vol. v, fol. 122; H. R. Trevor-Roper, 'Oliver Cromwell and his Parliaments', *Essays presented to Sir Lewis Namier*, ed. R. Pares and A. J. P. Taylor (London, 1956), p. 33.

[64] Eames, 'The poems of Sir William Kingsmill', ii. 50.

[65] *Calendar of the Committee for Compounding*, ed. Green, iii. 1659. *F. & R.*, ii. 1080.

[66] Eames, 'The poems of Sir William Kingsmill', i. 43; H.C.R.O., 19M61, nos. 1382, 1383, 1385.

[67] *Cal.S.P.Dom.*, 1658–9, p. 319.

[68] Marsh, *Memoranda*, p. 16.

[69] *Cal.S.P.Dom.*, 1655–6, pp. 78, 89, 172; *Cal.Clar.S.P.*, iv. 371.

in power' and might have escaped the decimation himself if he had attended them personally.[70] But the political impact of such friendship seems to have been muted.

Whatever its future potential might have been, the immediate impact of Richard Cromwell's Protectorate was to rally the bulk of former parliamentarians in Hampshire to support the government. Sir Henry Worsley, the sheriff of the county and a secluded member of the Long Parliament, featured prominently in the celebrations of his accession at Newport in the Isle of Wight. In November 1658, some knights, gentlemen, ministers and inhabitants of the island made a strongly pro-Cromwellian address.[71] Anglican royalists can only have been alienated by the measures which Richard Cromwell was obliged to take on account of his position, such as the lavish funeral for his father and the uncompromising religious proclamation of November 1658.[72] Conversely, those who stood four square behind the religious changes of the 1640s would have regarded the proclamation as a good sign, that the new protector would have no truck with traditional Anglicanism. Some ministers in Hampshire, who were clearly of this mind, composed an address to Richard Cromwell in December, praising him for the way he seemed set to follow in the footsteps of 'your illustrious and most renowned father'.[73]

The majority of the Hampshire bench sitting at Epiphany sessions 1659, which included several veterans of the parliamentarian cause in Hampshire, drew up an address to congratulate Richard Cromwell on his accession, which was supported by the grand jury and other local people.[74] But not all the JPs who attended the quarter sessions were enamoured of the new protector and his regime. Robert Reynolds and Nicholas Love, who had both held high office under the Commonwealth began to make their opposition clear, looking to the leadership of Robert Wallop, who, though he was *custos rotulorum* did not attend the Epiphany sessions. They were heavily outnumbered on the bench, and when Wallop made clear his intention of having Sir Henry Vane, another enemy of the regime, returned for the pocket borough of Whitchurch in the forthcoming general election, he was challenged. A majority of JPs, the 'court faction' as Ludlow dubbed them, subscribed a letter to Wallop threatening to contest his election if he persisted

[70] H.C.R.O., 19M61, no. 1375.
[71] *A True Catalogue or An Account of the several places and most eminent persons in the three nations, and elsewhere and by whom Richard Cromwell was proclaimed Lord Protector of the Commonwealth of England, Scotland and Ireland* (London, 1659), pp. 17, 35.
[72] Richard Morley noted the former with disapproval, Marsh, *Memoranda*, p. 12.
[73] *Original Letters and Papers of State Addressed to Oliver Cromwell concerning the Affairs of Great Britain from the year 1649 to 1658 Found among the Political Collection of Mr John Milton*, ed. John Nickolls (London, 1743), p. 163.
[74] *A True Catalogue*, p. 34.

in his plan. But in the event, this challenge did not materialize, and Robert Wallop was returned as one of the knights of the shire, along with Richard Norton, who was now unequivocally supporting the Protectorate. A belated bid, sponsored by Richard Cromwell himself, to question the Whitchurch election on the basis of alleged improprieties by Wallop did not come to anything either, so that Sir Henry Vane and Robert Reynolds were returned.[75] Thus the enemies of the 'single person' carried their opposition into Richard Cromwell's Parliament. It is easy to see these men as motivated solely by thwarted ambition, and Reynolds for one does appear to have been a political opportunist. But Wallop seems to have developed some genuine republican sentiments, which he would maintain long after it was safe to do so.[76] On the other side, the Cromwellian faction were far from being a group motivated solely by political principle. William Wither of Manydown was the son of a local parliamentarian gentleman. Richard Cromwell had hoped to use him to stand in the Whitchurch election because he was 'an active man, and one that Wallop hath disobleiged'.[77] But there had been some genuine converts to the Cromwellian cause from amongst the former opponents of the Protectorate, for example, John Bulkeley. He played a prominent part in the Parliament of 1659, working hard for agreement between it and the court. He frankly admitted, 'I come to bring court and countrey together', though he had not totally lost his 'country' principles, as he also pressed for the ultimate abolition of the excise. But as astute Cromwellians like Richard Norton realized, the real threat to settlement lay in the army. Finding themselves isolated in the Commons, republicans, like Robert Wallop, conspired to stir up disaffection amongst the military, and in the end were successful.[78] The army turned against Parliament, secured its dissolution, and overthrew the Protectorate.

Some rank-and-file parliamentarians in Hampshire supported the change, addresses of support for the restored Rump coming from the 'well affected' in the Portsmouth area and in the county more generally.[79] But the return of the Rump was extremely unpopular with those Hampshire gentry whose

---

75 H.C.R.O., QO 4, p. 6; *Ludlow's Memoirs*, ed. Firth, ii. 51; *Collection . . . of Alfred Morrison*, ii. 396; *Return . . . of Every Member of the Lower House of Parliament, 1213–1874* (1898), pt i. p. 509.

76 *Edmund Ludlow: A Voyce from the Watch Tower: Part Five 1660–1662*, ed. A. B. Worden (Camden Society Fourth Series 21, 1978), pp. 99, 102–3.

77 *Collection . . . of Alfred Morrison*, ii. 396.

78 *Burton's Diary*, ed. Rutt, iv. 296, 316, 347; Brit. Lib., MS Lansdowne 823 (Henry Cromwell's papers), fol. 208; *Ludlow's Memoirs*, ed. Firth, ii. 66.

79 *To the Parliament of the Commonwealth of England . . . the Humble Petition and Representation of Divers well affected of the county of Southampton* (London, 1659); *To the Supream Authority The Parliament of the Commonwealth of England The humble Petition of divers well affected Persons Inhabitants of the Town of Portsmouth and Places Adjacent* (London, 1659).

hopes of a settlement had rested upon the Protectorate. Richard Norton 'let fall some expressions of discontent' at the change, and was hastily removed from the governorship of Portsmouth on that account.[80] The overthrow of the Protectorate brought about a coalescence of view between the non-republican parliamentarian gentry of Hampshire, including a majority of JPs, and the royalists. With the last hope of settlement gone it was logical for the parliamentarians to turn to the Stuarts. Indeed, Richard Cromwell himself was alleged to have done so.[81] This movement is well attested by a hostile local source, a Leveller petition of November 1659, purporting to come from the people of Hampshire. It observed how 'many that have heretofore been opposers of the same [i.e. the Stuarts] through the subtelty and insinuations of the said Party, are ready to comply with them, under pretence that there is no other possibility of Settlement'.[82]

Many former parliamentarian gentry became involved in conspiracy against the government in the summer of 1659, under Lord De la Warr's overall command, and though few were actually caught, it is clear that many more were implicated. According to one report most of the gentry of the county were involved, and according to Thomas Muspratt, a sequestration official, many more than the handful that did so, would have joined Booth's rising if it had been nearer to hand and better supported. At the same time, members of Hampshire's royalist aristocracy like Lord St John and Sir Robert Howard were joining the hitherto rather disreputable ranks of conspirators.[83]

It is well known that it is wrong to talk of anarchy breaking out in England in 1659. Perhaps it is appropriate to emphasize here that it was not even the fear of anarchy and disorder which alienated the majority of Hampshire gentry from the Commonwealth. Indeed, much of the violence to take place in 1659 in Hampshire was provoked by the enemies of the republic in one way or another, be they De la Warr's confederates, or a collection of gentry and twenty-five others who staged a riot earlier in the summer to retain control of Alice Holt and Woolmer forests for Richard Norton, when the

[80] *Ludlow's Memoirs*, ed. Firth, ii. 80.
[81] Richard had first offered to recognize Charles II at the time of his fall in the spring, Hutton, *The Restoration*, p. 40; *Cal.Clar.S.P.*, iv. 355, 362.
[82] *England's Standard: To which all the Lovers of A just and speedy Settlement & A safe Parliamentary Authority . . . are desired to repair or A Remonstrance of the Lovers of the Commonwealth, Inhabitants of Hampshire* (London, 1659), p. 1; Dr Ronald Hutton is strictly speaking incorrect to write that the General Council received no loyal addresses from anyone, as this appears to be one, but how many people it really spoke for is open to question, Hutton, *The Restoration*, p. 74.
[83] *Cal. Clar.S.P.*, iv. 274, 307, 313, 316–17, 321, 323–4, 343, 351, 355–6, 361–2, 369–71, 380; P.R.O., S.P. 23/263/79; Underdown, *Royalist Conspiracy*, p. 296; *The Letter Book of John, Viscount Mordaunt 1658–1660*, ed. M. Coate (Camden Society, Third Series, lxix, 1956), pp. 11, 18.

Rump wished to restore them to Sir Henry Mildmay. Another riot took place in the autumn at Faccombe on the Berkshire border, but this time it had been organized by Francis Reade, a royalist, and two of his relations taking the law into their own hands in a property dispute with a neighbour.[84]

Back in 1653, Hampshire's parliamentarian gentry had belatedly rallied to the Rump because it seemed to be the bulwark of the national church and of property. But it patently failed to resume this role in 1659. On the contrary, it patronized Quakers and gave equivocal responses to their petitions calling for the abolition of tithes.[85] In these circumstances, it is hardly surprising that few gentlemen rallied to the Rump's defence in the autumn and winter of 1659. The gentry largely remained aloof from the Rumpers' rebellion at Portsmouth in December. Richard Norton, though personally approached, utterly refused to co-operate with his erstwhile republican opponents in challenging the military government. Lacking gentry support, individual Rumpers fielded their servants and dependents. Robert Wallop brought fifty such men into Portsmouth.[86]

Richard Norton and other former parliamentarians were now totally committed to a free Parliament. By February 1660, Norton was involved in negotiations for the re-admission of the secluded members of the Long Parliament. When Monck wanted the secluded members to promise not to bring in Charles II, Norton told him, 'that freedome of Parl[iamen]t was the just right & interest of the nation, & if they thought it fitt to bring in the Turke they ought not to be imposed on to the contrary'.[87] Norton was restored to the governorship of Portsmouth by the filled out Long Parliament and elected to its Council of State, where he was joined by Sir William Lewis, the formerly secluded MP for Petersfield.[88] But by contrast with their activism, another secluded MP, Sir Henry Worsley, as he explained to the corporation at Newport, had no mind to resume his seat.[89]

Events at the centre in February 1660 provoked considerable excitement in Hampshire, as they did in other counties. Monck's ultimatum to the Rump of 11 February calling for fresh elections and a dissolution raised expectations which Captain William Angell, an army officer stationed at Winchester, did his best to stifle. In the counties to the west of Hampshire there were open

[84] P.R.O., S.P. 18/203, fols. 34–5; H.C.R.O., QI, fols. 141–4.
[85] *The Humble Petition of Many Well-affected Persons of Somerset, Wilts and some part of Devon, Dorset and Hampshire to the Parliament of the Commonwealth of England against Tythes* (London, 1659); Reay, 'The Quakers, 1659, and the restoration of the monarchy' in his *The Quakers and the English Revolution*, ch. 5, pp. 81–100, which also appears in *History* 63 (1978) cited above, p. 63, n. 173.
[86] D. Dymond, *Portsmouth and the Fall of the Puritan Republic* (Portsmouth, 1971), p. 9.
[87] Brit. Lib., Verney MSS microfilm, M/636, reel no. 17: Dr Denton to Sir Ralph Verney, 18 Feb. 1659/60.
[88] *Cal.Clar.S.P.*, iv. 671; *Cal.S.P.Dom.*, 1659–60, p. xxvi.
[89] I.W.C.R.O., 45/16b, p. 13.

celebrations.[90] By the 14th, the rumours of Monck's stand had been confirmed by newsheets circulating in Hampshire. John Stewkeley at Preshaw
House not far from Winchester, having heard that Monck had declared for a
single person, was already looking forward to a Stuart restoration.[91] By the
end of the month Andrew Henley of Bramshill, son of a royalist, was looking
forward to the new Parliament to be summoned after the dissolution of the
Long Parliament, as 'like to bee soe profittable to the nation'.[92]

In the months leading up to the Restoration, the county's political life continued to be dominated by former parliamentarians. John Bulkeley and
Richard Norton were elected knights of the shire to the Convention, having
persuaded Andrew Henley to abandon the poll which he had initiated.[93]
Andrew Henley was promised Norton's interest at Portsmouth, on which he
was elected in due course. In the boroughs, the republicans were generally
seen off, though Robert Wallop managed to have himself returned for
Whitchurch. Thomas Muspratt, who had stayed in office as a sequestration
official under the military government was routed in a poll at Winchester
obtaining only five votes and coming way behind John Hooke and Thomas
Cole, the successful candidates. John Braman, a radical army officer from
Alton, despite great confidence of success, was not elected for Stockbridge.[94]

The vast majority of Hampshire MPs seem to have been committed to a
Stuart restoration, yet the unity of purpose amongst a majority of the gentry
at this stage was rather superficial. Bulkeley, Norton and their allies wished
to preserve the ecclesiastical reforms of the 1640s.[95] They certainly did not
want an unconditional return to the traditional Anglican church, and did not
believe that this was the inevitable consequence of a Stuart restoration (they
might have reacted very differently if they had). But this was precisely what
royalists like John Stewkeley expected and hoped for.[96] Richard Norton may
not even have favoured an unconditional restoration of the monarchy. He
was on record as favouring terms being imposed upon the king as recently as

[90] *Cal.S.P.Dom.*, 1659–60, p. 369; Hutton, *The Restoration*, p. 94.
[91] This was premature as Monck was still outwardly favouring a commonwealth, Brit. Lib.,
Verney MSS microfilm M/636, reel no. 17, John Stewkeley to Sir Ralph Verney, 14 Feb.
1659/60; Hutton, *The Restoration*, p. 95.
[92] Brit. Lib., MS Sloane 813, fol. 3.
[93] *Ibid.*, fol. 16.
[94] H.C.R.O., W/B1/5, fol. 187; *The House of Commons 1660–1690*, ed. B. D. Henning
(3 vols., London, 1983) [hereafter *H.C.*], i. 257–8.
[95] Andrew Henley, though the son of a royalist, had denied any desire to oppose Norton in the
election and had originally intended to stand with him; his religious views are obscure but
as he had invested more than £2,000 in episcopal lands in Dorset he had a substantial stake
in the maintenance of the status quo in religion, Brit. Lib., MS Sloane 813, fol. 16; *Collectanea Topographica et Genealogica* (8 vols., London, 1934–43), i. (1834), 286.
[96] Brit. Lib., Verney MSS microfilm M/636, reel no. 17: John Stewkeley to Sir Ralph Verney,
14 Feb. 1659/60.

1658, and when he met Edmund Ludlow in May 1660 after the chance had been missed, he seemed unhappy with the turn events had taken. He blamed men like Ludlow rather than the royalists for this.[97] But the unity of even the majority of the gentry at this time should not be over-stated.

[97] *Cal.Clar.S.P.*, iv. 29; *Edmund Ludlow: A Voyce from the Watch Tower*, ed. Worden, p. 121.

Part II

THE RESTORATION

The restored monarchy
and the role of government

Many parts of the traditional structure of royal government were revived in 1660, at least nominally. The Privy Council, the Exchequer, the secretaries of state, were all re-established, though these institutions or ones closely resembling them had existed in the 1650s, or at least during the Cromwellian Protectorate. In other respects, the restoration was only partial. Some of the most effective instruments of central government in the pre-Civil War period, Star Chamber, High Commission, the Council of the North, were not revived. Nor did institutional development cease at the Restoration, as the Privy Council continued to decline, whilst other departments, like the Treasury and the secretary of state's office rose in importance.[1] The royal court, informal and pluralistic though it was, was once again the centre of patronage and policy making; but the existence of a 'standing Parliament' for much of the first twenty years of Charles II's reign meant that it did not operate as such in a vacuum.

The Restoration government deserves to be taken seriously as it sought to tackle the problems facing the post-Civil War state: defence, security, finance and religion, in the localities. The constraints upon the regime were largely psychological after the failure of some 'Presbyterian' politicians to impose terms upon the king, and opportunities existed for really effective government. Dr Morrill has rightly observed, 'Charles II's government had everything in its favour in the overwhelming desire of the majority of the population for permanent and firm rule.'[2] Ollard has written, 'Charles was now embarking on the role of a monarch ruling by law and precedent, not by arbitrary power or military force.'[3] This was a role consciously and voluntarily adopted. In many ways, the king enjoyed considerable freedom of movement. Historians who fondly believe that the chance for a strong,

---

[1] Baxter, *The Development of the Treasury 1660–1702*; H. Roseveare, *The Treasury 1660–1870: The Foundations of Control* (London, 1973); Fraser, *The Intelligence of the Secretaries of State 1660–88*.

[2] Morrill, *Cheshire*, p. 328.

[3] R. Ollard, *The Image of the King: Charles I and Charles II* (London, 1979), pp. 127–8.

assertive government had disappeared by 1660 usually ignore this aspect of the situation after the Restoration, and fail to observe the advantages which the Restoration government enjoyed over its predecessors.

The consent of the majority of the landowning classes, which, for various reasons outlined above, had eluded the regimes of the Interregnum, was accorded to the restored monarchy from its inception, and articulated in Parliament. Charles sought to enhance this by ruling according to law, abiding by statutes and, at least before 1672, not asserting his prerogative at the expense of statute law. But it should be stressed that neither Charles nor his ministers were being simply high-minded by pursuing this policy. Ruling by statute, made possible through the co-operation of Parliament, greatly facilitated rather than impeded effective government in the provinces. Parliament, indeed, was a far better instrument for ruling the localities than a standing army had been. An unimpeachable statutory basis would prove an incomparable advantage, for example in the Restoration government's fiscal and militia administration at local level.

It will be shown in the following part how the government after 1660 was just as involved as its Interregnum predecessors had been in the localities, in the pursuit of its policies and needs. On the basis of the Hampshire evidence, it will be seen that in several important respects, the Restoration saw a re-assertion of central control over the localities, with the active co-operation, or tacit support, of large elements of the landed classes. In general, it will be demonstrated how at least in relation to Hampshire, the Restoration regime was more successful in its handling of the localities than its Interregnum predecessors, though the resurgence of opposition in the 1670s and the reasons for it will be examined in the last section.

4

Local office-holding 1660–78

It is the object of this section to explore the impact of the Restoration upon local office-holding and the structure of local patronage in Hampshire, drawing some comparisons with the 1650s. The Restoration government stood in a very different relationship with the provinces from its Interregnum predecessors. With the wide support of the landed classes, it lacked the incentive to use patronage to win over enemies. There was considerable freedom of choice over who was appointed. But the government was also heir to the partisan attitudes engendered by the Civil War, and was just as interested in the loyalty of local office-holders as its Interregnum predecessors had been.

The Restoration government, even before the election of the Cavalier Parliament, tended to rely on men of proven loyalty, and in many cases with royalist pasts, to perform important tasks in Hampshire. The lieutenancy was a more compact, more carefully hand-picked, and no less partisan body than the militia commissioners of the 1650s. Lord Treasurer Southampton, the lord lieutenant, was one of the more conciliatory of former royalists, but four out of his six deputies had been active royalists, and the fifth was the son of a royalist.[1] Richard Norton was the isolated, one is tempted to say token, former parliamentarian. The same partisan spirit is discernible in the appointment of officers. Royal policy, as Southampton made clear to Sir Robert Howard, was for the maximum number of officers to be commissioned, but it was understood that this should not be interpreted to mean the admission to commands of men whose loyalty was in any doubt. As the deputies explained to Southampton, in October 1660, there was a shortage of gentry suitable to command regiments in the local militia, 'either for want of experience in most of the Gentry: or of such opinions & temper as may secure

---

[1] Sir Humphrey Bennet, Sir Robert Howard and Lord Henry Paulet had been commissioned officers and Sir John Norton had been an active royalist; Sir Andrew Henley was the son of a royalist; P. R. Newman, *Royalist Officers in England and Wales, 1642–60* (New York and London, 1981), pp. 23–4, 200; W. H. Black, *Docquets of Letters Patent . . . 1642–6* (2 vols., privately printed, 1837), i. 65; Brit. Lib., Addit. MS 25302, fol. 143; G. E. Aylmer, *The King's Servants* (2nd edn, London, 1974), p. 419.

in us such a confidence, as becomes the careful endeavours of his Ma[jes]ties & the Nacons safety'. Southampton agreed and accepted the proposal that they themselves should command regiments in accordance with pre-Civil War practice.[2] Considerable care was taken in the appointment of lesser officers, with some men being rejected after consideration.[3] Some former parliamentarians were employed, but they were very much on probation, as Sir Robert Howard wrote to Sir Andrew Henley in January 1661, 'I sesire to trie the temper of men by engagement.'[4]

Subsequent militia legislation made the loyalty of the militia a statutory requirement and enhanced the Crown's control over the lieutenancy. The Militia Act of 1662 required not only all members of the lieutenancy, but officers and soldiers as well, to take the oaths of supremacy and allegiance and a non-resisting declaration, which was so unconditional that Lord Treasurer Southampton had tried to amend it in the House of Lords. By the same act, the Crown had a right of veto over the appointment of deputy-lieutenants which, as the earl of Derby discovered in Lancashire when he tried to appoint several former parliamentarians, was no mere formality.[5]

The Restoration government also oversaw a campaign to purge men of dubious loyalty from the commissions of the peace. In Hampshire, in the early years of the Restoration, some thirty-five Interregnum JPs were removed from the bench, a figure comparable with neighbouring Sussex. But proportionately the survival rate in Hampshire, at 36 per cent seems to have been higher than many other counties.[6] This may be on account of Southampton's moderating influence. But the purge was definitive, only one of the purged making his way back on to the commission in the 1660s.[7] The influx of men to replace those who were removed did not simply represent the reinstatement of an old elite. Of the forty-two Restoration appointees, less than half came from families which had been represented on the commission of the peace on the eve of the Civil War, a phenomenon which has parallels in other counties. But it is harder to detect a partisan intent in the commission of the peace than in the lieutenancy. Indeed some moderate

---

[2] Brit. Lib., Addit. MS 21922 (Norton of Rotherfield lieutenancy book), fol. 243.

[3] P.R.O. (Kew), Treasury T51 (Lord Treasurer Southampton's General Entry Book) No. 1, pp. 210–11.

[4] Brit. Lib., MS Sloane 3299, fol. 24.

[5] M. P. Schoenfeld, *The Restored House of Lords* (The Hague, 1967), p. 215; D. P. Carter, 'The Lancashire Lieutenancy 1660–1688' (Oxford Univ., M.Litt. thesis, 1981), pp. 29–32.

[6] P.R.O., C193/13/5; C220/94; C231/6; Fletcher, *Sussex*, p. 134; Holmes, *Lincolnshire*, p. 219; P. Jenkins, ' "The Old Leaven": the Welsh Roundheads after 1660', *H.J.*, 24 (1981), 815–16; G. C. F. Forster, 'Government in provincial England under the later Stuarts', *T.R.H.S., Fifth Series*, 33 (1983), 31; Hutton, *The Restoration*, p. 129.

[7] Francis Tilney in February 1664, P.R.O., C231/7, p. 223.

parliamentarians, like Sir William Lewis, who had been removed from the commission before 1660, were now reinstated.[8]

The government was uncertain what policy to adopt towards the borough corporations, and while it hesitated local Anglican royalists seized the initiative. Four hundred men under the command of former royalist officers appeared in arms at the proclamation of Charles II at Winchester. Next month, excluded royalist magistrates and other inhabitants petitioned the House of Lords against the intrusion and misrule of the Rump's nominees.[9] After the mediation efforts of the marquis of Winchester and Lord Robartes had failed, the Lords ordered Thomas Muspratt and two other recalcitrant officials to be removed from the corporation.[10] But even without this intervention, the hold of former parliamentarians over the corporation was clearly at an end. In June 1660, Lord St John of Basing, the son and heir of the marquis of Winchester, was admitted as a freeman and returned in a by-election to the Convention. And in September, several other local royalist gentry were admitted as freemen. Ferdinando Bye, the royal nominee for town clerk in 1647, was admitted to that office, displacing Stephen Welstead, who had been put in by the county committee. Another group of gentry freemen, admitted the following March, included three Catholics. Discontented elements, anxious at the way the corporation appeared to be moving, tried to disrupt its proceedings. In November 1660, the corporation voted that these 'Turbulent & contentious Spiritts' would be fined twenty shillings each for such conduct.[11]

Elsewhere, notably in Basingstoke and Southampton, the change of regime at the centre prompted the implicit Anglican royalism of a majority of the corporations to become overt, with only minor changes in their membership. Southampton had given a hint of its true sympathies even before the Restoration by returning William Stanley, one of the royalists purged in 1655, to the Convention.[12] He and two other victims of the purge had since been reinstated in the corporation. One of them, Edward Downer, was elected mayor in September 1660. By the following May, the corporation was prepared to burn the Covenant, Mayor Downer telling the people 'What a world of Perjury, Blood and Mischief that cursed oath had begotten in all three Kingdomes.'[13] At Basingstoke, John Millet was removed as lecturer on

[8] P.R.O., C220/9/4; H.C.R.O., 5M53, no. 964; Hutton, *The Restoration*, p. 129.
[9] *Mercurius Publicus*, no. 21, 17–24 May 1660, pp. 323–4; *Hist. MSS Comm. Seventh Report App. pt I* (House of Lords MSS), pp. 93, 100.
[10] *L.J.*, xi. 130–1, 138–9.
[11] H.C.R.O., W/B1/5, fols. 139–40, 142–7, 157, 162.
[12] *H.C.*, iii. 475.
[13] *The Kindgomes Intelligencer*, no. 24, 10–17 June 1661, pp. 369–70.

2 January 1662 for not being 'conformable to the Governem[en]t of the church of England'.[14]

But in some places, the hold of former parliamentarians and present non-conformists proved stronger, and external help was needed against them. Court candidates were defeated in the elections for the Cavalier Parliament at Lymington and Newtown and the corporation of Portsmouth hesitated to accept the duke of York's candidate, Sir George Carteret.[15] Royalists at Christchurch petitioned Lord Treasurer Southampton against the 'dis-affected' persons who had dominated their corporation since the early 1640s.[16] Southampton passed their petition on to the Privy Council who referred the matter to two local gentlemen, Sir Humphrey Bennet, a burgess of the borough and former royalist, and Richard Compton, in February 1661. However, these gentlemen subsequently exceeded their brief, threaten-ing to suspend six of the Hildesley faction, unless they would admit eleven of their nominees to the corporation, against which Mayor Thomas Grew and eleven of the burgesses protested. It also alarmed Lord Baltimore, who was in the process of re-establishing his interest in the borough, as lord of the manor. Southampton regarded the conduct of Bennet and Compton as most indis-creet in the light of the forthcoming elections to the Cavalier Parliament. The mayor and burgesses petitioned the Privy Council, which put a stop to the intervention in the borough, whose government was not finally settled until the enforcement of the Corporation Act.[17]

Similar caution was shown by the central authorities in the granting of a new charter to Newport in the Isle of Wight, which was arranged through the mediation of the governor of the island, the earl of Portland, in 1661. It con-tained some modest alteration to the structure and jurisdiction of the borough, at the request of the corporation, whose governing body now included aldermen. There was a slight expansion in crown influence, with a royal veto over the appointment of the recorder and town clerk. But the effect of the new charter was to perpetuate the present corporation in power. Only Henry Ringwood, a former mayor and one of the newly appointed aldermen, was excluded for refusing to take the prescribed oaths on 10 January 1662. The charters of Hampshire's other boroughs were simply continued.[18]

But the government's hesitation and caution should not be seen as representing any sympathy for local magistrates or inhabitants of the corpor-

---

[14] H.C.R.O., 148M71 (Basingstoke Town Council Minutes 1641–1700), 1/3.
[15] *H.C.*, i. 248, 251, 253.
[16] *Cal.Treas.Bks.*, i. 120.
[17] P.R.O., P.C. 2/55, pp. 138, 169; Christchurch Civic Offices, council minute book 1615–1857 – sheet attached to page 99; *Cal.Treas.Bks.*, vii. 1539.
[18] I.W.C.R.O., 45/16b, pp. 28, 48; Copy of Translation of Charter of 1661; *Cal.S.P.Dom.*, 1661–2, pp. 44, 66.

ations who were of dubious loyalty. The king went along with the Corporation Act, and some of the court's supporters in the Lords even proposed to strengthen the measure and the Crown's influence by amendment to it.[19] Even before the measure was enforced in Hampshire, Secretary Nicholas wrote to the mayor of Southampton ordering him to report the names of local people 'of froward & obstinate temper' who were disrupting the government of the corporation.[20] The Corporation Act was a very useful measure for a government anxious about disaffection. The commissions which the Crown appointed to enforce the measure in Hampshire and elsewhere were dominated by royalists or their own sons, and were filled out with neuters rather than balanced with former parliamentarians. The names of thirty-one commissioners who were nominated in Hampshire are known. This included the surprisingly high number of twelve members of Southampton corporation. The nineteen gentry commissioners included nine who had been active royalists before 1660 and two more were the sons of royalists. The Southampton contingent did include the parliamentarian Edward Exton and even the republican James Capelin, but they were balanced by two of the royalists ejected in 1655 and swamped by their neutral colleagues, quite apart from the three royalist gentry who were also named in the commission at Southampton.[21] Given their complexion and wide powers, the court must have expected the commissions to root out dissenting and former parliamentarian influence in the boroughs. As Professor Aylmer has observed, the act 'gave the Anglican-Cavalier gentry a brief opportunity to interfere in and to purge the governments of incorporated boroughs at least as efficiently as had successive ordinances and acts . . . between 1647 and 1653'.[22] In Hampshire, and apparently in the west country, the impact of the Corporation Act was rather greater than the efforts of Interregnum governments to remove their enemies from the boroughs.[23]

As might have been expected, the commissioners did their work very thoroughly between the late summer of 1662 and the spring of 1663, when their powers expired. The commissioners at Southampton drew up a six-point charge against James Capelin, the former mayor, demonstrating his

[19] J. H. Sacret, 'The Restoration government and municipal corporations', *E.H.R.*, xlv. (1930), 249.

[20] P.R.O., S.P. 44/3, p. 61.

[21] East, *Portsmouth*, p. 169; *Hist. MSS Comm. Eleventh Report App. pt III. Southampton MSS*, p. 55; I.W.C.R.O., 45/16b, p. 60; A. H. Estcourt, 'The ancient borough of Newtown alias Franchville, Isle of Wight', *Proceedings of the Hampshire Field Club*, ii. (1891), 98.

[22] G. E. Aylmer, 'Crisis and regrouping in the political elites in England from the 1630s to the 1660s', *Three British Revolutions 1641, 1688, 1776*, ed. J. G. A. Pocock (Princeton, 1980), p. 156.

[23] Williams, 'County and municipal government in Cornwall, Devon, Dorset and Somerset', ch. 2, pp. 65–119.

strong republican and dissenting sympathies from events going back more than a decade. They voted by eight to two to remove him. The commissioners at Lymington held several hearings, though here, as at Winchester, many suspect members of the corporation failed to attend them.[24]

The resultant purges were in many cases very far-reaching. The removal of ninety-three members of the corporation of Portsmouth was exceptional. But other large scale expulsions did take place, like the twenty-one removed at Lymington, or the eighteen removed at Winchester (apart from the three already marked out for ejection by the House of Lords) which amounted to a purge of 30 per cent of the corporation since the Restoration. There were more moderate purges at Southampton, where nine burgesses along with Alderman James Capelin were removed; and at Newtown, eight members of the admittedly small corporation were removed, whilst at Newport only four fell foul of the act, one sixth of the corporation's total strength.[25] Direct evidence does not survive for Christchurch, but a minor purge seems to have taken place there, as John Hildesley disappeared from the corporation.

Some were removed for failure to take the prescribed oaths. This was the case with John Hall, mayor of Newtown, Henry Dore, mayor of Lymington, the four men ejected at Newport and the nine burgesses purged at Southampton. At Newport it seems likely that the dissidents objected to the declaration against the Covenant, and this was certainly true of those at Southampton. But evidence as to the exact objections of those who refused to comply with the act is unfortunately very rare.[26]

The majority of those purged in the boroughs of Hampshire seem to have been removed at the disrection of the commissioners regardless of whether they took oaths or not, on the grounds that they were disaffected to the royal government. Some were merely the professional servants of previous regimes, as were a large proportion of those removed at Portsmouth.

The impact of the purges on the social hierarchy varied considerably from place to place. Most of those removed at Southampton had only recently obtained their burgess-ships, so that the purge made little impact on the traditional oligarchy. But elsewhere the changes were more far-reaching.

---

[24] Davies, *History of Southampton*, pp. 494–5; H.C.R.O., 27M74A, DBC/283; W/B1/5, fol. 177.

[25] East, *Portsmouth*, p. 169; H.C.R.O., 27M74A, DBC/283; A. B. Rosen, 'Economic and social aspects of the history of Winchester 1520–1670' (Oxford Univ., D.Phil. thesis, 1975), p. 275; S.C.R.O., SC2/1/8, fol. 185; Estcourt, 'The ancient borough of Newtown', p. 98; I.W.C.R.O., 45/16b, p. 62.

[26] All four of the Newport men had taken the oaths of supremacy and allegiance under the charter of 1661, I.W.C.R.O., 45/16b, pp. 43–5; a contemporary source makes clear that abjuring the Covenant proved the stumbling block at Southampton, Brit. Lib., MS Egerton 868, fol. 49; for the lack of evidence see Hutton, *The Restoration*, p. 161.

Thirteen of the burgesses removed at Lymington had been admitted to the corporation before 1649, and seven had been elected before 1640.[27]

Nor were all those purged socially insignificant. Indeed, the enforcement of the Corporation Act was in one sense, another round in the conflict between royalist and parliamentarian gentry going back to 1642. Important moderate parliamentarians like the Whiteheads, Sir William Waller and John Maynard were amongst the purged as well as disgraced republican gentry like Robert Wallop, John Lisle and Nicholas Love. Sir John Barrington was removed from the corporation of Newtown, though he continued to sit for the borough in Parliament. John Hall, the ejected mayor, was steward of Barrington's manor of Swainston.[28]

The commissioners did not only purge substantial numbers of borough office-holders, but put in others to replace them. In some cases, this involved simply the formal re-instatement of previously excluded royalists, like the three at Southampton, or John Colson 'ejected for loyalty' who was restored as an alderman of Winchester.[29] But the commissioners also made new appointments, nominating four new aldermen at Portsmouth, and six new burgesses at Lymington. Four new members of the 'Twenty-Four' were elected at Winchester for their loyalty, at the specific request of the commissioners. At Newtown, the commissioners installed eight new members of the corporation, including five of their own number. Besides this, no less than three mayors, Anthony Habberly (previously excluded for royalism) at Portsmouth, John Colson at Winchester and Francis Guidott at Lymington owed their elections directly to the commissioners.[30]

The motivation for these wide-ranging changes was essentially political, and the dividends were parliamentary. At Lymington, the purge had the effect of transforming the complexion of the borough, and of reversing the election result of 1661. When a by-election occurred in 1663, Sir Nicholas Steward, the formerly defeated court candidate, was returned.[31]

The purge of borough government, like that of county government in Hampshire, was decisive. Outside Portsmouth, few of the excluded officials made their way back into the corporations. The Portsmouth purge was really too drastic to be sustained, and ejected burgesses were being re-admitted as early as September 1663.[32] But elsewhere the position was different. Of the

[27] S.C.R.O., SC3/1/1; St Barbe, *Lymington*, pp. 7–8.
[28] East, *Portsmouth*, p. 169;; Estcourt, 'The ancient borough of Newtown', p. 98; B. Carpenter-Turner, *Winchester* (Southampton, 1980), p. 214; H.C.R.O., 27M74A, DBC/283; I.W.C.R.O., Jerome Collection, Hall Letters: this marked the beginning of an eclipse of the Barrington interest in the borough.
[29] S.C.R.O., SC3/1/8, fol. 185; Carpenter-Turner, *Winchester*, p. 213.
[30] East, *Portsmouth*, p. 169; H.C.R.O., 27M74A, DBC/283; W/B1/5, fols. 177, 179.
[31] H.C., i. 249.
[32] Dymond, *Portsmouth and the Fall of the Puritan Republic*, p. 19.

burgesses ejected at Southampton, William Braxton was re-admitted in October 1673, only to be removed again within five years for frauds in the customs. The others do not seem to have sought re-admission. Those excluded at Lymington remained out of office until 1677–8, when Bartholemew Bulkeley and Philip Dore regained admission. But Bulkeley, and Braxton at Southampton, had been involved in protracted litigation against their respective corporations, and their re-admission can be seen as attempts to bring them under control in the interests of local peace.[33] Thomas Muspratt regained his place on Winchester's corporation as early as 1665, but only through the special intervention of Lord St John, and his was an isolated case.[34]

Nationally, the royal government stood by the Corporation Act and the work of the commissioners. In 1668, the Privy Council issued a circular letter to sheriffs to ensure that it was being complied with. The Council also took a local initiative in the case of Romsey, where dissent was strong, early in 1669, ordering Thomas Knowles and Edward Hooper to investigate a report that Richard Weale, the newly elected mayor, had not taken the statutory oaths and sacrament.[35] In boroughs with full records there is evidence of continuing enforcement. At Christchurch, it is clear that the act was being enforced to the letter throughout the period. At both Winchester and Southampton, all the statutory oaths and declarations were taken by the annually elected corporation officers, and purged officials and conscientious dissenters were thus kept out, though occasional conformists could not be excluded. Edward Hooker, a prominent dissenter, managed to survive on Winchester corporation.[36]

When the central government came up against serious obstruction to its policies, it was prepared to contemplate further purges. When the magistrates of Portsmouth proved uncooperative over plague relief in April 1666, Secretary Morice wrote to Sir Philip Honeywood, acting governor of the town, and himself a burgess since 1662, ordering him to remove any recalcitrant aldermen.[37]

But there was no new initiative towards the boroughs after 1663, except in individual cases. In 1670, the Crown acceded to the request of certain members of Christchurch corporation for a charter, but it provoked the antagonism of Lord Cornbury (Clarendon's heir) whose interests as lord of

---

[33] S.C.R.O., SC2/1/8, fols. 283–4, 288, 338; H.C.R.O., 27M74A, DBC/2, fols. 67–8, 74; St Barbe, *Lymington*, p. 9.

[34] Rosen, 'Economic and social aspects of the history of Winchester', p. 273.

[35] Sacret, 'The Restoration government and municipal corporations', pp. 254–5; P.R.O., P.C. 2/61, p. 217.

[36] Christchurch Civic Offices, council minute book 1615–1857 *passim*; H.C.R.O., W/B1/6 *passim*; S.C.R.O., SC2/1/8, fols. 260, 311; Mildon, 'Puritanism in Hampshire', p. 413.

[37] *Cal.S.P.Dom.*, 1665–6, p. 355.

the manor were thereby threatened, so it was rapidly withdrawn. However, a new charter was granted to Basingstoke in 1671, which granted a fair on Basingstoke down, causing no local controversy.[38] In 1672, *quo warrantos* were being contemplated against Southampton, Andover and Winchester along with several other boroughs, but at least in these cases they were not carried out. Rumours of a new charter with fresh privileges being granted to Andover persisted during the 1670s but were not realized. Another initiative towards Andover, to make Lord De la Warr, Lord Sandys and four local gentlemen justices within the borough by letters patent in July 1674 was also rapidly abandoned.[39]

But this reversion to prevarication should not distract attention from the fact that during the 1660s, the royal government had looked for and obtained in Hampshire a new power base in local government. The impact of the profound changes in office-holding was not simply to restore the pre-Civil-War elites in county and borough; some members of these elites actually lost office and influence through the purges, and many new men were promoted. Eligibility for office was not simply defined by social status, but by sworn or proven loyalty to the regime. A positive commitment was required.[40]

The Restoration also had a profound impact on the structure of patronage, which linked the centre with the localities. The result was a subtle mixture of centralization and decentralization. The re-establishment of the royal court as the centre of political life made influence there of paramount importance for anybody hoping to gain office locally. But considerable influence was devolved to the aristocratic leaders of local society, particularly the lord lieutenant, who as Professor Aylmer has observed 'came to be something a little nearer to a viceroy than merely the titular head of the militia in his county'.[41] But the lord lieutenant himself owed his position and his success as a channel for patronage to the influence which he enjoyed at court.

The influence which the lord lieutenant exercised locally enabled him to promote his friends, relatives or clients. Lord Treasurer Southampton, who combined central office with local office in Hampshire, was able to protect his relative Henry Wallop from the consequences of his father's disgrace,

---

[38] P.R.O., P.C. 2/62, pp. 319, 326; H.C.R.O., 148M71, 1/1/4 (Basingstoke Charter, 24 June 1671).

[39] P.R.O., E148, no. 8, pt 2 (Exchequer Informations Chas II). *Cal.S.P.Dom.*, 1672, pp. 543–4, 589, 612; *Cal.S.P.Dom.*, 1672–3, p. 16; *Cal.S.P.Dom.*, 1677–8, p. 281; H.C.R.O., 37M84, 2/QS/4.

[40] Dr Taylor's analysis of the personnel of the corporations of Romsey in the 1651 to 1680 period and Andover in the 1660s shows that although the men who governed these two towns were mainly drawn from the richer element, this was not exclusively so, 'Population, disease and family structure in early modern Hampshire', pp. 211–15.

[41] Aylmer, 'Crisis and re-grouping in the political elites in England', in Pocock, *Three British Revolutions*, p. 156.

ensuring him a place in the commission of the peace and a senior command in the militia. After Southampton's death, he was removed from the commission of the peace.[42]

Southampton's successor as lord lieutenant (though not initially as *custos rotulorum*) was Charles, lord St John of Basing, the Protestant heir of the marquis of Winchester, a follower of the duke of Buckingham in politics. He too patronized men with embarrassing political pasts, like Thomas Jervoise, heir of the Rumper Sir Thomas Jervoise (d. 1654), who held no post in the militia until Lord St John made him a deputy-lieutenant and senior militia officer in 1673. As high steward of Winchester from March 1668, Lord St John also patronized ejected officers of the corporation. He deployed his influence as lord warden of the New Forest to promote friends and relations. Presumably he was also responsible for the inclusion of several former Interregnum officials in the commission of inquiry into wastes and spoils in the New Forest in 1672.[43]

To alienate a man of Lord St John's influence could be fatal to the career of a local gentleman. Sir Andrew Henley's feud with Lord St John had begun in 1666, for reasons which are not entirely clear. But it was still raging on through the courts as late as May 1668, by which time Lord St John had become lord lieutenant. Not surprisingly, Henley did not keep his place in the lieutenancy.[44]

But Lord St John's local dominance depended heavily on the Crown's favour. When he lost this through siding with the opposition in Parliament from 1673 onwards, his position was undermined. His influence over the commission of the peace became circumscribed, and new appointments became fewer between 1673 and Lord St John's eventual dismissal in 1676.[45]

Meanwhile, other men, notably churchmen, who enjoyed favour at court during the Danby era, began to gain control over local patronage. Henry Compton, former master of St Cross and an active JP in Hampshire, who had subsequently been promoted to the bishopric of Oxford and ultimately that of London, used his influence to get Henry Whitehead, a sympathizer with dissent and the 'country' interest, removed from the commission of the peace.[46] When James, lord Annesley, wished to gain Lord St John's place as

---

[42] P.R.O., C220/9/4, fol. 76; C231/7, p. 372; *Cal.Treas.Bks.*, i. 82, 378; *D.N.B.*, Robert Wallop.

[43] *H.C.*, iii. 277; H.C.R.O., 44M69 F11 (Personal Papers of Captain Thomas Jervoise) on Jervoise see below, pp. 153–4; W/B1/6, fol. 45; *Winchester College Muniments*, comp. Himsworth, i. 22; *A Calendar of New Forest Documents: The Fifteenth to the Seventeenth Centuries*, ed. D. J. Stagg (Hampshire Record Society, 1983), Appendix B, pp. 285–7; *Cal.Treas.Bks.*, iii. 1204.

[44] *Cal.S.P.Dom.*, 1667–8, pp. 92, 371–2.   [45] P.R.O., C231/7, pp. 456–507.

[46] H.C.R.O., 'Quarter sessions orders summary 1649–58, 1659–72', by J. S. Furley: *Hist. MSS Comm. Finch MSS* (1670–90), ii. 45; *H.C.*, iii. 708.

custos rotulorum (which he had held since 1670), he addressed himself to Archbishop Sheldon, describing himself as 'a most obedient sonne of the Church'. Despite his lack of experience on the bench (he had only been in the commission of the peace eighteen months) Annesley gained his prize on 27 April 1676.[47]

The post of lord lieutenant went to Edward Noel, the heir of Viscount Campden, who was brother-in-law to Lady Danby. In 1660, Noel had married Elizabeth Wriothesley, daughter of the earl of Southampton. Though he had only been in the commission of the peace since July 1669, the king had been grooming him to replace Lord St John, now marquis of Winchester, at least since July 1675. He was certainly a substantial figure, though his links with Hampshire were so comparatively recent. In 1660, 16,490 acres in Middlesex, Kent, Gloucestershire and Rutland (the family's home county) had been settled on him, besides the Titchfield estate which he inherited in 1667. As a man obviously enjoying the court's favour in the county he soon began to obtain offices and influence in the local boroughs.[48]

The Restoration had had a profound effect on local office-holding and an equally significant impact on the structure of local patronage. Nevertheless, in Hampshire at least, the central government continued to employ a substantial number of professional servants, some of whom became involved in local government, as their Interregnum predecessors had done. This did not really threaten local administration with centralized control, any more than it had done in the 1650s. But for all that, it is worth examining in order to put the experience of the Interregnum in perspective, and to identify the true significance of the Restoration.

The early 1660s witnessed a considerable demilitarization of the Solent. Hurst castle's garrison was reduced to a few gunners, and Calshot's was little more (see Table 2).[49] The Portsmouth garrison was retained, with the old soldiers apparently re-enlisting, though political suspects were subsequently weeded out.[50]

Officers were appointed to garrison commands by virtue of influence at court. Lord Culpeper became governor of the Isle of Wight in 1661, because of the king's debt of gratitude to his father. Richard Norton was displaced by the duke of York as governor of Portsmouth, and thereafter officers of the

[47] Bodl., MS Tanner 42, fol. 225; P.R.O., C231/7, pp. 369, 484, 511.
[48] H.C., iii. 144; P.R.O., C231/7, p. 348; *Cal.S.P.Dom.*, 1675–6, p. 197; Schoenfeld, *The Restored House of Lords*, p. 107; St Barbe, *Lymington*, p. 9; S.C.R.O., SC3/1/1, fols. 234, 236; SC2/1/8, fols. 320, 330.
[49] *Cal.Treas.Bks.*, i. pp. 257, 290, 295; *Cal.S.P.Dom.*, 1660–1, p. 486.
[50] H.C.R.O., 24M54/14, fol. 13; *Cal.S.P.Dom.*, 1661–2, p. 551.

Table 2. *Garrison establishments on the
Solent 1661–79*

	1661	1679[c]
Calshot castle	13[a]	5
Hurst castle	5[b]	5
Isle of Wight	c. 50[b]	165
Portsmouth	c. 707[b]	152

[a] *Cal. Treas. Bks* i. 295.

[b] These are approximations based on company muster rolls and other partial lists, Sir Robert Holmes' account for Sandham fort (1662–6), P.R.O. (Kew) A.O.1 311/1231; the muster roll of the duke of York's company in the garrison of Portsmouth Aug. 1661, Brit. Lib., Addit. MS 18764, fol. 36; the muster roll of Captain Robert Busbridge's company in the garrison of Portsmouth, 10 Aug. 1661, Brit. Lib. Addit. MS 33278, fols. 29–30; I.W.C.R.O., 'A true copy of the schedule annexed to the patent of Sir Robt Holmes Gov. of the Isle of Wight'; contained in Carisbrooke Parish Register no. 5 (1766–1813).

[c] P.R.O. (Kew), W.O. 24/5, fols. 6–9.

garrison tended to be his clients.[51] According to a local enemy of Sir Philip Honeywood, who was acting commander of the Portsmouth garrison from April 1662, he was a coward who 'by favour of a lady of the Court became a captain of a foot company and by Sir Cha[rles] Berkeley's favour Deputy Governor of Portsmouth'.[52] Sir Charles Berkeley was the duke of York's lieutenant-governor. Court influence may also have had a part to play in the appointment of Sir Robert Holmes as governor of the Isle of Wight in 1668. Most of the officers commissioned in local garrisons after 1661, were strangers to the locality.[53]

However, the local gentry were not totally excluded from garrison commands or influence over who was appointed. Henry Paulet was made captain

---

[51] S. S. Webb, ' "Brave men and servants to his Royal Highness": the household of James Stuart in the evolution of English imperialism', *Perspectives in American History*, viii. (1974), 60–1.

[52] *Portsmouth Sessions Papers*, ed. Hoad, p. 28.

[53] C. Dalton (ed.), *English Army Lists and Commission Registers 1661–1714* (6 vols., London, 1892–1904), i. 27, and *passim*; *Life of James II . . . collected out of memoirs writ of his own hand*, ed. J. S. Clarke (2 vols., London, 1816), i. 445.

of Calshot castle in June 1661. Sir William Oglander was a deputy-governor to Lord Culpeper from 1664, and Sir Edward Worsley was the sole lieutenant-governor to Sir Robert Holmes from 1675. Culpeper, tactless and imperious though he was, sought 'the countryes recommendation' before appointing a man as his chief gunner. The king subsequently decided to remove Culpeper himself because he was not respected by the local gentry.[54]

Hampshire's garrison officers hardly provided the potential for military based centralization. Culpeper was lazy, volatile and a resister of taxes.[55] Edward Strange, governor of Hurst castle, also obstructed the revenue. Henry Paulet went mad before he died in 1672.[56] Even the otherwise effective Sir Robert Holmes indulged in false musters, and several junior officers proved insubordinate, or dishonest.[57]

Yet several of the more reliable officers were actively involved in local government in the areas where they served. Even Culpeper proved capable of acting as a Corporation Act commissioner, along with his deputy, Colonel Walter Slingsby. Culpeper and three other locally stationed military officers were appointed to the Sandham local commission for sewers in 1662. Culpeper and Slingsby were in the commission of the peace in 1664; Sir Philip Honeywood was appointed to the same in 1668, and soon joined by Sir Robert Holmes. James Halsall, another locally based military commander, was appointed in 1673 and George Legge, new governor of Portsmouth, in 1674.[58]

Some of these men were active in local government. Colonel Walter Slingsby was one of the most active JPs in the Isle of Wight in the mid-1660s. Sir Robert Holmes was equally active between 1668 and 1672.[59] Sir Philip Honeywood, who had been given a commission in the Hampshire militia in 1667, was an active JP in the Portsdown division by 1672.[60] The appointment and the activity of military men does not seem to have been controversial, as they were appointed as tax commissioners in acts of Parliament. Sir Philip Honeywood was named and acted as a subsidy commissioner in 1663–4. Colonel Walter Slingsby, Alexander Culpeper, James Halsall, George Legge, Sir Robert Holmes were named in subsequent legislation before 1678.[61]

[54] *Cal.S.P.Dom.*, 1661–2, p. 22; I.W.C.R.O., OG/19/82; OG/73/16; MS Ward, no. 906; Sir R. Worsley, *The History of the Isle of Wight* (London, 1781), p. 138.

[55] See below, pp. 107, 118, 144.

[56] P.R.O., P.C. 2/63, p. 290; *Cal.S.P.Dom.*, 1672, p. 76.

[57] See below, p. 169; P.R.O., P.C. 2/62, p. 314; Webb, ' "Brave men and servants to his Royal Highness" ', p. 67; *Cal.S.P.Dom.*, 1671, p. 186.

[58] Estcourt, 'The ancient borough of Newtown', p. 98; P.R.O., C181 (Crown Office Entry Book), 7, p. 174; P.R.O., C231/7, pp. 226, 326, 343, 456, 481.

[59] *Cal.S.P.Dom.*, 1664–5, pp. 47, 108–9, 446; H.C.R.O., QO 4, pp. 322, 333; I.W.C.R.O., BRX/PR/4.

[60] *Cal.S.P.Dom.*, 1667, p. 248; H.C.R.O., QO 5, p. 9.

[61] *S.R.*, v. 466, 540, 589, 769, 822; P.R.O., E179/247/28.

Though Parliament was becoming increasingly alarmed at the prospect of a standing army in this period, it does not appear to have connected the threat with the participation of individual officers in local government.

The military were also nominated as members of local corporations. Samuel Williams, who was a store-keeper attached to the duke of York's company at Portsmouth in 1661, was one of the aldermen appointed by the Corporation Act commissioners the next year. It became standard procedure for deputy or lieutenant-governors to be elected burgesses. Colonel Walter Slingsby was made an 'out burgess' of Newtown in the Isle of Wight in 1663, by the Corporation Act commissioners of whom he was one. And in 1676, Sir Robert Holmes, and his brother Sir John, both became involved in this administratively irrelevant but politically significant borough.[62]

Portsmouth continued to be an important naval base, and members of the local naval establishment continued to be nominated and to be involved in local government. There was a naval contingent on the Hampshire commission of the peace, though none of those named seem to have acted. But several naval officials became actively involved in the government of Portsmouth, including Thomas Middleton, the resident navy commissioner (from 1664). But the Navy Board disapproved of such involvement, regarding it as needless distraction from navy business and did everything in its power to discourage it. But Middleton considered such a policy futile, and it certainly never succeeded. The naval magistrates did not prove noticeably more compliant to the wishes of central government than their civilian colleagues. But Sir John Kempthorne, resident commissioner, was able to use his membership of the corporation to good effect in pursuit of those who embezzled naval stores in 1677.[63]

As was seen above, the revenue esitablishments of the 1650s had been at least partially drawn from and integrated with the local communities in Hampshire. In its early years, the Restoration government made much of putting local revenue collection into respected local hands. But in due course, financial and political necessity caused this to change.

When the excise was put out to farm in 1662, the Treasury solicited nominations for county farmers from the JPs at quarter sessions (as the Rump had tried to do in 1652).[64] Hampshire's JPs were heartened by the 'cleere expressions of favour to o[u]r Country' which they found in the Treasury's letter, and appointed two local gentlemen as suitable candidates. The hearth

[62] Brit. Lib., Addit. MS 18764 (Exchequer Accounts 1566–1755), fol. 36; East, *Portsmouth*, pp. 169, 357, 360; Estcourt, 'The ancient borough of Newtown', p. 98; I.W.C.R.O., Jerome Collection, Newtown assembly book, 1671–96, fol. 4; see below, p. 151.
[63] P.R.O., C220/9/4, fols. 76–7; C193/12/3, fols. 90–1; *Cal.S.P.Dom.*, 1665–6, pp. 308, 317, 319, 323, 547–8; *Cal.S.P.Dom.*, 1666–7, p. 136; *Cal.S.P.Dom.*, 1667, p. 467; *Portsmouth Sessions Papers*, ed. Hoad, p. 65.
[64] C. D. Chandaman, *The English Public Revenue 1660–1688* (Oxford, 1975), p. 54.

tax was initially collected through sheriffs, but when this proved too slow, the Crown insisted on appointing special receivers. But in the case of the Isle of Wight, the Treasury chose Thomas Worsley of Bembridge, member of an established local gentry family, to perform the task. At the same time, Sir John Norton was appointed receiver-general for the taxes Parliament was granting for the Dutch War. The patent officers of the customs were generally respectable local merchants.[65]

But as the 1660s progressed, and the financial needs of the regime became more acute and its political difficulties greater, local gentlemen and merchants were ousted from local revenue departments. The local excise farmers soon found themselves outnumbered and ultimately displaced by city financiers, in Hampshire as in other counties; these men were better able to meet the terms which the Treasury was now demanding. When the hearth tax went out to farm after 1666 it was the same story, with advertisements being placed in the *London Gazette* for would-be farmers. Even when direct collection resumed briefly in the 1670s, and it did not return to local hands.[66]

It was not only the financial needs of government which had the effect of removing local revenue offices from local hands. As Parliament became less tractable, new revenue offices were used to influence MPs. So, for example, the sub-commissioners for prizes at Southampton in the Dutch Wars were mostly MPs and outsiders, though their employees were recruited locally. The sub-commissioners of prizes at Southampton in 1666 showed scant regard for local privileges, warning the corporation not to assert its rights too rigorously to the detriment of the royal government.[67]

But there was no systematic policy of centralization. The restoration government had simply reacted to changing financial and political circumstances, without any particular idea of undermining local involvement in revenue collection. Nor were the farmers and officials whom it came to employ generally more committed to central government than the locals whom they had displaced.

The Restoration had a radical impact on office-holding in Hampshire, sweeping from power many who had held office during the previous twenty years. Men were promoted to take their place on the grounds of their proven loyalty to the regime, and the favour they could deploy at court. As new political conflicts emerged this inevitably had an impact upon local office-holding, but systematic purging was not revived until the Exclusion Crisis.

[65] H.C.R.O., QO 4, p. 124; *Cal.Treas.Bks.*, i. 3, 7, 58, 656; *Cal.Treas.Bks.*, ii. 175.
[66] *Cal.Treas.Bks.*, i. 430; ii. 190; iii. 833–6, 864; Chandaman, *The English Public Revenue,*. pp. 54–64; *The London Gazette*, no. 229, 23–7 Jan. 1667; no. 263, 21–5 May 1668: I am grateful to Dr J. H. Thomas for these references.
[67] K. H. D. Haley, *The First Earl of Shaftesbury* (Oxford, 1968), p. 176n; *Cal.S.P.Dom.*, 1666–7, pp. 333, 472, 475; *Cal.S.P.Dom.*, 1672–3, p. 535; Davies, *Southampton*, p. 499.

5

The enforcement of policy 1660–78

DEFENCE AND INTERNAL SECURITY

The Restoration saw changes in the structure of local defence and security arrangements. But these should not distract attention from the fact that the Restoration government was just as involved in the provinces for these purposes as its Interregnum predecessors had been, at least for the first seven years of Charles II's reign. The government was equally capable of interfering in the localities to ensure its own safety and was in many ways more successful in the policies which it pursued than the regimes of the 1650s.

In the years which immediately followed the Restoration, the hand-picked lieutenancy in Hampshire was plied with detailed instructions from the Privy Council. These concerned the mustering of militia, the observation, disarming and detention of those disaffected to the government, and the suppression of false news. Though the earl of Southampton was confined to London by government business or illness, his deputy-lieutenants were not simply left to their own devices, but were expected to return detailed accounts of their proceedings to Southampton and the Privy Council, a requirement which they gladly fulfilled.[1] This stream of orders, which slowed down somewhat between 1663 and the outbreak of the second Dutch War, thereafter resumed until peace was concluded, with a new emphasis on the defence of the coast. But again, the central government, in the form of the Privy Council, did not just leave this concern to local deputy-lieutenants unsupervised, but orchestrated defensive strategy, ordering contingents of militia from Berkshire, Wiltshire and mainland Hampshire down to the Isle of Wight in 1666 and 1667.[2] The Restoration government was also capable of initiatives

---

[1] Brit. Lib., Addit. MS 21922, fols. 239–40, 244–6, 249, 253 (this letter book belonged to the Nortons of Rotherfield and not, as Dr Green suggests, to Richard Norton of Southwick, their cousin), I. M. Green, *The Re-Establishment of the Church of England 1660–1663* (Oxford, 1978), p. 182; MS Sloane 813, fols. 26–7, 68–9; P.R.O., P.C. 2/56, pp. 53–8, 185–6, 498–9; *Cal.Treas.Bks.*, i. 312, 315–16.

[2] P.R.O., P.C. 2/59, pp. 93, 98, 115, 442; S.P. 44/20, p. 82; *Cal.Treas.Bks.*, i. 675–6; *Cal.S.P.Dom.*, 1665–6, pp. 466, 538; P.R.O., S.P. 29/165, fol. 121; S.P. 29/204, fol. 50; S.P. 29/205, fol. 118.

to direct local defence, which were similar to ones made during the Interregnum. In the crisis of 1666–7, various aristocrats having military experience or with commissions in the Guards were appointed to command the militia in various sensitive regions, in a way very reminiscent of the experiments of the 1650s.[3] Lord Gerard of Brandon was appointed to command the militias of both mainland Hampshire and the Isle of Wight: a degree of rationalization of which no Interregnum government had thought.[4] Lord Gerard was down inspecting the fortifications of the Isle of Wight by 13 April 1667, and he spent the rest of the spring and summer in the Solent area improving fortifications and finalizing defence plans. In mid-June, at the time of the Medway disaster, his brief was expanded to include the command of the militia in neighbouring counties as well as Hampshire and the Isle of Wight, and the overall command of regular forces in the area too. He was given detailed instructions as to his powers and his duties, which were further clarified in response to his queries. Lord Gerard stayed in the county until the middle of August.[5]

After the Restoration, the lieutenancy and the local militia were the mainstays of defence and security in the provinces. Nevertheless, the regular forces which remained also had a vital policing role to perform. Even before its disbandment and re-enlistment, members of the Portsmouth garrison were busy reporting the seditious words of republican sympathizers amongst townspeople, and they continued to do so after 1661. Major Wyndham's troop of Horse Guards was delegated to assist the Hampshire deputy-lieutenants during the summer of 1661 in the suppression of disaffection.[6] Certain garrison commanders excelled in the pursuit of republican plotters. Colonel Walter Slingsby, deputy-governor of the Isle of Wight, was particularly active and effective. He also performed the traditional task of a deputy-governor in organizing the island's militia and defences.[7] In this role he was succeeded by Sir Henry Jones, who came to the island with his troop of Horse Guards in the summer of 1666. He was appointed deputy-governor the following March.

---

[3] Lord Berkeley of Stratton in Suffolk, Cambridgeshire and Ely, *Cal.S.P.Dom.*, 1667, p. 167; Lieutenant-General Middleton in Kent, Clarendon, *Continuation of the Life*, iii. 247; the earl of Carlisle in the northern counties, S.S. Webb, *The Governors-General: The English Army and the Definition of Empire 1569–1681* (Chapel Hill, 1979), pp. 89–90; the earl of Oxford, colonel of the Royal Regiment of horse and lord lieutenant of Essex, Oxfordshire and Hertfordshire was sent down to Harwich by the king in June 1667, 'to raise the country', *The Diary of Samuel Pepys*, ed. R. Latham and W. Matthews (11 vols., London, 1970–83), viii (1667), 254–5.

[4] *Cal.S.P.Dom.*, 1666–7, p. 441.

[5] *Cal.S.P.Dom.*, 1667, pp. 30, 372; P.R.O., S.P. 29/205, fols. 116, 118, 120.

[6] *Portsmouth Sessions Papers*, ed. Hoad, pp. 14, 15, 19, 20, 21, 33; Brit. Lib., Addit. MS 21922, fols. 248–9.

[7] *Cal.S.P.Dom.*, 1663–4, pp. 193, 202, 298, 302, 352,. 361, 366–7; P.R.O., S.P. 29/125, fol. 89.

Regular forces played an important role in defending the Solent in the summer of 1667.[8]

The secretaries of state built up an intelligence network in the area during the 1660s, which was quite as good if not better than Thurloe's. Colonel Walter Slingsby, Sir Philip Honeywood and ultimately Sir Robert Holmes all provided regular reports. Their information was supplemented by Hugh Salisbury, a naval official and member of Portsmouth corporation, John Lysle, a public notary from West Cowes, and Sir Robert Dillington, a deputy-lieutenant in the Isle of Wight, who was an old friend of Sir Joseph Williamson, Arlington's secretary.[9] Not only did these men provide accurate reports of local events and the movement of potential conspirators, they also gave the central government vital insights into the mood of the local people, a dimension which was largely lacking from the intelligence of the Interregnum period. In other respects though, parallels with the 1650s are close; lists of suspected persons were drawn up at the centre.[10] In the early 1660s, almost every loose word in the locality seemed likely to be reported to the government: some words which one gentleman happened to say to another in a private conversation, which was embarrassing for all concerned when the gentleman in question happened to be Richard Norton, one of the deputy-lieutenants, and his words, which Colonel Walter Slingsby thought treasonable, consisted of a prediction that he would live to see England a commonwealth again.[11]

It would be wrong to think that local people resented government involvement in and control over the defence and security of their area. A wide cross-section of the local community actively favoured the military presence and governmental initiatives to safeguard their locality. The mayor, aldermen, merchants and inhabitants of the town of Southampton petitioned the Privy Council in June 1661 that Hurst and Calshot castles be continued as garrisons as a deterrent to pirates.[12] The deputy-lieutenants asked the earl of Southampton that they might have a regular troop of horse with them again in 1662, to help to suppress sedition.[13] But the appeal was rebuffed. There was no sense of rivalry apparent between the deputy-lieutenants and the regular forces, indeed, two members of the lieutenancy, Richard Norton and Sir Robert Howard, were commissioned to raise regiments of regulars in

[8] P.R.O., S.P. 29/162, fols. 245–6; S.P. 29/163, fol. 118; I.W.C.R.O., M. 41, p. 21; *Cal.S.P.Dom.*, 1667, pp. 190–1, 351.

[9] Fraser, *Intelligence of the Secretaries of State*, Appendix III; *Cal.S.P.Dom.*, 1660–70, *passim*.

[10] E.g. P.R.O., S.P. 9/32, 'Williamson's Spy-Book' – which does not contain any Hampshire names, but S.P. 29/88/60 contains several.

[11] P.R.O., S.P. 29/103, fol. 286.

[12] P.R.O., P.C. 2/55, p. 254.

[13] Brit. Lib., Addit. MS 21922, fol. 252.

1667, and the latter hoped to use 'the creditt he had in Hampshire' to raise men.[14] Some people in the Isle of Wight drafted a petition to Albemarle in 1665 or 1666 that locally stationed regular soldiers might be ordered to help them in keeping up the watch against the spread of the plague.[15] The gentry and people of the Isle of Wight were looking for strong military leadership to supervise the defence of the island during the second Dutch War. They found it to some extent in Colonel Walter Slingsby, whom they strongly supported, but not in the governor Lord Culpeper, who was more of a courtier than a military leader. While he was away at court pleading the cause of the island's defence, early in 1666, a petition was drawn up and subscribed by the bulk of the island's leading inhabitants. It was presented to the king in April. Apart from complaining against Culpeper's attitude and actions, the petitioners claimed that the island was not as well defended as it should be, the magazines were not as well stocked, nor the militia in the state of readiness it ought to be, 'for your Ma[jes]ties service and the defence and safety of this your Kingdome'. The government appeared to reject the petition, but in fact it had already resolved to strengthen the island, with regular troops, engineers and ordnance stores.[16] By May, Culpeper was also down in the island and giving a more positive lead than ever before, though he was soon effectively replaced by Sir Henry Jones, and ultimately by Lord Gerard of Brandon. Understandably, Lord Gerard was welcome on both sides of the Solent; the deputy-lieutenants of Hampshire, along with many gentry, all attended him to consult about local defence. He made several visits to the Isle ot Wight to inspect the fortifications there, while his presence dispelled the fear that the island was forgotten in Whitehall.[17]

But unlike its Interregnum predecessors, the Restoration government did not rely mainly on army officers or regular soldiers to police and guard the localities. Its achievement lay in the way it managed to involve local people in their own defence and security, whilst keeping over-all supervision firmly in its own hands. The government's success owed much to the zeal of its supporters in Parliament and in the lieutenancies, many of whom had a royalist past. The tone of the correspondence between Lord Treasurer Southampton and his deputies is one of trust and shared enthusiasm for the preservation of the regime. The deputy-lieutenants saw themselves as involved in a national

---

14 *Cal.S.P.Dom.*, 1667, pp. 181, 183; P. H. Hardacre, 'Clarendon, Sir Robert Howard and Chancery office-holding at the Restoration', *Huntingdon Library Quarterly*, xxxviii (1974–5), 213.
15 Brit. Lib., Addit. MS 46501, fol. 29.
16 P.R.O., S.P. 29/136, fol. 126; P.R.O., S.P. 29/153, fols. 192–3; I.W.C.R.O., OG/19/84.
17 I.W.C.R.O., OG/19/77; *Cal.S.P.Dom.*, 1667, pp. 225, 274, 294; *Cal.S.P.Dom.*, 1670 and Addenda, 1660–70, p. 708; P.R.O., S.P. 29/163, fol. 118; S.P. 29/208, fol. 63; S.P. 29/209, fol. 169.

struggle against sedition and republicanism; in late August 1662 they wrote to the earl of Southampton, 'for the security of the Nation in Generall we shall not be wanting in o[u]r utmost endeavours to keepe o[u]r Militia in the best readinesse we can'.[18] Nor was the deputies' loyal language a mere front designed to appease Whitehall. Their concern is apparent from the correspondence which passed amongst them. Sir Andrew Henley wrote to his colleagues in response to an order from the Privy Council in August 1661, 'I . . . doe think it most meet accordingly that all care and industry should be used to settle the Militia.' However, acting without clear statutory backing and on the basis of out-dated records and assessments, the deputy-lieutenants had considerable difficulty in doing this. But despite these major handicaps, by the autumn of 1661, they were in the process of mustering the foot regiments from Basingstoke, Kingsclere, Alton and Andover divisions, and the horse troop raised from the Portsdown and Alton divisions was ordered to muster under the command of Sir Humphrey Bennet on 5 November 1661.[19]

The militia legislation of the Cavalier Parliament effectively solved the problems which had beset the local lieutenancies. As Dr Hassell-Smith has written, 'These Acts resolved the tensions and contradictions within militia administration which had been largely created by the 1558 Arms Act and which had been, if anything, aggravated by its repeal in 1604.'[20] The act of 1662 paved the way for a complete re-assessment, which greatly facilitated the mustering of the militia. Three deputy-lieutenants sitting at Winchester on 7 November 1662 ordered this part of the act to be carried out in Hampshire, by militia officers in each division. Appeals against assessments for the provision of horses and arms were to be made to the deputy-lieutenants.[21] The legislation helped to establish a smaller but more effective militia in Hampshire than had existed in the traditional trained bands. By 1679, it consisted of six divisional regiments of foot, plus the town companies of Southampton and Winchester and two troops of horse, numbering in all 3,330 men, about 2,000 fewer than the pre-Civil-War figure. But the weaponry had been modernized, and by 1666 at least part of the Hampshire militia were in uniform.[22] The 'Trophy money' for which provision was made in the 1662 statute, combined with the generosity of some militia officers, helped to equip units with the drums and flags requisite for a proper fighting

[18] Brit. Lib., Addit. MS 21922, fol. 255.
[19] Brit. Lib., Addit. MS 21922, fols. 240–1, 247–8; H.C.R.O., 37M,84, 4/AC/8.
[20] A. Hassell Smith, 'Militia rates and militia statutes 1558–1663', *The English Commonwealth 1547–1640*, ed. P. Clark, A. C. R. Smith and N. Tyacke (Leicester, 1979), p. 109.
[21] Brit. Lib., MS Sloane, 813, fol. 50.
[22] Brit. Lib., Addit. MS 21922, fols. 59–63; *Cal.S.P.Dom.*, 1679–80, pp. 60–1; the 'royal white trained bands' in Hampshire are referred to in *Verney Memoirs*, iv. 136; Andover Corporation purchased a yellow coat for its militiamen on 20 July 1665, H.C.R.O., 37M84, 4/AC/10.

force.[23] The fact that the legislation did not apply to the Isle of Wight militia helps to explain the problems which were encountered in reconstituting it, at least before 1666.[24]

But it would be wrong to ascribe the success of the Retoration government in policing the provinces exclusively to the legislation of the Cavalier Parliament, or even the enthusiasm displayed by the lieutenancies. There was no magic in the mere existence of militia legislation, as the Rump had learnt to its cost, and the loyalest of servants might be rendered impotent if he was isolated in a community which was indifferent or hostile to the central government, as the militia commanders of the 1650s had been. This was not the situation which the deputy-lieutenants in Hampshire found themselves in, as they sought to immobilize and disarm republican sympathizers in the early years of the Restoration. A wide body of opinion amongst the county's gentry and people had no desire to see a return to the Commonwealth, and endorsed the lieutenancy's efforts to prevent this. John Bulkeley, a knight of the shire, praised its early initiatives to maintain local order, in the Convention.[25] In the hiatus before the full militia could be mustered, many gentry and others flocked to join volunteer militia horse troops. A troop of 200 volunteers 'well hors'd, well armed and accommodated in all repsects like a troop of honour' was raised in the Isle of Wight under the command of Colonel Walter Slingsby. At a muster on St George's Down (near the centre of the island) on 23 April 1661, they were attended by the leaders of local gentry society, including several former parliamentarians.[26] Five volunteer troops had been raised in mainland Hampshire by the end of March 1661, and according to press reports this had not exhausted the supply of potential recruits. By May 1662, when these troops turned out to attend the king on his way to Portsmouth, they could plausibly be described as a regiment of horse. And in the summer of 1662, they were put on stand-by in case a crisis arose.[27] Paradoxically, it was the apparent vulnerability of the Restoration regime which was its greatest strength, eliciting the active support of many local gentry keen to avoid a return to the Commonwealth. Many identified their

---

[23] Unfortunately the only direct evidence for this before 1678 relates to the Andover division, but it may be assumed that this was a widespread phenomenon before the Exclusion Crisis; Bodl., MS Top. Hants. e. 11 (Richard Ayliffe's account book 1664–7 [copy]), pp. 72, 82; *Don Quixote Redivivus encountering a Barnsdoor* [?London], p. 2 and *passim*.

[24] No general muster appears to have been held before 1665, P.R.O., S.P. 29/125, fol. 89; for a more general survey of the reform of the militia in the seventeenth century, see A. Fletcher, *Reform in the Provinces: the Government of Stuart England* (New Haven and London, 1986), chapter 9, pp. 282–347.

[25] H.C., i. 744.

[26] *Mercurius Publicus*, no. 17, 25 April–2 May 1661.

[27] *Mercurius Publicus*, no. 13, 28 March–4 April 1661; *Mercurius Publicus*, no. 21, 22–9 May 1662; Brit. Lib., Addit. MS 21922, fol. 254.

fortunes with those of the central government in a way they had not done during the 1650s.

During the second Dutch War, this identification became even closer, under the threat of invasion. Once the debacle of Culpeper's lack of leadership had been overcome, the gentry and people of the Isle of Wight showed that they were very ready to come to the defence of their island. All sixteen companies of the Isle of Wight militia, numbering 1,800 men, appeared at a general muster on St George's Down on 12 July 1666 and, according to one deputy-lieutenant, Sir Robert Dillington, showed 'much readiness to protect their King & Country'. Nearly 2,000 islanders turned out to watch this impressive array. According to Dillington, the gentry were prepared to mount a troop of volunteer horse at their own expense, which after one month's service would go on to the Crown's payroll until the end of the war.[28] Dillington and the other deputies, when they received a supply of weapons, listed and trained the spare men not charged with arms, which added a third, perhaps 600 men, to the strength of the militia. But the islanders were still looking for external support, which duly materialized in the form of three companies of the Berkshire militia, for which Dillington and others were duly grateful.[29]

In the crisis of the following summer the royal government made every effort to maximize local involvement in the defence of the coasts, which had been left exposed by the mistaken policy of laying up the fleet before peace had definitely been concluded with the Dutch. Arlington wrote to the lords lieutenant of all the south-eastern maritime shires and to the deputy-lieutenants of Hampshire (the earl of Southampton being recently dead) ordering them to deploy every possible man to deter a Dutch invasion. The militia of Hampshire were mustered and marched to the Solent, and contingents from inland counties marched to the Isle of Wight. Though the town was already full of regular soldiers, Sir Philip Honeywood called upon inhabitants to defend Portsmouth and six hundred immediately enlisted and swore to defend the place with their lives and fortunes.[30] The mayor of Southampton supervised the inhabitants of the town in digging fortifications there. The dean and chapter of Winchester provided Sir John Clobery's independent horse troop with fourteen horses, at their own expense.[31]

When a Dutch fleet actually appeared off the coast in mid-July, looking to

[28] P.R.O., S.P. 29/162, fols. 245–6; P.R.O., S.P. 29/163, fol. 118.
[29] P.R.O., S.P. 29/162, fol. 246; S.P. 29/165, fol. 121.
[30] *Cal.S.P.Dom.*, 1667, pp. xii, 207–8; P.R.O., S.P. 29/204, fol. 50; S.P., 23/205, fol. 118; Bodl., MS Top. Hants. e. 11, p. 83.
[31] Brit. Lib., MS Egerton, 868, fol. 53; *Documents Relating to the History of the Cathedral Church of Winchester in the Seventeenth Century*, ed. W. R. W. Stephens and F. T. Madge (2 vols., Winchester, 1897), ii. 117.

follow up its recent victory in the Medway, the amalgamated forces in the Isle of Wight shadowed its progress along the island's coast, while Lord Gerard of Brandon was active in deploying the trained bands. On the mainland, the deputy-lieutenants and militiamen 'showed much courage and resolution in case the enemy had made an attempt'. But seeing the martial array on the coast, the Dutch fleet thought better of attempting a landing.[32] An even worse disaster than the Medway had been averted by a timely government initiative in the mission of Lord Gerard of Brandon, combined with the rallying of the localities to their own defence.

After 1667, the royal government could afford to take a more detached view of local defence and security arrangements. At home, it attained a degree of security which had never been enjoyed by the regimes of the Interregnum. Republicanism, having failed to exploit the crisis of the second Dutch War, was no longer perceived as being such a threat. In 1672, the government sought to defuse disaffection at home by granting toleration to dissenters, rather than by vigorous policing. Abroad too, Charles II's government was never again to be as hard-pressed as it had been in the summer of 1667. England's diplomatic isolation, which had been a prime factor in creating the crisis of 1666–7, was ended first by the Triple Alliance of 1668, and then by the French alliance of 1670.

It was still sometimes necessary to put the militia into a state of readiness. On 10 March 1668, the Privy Council sent a letter to Lord St John, the new lord lieutenant of Hampshire, to put the militia on stand-by to defend Portsmouth if necessary. A similar order was issued by the king in May 1673 during the third Dutch War. The year before, some of the militia in the Isle of Wight had been drawn into the forts and castles there. They were said by Colonel James Halsall, temporary military commander in the island, to be in a good posture.[33] But these were only precautions.

However, the government had not totally neglected the defence of the Solent between the two Dutch Wars. Indeed, unlike the military governments of the 1650s, which had allowed them to decay, the government of Charles II devoted considerable care and resources to building up and modernizing Hampshire's fortifications. According to the historian of Hampshire's coastal defences 'Charles II . . . initiated a fortress building programme on a massive scale which paralleled Henry VIII's precautions more than a century before'. The achievement was to be unequalled until the eighteenth century and much of the work was done between the Dutch Wars. A vigorous start had been made under Sir Philip Honeywood and Lord Gerard of Brandon

[32] P.R.O., S.P. 29/209, fol. 169; S.P. 29/210, fol. 208; *Cal.S.P.Dom.*, 1667, p. 321.
[33] P.R.O., P.C. 2/60, p. 221; *Cal.S.P.Dom.*, 1671–2, p. 533; *Cal.S.P.Dom.*, 1672, p. 76; *Cal.S.P.Dom.*, 1673, p. 270.

during the second Dutch War, using funds diverted from the special militia tax of £70,000. Designs for Portsmouth's fortifications were made by Sir Bernard de Gomme in accordance with the latest European ideas. On 30 June 1667, Hugh Salisbury wrote to Williamson from Portsmouth predicting that 'this place wilbe Invincible when finished'. And the town did look sufficiently strong to deter a Dutch attack two weeks later. The work continued after the war. Then the systematic improvement of the Isle of Wight's fortifications was undertaken in the light of a survey by Sir Robert Holmes in 1668. Work began in May 1670, and over the next six years Holmes spent nearly £3,000 on the fortifications.[34]

Such defence plans could be pursued without reference to or co-operation from local magistrates, but when maritime war was resumed in 1672, the royal government was just as dependent upon them, as its Interregnum predecessors had been, to provide support services. Large scale impressment of seamen had been practised during the second Dutch War, nationally and locally. A structure of control based on the Privy Council and local vice-admiralties was devised, which was deployed again in 1672, lords lieutenant being ordered to write to the secretaries of state in case of difficulty. JPs were called upon to draw up lists of resident seamen in their areas. The system appears to have worked reasonably well in Hampshire, under the care of Sir Robert Holmes' deputy vice-admirals. Only Southampton once again caused problems by claiming a separate vice-admiralty jurisdiction, though the corporation was actively listing seamen, presumably for the state's service by November 1672.[35] Heavy demands were made on the boroughs in providing accommodation for sick and wounded seamen and prisoners. As early as 22 March 1672, the Privy Council wrote to the mayor of Winchester to make places ready in the city to receive prisoners.[36] Apart from the billeting of soldiers, Portsmouth also had to accommodate large numbers of sick and wounded during the third Dutch War, and more than £700 was still owing to some inhabitants on that account, more than a decade after the conclusion of peace.[37]

But with the end of hostilities in 1674, there was a significant decline in government involvement and indeed in local activity concerned with defence and security. Lord St John had been alienated from the court and Danby

---

[34] A. D. Saunders, *Hampshire Coastal Defence since the Introduction of Artillery* (Royal Archaeological Institute, 1977), p. 13; H. J. Sparkes, 'The development of Portsmouth as a naval base' (London Univ., M.A. thesis, 1911), p. 169 and note; Brit. Lib., MS Sloane 873 (Sir P. Honeywood's Account for Portsmouth Fortifications 1665–7); P.R.O., S.P. 29/207, fol. 185; S.P. 29/210, fol. 208; *Cal.S.P.Dom.*, 1667–8, p. 218; I.W.C.R.O., DOI/11.

[35] P.R.O., (Kew), Adm. 1/5246, pp. 80–2; I.W.C.R.O., OG/19/40; *Cal.S.P.Dom.*, 1672, p. 232; *Cal.S.P.Dom.*, 1673, pp. 58, 331; S.C.R.O., SC2/1/8, fol. 281.

[36] P.R.O., P.C. 2/63, p. 201.   [37] P.R.O., P.C. 2/71, pp. 92–3.

simply ignored him as lord lieutenant. Though it is wildly premature to talk of eighty years of decay beginning in 1670, as J. R. Western does,[38] in Hampshire there may have been a hiatus in militia administration as a result of governmental indifference and Lord St John's opposition. Deputy-lieutenants continued to be appointed and local musters may have continued as they did in Lancashire, but no militia rate seems to have been raised in the Basingstoke division between 1670 and 1678, though this may initially have been because there was a surplus from rates already raised. Andover corporation made no contribution towards the muster-master's pay between 1671 and 1677.[39] Such military preparations as were made locally were hardly useful to the central government. On 4 April 1676, the Hampshire quarter sessions ordered Weyhill parish to provide butts and bows and arrows for archery practice according to ancient statute.[40] But the ease and apparent thoroughness with which the militia was revived in 1677–8 should warn one against any hasty judgement as to its decline. The Hampshire militia was re-invigorated by the new leadership of Edward Noel and his deputies after 1676, and the Isle of Wight militia, which suffered no comparable hiatus, was fully active after April 1677.[41]

The Restoration government was generally far more successful and effective than its Interregnum predecessors in its management of local security and land-based defences. This was the result of a number of factors. Whilst retaining a regular military arm, the Crown had obtained the support of Parliament in putting local militia administration onto a sound statutory footing. But these factors would not alone have produced effective defence or policing in the provinces. Interregnum regimes had had a much larger army and passed numerous militia acts. The Restoration government supervised local defence and security up to 1667, and to a lesser extent up to 1674, and its endeavours in these areas were fully supported not only by its partisans who dominated the lieutenancies but also by the wider community in Hampshire as elsewhere. Governmental neglect on the other hand could have a damaging effect on the local militia, as it appears to have done, if only for a short time, in the mid-1670s.

---

[38] J. R. Western, *The English Militia in the Eighteenth Century* (London and Toronto, 1965), pp. 52ff.

[39] Carter, 'The Lancashire Lieutenancy 1660–88', pp. 103–4; H.C.R.O., 44M69 021 (Box contains bundle of militia tax ratings); 37M84, 4/AC/13.

[40] H.C.R.O., QO 5, p. 123.

[41] H.C.R.O., 37M84, 4/AC/13; Brit. Lib., Addit. MS 26774 (Latham papers), p. 185; P.R.O., S.P. 30 Case G (Richard Cobbe's Account 1683); P.C. 2/66, p. 301; I.W.C.R.O., Fitzherbert-Brockholes Collection, no. 207; DOI/22.

FINANCE

The raising of revenue had been a major area of governmental concern in the provinces during the 1650s. Interregnum regimes had taken steps to ensure that their money continued to flow in, and huge sums had been raised with a minimum of open resistance. But payment was often slow and in arrears, and the cost in terms of unpopularity had been vast. How then did the Restoration government fare in this vital area?

Perhaps the most fundamental difference between the fiscal system of the Restoration government and that of its predecessors was its irreproachable parliamentary basis. No taxes since 1642 had been voted by a full and free Parliament. All the taxes which the Restoration sought to raise had this mandate, at least until 1685. In 1660, the last significant non-parliamentary revenue, feudal dues, was replaced by an excise voted by Parliament. A package of revenues, including the excise, customs revenue and a new tax on hearths were supposed to ensure the Crown a permanent annual revenue of £1.2 million.[42] Unparliamentary taxation was now largely a thing of the past, as much for pragmatic reasons as any other. Would either Charles I or Oliver Cromwell have risked the alienation of the political nation through arbitrary taxes, if they had had as an alternative the sort of grants which Parliament was prepared to make to Charles II?

The statutory basis of taxation was at once a weakness and a strength: its formal legal basis could be appealed to by government when it met with obstruction or uncertainty in the provinces. But having once been granted by Parliament, these taxes could be withdrawn in the same way. The opposition in the Commons made numerous attempts to abolish or modify the hearth tax between 1666 and 1680, though its abolition was not finally achieved until 1689.[43] All other taxes were subject to parliamentary criticism and revocation.

The Restoration also saw important developments within government itself in the area of revenue control and management. The government machinery which dealt with revenue collection was more streamlined and more centralized within itself than it had been during the 1650s. The Exchequer was fully and finally re-established as a clearing house of government money. In this period, as Meekings has observed, it was, 'a great department which, although jealous of its traditions, could still be imaginative and resourceful'. But ascendancy in revenue control was soon established by the Treasury, under the Commission of 1667, supported by crucial orders in

---

[42] Chandaman, *The English Public Revenue*, p. 200.   [43] *Ibid.*, pp. 86–8.

Council in 1668.[44] It would be behind much of the Restoration government's involvement in the localities.

But the Exchequer also had an impact on the localities. Its full restoration ensured that there were now adequate means to bring revenue collectors to account. As was seen above, the success of Interregnum governments in this important area had at best been partial. The Restoration government demonstrated its potential for effective action by the way it made Interregnum revenue collectors account for the money they had raised. Again, the way was cleared by statute. The Indemnity Act excepted certain named revenues from its provisions, making their collectors liable to proceedings. This was followed up by a further explanatory act in 1662. Meanwhile preliminary steps had been taken by Lord Treasurer Southampton, to make revenue collectors pay in money known to be in their hands. Excise collectors were allowed to compound for their arrears. At the same time, private individuals were commissioned to recover sums in Hampshire and other counties, to repay debts due to them. Colonel Thomas Napier was granted £2,000 out of money he should find in the hands of John Woodman.[45]

But Lord Treasurer Southampton's preference was for the normal course of the Exchequer, and this was deployed against large numbers of Interregnum revenue collectors, though unfortunately the proceedings were more productive of information than of hard cash. Nationally Chandaman has reckoned that less than £9,000 of Commonwealth taxation was recovered during the 1660s, apart from the substantial arrears of customs and excise which were accounted for separately.[46]

Some former revenue collectors, like John Hildesley, had taken notice of the provisions of the Indemnity Act and came into the Exchequer to clear their accounts, before being ordered to do so. But others would need to be investigated. To this end, commissions were issued from the Exchequer, one for Hampshire, consisting mostly of Winchester-based royalists, and one for the Isle of Wight. A preliminary list of revenue collectors in Hampshire was drawn up containing thirty-six names. As a result of the commissioners' investigations, which at least in the Andover division appear to have been quite thorough, a bill was exhibited in the Exchequer with the names of 203 defaulting accountants attached. These men were obliged to make sworn

[44] *Dorset Hearth Tax Assessments 1662–1664*, ed. C. A. F. Meekings (Dorchester, 1951), p. xviii; Roseveare, *The Treasury 1660–1870*, pp. 18–33.
[45] *S.R.*, v. 228–9, 409; *Cal.Treas.Bks.*, i. 170, 174, 573, 576, 637, 703; *Cal.S.P.Dom.*, 1661–2, p. 61; *Cal.S.P.Dom.*, 1664–5, p. 98; P.R.O., E134/13 & 14 Chas II Hil. 16: Deposition of Robert Woodward.
[46] Chandaman, *The English Public Revenue*, pp. 126–7; for an account of the process based largely on Devon material see S. K. Roberts, 'Public or private? Revenge and recovery at the Restoration of Charles II', *B.I.H.R.* 59 (1986), 172–88.

answers, either before commissioners in the locality or at the Exchequer itself. The answers of eighty survive, though it is clear that more were made. Replications were issued against eight for unsatisfactory answers, and they had to supply further ones.[47] The impact of the investigation was far-reaching in Hampshire, as it was in Devon, and doubtless in other shires. Much of the class of documents known as the Commonwealth Exchequer Papers (S.P.28) only found their way to the centre as a result of this investigation. Interregnum governments had been totally ignorant about several of the sums which were now accounted for. Several accountants from Hampshire were made to draw up full declared accounts of the sums they had raised.[48]

However, when it came to dealing with the few hard cases of corruption and embezzlement, the Restoration government got little further than its Interregnum predecessors. John Woodman was prosecuted through the Exchequer, but his case seems to have ended inconclusively. The sequestration sub-commissioners of 1649–53 were reckoned to be liable for £1,772 5s 1½d which was unaccounted for by them. But there is no evidence that this money was ever paid.[49] However, Exchequer accounting was an important means for central government to control provincial tax collection and it would be applied to those responsible for raising the Restoration regime's own revenue.

One of the most radically different things about the fiscal system of the Restoration, at least before 1672, was the improvement of government credit. During the 1650s, public faith bills had circulated at uniquely low prices, and the government had been able to raise loans only by threatening to repudiate its debts.[50] After the Restoration, the regime was sufficiently secure at least to raise loans on the basis of the taxes which Parliament had granted, not only from city financiers, but from country gentlemen as well.[51] Tax-farming was a form of credit, by which central government was able to raise large sums in advance on the basis of the taxes which Parliament had granted it. In 1662, both the customs and the excise were put out to farm, and the hearth tax was more often out to farm than not between 1666 and 1684.

[47] P.R.O., E112/564, nos. 345–9, 362; E113/14: Hampshire; E178/7346; S.P. 28/154 (Hampshire); S.P. 28/351.

[48] P.R.O., S.P. 28/230 (Hampshire), note on back of account by Thomas Bettsworth; S.P. 28/154, Richard Webb's Account Book; E360/208, fols. 82–4; E179/176/554.

[49] P.R.O., E134/13 Chas II, Mich. I; 13 & 14 Chas II, Hil. 16; Hil. 20; Round Room, Exchequer (K.R.) Decrees Calendar iii. (16 Chas II, East.–29 Chas II, Trin.), fol. 3; *Cal.S.P.Dom.*, 1667–8, p. 212.

[50] H. J. Habakkuk, 'Public finance and the sale of confiscated property during the Interregnum', *Economic History Review, 2nd Series*, 15 (1962–3), 82–3.

[51] In Hampshire, Lord St John, Sir Robert Howard, Richard Norton and Sir Henry Worsley all lent substantial sums at the time of the second Dutch War, and many other gentlemen seem to have done the same; *Cal.Treas.Bks.*, i. 656, 700; Brit. Lib., Addit. MS 46501, fol. 30; microfilm Verney MSS, M 636, reel no. 21, Cary Gardiner to Sir Ralph Verney, 25 June 1666.

Interregnum governments had resorted to farming especially of the excise, but generally on a limited and localized basis. But the farming of Restoration taxes became increasingly confined to a few hands as time went on. By the mid-1670s, Danby was able to raise huge sums in advance from the tax-farmers.[52]

The structure of its credit put central government into an ambivalent position over the money which was raised in its name in the localities. On the one hand, the collection of indirect taxes for the period before the 1680s was mostly in the hands of the staffs of the farmers, who were only indirectly responsible to the government. On the other hand, the need to bring money into the Exchequer to repay loans, especially after Downing's pioneering credit provisions in the Additional Aid of 1665, gave a big incentive for interference in the localities to hasten the payment of taxes. And it is fair to say that the system was far less hand to mouth than Interregnum revenue collection. Some revenue was assigned to pay off debts in the locality where it was raised. But this practice was not nearly as common as it had been in the 1650s. The pay of the garrisons at Portsmouth and in the Isle of Wight came to rest on the personal credit of Sir Stephen Fox, paymaster of the Guards and garrisons.[53]

But great though the differences were between the financial system of the Interregnum and that of the Restoration regime, many of the problems with revenue collection were very much the same. Quite apart from its ordinary revenue, the Crown obtained substantial grants of extraordinary, direct taxation during the first two decades after 1660. Direct taxation was not continuous as it had been during the 1650s, but the spacing out of instalments meant that direct taxation was levied almost every year until 1675, and on top of this militia rates were raised.[54] During much of the 1660s, it was at a level comparable with the later years of the Interregnum, and more than £8 million was raised from the nation at large. Apart from the subsidies of 1663 and 1671, and poll taxes of 1660, 1667 and 1678, money was raised through the assessment system, with fixed irrevocable quotas for each county. Worse, from Hampshire's point of view was the fact that its quota was increased by more than 10 per cent in the general re-assessment of 1665.[55] Many people in the localities must have expected to see a dramatic reduction of taxation in 1660, but no such cut took place, at least in the short term.

In these circumstances, it is not surprising to find the problems which had dogged Interregnum tax-collection recurring. Direct taxes were collected by

[52] Chandaman, *The English Public Revenue*, pp. 23, 54–64, 92–104.
[53] *Ibid.*, App. 1, pp. 295–302; *Cal.Treas.Bks.*, i. 284, 530, 656; C. Clay, *Public Finance and Private Wealth: The Career of Sir Stephen Fox, 1627–1716* (Oxford, 1978), pp. 43–4.
[54] Chandaman, *The English Public Revenue*, Table 2, p. 157.
[55] *Ibid.*, pp. 162, 189–90; *C.J.*, viii. 589.

amateur officials, under the auspices of commissioners who could not be coerced by central government, and whom, except in 1671, it did not even appoint directly. People were slow to pay their taxes, and instalments fell into arrears from the very beginning of the Restoration period. No money had come in under the Poll Act in Hampshire by the end of October 1660, though payments had been due to begin at the end of August. And despite the fact that the money only had to reach Portsmouth, taxation for the disbandment of the forces continued to come in very slowly from Hampshire.[56] The slow payment of direct and indirect taxes in Hampshire continued to be a problem for the rest of the decade.[57]

Initially too, localism and rating disputes posed problems. When the county commissioners for the poll tax ordered the constables of Southampton to attend them at Winchester in September 1660, the corporation voted it 'contrary to the liberties and privileges of the town' and forbade them to attend, though there was no separate commission for Southampton under the act. When the constables disobeyed and attended the commissioners, they were each fined £5. By 1663, Southampton had its own commission, but even this did not eliminate tension between the county and the borough over-night. As late as 1678, the corporation was asking that militia assessments raised within the town should be spent on its own trained bands. But the corporation of Southampton was itself challenged in 1661 for the unfair apportionment of taxes, which it was supposed to have imposed on the parish of St Mary's, near Southampton. The inhabitants of the parish appealed to the Privy Council, which referred the case to the nearest JPs.[58] A series of rating disputes were brought before the Hampshire quarter sessions in the early years of the Restoration.[59]

But, as during the Interregnum, so after the Restoration, actual resistance was rare, and most of the money demanded from the county was ultimately paid. Lord Culpeper's imprisonment of a hearth-tax official in the Isle of Wight in April 1665 provoked an isolated tax-payers' strike there. But all the money due from the island under this collection had been paid in or accounted for by the end of July 1667, despite the added disruption of plague and war.[60]

Lord Treasurer Southampton had complained of the slow payment of the eighteen months assessment in 1662 and 1663. But by the time Sir Hugh

---

[56] *Mercurius Publicus*, no. 44, 25 October–1 November 1660; *Mercurius Publicus*, new series, no. 10, 7–14 March 1661.

[57] *Cal.Treas.Bks.*, i. 394, 539; ii. 22, 38, 48, 74, 83, 149; iii. 16.

[58] *S.R.*, v. 219, 466; S.C.R.O., SC 2/1/8, fols. 161, 340; P.R.O., P.C. 2/55, p. 540.

[59] H.C.R.O., QO 4, pp. 58, 142, 147–8.

[60] Bodl., MS Clarendon 84, fols. 98, 104; C. A. F. Meekings, *Analysis of Hearth Tax Accounts 1662–5* (List and Index Society, vol. 153, 1979), p. 116.

Stewkeley declared his account in June 1664, the only sum outstanding of the county's quota of nearly £36,400 was £131 18s 0d due from the town of Southampton.[61] Of the £39,765 10s 0d due from the county under the Additional Aid of 1665–7, £35,713, or nearly 90 per cent had been received within eight months of the statutory deadline for the last instalment.[62]

But central government could not afford to be complacent. If it wanted its money to be paid in efficiently, and punctually, it would have to be constantly vigilant and as ready as its Interregnum predecessors to interfere in the provinces. Almost from the beginning, the Restoration government showed a determination to exert control over the money raised in its name. In 1664, because of the shortfall in the hearth tax, royal ministers insisted on taking it out of the hands of sheriffs and other local government officers, and vesting it in a separate administration of its own.[63] The next year, the government incurred considerable suspicion and hostility by trying to gather in the remains of the three annual assessments of £70,000 raised to cover the contingencies of the militia. The attempt was only partially successful. But when Lord Treasurer Southampton wrote to the deputy-lieutenants in Hampshire remonstrating with them for their neglect to pay the money left over in Hampshire to Sir Philip Honeywood, they immediately paid in £1,684 8s 0d.[64]

But it needed more than letters, if the government were really to enforce its fiscal policy in the localities. As the 1660s progressed a constant two-way traffic developed between the Treasury and the localities. Messengers and sergeants were sent down into Hampshire to bring up defaulting revenue collectors in custody. In 1666 Francis Stevens, the sergeant at arms, was sent to arrest some excise collectors for detaining money in their hands. And on 22 July in the following year, it was ordered that Thomas Gallet, formerly receiver-general of assessments 1655–60 and now deputy receiver-general, be taken into custody, for failing to pay in the arrears of the royal aids in his hands. Nor were the Treasury Commissioners of 1667 afraid to summon and browbeat men from established county families like Sir John Norton, the receiver-general. He was obliged to attend the Commissioners on several occasions, and was threatened with dismissal for his supposed recalci-

[61] *Cal.Treas.Bks.*, i. 394, 529; P.R.O., E360/145; Declared Account of Sir Hugh Stewkeley.
[62] P.R.O., E401/1938–41, much of the rest of the money would have been accounted for by poundages paid to the receiver-general, head-collectors and sub-collectors and retained in the locality; it is impossible to estimate the rate of payment of the Royal Aid of 1665 and the month's assessment of 1667–8, because the recorded receipts were falsified on account of the exigencies of the government's credit, Chandaman, *The English Public Revenue*, pp. 178–9.
[63] L. M. Marshall, 'The levying of the hearth tax 1662–1688', *E.H.R.*, li. (1936), 629.
[64] Western, *The English Militia*, pp. 45–8; *Cal.Treas.Bks.*, i. 675–6; Brit. Lib., MS Sloane 873, fol. 2.

trance.[65] Those who obstructed taxes were liable to harsh treatment. When John Howard, keeper of the common gaol at Winchester, persistently refused to pay the excise on beer brewed in the gaol in January 1664, and the sheriff failed to act, Francis Stevens was ordered to arrest Howard, though the JPs of Hampshire were given the option of dealing with him themselves. Central government employed a wide variety of agencies in chasing up the collection of direct or indirect taxation in the provinces, from bishops to assize judges.[66]

Government also developed new machinery with the specific intention of hastening the payment of taxes in the provinces. In 1665–7, it established the Tax Office, an exchange office and office for the paymaster of wagons, the latter being in charge of bringing the money physically up to London.[67] At the same time, solicitors were appointed to go down into particular localities to encourage the forwarding of money to the centre, their function being similar to the agents employed by the Army Committee in the 1650s. In January 1668, Thomas Browne was appointed solicitor of the aids in Hampshire, Berkshire, Oxfordshire and Buckinghamshire at a salary of £200 p.a. Similar appointments were made with each new parliamentary grant. In 1670, the Tax Office was re-organized and applied to the task of reforming the administration of the hearth tax, but it continued to have a supervising role over direct taxation.[68] Finally, in the assessment legislation of the 1670s, the government managed to increase the authority of the receiver-general, the official over whom it exerted the greatest control.

These initiatives certainly had some impact upon the pace and efficiency of local revenue collection. Chandaman has noted a nationwide improvement in the speed with which assessments were paid in the 1670s.[69] The 1673 assessment began well in Hampshire, with almost all the first instalment being paid within eleven weeks of the statutory deadline. Rates of payment fell off in subsequent instalments, until the fifth instalment, due on 3 June 1674, which was paid almost as rapidly as the first.[70] This is especially impressive when it is remembered that the average time taken for the remittance of land taxes from the country at large during the period 1693–1798 was 1.64 years.[71] The assessment for building thirty warships in 1677 also began well in Hampshire, the first two instalments being fully paid within the year. The third

---

[65] *Cal.Treas.Bks.*, i. 729, 735; ii. 7, 18, 22, 36, 43.
[66] *Cal.Treas.Bks.*, i. 560, 579, 670; iv. 604; P.R.O., E179/278/67; Marshall, 'The levying of the hearth tax', p. 640.
[67] W. R. Ward, 'The Office of Taxes 1665–1798', *B.I.H.R.*, 25 (1952), 204–5.
[68] Chandaman, *The English Public Revenue*, p. 182; *Cal.Treas.Bks.*, ii. 227; *Cal.Treas.Bks.*, iii. 387, 397, 577; iv. 102, 166; Ward, 'The Office of Taxes', p. 205.
[69] Chandaman, *The English Public Revenue*, pp. 185–6.
[70] *S.R.*, v. 752–3; P.R.O., E401/1951, pp. 134, 190, 238, 260; E401/1952, pp. 12, 44, 130–1, 191, 210, 277, 285, 336; E401/1953, pp. 39, 147, 218, 225; E401/1955, p. 13.
[71] Beckett, 'Local custom and the "New Taxation"', p. 107.

instalment was virtually paid within six months, but thereafter remittance slowed down somewhat. During the 1670s, members of the Tax Office were involved in chasing up arrears. Sir Richard Mason performed this role on several occasions in Hampshire.[72]

The early 1670s also saw a tightening of control over indirect taxes. The customs reverted to direct exploitation in 1671, and never went back to farm. The government began to take more of an interest in discovering frauds and smuggling. To this end, Thomas Cole, a customs officer at Southampton (who by 1671 was in receipt of government newsletters) was a useful agent. He reported on local smuggling operations, and was responsible for several seizures. The expanded staff of customs officers were subject to closer scrutiny by the Treasury and Customs Commissioners, and anyone found conniving in fraud was disciplined. Local garrison commanders who failed to support customs officers, like Edward Strange, governor of Hurst, were liable to be summoned before the Privy Council to answer for their conduct.[73] By the autumn of 1671, the wine licence administration under recently reformed management, was also having an impact on Hampshire and neighbouring counties. The agents Richard Booker and Nathaniel Barnard were instrumental in the fining of six innkeepers in Hampshire and the arrest of six others for illegal liquor sales. They had similar success in Surrey and Dorset.[74]

What then was the local reaction to the Crown's revenue demands and their enforcement? The hearth tax was particularly unpopular, provoking riots in several counties, though not in Hampshire. Some people in the Isle of Wight were quick to follow the example of Lord Culpeper in 1665 in refusing to pay the hearth tax.[75] Opposition did not die down overnight, and payment continued to be slow. In the hearth-tax account running from Michaelmas 1671 to Lady Day 1673, which was declared in February 1674, there were eighty-three defaulters named for the Isle of Wight, besides 534 for mainland Hampshire.[76] But opposition to the excise was less violent than it had been during the 1640s and 1650s, partly because of the reduction in the com-

---

[72] S.R., v. 803, 829; P.R.O., E401/1953, p. 210; E401/1956, p. 11; E401/1959, pp. 180, 197, 217; E401/1960, pp. 2, 69, 98, 104, 188, 225, 306; E401/1961, p. 126; E360/145, Accounts of Samuel Williams.

[73] *Cal.S.P.Dom.*, 1671, pp. 322–3; Brit. Lib., Addit. MS 33278 (Madden Collection), fol. 40; P.R.O., E401/1947, pp. 75, 175; E401/1956, p. 105; E401/1960, pp. 203–4; *Cal.Treas.Bks.*, iv. 132, 297; v. 208, 1409; P.R.O., P.C. 2/63, p. 290.

[74] P.R.O., E122/218/11; Chandaman, *The English Public Revenue*, pp. 117–18.

[75] Marshall, 'The levying of the hearth tax', pp. 631–2; Bodl., MS Clarendon 84, fol. 98.

[76] *The Hearth Tax Returns for the Isle of Wight 1664–1674*, ed. P. D. D. Russell (Isle of Wight County Record Office, 1981), Appendix, pp. 230–1; the payment of the £3,884 12s 6d due for the year ending Lady Day 1674 into the Exchequer did not take place until nearly three years later at the beginning of March 1677, P.R.O., E360/145: Account of Simon Smith for the hearth tax in Hampshire for the year ending Lady Day 1674; C. A. F. Meekings, *Analysis of Hearth Tax Accounts 1666–99* (List and Index Society, vol. 163, 1980), fol. 44.

modities to which it was applied. According to Beloff, there were no excise riots in the Restoration period.[77] Cases of opposition by individuals to the excise abound in the Treasury books, but these are not always what they seem. In October 1671, Joseph and Matthew Phripp of Cowes assaulted a local excise officer on only a slight provocation, Joseph describing the excisemen generally as a company of rogues who came to abuse 'the country'. This may have been a cry of wounded innocence, but Matthew Phripp's case was rather more complex. He had failed to pay the hearth tax upon his empty house in West Cowes in 1669 and 1670, and as an innkeeper was simultaneously in trouble with the wine licence authorities for failure to pay that duty. During the second Dutch War, Phripp, whilst serving as an ensign in locally stationed forces had abused his position to steal prize goods, which also came to light in the early 1670s. Matthew Phripp in other words was simply a dishonest man with a strong aversion to paying taxes. One wonders how many more of those who came before the Treasury for evading taxes were of the same ilk. Nevertheless, the Treasury Commissioners agreed that there was wrong on both sides in the Phripp case, and effectively defused the situation. But the excessive zeal of revenue men could and did provoke widespread resistance in the Isle of Wight community. The islanders resented the checks placed upon their trade with the mainland by customs officers at Southampton in their determination to eliminate smuggling. Again the Treasury was obliged to mediate.[78]

In the successful and efficient raising of Crown revenue, much depended on the attitude of the gentry, or more particularly, the magisterial element within that class. JPs had a vital role in the management of revenue collection in the counties. Until 1664, they had an important part to play in the raising of the hearth tax, and they continued to have an important supporting role. Magistrates were also in charge of adjudicating matters arising from the excise, though this of course was by no means a new development in 1663, when the Cavalier Parliament passed an act for the better ordering of the excise. JPs had other miscellaneous tasks under early Restoration legislation, for example, issuing warrants for the levying of carriage upon the counties.[79]

Historians who have studied the central administration of the Restoration period generally have a pessimistic view of the attitude of JPs towards the government's revenue. Professor Baxter has spoken of JPs in general in this period as 'certainly less than sympathetic to the needs of the central adminis-

---

[77] M. Beloff, *Public Order and Popular Disturbances 1660–1714* (London, 1938), pp. 93–4.
[78] *Cal.Treas.Bks.*, iii. 1042, 1046, 1047, 1178, 1184; *Cal.Treas.Bks.*, iv. 335, 337, 346, 821, 844; v. 113, 647–8, 1376; *The Hearth Tax . . . Isle of Wight*, ed. Russell, Appendix, p. 227; P.R.O., E122/218/11; *Cal.S.P.Dom.*, 1671, p. 186–7.
[79] Chandaman, *The English Public Revenue*, pp. 43–4, 81–6; *S.R.*, v. 413–14.

tration'.[80] But though some justices were clearly irresponsible and uncooperative, can this really be said to have been true of JPs in general? Acting as a body, Hampshire's magistrates seem to have been far from unsympathetic to the government's needs.[81] In 1662, they held a special sessions in order to settle the excise and hearth tax in their county. And in 1663, the quarter sessions issued a special order 'for the more perfect and exact making up of the returns for fire hearths', and laying down that divisional meetings be held for that purpose.[82] If the initial returns of the hearth tax were not as good as they might have been, this does not appear to have been the fault of JPs, at least in Hampshire. At the same time, their initial response to the need to levy carriage on the county for ships' timber was positive, meeting naval officials and promising to make examples of defaulters. However, the enthusiasm of some waned as they faced strong opposition from the local population, and they incurred a sharp rebuke from the Privy Council for their pains.[83] But the JPs did not necessarily oppose central government even when its fiscal demands encroached upon county government. In 1671, the Crown obtained a ruling from the lord keeper and some of the judges, that the recently granted law duty could be raised from the recognizances given by alehouse-keepers in the counties. The Privy Council dispatched a letter to JPs ordering that returns be made of all recognizances from alehouse-keepers so that they could be taxed at 2s 6d each, and also that unlicensed alehouses be suppressed. At their next quarter sessions, Hampshire's JPs complied with the orders they had received, delegating a JP to communicate them to each division.[84]

JPs seemed to show a similarly responsible attitude when acting as subsidy commissioners in 1671. (The Crown seems to have recruited these men from the bench.) Sir George Downing, the secretary to the Treasury, thanked the commissioners in Hampshire for their care in setting and assessing the subsidy locally. If subsequent performance did not live up to expectation this was probably the fault of lesser officials.[85]

There were of course some justices who, acting out of sessions, were capable of making judgements which were detrimental to the government's interest. On 26 November 1663, Sir Andrew Henley and Benjamin Rudyard sitting out of sessions, gave a judgement in favour of three innkeepers (two

[80] Baxter, *Treasury*, p. 80.
[81] Dr Ronald Hutton, while generally endorsing the pessimistic views of earlier historians, acknowledges that Hampshire's JPs were more dutiful, Hutton, *The Restoration*, pp. 238, 359 n. 87.
[82] H.C.R.O., QO 4, p. 124; Brit. Lib., MS Sloane, 813, fol. 65.
[83] *Cal.S.P.Dom.*, 1663–4, pp. 25, 59–60, 263; S.P. 29/68, fol. 315; *Cal.S.P.Dom.*, Add. 1660–85, p. 101.
[84] P.R.O., P.C. 2/63, pp. 40–2; H.C.R.O., QO 4, p. 333; *Cal.Treas.Bks.*, iv. 24–5.
[85] *Cal.Treas.Bks.*, iii. 875, 1143.

from Hartley Row and one from Elvetham) who were charged with refusal to pay the excise. This decision was upheld at the Epiphany quarter sessions following, but only because the excise officials failed to appear to make good their charge. Again, acting out of sessions, Richard Norton failed to countenance the levying of the duty on alehouse recognizances at the beginning of 1673, and his attitude delayed its payment, so Sir Robert Howard, now secretary to the Treasury, wrote to remonstrate with him.[86]

But when government had the law on its side (and this was where the statutory basis of taxation was so vital) and it appealed to magistrates to conform with its wishes, it usually had its way. Lord Treasurer Southampton wrote to Hampshire's JPs remonstrating with them about their decision in the case of the three innkeepers in January 1664, referring them to the excise legislation, and pointing out that one of the innkeepers had tried to use their order to encourage others to resist the tax. Southampton was hopeful of their compliance, and he was not disappointed. In response to his appeal, the offending order was declared void and the proceedings of the excise sub-commissioners against the innkeepers therefore legal. In subsequent cases, government ministers rested their argument upon what the statutes actually said, which seemed to be compelling with local justices.[87] But legislation cut both ways. JPs too were capable of reading the statutes and basing their arguments upon them, as for example when the Epiphany quarter sessions of 1675 in Hampshire decided that kilns which the hearth-tax officers were charging did not come within the scope of the relevant act of Parliament.[88] But JPs were not as a body unsympathetic to central needs. They were generally keen that government should raise the money to which it was entitled from the provinces. Writing to Sir Joseph Williamson in 1676, about the matter of local customs dues, Sir Robert Dillington of the Isle of Wight drew attention to the recently discovered frauds in local customs administration. He added, 'I could heartily wish undue practices might be severely punished, for through these abuses a scandall reflects on the country . . .'[89]

But if local communities closed ranks against them, both government and justices might be powerless. The excise officers had no difficulty obtaining a warrant from Richard Compton and Henry Bromfield, JPs, against Henry Swettingham of Sopley, for selling beer without paying excise on it in 1665. But most of the parishioners of Sopley then signed a certificate to say that Swettingham had never sold beer there. The quarter sessions court had no alternative but to suspend the warrant against Swettingham and refer it to local justices to investigate.[90]

[86] H.C.R.O., QO 4, pp. 163–4; *Cal.Treas.Bks.*, iv. 28.
[87] *Cal.Treas.Bks.*, i. 579, 595; iii. 1047; iv. 29; H.C.R.O., QO 4, p. 169.
[88] H.C.R.O., QO 5, p. 76.
[89] P.R.O., S.P. 29/381, fol. 258.   [90] H.C.R.O., QO 5, p. 76.

In a number of ways, central government was heavily involved in the localities after 1660 to ensure that its revenue was effectively collected and paid in. In fact, the fiscal system of the Restoration was in some ways more centralized than that of the 1650s. Heavy taxation which persisted during the 1660s and into the 1670s was unpopular, and tardily paid. But at least in Hampshire, the gentry or those who acted as JPs were generally sympathetic to government's needs and obedient to its will. The Restoration regime did not resort to using troops to raise its taxes, and the mere existence of an unpaid army did not necessarily have the impact on Hampshire that one might have expected. One of the worst paid direct taxes of the reign of Charles II in the county was that raised to pay off the army in 1660–1. One invaluable asset which the Restoration government did have and use, was an unimpeachable statutory basis to all its taxes which it tried to raise from the country, which in practice more than made up for the lack of a large standing army to aid collection.

LOCAL GOVERNMENT AND THE PRESERVATION OF ORDER AFTER THE RESTORATION

The Restoration has been associated with the waning of government interest in the supervision of local social administration.[91] But what is often lost sight of is the extent to which order had been redefined in political terms since 1640, at least in the mind of central government. The major-generals experiment was more concerned with security than with social policy, and its impact in the latter area was generally limited. The change of perspective from the centre also needs to be put firmly in its economic and political context. The passing of dearth crises and the stabilization of prices from the mid-century reduced the threat of disorder amongst the poorer sections of the population, who had already shown themselves to be much less of a danger to the government than ideologically inspired rebels of one sort or another. So the Restoration government in its early years was keen to revive the militia to guard itself against republican conspiracy rather than vagrants, although the royal instructions to the earl of Southampton as lord lieutenant in 1660 contained an order to suppress vagrancy and idle persons without a profession or trade.[92]

The primary concern of central government in this period was the prevention of politically inspired disorder and rebellion in the provinces. The routine maintenance of order was left to local magistrates and the forces at

---

[91] K. Wrightson, *English Society 1580–1680* (London, 1982), p. 228; Fletcher, *Reform in the Provinces*, pp. 47, 358.
[92] Brit. Lib., Addit. MS 21922, fol. 240.

their disposal. But if they had difficulty containing a disorder, they might appeal to their superiors at county or national level for assistance. The magistrates at Southampton in the early Restoration period faced a dual threat from disaffection on the one hand and popular turbulence on the other. In 1661, twenty-two disorderly persons were cited before sessions for indulging in a skimmington ride. In June 1662, Secretary Nicholas wrote to the mayor to encourage him in his struggle against 'severall persons of froward & obstinate temper who continue to oppose or disturbe' the good government of the town, and to report their names to the Council.[93] It was doubtless this which encouraged the next mayor in the following February to report the occurrence of a corn riot at the town to the Privy Council. From the Council's reply it appears that 'some multitudes of the Common sort of people have tumultuously assaulted and offered violence to such as bring corne the [sic] markett at Southampton'.[94] But the town trained bands were rapidly mustered and the tumult effectively dealt with, without intervention by the government. To prevent such disorder recurring the Council ordered the mayor to prevent the export of grain locally unless prices fell below the statutory level when it could be exported. A grain riot which occurred at Christchurch at about the same time was dealt with by the courts of the borough and of the county, though there was talk at one point of raising *posse comitatus* against the rioters.[95] The trained bands generally showed themselves capable of dealing with such localized disorders. When some people broke out of the houses which had been shut up in plague-ridden Winchester in July 1666 to raid the houses of the better sort and open the gaol, they were surprised by a detachment of the militia which had been posted in the city. One of the rioters was killed and three were wounded.[96] But when the county militia itself was the target of a riot at Southampton in March 1678, Edward Noel, the lord lieutenant, found it necessary to appeal to the Privy Council to order local JPs to help bring five named culprits to justice.[97]

The drive for order of the pre-Civil-War period, far from being blunted by the Restoration, was actually fulfilled under it. The immobilization of the poor, which was a crucial part of it, came a step nearer with the law of settlement in 1662, which codified the results of local initiatives going back some decades.[98] The role of central government in such measures and their enforce-

[93] S.C.R.O., SC2/1/8, fol. 170; P.R.O., S.P. 44/3, p. 61.
[94] P.R.O., P.C. 2/56, p. 317.
[95] *Cal.S.P.Dom.*, 1663–4, pp. 74, 130–1; H.C.R.O., QO 4, pp. 132–3, 142–3.
[96] *Verney Memoirs*, iv, 136; Dr Slack cites this incident but misplaces it in Portsmouth rather than Winchester, P. Slack, *The Impact of Plague in Tudor and Stuart England* (London, 1985), p. 302.
[97] P.R.O., P.C. 2/66, p. 301.
[98] P. Styles, 'The evolution of the law of settlement', *University of Birmingham Historical Journal*, 9 (1963–4), 33–63.

ment was limited. But the Crown did have a part to play in backing up such legislation, for example by naming sufficient JPs and encouraging them to act. There was a far better spread of JPs in Hampshire's commission after the Restoration than before, so that petty sessions were kept up in the divisions.[99] The activity of JPs was a sure bulwark in the preservation of order and the government realized this. On 25 March 1665, at the king's request, Lord Chancellor Clarendon wrote a long circular letter to JPs in which active justices were warmly praised, the king thinking himself 'to be p[ar]ticularly beholding to every good Justice of the peace who is cheerful & active in his place'. But the negligent who could not be bothered to be sworn or to attend quarter sessions would be disciplined by their removal from the commission of the peace. Monthly meetings and the watch were to be kept up. In this way the government hoped to suppress 'seditious meetings or Conventicles' and discover the plots of the 'ill-affected'.[100] The object of the government's anxieties was as ever republican conspiracy, but the proposed solutions to the problem had a strangely old-fashioned ring to them.

The Restoration government was capable of traditional forms of intervention in local administration, as is demonstrated by its handling of the plague in 1665–6. The country had been free from epidemics of the plague between 1654 and 1664, so this was a problem which the Protectorate government had been spared.[101] The plague of 1665–6 was regionally selective, leaving large areas of the country unaffected, but it spread rapidly from London to several towns in Hampshire in the summer of 1665.[102] The government soon became involved in trying to contain and relieve afflicted areas, sometimes in response to appeals from local magistrates. One such appeal to Lord Ashley from magistrates at Southampton on 4 July 1665 received a prompt response in the form of a letter from the Privy Council which catalogued the steps that had already been taken. These included a collection made for infected places on the monthly fast day, orders to the neighbouring justices to bring in provisions and the sending of a physician to Southampton at royal expense. A letter to the five local justices ordered them not only to supply Southampton with provisions, but also to keep watch and ward to prevent the plague from spreading. The Council took other measures

---

[99] H.C.R.O., QO 4, pp. 82, 156, 254.

[100] This letter was taken seriously locally – the bailiff of Andover ordered a copy for the borough from the deputy clerk of the peace at a cost of 5s, H.C.R.O., 37M84, 4/AC/10, 1664–5; for copies of the letter *Hist. MSS Comm. Various Collections*, ii. 379–80; All Souls College, Oxford, All Souls MS 239, fol. 165.

[101] Slack, *The Impact of the Plague*, p. 68.

[102] It was at Fareham near Portsmouth as early as May, in Southampton in June and in Alton soon after that, J. Taylor, 'Plague in the towns of Hampshire: the epidemic of 1665–6', *Southern History*, 6 (1984), 104–5.

like banning local fairs on 28 August 1665.[103] Meanwhile, the local informants of the secretary of state kept Williamson posted on the spread of the infection.[104]

The government appealed to or reprimanded local magistrates as yet more towns, including Portsmouth and Petersfield fell victim to the plague.[105] But such localized orders were of limited value. The justices appealed to might respond positively as they did near Southampton, but those further away proved recalcitrant in relieving afflicted areas.[106] What was called for was an updated version of the traditional plague orders which could be universally applied.

Characteristically, the Restoration government waited on Parliament to give a revised version of the plague orders clear statutory backing, but for once Parliament, which had so effectively codified local militia and poor law practices, failed to deliver. Instead the government was obliged to press ahead on its own, issuing the *Rules and Orders* as a proclamation from the king and Council on 11 May 1666, addressed to all magistrates. This produced results at Hampshire's summer quarter sessions, held by royal permission at Basingstoke instead of Winchester. One JP in each division was appointed treasurer to receive and disburse the money, and there is evidence that this was enforced in the New Forest division. Gentry who lived near Winchester found themselves paying a weekly tax for the second year running.[107]

Although cases of plague were reported in London as late as 1679, the epidemic of 1665–6 was the last of its kind in England. According to Dr Slack, this may at least in part be attributed to government action.[108] With the passing of the last major outbreak, another traditional form of central government interference in the localities was rendered redundant, although the Privy Council would continue to badger the mayor of Portsmouth about the need for cleanliness and public hygiene to prevent infections there for several years to come.[109]

[103] P.R.O., P.C. 2/58, p. 209; R. Steele, *A Bibliography of royal proclamations of the Tudor and Stuart sovereigns and of others published under authority, 1485–1714* (2 vols., Oxford, 1910), i. no. 3431, p. 414.
[104] E.g. Colonel Walter Slingsby [W.S.], *Cal.S.P.Dom.*, 1664–5, pp. 446, 515.
[105] *Cal.S.P.Dom.*, 1665–6, pp. 355, 374–5.
[106] *Cal.S.P.Dom.*, 1664–5, p. 510.
[107] Slack, *The Impact of Plague*, pp. 223–5; Steele, *Proclamations*, i. no. 3461, p. 417; H.C.R.O., QO 5, pp. 231–2; Christchurch Civic Offices, council minute book 1615–1857, warrant attached to p. 116; Brit. Lib., Verney MSS microfilm M/636, reel no. 21, Cary Gardiner to Sir Ralph Verney, 13 Aug. 1666.
[108] Slack, *The Impact of Plague*, pp. 69, 311–37.
[109] E.g. P.R.O., P.C. 2/63, p. 28.

RELIGIOUS POLICY

Interregnum governments had striven to establish a coherent religious policy. But under their rule, the church in England had been highly decentralized, with considerable parochial autonomy and a wide degree of toleration in practice. The laissez-faire policies of those in power at the centre were not based on accurate knowledge of the religious views or preferences of the majority in the provinces, but on an ideological commitment to the 'godly' minority there. From the point of view of the central direction of the nation's religious life, the 1650s had undoubtedly been the nadir. In the following section, the record of the restored monarchy in this highly sensitive area will be examined.

Recent accounts of the religious history of the reign of Charles II have stressed the failure of the king to carry out his policy of comprehension, or even toleration towards Protestant dissenters, or to obtain lasting relief for Roman Catholics. An intolerant Anglican settlement was forced on the king by the majority in the Cavalier Parliament, and Charles' attempts to modify it using his prerogative notably in 1662–3 and 1672–3, ended in failure. The provincial gentry outside Parliament have also been implicated in this set-back.[110] The defeat of the king's personal policy and the inconsistency of his government on the religious issue have been used to demonstrate its supposed weakness. Dr Hutton has gone as far as to suggest that they show 'the extraordinary ramshackle nature of the restored monarchy'.[111]

Some historians are understandably sceptical about this new emphasis, which certainly underestimates several vital factors in the situation.[112] No one has adequately addressed the problem of whether it was a viable policy to exploit the Cavalier spirit in connection with the Corporation Act, while resisting it over uniformity as Charles II tried to do. Insufficient account is often taken of the king's personal weakness in bringing about the defeat of his policy. As Ollard has aptly written of Charles' commitment to toleration, 'There is no reason whatever to doubt the sincerity of his opinions, but the evidence tells against their strength.'[113]

[110] Green, *The Re-Establishment of the Church of England*; R. A. Beddard, 'The Restoration church', *The Restored Monarchy 1660–1688*, ed. J. R. Jones (London, 1979), pp. 155–75; B. Reay, 'The authorities and early Restoration Quakerism', *Journal of Ecclesiastical History*, xxxiv. (1983), 69, 84.

[111] Dr Hutton makes this judgement in the context of the hardline episcopalian views which Sir John Berkenhead was able to voice through the official press, without any discouragement from the king, Hutton, *The Restoration*, p. 174.

[112] See for example Professor K. H. D. Haley's review of Dr Hutton's book, *History*, 71 (1986), 155.

[113] Ollard, *The Image of the King*, p. 106; to be fair Dr Green is fully aware of this factor in the making of the settlement, Green, *The Re-Establishment of the Church of England*, pp. 127–8.

The king was clearly involved in the revival of the traditional Anglican church in Hampshire, from soon after his restoration. The dean and chapter repossessed Winchester cathedral on 19 August 1660, and on the 28th, the king nominated Brian Duppa to the vacant see. Both bishop and chapter were soon appointing officials and collecting rents and in October, the king ordered all lay tenants to leave the close. Charles purported to stand for a form of modified episcopacy in his Worcester House Declaration of October 1660, yet did little to bring it about, and then assented to the restoration of bishops' coercive powers with only minor modifications in 1661. Following the passage of the Ecclesiastical Causes Act, the consistory court was revived at Winchester, holding its first meeting on 5 October 1661.[114] In 1662, it began calling Quakers before it for failure to attend their parish churches.[115]

As Dr Green has shown, Charles did make some effort to achieve a comprehensive church at parish level, through the balanced use of patronage between 1660 and 1662. Between 1 June and 9 September 1660, fifteen Interregnum incumbents were confirmed in their livings in Hampshire by means of royal presentment, and four other conformists were newly presented.[116] But at the same time, twenty Interregnum incumbents were removed to make way for ejected predecessors.[117] However, harassment of ministers for failure to use the Book of Common Prayer does seem to have been rare before the Act of Uniformity came into force.[118]

Charles retreated from his policy of comprehension and toleration albeit reluctantly, first by assenting to the uniformity bill, then by abandoning the idea of individual indulgences for ministers and finally by withdrawing his Declaration of Indulgence in 1663, under pressure from the majority in the Cavalier Parliament. As a result a narrow, intolerant Anglican church was established, and some thirty ministers were ejected from livings in Hampshire for failure to conform.[119]

---

[114] Green, *The Re-Establishment of the Church of England*, pp. 72–3, 106, 126–8, 134, 255; *Documents relating to the History of the Cathedral Church of Winchester*, ed. Stephens and Madge, ii. 105.

[115] H.C.R.O., 24M54/14, fol. 15.

[116] Green, *The Re-Establishment of the Church of England*, appendix 2, pp. 246–8.

[117] At least four more were removed before the Act of Uniformity came into force in 1662, A. G. Matthews, *Calamy Revised* (Oxford, 1934), *passim*.

[118] Dr Green found only two Hampshire ministers prosecuted for this at the autumn assizes of 1661, *The Re-Establishment of the Church of England*, p. 191; Basingstoke corporation removed its lecturer in January 1662 for failure to conform, see above, pp. 91–2; shortly before St Bartholomew's Day, two of the deputy-lieutenants were involved in hunting down Humphrey Ellis, a minister ejected at Winchester in 1660, who had since obtained a living in Dorset, from which he would shortly be ejected as well, Brit. Lib., Addit. MS 21922, fols. 252–3, 256.

[119] Matthews, *Calamy Revised*, *passim*; supplemented by Mildon, 'Puritanism in Hampshire', pp. 374–6.

The settlement may have been a personal defeat for Charles, but it was also a set-back for parochialism, and an opportunity for central control. Local religious life was again under the eye of a royal nominee, lacking local roots. The practices of the clergy and parochial officials were now subject to close external scrutiny, as the surviving churchwardens' accounts for Hampshire clearly testify.[120] Many churchwardens were unprepared for the loss of independence which the restoration of episcopacy represented and failed to attend George Morley's primary visitation as bishop of Winchester in 1662.[121] The restored church structure provided a means for government to acquire a greater awareness of local religious observance, an awareness which had quite eluded the governments of the 1650s. However, the diocesan machinery embarked falteringly upon its role of gathering information. When he wrote to Clarendon on 28 August 1662, Bishop Morley thought that there were only eight ministers in the whole of Hampshire who had failed to conform, and when he wrote again ten days later, towards the end of his visitation, he still thought there were only nine.[122] But gradually, through the diocesan machinery, Morley began to gain a more realistic impression of the extent of nonconformity in the county. In 1664, he had an abstract made of all the churchwardens presentments from his annual visitation for the county of Hampshire. This showed that 976 persons did not come to church of whom 599 were sectaries of unspecified sort, 29 were Quakers, 19 were Anabaptists, 1 was a Familist and 201 were Catholics. These figures were under-estimates, and there were gaps in them.[123] But at least the names and approximate geographical distribution of nonconformists were now known to the diocesan authorities.

This sort of information was increasingly placed at the disposal of central government. No returns of dissenters survive for Hampshire for 1665, and those of conventicles for 1669 are incomplete. But it was clear that several thousand people were attending conventicles of one sort or another. More detailed figures, at least of uncompromising nonconformists, were returned in 1676 in the Compton Census, which revealed 3,714 nonconformists and 846 Catholics in Hampshire, as against 70,660 conformists, over sixteen years of age.[124]

---

[120] E.g. H.C.R.O., 68M70 PW1; 1M70 PW1; 88M81W PW2.
[121] Green, *The Re-Establishment of the Church of England*, pp. 138–9.
[122] Bodl., MS Clarendon 73, fols. 216–17; MS Clarendon 77, fol. 207.
[123] For example there was a 'nil' return for Whitchurch where there is known to have been a Baptist church, Whitley, 'Early Baptists in Hampshire', p. 225; H.C.R.O., Winchester Diocesan Records B/1/A–4, no. 36.
[124] *Original Records of Early Nonconformity under Persecution and Indulgence*, ed. G. Lyon Turner (3 vols., London, 1911–14), i. 136–43; *The Compton Census of 1676: a critical edition*, ed. A. Whiteman with assistance of M. Clapinson (Records of Social and Economic History, new series, X,O.U.P., 1986), p. 96.

But it was one thing to gather this information, quite another to act upon it. Opinion at Whitehall was divided over religious policy for much of the first twenty years of the reign, as it had been for much of the 1650s. Some ministers like Arlington supported the king's Declaration of Indulgence in 1662–3, others like Lord Treasurer Southampton opposed it. But in 1665, Southampton argued against the Five Mile bill, while the court prelates Archbishop Sheldon and Bishop Morley supported it. Sir Thomas Osborne served in the tolerationist regime of 1672–3, only to complete the reversal of its religious policy in 1675 and after when he became earl of Danby.[125] These divisions did not necessarily weaken the government; in fact, as will be argued below, they paradoxically contributed to stability at least before 1672.[126]

As in the 1650s, so in the 1660s, much of the pressure for religious intolerance came from the provinces, especially through Parliament. Yet Charles and his ministers cannot be exonerated of the persecution which did take place, as at several points they clearly encouraged it for their own purposes. In January 1661, the king ordered all conventicles of Anabaptists, Quakers and Fifth Monarchy Men to be suppressed.[127] In Hampshire, members of the lieutenancy took the king at his word. On 13 January 1661, Sir Robert Howard wrote to Sir Andrew Henley from London, 'by this King's proclamation you see what strictness must be used. The Oath of Aleagence must be constantly tendred; and all Conventicle meetings of the Phanatiques disturbed & prevented.'[128] In May 1662, Charles assented to the act which effectively outlawed the Quakers.[129] He used the fear of nonconformist plots to get measures of which he approved through Parliament, and his irresponsible scare-mongering had its impact on MPs, who were also deputy-lieutenants in the counties. Two admittedly hardline deputy-lieutenants, Sir Humphrey Bennet and Sir John Norton, explained their zeal to Lord Treasurer Southampton in October 1662 as follows, 'for his Ma[jes]tie having acquainted the house of Commons [of which they were both members] with the unquiet motions of some restless spirits which were busy in several parts to designe us new troubles'.[130] In the wake of the plot of 1663, Charles gave

---

[125] Green, *The Re-Establishment of the Church of England*, pp. 219–20; D.N.B., Thomas Wriothesley, fourth earl of Southampton (1607–67); C. Robbins, 'The Oxford Session of the Long Parliament of Charles II, 9–31 October 1665', B.I.H.R., 21 (1946–8), 214–24; A. Browning, *Thomas Osborne, Earl of Danby and Duke of Leeds* (3 vols., Glasgow, 1944–51), i. 89–102, 146–84.

[126] See below, p. 148.

[127] For the proclamation, see Steele, *Proclamation*, i. no. 3278, pp. 393–4; this was followed by a conciliar letter calling on deputy-lieutenants to apprehend dangerous persons and tender the oaths of supremacy and allegiance to them, Brit. Lib., Addit. MS 21922, fol. 246.

[128] Brit. Lib., MS Sloane 3299, fol. 24.

[129] Reay, 'The authorities and early Restoration Quakerism', pp. 73–4.

[130] Brit. Lib., Addit. MS 21922, fol. 250.

his assent and support to the Conventicle bill in 1664, and even allowed the Five Mile Act to pass in 1665. Though the exact motivation for it is far from clear, Charles II's government returned to a policy of persecution in the late 1660s.[131] In 1668 and 1669, proclamations were issued against conventicles; Arlington wrote to Sir Robert Holmes, the new governor of the Isle of Wight, on 21 June 1669, ordering him to call together some 'discreet justices' to enquire into unlawful meetings, which were then to be suppressed and the leaders 'severely proceeded against according to law'.[132] Soon after this came the second Conventicle Act, which Charles fully endorsed and supported.

When the Caroline toleration finally became a reality in the Declaration of Indulgence of 1672, it was very different from the Commonwealth and Cromwellian models which had preceded it. Those nonconformist ministers who wished to profit from it had to apply personally to the government to obtain a licence, and particular premises had to be licensed for worship. The Restoration government's desire for information and control were evident, even when it was pursuing a policy of toleration. Forty-six nonconformist ministers (including four Baptists) obtained licences to preach within Hampshire and thirty houses were licensed for worship.[133]

But Charles abandoned his Declaration of Indulgence in 1673 in the face of parliamentary opposition and gradually returned to the policy of persecution in 1675 and after. In 1676, assize judges were ordered to charge justices to enforce the laws against recusants and conventicles.[134] This remained official government policy until the Popish Plot of 1678.

It is unfortunately very difficult to assess the full impact of government policy at local level, in Hampshire or in any other county in this period. There is a major problem of evidence about persecution.[135] County records are incomplete.[136] Under the Clarendon code, procedure against nonconformists became highly decentralized, taking place mostly through borough courts or

[131] For possible reasons, J. Miller, *Popery and Politics 1660–1688* (Cambridge, 1973), pp. 107, 113.

[132] R. Hutton, 'The making of the secret treaty of Dover 1668–70', *H.J.*, 29 (1986), 313–16; Steele, *Proclamations*, i. no. 3514, p. 424; no. 3529, p. 426; I.W.C.R.O., Jerome collection, MS Swainston 183.

[133] F. Bate, *The Declaration of Indulgence: a study in the rise of organized dissent* (Liverpool, 1908), appendix vii, pp. xxix–xxx, lxviii; Bate omits Robert Whitaker, licensed to preach at the house of William Bulkeley at Burgate, Fordingbridge, *Cal.S.P.Dom.*, 1671–2, p. 357.

[134] *Hist. MSS Comm. Twelfth Report, App. pt VII, Le Fleming MSS*, p. 125; I am grateful to Anthony Fletcher for this reference.

[135] See Hutton, *The Restoration*, p. 210, in the context of the Conventicle Act.

[136] Hampshire, as a county on the western circuit has no assize minute book, indictments or depositions relating to it in the 1660s, only a bail book covering the period 1654–77 survives and gaol books covering the period after 1670; see Green, *The Re-Establishment of the Church of England*, p. 191; at the level of quarter sessions, the situation is hardly better with no sessions rolls or record of presentments or indictments between 1660 and the 1680s, and only occasional references to conventicles in the order books.

county justices acting out of sessions. This process culminated in the second
Conventicle Act under which a single justice could convict, and was only
required to return a certificate of conviction at the quarter sessions.[137] No
Hampshire borough has a totally comprehensive set of judicial records for
this period, a deficiency which is partly compensated for by the records of
Quaker sufferings, but these of necessity only relate to this particular sort of
dissenter.[138] For another sort, the ministers ejected after the Restoration,
there are the works of Calamy.[139] Apart from these, there are occasional press
reports or pamphlets or documents in gentry collections, which throw some
light on the extent of persecution locally. But the gaps in the evidence make
it difficult, if not impossible, to be dogmatic about the exact limits of
persecution.

Nevertheless, piecing together the various bits of evidence, it is possible to
form an impression of the rhythm of persecution in Hampshire, in the first
eighteen years of Charles II's reign. Before January 1661, persecution even of
Quakers seems to have been a spasmodic phenomenon. John Pidgeon, a
Quaker from Crawley, was arrested on 10 October 1660 and brought before
justices sitting at Winchester and imprisoned for failing to take the oaths of
supremacy and allegiance or promise not to have more than five people meet
at his house. His relative Samuel followed him to gaol in November, and Sir
Humphrey Bennet boasted about the proceedings to Secretary Nicholas. The
only place where persecution seems to have been carried out systematically at
this time, even against Quakers, was at Portsmouth, under the auspices of
officers and soldiers of the garrison, men in the government's pay and under
its orders. This often sadistic persecution persisted during 1661.[140]

The most devastating persecution of the early Restoration period was
unleashed by a royal proclamation, when Parliament was not sitting, in
January 1661. There were sweeping arrests in Hampshire as elsewhere,
mostly carried out by the deputy-lieutenants and some Quakers were even
apprehended on the highway, as Ambrose Rigg was at Petersfield. The oaths
of supremacy and allegiance were tendered and on their refusal the Quakers
were imprisoned, eighty-one of them in Hampshire. Most of them were

---

137   S.R., v. 649–50.
138   H.C.R.O., 24M54/14 County Sufferings Book 1655–1799; 24M54/151 List of Friends
      imprisoned at Basingstoke 1667–1832.
139   E. Calamy, *An Abridgement of Mr Baxter's History of His Life and Times with an Account
      of the Ministers, Lecturers, Masters and Fellows of Colleges and Schoolmasters who were
      ejected or silenced after the Restoration in 1660, By or Before the Act of Uniformity* (2nd
      edn, 2 vols., London, 1713); and *A Continuation of the Account of the Ministers* [etc.]
      (2 vols., London, 1727); these works are cited below for anecdotal references to certain
      ministers which are not included in Matthews' revision.
140   H.C.R.O., 24M54/14, fols. 6–10, 12–14; *Cal.S.P.Dom.*, 1660–1, p. 319.

released at royal command at the time of the coronation.[141] At this stage, before the passage of the Act of Uniformity, dissent does not seem to have been sufficiently widespread to be alarming even to staunch royalists in Hampshire. The deputy-lieutenants reported in September 1661, 'wee cannot find (unless in some few places by the Quakers) any meetings that may give us grounds to feare the disturbance of the publique peace in this county'.[142]

It was a year before the vigorous persecution of nonconformists resumed in Hampshire, and when it did its targets were carefully selected. In the autumn of 1662, prominent individual Quakers were picked up under the Quaker Act. George Embree at Southampton had a moderate fine of ten shillings imposed upon him, and on his refusal to pay was sent home, pending distraint, and ultimately was imprisoned for nearly five weeks. In October, the deputy-lieutenants sent Humphrey Smith, a Quaker evangelist to the county gaol, where in November he was joined by John Bishop, a leading Quaker from the Isle of Wight, sent there by local justices for refusing the oaths of supremacy and allegiance. Smith died in prison the following May.[143]

Initially only those nonconformist ministers who drew attention to themselves seem to have been punished. Nathaniel Robinson, leader of the Independent church at Southampton, was detained after he confronted Bishop Morley on his primary visitation and called the confirmations he was conducting a 'stage play'. But on his humble submission and promise of reformation and conformity, he was dismissed with the payment of a small fine. James Wise, a Fifth Monarchist, was committed to gaol at Southampton for preaching, and when he continued to preach through the bars of his cell, he was sent to Calshot castle. The main priority of the local authorities in Hampshire at this stage seems to have been to prevent nonconformity from spreading. Benjamin Burgess, ejected minister at Portsmouth was bailed in November 1662, on his promise to leave the town and not draw any citizens into nonconformity.[144]

At Southampton, the policy of containment developed into a full-scale campaign against conventicles, whether Quaker, Baptist or Independent, but those who promised conformity were let off with small fines and a warning. But such a policy was useless when dealing with Quakers who would neither promise conformity, pay fines or even take their hats off in court, and so they suffered lengthy periods of confinement.[145]

[141] H.C.R.O., 24M54/14, fols. 6, 9–10, 12.   [142] Brit. Lib., Addit. MS 21922, fol. 247.
[143] H.C.R.O., 24M54/14, fols. 10, 15, 18.
[144] Brit. Lib., Addit. MS 21922, fol. 257; *Mercurius Publicus*, no. 39, 25 Sept.–2 Oct. 1662, p. 644; *Mercurius Publicus*, no. 49, 4–11 Dec. 1662; Matthews, *Calamy Revised*, p. 87.
[145] *Mercurius Publicus*, no. 49, 4–11 Dec. 1662; H.C.R.O., 24M54/14, fols. 11–12.

The following autumn, 1663, saw a similar campaign against conventicles in Southampton. At the quarter sessions in September, twenty men and several women, largely Independents and Baptists were presented by the grand jury for holding or attending conventicles. In October, an unspecified number of nonconformists were fined the minimum twelve pence for non-attendance at church. On his refusal to pay or promise to desist from meeting, Henry Cox, an Independent minister, was ordered to be committed or find sureties for his good behaviour. Six Quakers were also committed to prison because they would not promise to refrain from meeting. Two of them remained in prison until 10 December.[146]

The Quakers attracted persecution elsewhere in the county in 1663. On 31 May, a Quaker meeting attended by George Fox at Poulnar, near Ringwood, was broken up by the local militia regiment and thirteen were imprisoned. One of them died in prison, and ten others would spend much of the next eight years in prison for refusing to pay fines. Though they were paroled and their fines reduced, nine of them were not finally released until they were pardoned by the king in 1672.[147]

The Conventicle Act which passed in 1664 was quite widely enforced in its first year of operation.[148] In Hampshire, it was used against Quakers on the Isle of Wight and at Southampton during that period.[149] But those ejected ministers who continued to attend their parish churches seem to have escaped persecution almost entirely. The meetings which some of them held at their houses were ignored. Lord Treasurer Southampton wanted such men to be licensed to preach, though the majority of the Cavalier Parliament passed the Five Mile Act against them in 1665. Some ejected ministers in Hampshire sought to observe the act, but it seems to have been widely ignored by the local authorities in the county.[150]

There appears to have been a general lull in persecutiion in the county in the mid-1660s. The only Quaker sufferings recorded in Hampshire in 1665–6 were connected with failure to provide arms for the militia.[151] But some parts of the central government's campaign against nonconformity between 1668 and 1671 do seem to have had an impact locally. The royal proclamation of 16 July 1669 called on justices to proceed against nonconformist preachers in particular, under the Five Mile Act.[152] In August, the act was enforced against

[146] S.C.R.O., SC9/1/10; Brit. Lib., MS Egerton 868, fol. 50; H.C.R.O., 24M54/14, fol. 17.
[147] *Fox's Journal*, ed. Nickalls, pp. 440–2; P.R.O., ASSI 23/1.
[148] Hutton, *The Restoration*, p. 208.
[149] *Cal.S.P.Dom.*, 1664–5, pp. 47, 109; H.C.R.O., 24M54/14, fol. 17.
[150] Matthews, *Calamy Revised*, p. 139; Robbins, 'The Oxford Session of the Long Parliament of Charles II', p. 221; Calamy, *A Continuation*, i. 507.
[151] H.C.R.O., 24M54/14, fols. 16–17.
[152] Steele, *Proclamations*, i. no. 3529, p. 426.

nonconformist ministers at Southampton, two of whom were imprisoned and there were warrants out for the arrest of three more. As a result, conventicles were said to have been 'forborn in a very great measure' in the locality. Five Baptists were indicted for attending a conventicle at the house of Thomas Trodd, and 102 people were presented by the quarter sessions grand jury for absence from church for a month. The persecution continued at Southampton next year, in the wake of the second Conventicle Act, which the corporation ordered to be carried out within the borough. Nathaniel Robinson was convicted of preaching to a conventicle within the town's juris-diction, under the new summary procedure provided for by the act. Eleven Quakers were prosecuted in the same way, and imprisoned for contempt of court in September 1670.[153]

In July 1670, the Conventicle Act was employed against Quaker meetings in the north of the county at Froyle and Alton; in the latter place, the imprisonment of the teacher Nicholas Gates deterred them from meeting indoors for several months. In November 1670, the attenders at a burial at the Quaker grave-yard at Baughurst were fined and the fines distrained for. Meanwhile, justices were enforcing the Conventicle Act in the Isle of Wight and not just against Quakers.[154]

The issue of the king's Declaration of Indulgence of 1672, does seem to have brought persecution to an end in Hampshire. Elsewhere justices defied it and harried local ministers, but this does not appear to have taken place in Hampshire, while it was still in force.[155] But when the king cancelled it on 7 March 1673, the situation theoretically reverted to what it had been before the Declaration was issued.

Persecution duly resumed in several of Hampshire's boroughs during the summer and autumn of 1673. A quarter sessions grand jury at Newport presented thirty-six dissenters for absence from church. In the following July, thirty dissenters, mostly the same people, were presented along with four Catholic recusants.[156] In August, persecution of conventicles was resumed at Andover by a group of Anglican zealots there and continued into September. In August, Isaac Chancy and fourteen 'hearers' were convicted and in September, Samuel Sprint and twenty-seven 'hearers' suffered the same fate. The corporation was afraid that these proceedings might be challenged at the county assizes in July 1674 and prepared a legal defence of them.[157] At

---

[153] Matthews, *Calamy Revised*, pp. 139, 413; S.C.R.O., SC2/1/8, 248–9, 271; SC9/1/12; SC9/1/13; P.R.O., S.P. 29/264, fol. 39; H.C.R.O., 24M54/14, fols. 19, 22.
[154] H.C.R.O., 24M54/14, fols. 18–19, 21; QO 4, pp. 329, 332, 344.
[155] Miller, *Popery and Politics*, pp. 118–19.
[156] I.W.C.R.O., Newport sessions minute book (1673–1727) 45/59, under date.
[157] *Don Quixote Redivivus*, pp. 1–27; H.C.R.O., 37M84, 13/DI/1; Mildon, 'Puritanism in Hampshire', p. 414.

Southampton quarter sessions in September 1673, twenty-four people were presented for absence from church and the conviction of forty-three people for attending a conventicle at the house of Anne Knight was certified to the court. On 8 September, three of the same people, along with a fourth, were convicted again and Anne Knight and Nathaniel Robinson, the preacher, were each fined twenty pounds.[158]

In 1675, the central government reverted to a policy of persecution embracing both nonconformists and Roman Catholics, the latter having escaped fairly lightly in Hampshire, as in other counties, hitherto.[159] From July 1675, there was a stream of convictions for recusancy at Hampshire assizes, amounting to 475 in number by the summer of 1676 when there were another 280 convictions, though there were no sweeping confiscations of recusants' estates.[160] Persecution of conventiclers resumed in 1675–6 in boroughs like Southampton and Newport where it had been evident before, and took place at Portsmouth in 1676–7, where little appears to have been done against nonconformists since the early years of the Restoration period. The authorities at Winchester belatedly began to investigate the conventicle which met at Edward Hooker's house in 1677–8.[161] Paradoxically the Quakers seem to have escaped quite lightly in this period.[162]

Since 1660, the enforcement of the laws against recusants and nonconformists in Hampshire had mostly been spasmodic, selective and moderate in terms of the punishments inflicted. The rhythm of persecution within local communities was inevitably influenced by a number of local factors. Dr Reay sees 'the anti-dissenting, zealously pro-Anglican initiative as coming *from* the counties'.[163] And yet, several waves of persecution, notably those in 1661, 1669–70 and 1675–6 were the result of initiatives from the centre. Charles II cannot be freed from blame for what persecution did take place. By the acts

---

[158] S.C.R.O., SC9/1/17.

[159] Before 1671, only 286 recusants had been convicted at Hampshire's assizes, which represented almost exactly a third of the Catholic community as recorded in 1676, 'List of Catholic recusants in the reign of Charles II' [wrongly dated 1677, in fact dating from 1671] *Catholic Record Society Miscellany V* (Catholic Record Society, vol. vi. London, 1909), pp. 312–17; only £147 15s 7d seems to have been levied on the entire country in revenue from recusants in this period, at a time when recusancy laws were being increasingly used against Quakers, Miller, *Popery and Politics*, p. 106.

[160] P.R.O., E377/73, only six recusants appear to have suffered confiscation, one of whom, Robert Reeves of Swanmore, was a Quaker.

[161] S.C.R.O., SC9/1/20; I.W.C.R.O., 45/16b, p. 171; H.C.R.O., QO 5, pp. 83–4; *Portsmouth Sessions Papers*, ed. Hoad, pp. 65–7, 165–6; Mildon, 'Puritanism in Hampshire', pp. 410–13.

[162] The Quaker sufferings book is much thinner for this period and when some Hampshire Quakers petitioned their MPs in 1680, they admitted that they had escaped lightly, H.C.R.O., 44M69 07 'The Quakers' petition of Hampshire to the members of the county at Parliament, 1680'.

[163] Reay, 'The authorities and early Restoration Quakerism', p. 84.

to which he assented, the proclamations he issued and the orders which went out in his name, he was implicated in the sufferings of the nonconformists and Roman Catholics.

The gentry in Hampshire were by no means united in their commitment to an intolerant Anglican church, still less to the desirability of persecuting dissenters. Zealous persecuting magistrates were a minority in Hampshire, and in other counties as well.[164] Sir Humphrey Bennet took a murderous relish in persecuting Quakers, assuring Nicholas Finkley that if he refused to take oath at the next sessions in January 1661, he would be hanged as a traitor. Bennet was busily involved whenever persecution had the sanction of central government. But his fellow deputy-lieutenants were not as extreme, for example they tried hard in January 1661 to obtain the merest token of submission from the Quaker William Buckland to avoid having to punish him.[165] In the Isle of Wight in the early 1660s, the main persecuting justice was Colonel Walter Slingsby, Culpeper's deputy-governor, who like Bennet was a veteran royalist officer. He took upon him much of the local persecution especially of Quakers and Baptists, as part of his general work of policing and repression. He took a positively sadistic pleasure in the work, suppressing conventicles, and boasting to Williamson of how he had sent an English translation of the Koran to two Quakers in prison, hoping they would be converted and thus discredit the whole sect. Slingsby felt isolated, blaming the frequent conventicles of dissenters on the remissness of local justices, though there were some who were prepared to join Slingsby in the persecution of Quakers and to take action on their own initiative.[166]

At the other extreme, there were justices who were positively opposed to persecution, such as Henry Whitehead. However, these men were not necessarily effective in blunting persecution. Whitehead, Sir Kingsmill Lucy and Lady Sandys showed sympathy for the dissenters at Andover in 1673 and solicited the borough authorities on their behalf. But they failed to prevent them being punished. Open defiance of government policy could render such people even less able to help dissenters, through the loss of their local offices. Whitehead was removed from the commission of the peace in 1670 and again, after reappointment, in 1676, almost certainly for opposition to the government's religious policy.[167]

Acting collectively as the Hampshire quarter sessions court, the justices

---

[164] See below, pp. 147–8; A. Fletcher, 'The enforcement of the Conventicle Acts 1664–1679', *Persecution and Toleration: Studies in Church History*, 21, ed. W. Shiels (Oxford, 1984), pp. 235–46.

[165] H.C.R.O., 24M54/14, fols. 9, 12.

[166] *Cal.S.P.Dom.*, 1663–4, pp. 317, 332; *Cal.S.P.Dom.*, 1664–5, pp. 47, 108–9, 446; H.C.R.O., 24M54/14, fol. 18.

[167] *Don Quixote Redivivus*, p. 19; P.R.O., C231/7, pp. 372, 507; *H.C.*, iii. 708.

seem to have adopted a fair-minded, but essentially legalistic approach to the problem of dissent, despite the presence of keen persecutors and tolerationists on the bench. When an appeal came before it from the Isle of Wight in 1671, and there was some doubt as to whether the meeting concerned came within the Conventicle Act, the justices referred it back to the judges of assize. When it was referred back to them, the justices put the question to a jury which decided that the meeting had not been a conventicle; so the accused people were acquitted. In 1675, the court carefully debated whether it could hear appeals from Newport in the Isle of Wight which had quarter sessions of its own, and on perusal of the Conventicle Act and the borough's charter, decided it could not. The Conventicle Act was read and debated again the next year to decide if a meeting in Redbridge hundred was a conventicle or not, and it was decided that it was, so the constables were ordered to take action accordingly.[168] As in the area of fiscal policy, so with religion, the justices sought above all to uphold the statute law. When there was a conflict between this and the stated policy of the government, as in 1672–3, there was confusion. Most county justices, like those of Surrey, as Bishop Morley reported, even after the Declaration was withdrawn were 'not very forward to put those laws in Execution until some publick notice be given by way of Proclamation or otherwise'.[169] Some borough authorities needed no such prompting to resume persecution, but even at borough level keen persecutors appear to have been a minority in the corporations.[170]

But the attitude of the magistracy was not the only factor affecting the enforcement of religious policy in this period. There were jurisdictional problems at local level which could impede action. Benjamin Burgess was able to hold conventicles out of reach of the Portsmouth authorities over the water in Gosport in the 1660s. This problem would not be ironed out until the granting of a new charter to Portsmouth in 1682. In 1676, Thomas Walter, constable of the borough of Fareham, refused to execute a warrant to break up a conventicle nearby, on the grounds that it was in Fareham hundred and not part of the liberty of the borough.[171]

Worse than these were the problems posed by the recalcitrance, cowardice, corruption or complicity of lesser officials: constables, tithingmen, church-wardens and militia men.[172] In 1663, George Fox escaped detection at Poulnar, near Ringwood, because some militia soldiers seeing him in an orchard did not report it, having 'no mind to meddle'.[173] In the Isle of Wight

---

[168] H.C.R.O., QO 4, pp. 329, 344; QO 5, pp. 83, 97, 110, 138.
[169] Bodl., MS Tanner, 42, fol. 7.
[170] *Don Quixote Redivivus*, pp. 1–2.
[171] *Cal.S.P.Dom.*, 1667, p. 552; H.C.R.O., QO 5, pp. 142–3.
[172] Village officials were a problem in many counties including neighbouring Wiltshire, Fletcher, 'Enforcement of the Conventicle Acts', p. 244.
[173] *Fox's Journal*, ed. Nickalls, p. 441.

at the same time, Colonel Walter Slingsby found it necessary to employ spies to discover local conventicles.[174] The second Conventicle Act attempted to coerce constables with a threat of a £5 fine for failure to report or break up a conventicle.[175] But this failed to eliminate the problem. Constables at Southampton in 1670, though they had been witness to a meeting, failed to give evidence against some Quakers. At the same time, the tithingmen of Baughurst refused to drag James Park out of a Quaker meeting at the orders of the local clergyman, but waited until the meeting was over.[176] In August 1673, Richard Butcher, constable of Andover, failed to report a conventicle because he himself attended it, and a conventicle on the 31st of the same month escaped prosecution altogether through the inactivity of the church-wardens, though they had been warned about it. All suffered the £5 fine. The next week, the sheriff's bailiff at the same town proved so timorous that he ran away rather than help with the suppression of a conventicle.[177] In these circumstances, paid informers became increasingly important in the prosecution of dissent.

Such were the perennial problems in the enforcement of religious policy and no systematic attempt was made to tackle them until the Tory reaction in the 1680s. But even before 1679, there is a danger of exaggerating the degree of parochial autonomy in religious matters. Most of the examples of negligence by petty officials cited above occur in relation to their being called to account for them and in most cases disciplined.

---

[174] P.R.O., S.P. 29/103,148; *Extracts from State Papers relating to Friends (1664–9)*, ed. N. Penney (Supplement to the Journal of the Friends Historical Society, no. 10, 1912), p. 225.
[175] *S.R.*, v. 650.
[176] H.C.R.O., 24M54/14, fols. 19, 22, 23.
[177] H.C.R.O., 37M84, 13/DI/I, II, III; *Don Quixote Redivivus*, p. 3.

6

Court and county 1660–78

The Restoration was probably the single most popular political event of the seventeenth century in England. Public jubilation in 1660 is well attested in most contemporary sources and their accounts do not need to be re-iterated here. Suffice it to say that Hampshire was no exception to the national pattern. Many people turned out for the proclamation of Charles II at Winchester, and showed 'great joy and rejoycing'. Four thousand people including all the gentry joined in the celebrations in the Isle of Wight.[1] It is hard to determine the exact grounds for the popular enthusiasm for the restored monarchy. Some of it at least may have stemmed from false expectations as to what its rule would actually bring. Before the Restoration, Marchamont Nedham had attributed popular royalism to a belief that Charles II's return would mean 'Peace and no taxes'.[2] On both counts the people were to be rudely disillusioned.

Those who expected less government would also have been disillusioned. As has been seen hitherto in this part, the restoration of traditional institions such as the Exchequer, the lieutenancy and the episcopate did not herald a retreat of central government from involvement in the localities or a decline in effective government generally; in fact quite the reverse was the case. The Restoration in some respects saw a re-assertion of central control after the troubled years of the Interregnum. It is hard to know what ordinary people thought of this, but the bulk of their social superiors seem to have been strongly in favour of it. They saw strong government as the best guarantee against the return of the Commonwealth. Royalists amongst them saw political, ecclesiastical and social hierarchies as mutually supportive. Carew Reynell of Rivershill wrote in a panegyric to Charles II:

> The Nobles, Bishops, Gentry, Clergy all
> Join hands and hearts and centre in Whitehall.[3]

---

[1] *Mercurius Publicus*, no. 21, 17–24 May 1660.
[2] N. Jose, *Ideas of the Restoration in English Literature 1660–71* (London, 1984), p. 32.
[3] C. Reynell, *The Fortunate Change: Being a Panegyrick to His Sacred Majesty King Charles*

Such was the vision of harmony between court and country which some at least in Hampshire entertained at the Restoration.

The alliance between central government and local elites was made more secure once changes in the power structure in county and borough had been pushed through, with the help of the Cavalier Parliament. Those who, for one reason or another, had opposed the Restoration were rounded on and rendered incapable of doing the government any harm. Among the gentry, John Lisle and Nicholas Love fled abroad, whilst Robert Wallop was thrown in the Tower; all had their property seized.[4] Lesser gentry and former officials had their houses searched for arms and were implicated in unlikely conspiracies. Some were arrested. Indiscreet words reflecting on the royal government were seized upon and those who voiced them were punished, even before the passing of the stiff act to preserve the king's person and government in 1661.[5] Under these conditions, republicanism which had never been strong in Hampshire was soon eliminated as a serious political force.

But there was more to the period of comparative political stability which the Restoration ushered in than the mere elimination of republicanism. It arose to a large extent from the successful handling of the provinces by central government. Far from this peace with the localities being bought by a withdrawal of government to Whitehall, it stemmed from the renewal and growth of contacts between the Crown and the communities. The royal government was more sensitive to local feelings and better able to satisfy local aspirations than its predecessors had been. A structure of politics developed in which harmony rather than tension characterized relations between king and country.

Central to this structure of politics was the court, whose pluralism and informality were and are famous. There were several links between local elites in Hampshire and the court. The most important till his death in 1667 was Lord Treasurer Southampton, but there were others such as the earl of Portland, who resumed his post as captain/governor of the Isle of Wight in 1660. Even Lord Culpeper acted as a link to some extent after he succeeded Portland in 1661. Through these and other channels several individuals and groups were able to obtain favours for themselves and their localities.[6] The corporation of Southampton at last had its traditional sweet-wine levy restored to it, in accordance with an Elizabethan grant, through the intervention of Lord Treasurer Southampton. When the earl of Southampton

the Second Immediately on his Coronation, being the 23 of April 1661; reprinted in *Fugitive Tracts* (2nd series, 1600–1700, printed privately, 1875), no. xxiv.
4 Edmund Ludlow, *A Voyce from the Watch Tower*, ed. Worden, pp. 281–2, 293, 303–5; P.R.O., E178/6445: Commission to investigate the estates of J. Lisle and N. Love.
5 Brit. Lib., Addit. MS 21922, fols. 241, 245; MS Sloane 813, fol. 67; *Mercurius Publicus*, new series, no. 45, 31 Oct.–7 Nov. 1661; *Cal.S.P.Dom.*, 1663–4, p. 44; *Portsmouth Sessions Papers*, ed. Hoad, pp. 14, 15, 17.
6 See references to Newport's charter and Henry Wallop, pp. 92, 97–8, above.

made one of his brief trips to his seat at Titchfield in August 1664, the corporation responded by sending two hogsheads of French wine.[7] Lord Culpeper, apart from keeping Sir William Oglander up to date with political news, negotiated for him to get his baronetcy at a cheaper rate in 1666. Unfortunately Culpeper's failure to perform similar services for other gentlemen or to convince them that his lengthy stays at Whitehall were spent arguing the island's case there, turned them against him. His incompetence as a military leader and his habit of arbitrary imprisonment on the flimsiest grounds finally destroyed his local reputation. By the spring of 1666, the gentry were promoting a petition against his misrule, which Sir William Oglander, almost alone amongst the landed elite, omitted to sign. The petition was coolly received at Whitehall when it was presented,[8] but paradoxically the whole affair demonstrates how sensitive the regime could be to the feelings of local elites. For one thing, Charles himself, on a visit to the Isle of Wight in 1665, had observed that Culpeper was not respected by the gentry and had therefore thought fit to replace him. The petitioners had been able to consult Clarendon about the matter beforehand, though he failed to deter them from presenting the petition. The government had already resolved to redress the petition's principal grievances before it was presented, and even after it had been officially rebuffed, Clarendon wrote to the petitioners to tell them as much, and to admit that in certain actions Culpeper had been at fault. Over the question of Parkhurst forest which Culpeper had enclosed, on his own initiative without consultation, Clarendon assured them that the king was gracious, and 'the Lord Treasurer, the Lord Ashley and I myself, we are friends to the country'.[9]

But Culpeper had not been the Isle of Wight's only contact at court by any means. Sir Robert Dillington deployed the influence of his old friend Sir Joseph Williamson (Arlington's secretary) to improve the island's supply and defences in the wake of the Culpeper affair, and his pleas were echoed by Williamson's other contacts in the island, such as John Lysle of West Cowes. And when their lobbying achieved results, they were duly grateful to Williamson and Arlington.[10] Dillington continued to use Williamson's interest on the island's behalf. Even as late at 1676, by which time his relations with the government were somewhat strained, he wrote to Williamson over the dispute with the customs officers at Southampton, 'presuming on a fair occasion this Isle might not despaire of y[ou]r Patronage'.[11] Williamson's network included contacts on mainland

---

[7] S.C.R.O., SC2/1/8, fols. 182, 201.
[8] I.W.C.R.O., OG/19/82, 83, 84, 85; OG/66/16; P.R.O., S.P. 29/153, fols. 192–3.
[9] Worsley, *History of the Isle of Wight*, pp. 138–9; I.W.C.R.O., OG/19/86.
[10] *Cal.S.P.Dom.*, 1665–6, pp. 522–3, 533–4; P.R.O., S.P. 29/165, fol. 121.
[11] P.R.O., S.P. 29/381, fol. 258.

Hampshire and in many other parts of the country.[12] Dr Jenkins has aptly written of it: 'social contact lubricated the workings of effective government'.[13]

The king himself was aware of the need to keep local oligarchies sweet and took pains to bestow favours on them. In 1660, he presented a mace to Yarmouth corporation in the Isle of Wight for loyalty during his father's reign.[14] In July 1665, the king ordered that the Admiralty Court be adjourned to Winchester because of the plague, and saw to it that a letter was sent to the mayor and aldermen to explain that this action was 'intended as an instance of his Royall favour & an opportunity of Advantage & Benefit to the said Citty'.[15] The king's several visits to mainland Hampshire and the Isle of Wight kept him in touch with local feelings as well.

The court's greatest strength during the 1660s, apart from its wide local contacts, lay in its ability to contain different points of view and criticism within itself. This was particularly true of the religious issue but applied to other matters as well. Lord Treasurer Southampton was in many ways the moral conscience of the court until 1667, shunning the king's mistresses. He opposed excessively stringent oaths being imposed even on those of doubtful loyalty. As a tolerant Anglican with no belief in *jure divino* episcopacy, he strove for Protestant unity, and was a bitter opponent of Catholicism.[16] Many of his views would later be taken up by the country opposition in the 1670s.

But the court was not the only channel for local views and aspirations to reach the centre. Parliament, which met every year during the 1660s, provided another. Local and personal problems could be resolved by statutory means. Between 1660 and 1671, no fewer than 225 private acts reached the statute book, several of them relating to Hampshire. This was an extraordinarily high figure, both compared with the early Stuart period and with the 1670s, when only sixty-five more acts were added.[17] This was the corollary of Charles' policy of ruling with Parliament's consent. Local interests were carefully balanced, for example, in the Itchen Navigation Act of 1665. The rights of customary river users and the interests of the

---

[12] E.g. Randall Sanderson, vicar of Weyhill, who was able to use Williamson's influence to thwart the pretensions of Andover corporation over Weyhill fair, *Cal.S.P.Dom.*, 1672, pp. 543–4; *Cal.S.P.Dom.*, 1672–3, pp. 16–17; *Cal.S.P.Dom.*, 1677–8, p. 281; *Hist. MSS Comm. Twelfth Report App. pt VII. Le Fleming MSS*, pp. 35–150 for Sir Daniel Fleming of Rydal Hall's correspondence with Williamson.

[13] Jenkins, *The Making of a Ruling Class: The Glamorgan Gentry 1640–1790*, p. 120.

[14] This mace is still housed at the Town Hall, Yarmouth, I.W.

[15] P.R.O., P.C. 2/58, p. 205.

[16] Schoenfeld, *The Restored House of Lords*, p. 215; *A Letter from a Person of Quality to his Friend in the Country* (1675), p. 25; Clarendon, *Continuation of the Life*, iii. 239–40.

[17] *S.R.*, v. 434, 568–9, 623, 647, 751 and *passim*; only thirty-two private acts are listed for the entire reign of Charles I before the Civil War, *S.R.*, v. 52–3, 178.

corporation of Southampton were protected.[18] Bills which failed to take account of local interests, especially those which were represented in Parliament, were likely to fail. A bill by which Lady Wandesford sought to gain confirmation for a grant of marsh-lands in Hampshire from Charles I ran into difficulties for just this reason. Those who owned land in the Isle of Wight, like the Barringtons, were soon alerted to the potential dangers to their interests. All MPs from Hampshire and Sussex were named to the committee appointed on 11 January 1662, and they so amended the bill that it had to be redrafted.[19] The bill was abandoned, but when Lady Wandesford tried again with another bill in 1664, the local MPs were again ready, and Sir Henry Worsley, a member for Newtown, led an unsuccessful attempt to prevent the bill being committed. Again Sussex and Hampshire MPs were named en bloc to the committee and the bill was lost. Lade Wandesford pressed on with draining the land with the help of Dutch engineers.[20]

But Parliament's role as the outlet for local grievances and the watchdog for local interests was complicated by the influence of partisanship upon elections and the public measures which were passed. This could alienate significant elements in local society from the majority in the Commons. In 1660, while John Bulkeley was telling the Convention of the dangers of unrestrained hierarchy and the need for liturgical reform, the Hampshire assize grand jury was thanking the king for settling religion in accordance with the government of the church 'established in the Reign of Queen Elizabeth, King James and King Charles the first of ever blessed memory'.[21] As the Convention gave way to the Cavalier Parliament, Richard Norton and John Bulkeley were obliged to give way to Sir John Norton and Lord St John as knights of the shire, though they both found seats within the county. The new county members were both staunch Anglican royalists, who in the matter of religion were poles apart from their predecessors. Lord St John was soon acting as a teller for the public burning of the Solemn League and Covenant, the very document whose virtues John Bulkeley had been extolling to Richard Cromwell's Parliament, just over two years before. Richard Norton got into trouble with his colleagues for his refusal to take the Anglican sacrament on his knees.[22] Cavalier candidates did well in Hampshire's parliamentary boroughs in 1661. Eight of those elected had

---

[18] A. Samuels, 'The Itchen navigation: a lawyer's view of the legal issues', *Proceedings of the Hampshire Field Club*, xxxviii. (1982), 113; Rosen, 'Winchester in transition' in Clark, *Country Towns in Pre-Industrial England*, p. 152.

[19] The fact that Lady Wandesford regarded statutory confirmation as desirable for this perfectly legal prerogative grant is in itself revealing of the esteem in which statute law was held; I.W.C.R.O., Jerome Collection, Hall Letters, nos. 5 and 6; *C.J.*, viii. 343, 417, 418.

[20] The bill was defeated 98:86, *C.J.*, viii. 541; *Cal.S.P.Dom.*, 1668–9, p. 102.

[21] *H.C.*, i. 744; *The Parliamentary Intelligencer*, no. 38, 10–17 Sept. 1660.

[22] *H.C.*, i. 244, 744; iii. 160, 277; *Burton's Diary*, ed. Rutt, iii. 105–6.

been active royalists in the 1640s.[23] But a significant minority of Hampshire's delegation were opposed to the Cavalier religious policy, even after Henry Whitehead, elected on a double-return for Stockbridge, had fallen foul of a blatantly partisan disputed election decision. Richard Norton gave shelter to several ejected divines in 1662. Sir John Trott (MP for Andover) sheltered an ejected fellow of All Souls, and Giles Hungerford (MP for Whitchurch) opposed the hardline settlement in Parliament, though he was later involved in the persecution of dissenters in Wiltshire. John Bulkeley seems to have remained true to his principles until his death in 1662, and Sir John Barrington of Essex, who sat for Newtown, maintained a Presbyterian chaplain and nonconformist sympathies.[24]

However, such divisions did not necessarily endanger the stability of the Restoration regime. Local society might remain divided over religious policy, but it produced no fixed or formed opposition to the government, either in or outside Parliament, during the 1660s. The display of conformity to the Anglican church in Hampshire in 1662 was certainly impressive. According to Bishop Morley, 'all the considerable men of the county' were present at Winchester on Tuesday 26 August for the start of his primary visitation.[25] During that visitation Morley confirmed 200–300 people at Romsey, between 500 and 600 at Southampton and 1,000 in the Isle of Wight including virtually the entire gentry community.[26] On the mainland only a few gentry failed to conform.[27]

But outward conformity should not be seen as a necessary endorsement of the whole Cavalier policy. Richard Norton was amongst those who attended the start of Morley's visitation in 1662, no doubt with mixed feelings.[28] During the decade which followed the settlement of 1662, there emerged a group of gentry in Hampshire who, though not dissenters themselves, were nevertheless sympathetic to dissent, or at least hostile to the Anglican hierarchy. There were several gentry in the Andover area who were glad to welcome Samuel Sprint, the local nonconformist minister, to their dinner tables,

[23] Sir Humphrey Bennet (Petersfield), Sir Goerge Carteret (Portsmouth), Richard Goddard (Winchester), Sir Robert Howard (Stockbridge), Lawrence Hyde (Winchester), William Legge (Southampton), Robert Phelips (Stockbridge), Humphrey Weld (Christchurch); *H.C.*, i. 622; ii. 28, 402, 595, 630–1, 726; iii. 237, 682.

[24] *H.C.*, i. 601–2, 744; ii. 616–17; iii. 160, 608; for Giles Hungerford's involvement in the persecution of dissent, see E. A. O. Whiteman, 'The episcopate of Dr Seth Ward, Bishop of Exeter (1662 to 1667) and Salisbury (1667–1689) with special reference to the ecclesiastical problems of his time' (Oxford Univ., D.Phil. thesis, 1951), p. 419.

[25] Bodl., MS Clarendon 77, fol. 207.

[26] Bodl., MS Clarendon 73, fols. 216–17.

[27] E.g. Alice Lisle, Dorothy Cromwell, John Hildesley, William Bulkeley, Malachi Dudeney, H.C.R.O., Diocesan Records B/1/A – 4, no. 36; Lyon Turner, *Original Records*, i. 140–2; Bate, *Declaration of Indulgence*, p. lxviii; *Cal.S.P.Dom.*, 1671–2, p. 357.

[28] Bodl., MS Clarendon 77, fol. 207; Morley noted Norton's presence in particular.

where the corruptions of the episcopate were likely to be discussed.[29] Lady Sandys, Sir Kingsmill Lucy, the newly elected member for the borough, and Henry Whitehead showed sympathy to the persecuted dissenters at Andover in 1673.[30] Other conforming gentry who had parliamentarian pasts, like Thomas Bowreman of Brooke in the Isle of Wight, clearly remained suspicious of and hostile to the hierearchy.[31] Other former parliamentarians, such as Thomas Jervoise of Herriard, though conforming, seem to have favoured comprehension.[32] Former royalist politicians, notably Sir Robert Howard and Lord St John, developed a belated sympathy for dissent, and looked covetously upon ecclesiastical property.[33]

During much of the first decade of Charles II's reign, a degree of political stability was ensured by the fact that no religious group within local society could be entirely confident of, or totally despair of, royal favour. No one seemed to hold the king responsible for the religious policy which was adopted. Carew Reynell, in his panegyric to the king, took the opportunity to extol the virtues of traditional Anglicanism and to denounce the 'Linsy–Woolsey–Church' which he accused the Presbyterians of wanting to create.[34] Some commanders of the militia in Hampshire were said by Bishop Morley to be 'much troubled' at the idea of an indulgence to ministers who failed to conform in 1662.[35] But Charles soon abandoned the scheme of individual dispensations to ministers, which had provoked this reaction, and the subsequent Declaration of Indulgence did not last either.[36] Local dissenters for their part blamed the intolerant majority in Parliament for their lot. Some dissenters in the Isle of Wight described the religious measures of the Cavalier Parliament by 1663 as 'the arrogant impositions of the sons of pride'. But dissenters did not necessarily despair even of Parliament. Nonconformists at Gosport were said to be looking to it for relief by October 1667.[37] Nor, despite all Charles II's perfidy, did local dissenters despair of the king, even when he was in the middle of authorizing a policy of persecution in 1669. In the returns of conventicles in that year for Hampshire it appears that many dissenters were claiming the king's toleration, connivance or at least sympathy to justify their meeting.[38]

[29] Calamy, *Abridgement*, ii. (An Account), 341–2.
[30] See above, p. 139.
[31] Brit. Lib., Addit. MS 46501, fol. 228.
[32] Jervoise's library contained several tracts advocating comprehension, H.C.R.O., 44M69, Herriard/K/Pamphlets, nos. 222d, 223.
[33] *H.C.*, ii. 597; iii. 278; Bodl., MS Tanner 43, fol. 17.
[34] Reynell, *Fortunate Change* (1661).
[35] Bodl., MS Clarendon 77, fol. 207.
[36] Pepys, *Diary*, ed. Latham and Matthews, iii. 186 and note.
[37] P.R.O., S.P. 29/83, fol. 90; *Cal.S.P.Dom.*, 1667, p. 552.
[38] Lyon Turner, *Original Records*, i. 137–8, 141.

During the 1670s, all those aspects of the relationship between central government and the localities which had made for stability during the 1660s were to some extent undermined. First, and perhaps most dangerous of all, the religious policy of the Crown came to have an unprecedented and uncomfortable air of permanence about it. In 1672, Charles II issued his Declaration of Indulgence which established toleration for dissenters on the basis of the royal prerogative without reference to subsequent parliamentary approval. In this way it was very different from the Declaration of ten years before.[39] The Declaration of 1672 was in force for almost a year before Parliament even had the chance to debate it. In response to such unprecedented royal determination, intolerant Anglicans in the localities had their loyalty tested to the limit. When, after the Declaration had been withdrawn, dissenters at Andover still pleaded their licence against renewed persecution, Thomas Westcombe, a local persecuting magistrate, told them, 'the king had no power to give any such licence and made a pish at it'. The magistrates told the dissenters that they had to submit to Parliament, and deployed the opinion of three supposed MPs who happened to be staying in the town to support their view.[40] But the adoption of a policy of sustained persecution by the government under Danby did little to restore stability, as the body of opinion in the localities which favoured toleration was now considerable. The majority of people at Andover seem to have strongly disapproved of the resumption of persecution there. The dissenter who wrote up the affair in a satirical pamphlet observed that there was no more 'than a pair of sheers between Papists and such Protestants that are sick of the overflowing of the Gall' (i.e. persecutors).[41] Yet it was with such Protestants that the regime associated itself in 1675 and after. There is evidence of growing sympathy even towards Quakers in Hampshire.[42] The gentry who sympathized with dissent were sufficiently influential to get Sir Francis Rolle, a well-known patron of dissenters, returned as knight of the shire, in succession to Lord St John when he went to the Lords as marquis of Winchester in 1675.[43] But the government's policy remained one of persecution towards dissenters.

Also during the 1670s, other factors which had brought harmony to the relationship between central government and the localities was eroded. The Crown's commitment to ruling with the co-operation of Parliament seemed, for the first time since 1660, to be in question. From this point of view, the constitutional aspect of the Declaration of Indulgence was alarming, even to those like Lord St John who favoured relief for dissenters.[44] The existence of

[39] *The Stuart Constitution 1603–1688*, ed. J. P. Kenyon (Cambridge, 1980 reprint) pp. 403–8.
[40] *Don Quixote Redivivus*, pp. 15–16, 35.
[41] *Don Quixote Redivivus*, pp. 4–5, 25–6, 31.
[42] H.C.R.O., 24M54/14, fols. 19, 24.   [43] *H.C.*, i. 244; iii. 347.   [44] *H.C.*, iii. 278.

large-scale regular forces in the Crown's pay gave rise to fears that Charles would try to use them to coerce Parliament, fears which, if the duke of York had had his way, would have been well founded.[45] By November 1672, Bishop Morley feared that the court would use the army in some sort of coup d'etat.[46] In 1674, Lord St John claimed to have heard it from the lips of one of the Cabal that there was a plan to coerce the Commons to pass bills by force. And he accused councillors of wanting to set up a French style absolutism with the help of the army.[47]

But even when the forces had been disbanded, the court seemed intent on manipulating Parliament for its own advantage and to the detriment of the provinces. Parliament sat less frequently. It became more difficult for private acts or local bills to pass during the truncated sessions and the number that did declined markedly. One of the casualties was a bill promoted by Richard Norton for paving the streets of Portsmouth and erecting a workhouse or an almshouse there, which was lost in the prorogation of 1674–5. Proceeding without statutory backing, the mayor faced accusations of acting illegally in the locality.[48]

With parliamentary sessions scarcer and shorter, the court became increasingly insensitive to local grievances. Back in 1667, Lord Gerard of Brandon had been ordered by the king to pay for the quarters of the forces sent to the Isle of Wight, borrowing money on his own credit if necessary.[49] Sir Henry Jones spent £220 for just this purpose, for which he was later reimbursed.[50] But when soldiers were marched to the Portsmouth area in large numbers in the autumn of 1672, ready to embark for the proposed invasion of Holland, which never took place, free quarter was widely resorted to.[51] Only in March 1673, with a belatedly reconvened Parliament, were the knights of the shire, Lord St John and Sir John Norton, able to plead the case of the poor victuallers, unpaid since the previous November, who had been obliged to put up twenty or thirty soldiers apiece. According to Sir John Norton, even some private citizens were being compelled to quarter soldiers. Other MPs who sat for seats in the county, like Sir Robert Dillington, joined in the chorus of protest.[52] These men had hitherto been the loyal servants of the regime, but their loyalty was now being severely tested.

[45] J. Childs, *The Army, James II and the Glorious Revolution* (Manchester, 1980), p. 104.
[46] Bodl., MS Tanner 43, fols. 31–2.
[47] *H.C.*, iii. 278.
[48] *C.J.*, ix. 303, 308, 309; H.C.R.O., 5M50 (Daly MSS) no. 1608; *Portsmouth Sessions Papers*, ed. Hoad, p. 165.
[49] P.R.O., S.P. 44/20, p. 176.   [50] *Cal.Treas.Bks.*, ii. 204.
[51] *Cal.S.P.Dom.*, 1672–3, p. 502; *Cal.S.P.Dom.*, 1673, p. 30.
[52] A. Grey, *Debates of the House of Commons from the year 1667 to the year 1694* (10 vols., London, 1763), ii. 131; *The Parliamentary Diary of Sir Edward Dering 1670–73*, ed. B. D. Henning (New Haven, 1940), p. 144.

At the same time the court seemed to be set on the corruption of the Commons, filling it with pliant placemen as opposed to the genuine representatives of local communities. This provoked division in the constituencies between court supporters and their country opponents. When in October 1669, the leaders of Winchester corporation wished to return Sir Robert Holmes, the recently appointed governor of the Isle of Wight in a by-election, thirteen junior members of the corporation contested it and sought to return Sir John Clobery, a former Cromwellian officer who had settled in the city at the Restoration. But they were easily outvoted by thirty-seven other members of the corporation, including several local gentry.[53] Among them were Sir John Norton, a deputy-lieutenant and former royalist, Sir Richard Knight and Sir Henry Tichborne, a local Roman Catholic gentleman, who was becoming increasingly involved in borough politics at this time.[54] All three had been proposed as knights of the Royal Oak at the Restoration.[55] Sir Robert Holmes aroused further suspicion when he got involved in the politics of Newtown corporation in the Isle of Wight, which had been under the unchallenged control of two gentry families, the Barringtons and the Worsleys for a generation. Holmes set out to revive the dormant governor's interest and to this end became active in the politics of the borough in 1676. He managed to isolate Sir William Meux, the only member of the corporation to oppose him. Meux, son of a sequestered royalist but related to the Barringtons, began to look for allies in the wider community; according to Holmes, although he had formerly associated with men of similar political backgrounds to himself, Meux was now consorting with 'suspicious persons'. When a by-election loomed, those in Hampshire who suspected Holmes of trying to create a court borough did their best to thwart him. 'All the active people in Hampshire' Holmes observed, had been to Newtown, 'but I think to no purpose'.[56] In the event Holmes managed to remove Meux from the mayoralty of the corporation as well as his militia command and got his brother Sir John Holmes returned as MP. Appeals by Meux to both Parliament and Council failed to reverse these *faits accomplis*. In fact, Holmes was building his own local interest, independent of the court, but this was not clear to his opponents. In *A Seasonable Argument* in 1677 he was presented as the 'bashaw of the Isle of Wight'.[57]

---

[53] H.C.R.O., W/B1/6, fol. 60.
[54] Tichborne and Knight appear as members of the court faction at Lymington, H.C.R.O., 27M74A, DB2, fol. 87.
[55] Knight's name is wrongly given as Edward, Sir William Dugdale, *The Antient usage . . . of Bearing Arms*, ed. T. C. Banks (London, 1811), pp. 170–2.
[56] Brit. Lib., Bath–Coventry MSS microfilm M 863, reel no. 3, fols. 78, 83.
[57] H.C., i. 251; *Cal.S.P.Dom.*, 1676–7, pp. 578–9; I.W.C.R.O., Jerome Collection, Newtown assembly book 1671–96, pp. 4–5, 7–9; *English Historical Documents 1660–1714*, ed. A. Browning (London, 1953), p. 241.

At Lymington, growing factionalism is evidenced by an attempt to have parliamentary elections held by secret ballot in 1677, though it was overruled before any elections were held. The factions were therefore pushed into the open when it came to electing a replacement for the deceased Sir William Lewis, whom Shaftesbury had accounted 'thrice worthy'. The embryonic court faction carried it by two votes in returning Sir Richard Knight, who supported Danby. His main challenger was John Button, who was subsequently dubbed 'honest' by Shaftesbury, and who regained admission to the corporation at this time after sixteen years of exclusion under the Corporation Act.[58]

Lists of court supporters in the Commons were circulating in the provinces by the early 1670s. One such list dating from May 1671 may have existed in Hampshire at this time.[59] By 1675, the country opposition to Parliament was fully awake to the dangers and promoted a place bill in that year. In the debate on the non-resisting test bill in 1675, the newly elevated marquis of Winchester countered Danby's proposal with another, for putting an oath to all MPs not to be influenced by fear or favour in casting their votes. Those who sympathized with the country opposition would have read with alarm in *A Seasonable Argument* that ten out of Hampshire's twenty-six MPs were court dependants, though by no means all were dependable lobby fodder.[60]

As the 1670s progressed, the court became politically narrower and more intolerant of criticism. Placemen were expected to support ministers in Parliament and were liable to be dismissed if they refused.[61] There was no one in the government now of the stature of Lord Treasurer Southampton, who in the previous decade had embodied many country values. Favour at court came to be confined to fewer and fewer hands, and the range of views represented at Whitehall decreased. Even in the Cabal period this process had been discernable. Some churchmen had a difficult time after Clarendon's fall. Bishop Morley, who had close connections with the Hyde family, and who had hitherto been an influential court prelate, was ejected from Whitehall and his court offices.[62] Then in 1671, Lord St John nearly lost favour through his opposition to the new foreign policy which was taking shape. According to

[58] H.C.R.O., 27M74A DBC 2, fols. 48, 86–7; K. H. D. Haley, 'Shaftesbury's Lists of the Lay Peers and Members of the Commons 1677–8', *B.I.H.R.*, 43 (1970), 101; *H.C.*, i. 248.

[59] H.C.R.O., 39M69/PZ7 is the same as Brit. Lib., MS Harl. 7030, fols. 33–48; it is not clear when the Hampshire document arrived at Hursley, but it may well have been soon after its compilation; Oliver Cromwell, grandson of the protector and a future Whig, settled on the family estate there in 1675; Marsh, *Memoranda*, p. 14; I am very grateful to Norman Barber Esq. for help in tracking down this document.

[60] G. E. Aylmer, 'Place bills and the separation of powers: some seventeenth-century origins of the "Non-Political" Civil Service', *T.R.H.S.*, Fifth series, 15 (1965), 59; *A Letter from a Person of Quality*, p. 28; *English Historical Documents*, ed. Browning, pp. 240–1.

[61] Aylmer, 'Place bills', pp. 59–60.   [62] Bodl., MS Clarendon 87, fol. 84.

the French ambassador it was this that lay behind the failure of the customs farm contract in which Lord St John was involved. Indeed, his loss of favour was rumoured then.[63] The estrangement may have continued over the next few years, which could explain why he had to take his complaints against billeting to the floor of the House of Commons in 1673. By 1675, the rise of Danby and the continued opposition of Lord St John put the latter's offices at risk, and despite rumours of a rapprochement, he lost them the following spring.[64]

By alienating and finally purging a man of Lord St John's stature, the government was making a formidable political enemy. His interests and influence were by no means confined to Hampshire. He had political influence in counties as far apart as Cornwall and Yorkshire, and by 1677, he was even involved with the opposition in Scotland.[65] If the government was obliged to call a general election the opposition of such men could have a dire impact on the result. Even the second earl of Clarendon, who had retained enough influence at court to fend off the attack on his family's borough of Christchurch in 1670, fell from favour in 1675. His fall was noted locally,[66] but he continued to control Christchurch.

Danby's purges had wide repercussions in Hampshire. The marquis of Winchester's eclipse led to an increase in episcopal influence in the county, which combined with the persecution of dissenters must have seemed highly ominous to some gentry.[67] Former parliamentarians who had been rehabilitated were once again alienated from Stuart government. The case of Thomas Jervoise provides a classic example of this process. One of the JPs who survived the purge of 1660, he had had an anxious few months during that year when it seemed that a bill to compensate the fifth marquis of Winchester out of his and Robert Wallop's estates might pass the Convention.[68] But he subsequently obtained the patronage of the marquis' Protestant son, and was by him admitted to the lieutenancy in 1673, only to be dismissed with his patron in 1676. In November 1672, his agent William Guidott had advised him to develop an interest with the new Lord Chancellor, Lord Ashley (now earl of Shaftesbury) to prosper his several suits in Chancery. But Shaftesbury

---

[63] H. J. Oliver, *Sir Robert Howard (1626–98): A Critical Biography* (Durham, N.C., 1963), p. 178.

[64] *Hist. MSS Comm. Laing MSS*, i. 403; see above, p. 98.

[65] *H.C.*, iii. 276–9; *Cal.S.P.Dom.*, 1677–8, pp. 16–17.

[66] H.C.R.O., 44M69, E77; J. Daniell to Wm Wilmot, 29 April 1675.

[67] See above, pp. 98–9.

[68] The measure which was in revenge for the act of 1649 (see above, p. 70) passed the Lords but seems to have been sabotaged in a Commons committee, to which it was referred, by Giles Hungerford, who was related to Jervoise, and other local MPs, *C.J.*, viii. 110–11, 115, 134, 140, 185; *H.C.*, ii. 616–17; the bill was briefly and abortively revived in the Cavalier Parliament, but by then Jervoise seems to have been omitted from its provisions, *L.J.*, xi. 254, 307.

fell from office the very next year. By 1676, all passages to the court were blocked to Jervoise, but as his personal papers testify this did not in any way reduce his interest in central politics.[69] He would have to wait for a new Parliament if he wished to make his views heard. The same can be said of Henry Whitehead, son of a parliamentarian and protagonist against Holmes in the Newtown by-election, who was even removed from the commission of the peace in 1676, along with Sir Robert Henley of the Grange, Northington. All three would later be exclusionist MPs.[70]

But the growing unpopularity of the court with some sections of local society was not simply a product of distortions in the patronage system induced by the rise of Danby. Its associations with Catholicism and the French interest were even more damaging, and Danby's efforts to efface them only partly successful. In the autumn of 1673, in relation to the duke of York's Modena match, Lord St John observed, 'a lady so nearly related to the court of Rome must be a very inconvenient match', for the heir to the throne. He was appointed to the Commons committee to draw up an address against it. Next year, Lord St John mercilessly harried Samuel Pepys on the grounds that he was a crypto-Papist, and accused members of the Cabal of wanting to set up an absolute government on the French model.[71] His francophobia was echoed in the county, where the corporation of Lymington spent nearly a third of its annual budget in 1674 celebrating the peace with the Dutch,[72] and Carew Reynell, of Rivershill, writing in a tract entitled *The True English Interest* (1674) called upon Charles II to be the protector of international Protestantism against arbitrary power.[73] Danby's anti-French foreign policy seemed to conform to this programme and yet some in the localities rightly feared that the court was playing a double game. In 1677, the country people of the Portsmouth area were convinced that Louis XIV had visited the garrison incognito.[74] The fear of court Catholics grew in and outside Parliament. In 1674, Lord St John and Giles Hungerford, MP for Whitchurch, were named to a committee for a general test. In 1675, Hungerford was deputed to remind the Lords about a bill to hinder Catholics from sitting in Parliament, and was appointed to a committee to prevent the growth of popery.[75] In June 1676, Samuel Moone of Portsmouth was accused of saying that 'the Duke of York had declared himself a papist and that . . . he . . . would be the first to

[69] See above, p. 98; H.C.R.O., 44M69 E77; William Guidott to Thomas Jervoise, 19 November 1672; John Daniell to Wm Wilmot, 29 April 16750 44M69 06, copy of votes of the House of Commons, March 1676; copy of king's speech, 1677.

[70] See above, p. 139; *H.C.*, i. 251; ii. 525, 651–2; iii. 708.

[71] *H.C.*, iii, 278.

[72] H.C.R.O., 27M74A, DBC/2, fol. 80.

[73] C. Reynell, *The True English Interest* (London, 1674), pp. 70–1.

[74] *Hist. MSS Comm. Seventh Report App. pt I, Verney MSS*, p. 469.   [75] *H.C.*, ii. 617.

fight against him according to the oaths of allegiance and supremacy he had taken'.[76]

The policies of the Danby period, and the unfortunate image of the court, which Danby proved unable to change, had alienated a significant body of opinion not only in Parliament but in the localities also. By 1677, both Hampshire's knights of the shire were openly siding with the opposition, as were the county's principal resident aristocrats (the marquis of Winchester, Lord De la Warr and Lord Sandys). They were joined in opposition by nine of the MPs who sat for seats within the county.[77] More dangerously, there were several gentlemen and others outside Parliament determined to exploit the first opportunity to force changes of policy upon the court, which was increasingly isolated from their views. It was not the closeness of central government to the localities that engendered the resurgence of opposition, rather it was the growing distance between court and country, which led to tension. Links between the centre and the localities had withered and mutual incomprehension grew.

[76] *Portsmouth Sessions Papers*, ed. Hoad, p. 56.
[77] Haley, 'Shaftesbury's Lists', pp. 92, 94, 100–1.

Part III

FROM THE POPISH PLOT
TO THE REVOLUTION OF 1688

Local office-holding 1679–88

Central government during the 1680s in England has attracted considerable scholarly interest over the years and yet there is much about its relationship with the localities that is still obscure. This is partly because of the inordinate amount of attention which has been directed towards the necessarily ambiguous motivations of kings and such elusive concepts as 'absolutism'. This is surprising, as all historians agree that an absolute monarchy was not established in England in the 1680s, and Dr Miller has recently questioned whether the concept is a useful one in this particular context.[1] Equally all historians agree that the 1680s did see the rise of a stronger more authoritarian central government in Britain, but the discussion about the impact of successive regimes upon the country has been circumscribed and little of the surviving local evidence has been tapped to answer crucial questions about the period which have hardly yet been formulated. For example, it is still unclear to what extent local government continued to function in the period 1687–9 under the strain of successive purges and re-instatements.[2] The relationship between localism and the opposition to James II has not been explained in any depth, and it is hard on the basis of present knowledge to generalize intelligently about the continuities and contrasts between this period and those which preceded and followed it. The object of this part is to examine the impact of the central government in Hampshire between 1679 and 1688, to explore the changing attitudes there towards Whitehall, and above all to compare the regimes of this period, if only on a localized basis, with their Restoration and Interregnum predecessors.

It is generally acknowledged that the period from 1679 to 1688 saw an unprecedented degree of interference and manipulation of local office-

---

[1] Miller, 'The potential for absolutism', pp. 206–7.
[2] Forster has made a pioneering effort to estimate the extent of the breakdown, but only cites a relatively small number of counties, Forster, 'Government in provincial England under the later Stuarts', p. 47.

holding and institutions by central government. More debatable are the objectives that lay behind these intrusions and the impact which they had at local level. First, there was the desire to see men loyal to the regime and its policies prominent in, if not solely in control of, local offices. Secondly, there was a desire to increase central control over local institutions and officials. Thirdly, there was the intention to promote the election of a Parliament which would be agreeable to the government and its current policies. It is often hard to disentangle these elements at the centre, and perhaps artificial to do so.

The amount that can be learned about central intentions from a local study such as this is necessarily limited. So the main intention of this section is to establish what impact these decisions of central government and the initiatives which they inspired had on local office-holding and officialdom in Hampshire, between the Popish Plot and the Revolution of 1688. However, it is hoped that some light will be shed on the intentions of central government, in anticipation of a more general re-appraisal of central government and the localities in this crucial decade.

The Exclusion Crisis had several important effects on the structures of power and patronage in Hampshire, through the acceleration of trends which had been apparent before 1678. Edward Noel continued to enjoy royal favour, even after his humiliation in the county election for the second Exclusion Parliament, through the mediation of Danby and Colonel George Legge.[3] He continued to collect honours and local offices, and thus increased his hold over local patronage. Noel was made a baron in time to attend the Oxford Parliament, through Danby's influence. In July 1681, he replaced Lord Annesley as *custos rotulorum*. And by the beginning of October, the king had offered him the post of governor of Portsmouth, in succession to George Legge, though the duke of York was less happy about the prospect of his client relinquishing this command. Noel was unable to meet the purchase price of £5,000 which Legge was asking and sought Danby's intercession with his father Viscount Campden to make a contribution. The money was obtained and Lord Noel duly took up his command. On his father's death in 1682 he succeeded to his offices in the family's home county of Rutland, and was created earl of Gainsborough in December of that year, amongst a spate of Tory creations.[4]

Gainsborough now enjoyed considerable power and patronage under the Crown, nominating deputy-lieutenants and sheriffs in Hampshire (as well as in Rutland) and approving nominees for commands in Portsmouth garrison,

---

[3] For Noel's electoral humiliation, see below, p. 209.

[4] Browning, *Danby*, i. 345n; P.R.O., C231/8, pp. 42, 51; Brit. Lib., Addit. MS 28053 (Leeds papers), fols. 279, 287; *Hist. MSS Comm. Eleventh Report App. pt. V Dartmouth MSS*, i. 72; *Cal.S.P.Dom.*, 1682, p. 527; *H.C.*, iii. 144–5.

not to mention offices connected with the New Forest. He was able to groom his son to succeed him, making him his joint lord lieutenant, and deputy-governor of Portsmouth.[5] His caution in electoral and borough politics should not be taken to signify a lack of commitment to the regime, but is entirely understandable in the light of his experience as recently as 1679. His support for the government and its policies before 1687 was quite unequivocal. To return to Professor Aylmer's metaphor, Gainsborough was indeed something of a local viceroy, enjoying huge local power, by virtue of royal favour.

Despite his ultimate break with the Tories, James II preserved the structure of patronage which had developed during their ascendancy. Initially of course, Gainsborough was continued in all his offices, but when in spite of being summoned to London and personally closeted by the king, he refused to agree to the repeal of the Test Acts and penal laws, he was unceremoniously dismissed from all of them.[6] The extent of aristocratic opposition to the king's policy made it imperative for the king to change the structure of local patronage, which depended so much on aristocratic support.[7] Yet he failed to do this, choosing instead to load offices and responsibilities on to the shoulders of the few peers who would support him, many of them Catholics. So in Hampshire, the duke of Berwick, the king's illegitimate son, succeeded to all Gainsborough's offices, including the *custos*-ship. This seventeen-year-old Catholic prince, who had recently returned from Hungary, totally lacked local knowledge or connections, and was quite unsuitable for the role he was now called upon to play. His appointment resulted in a loosening of the royal grip upon the county and his developing smallpox in March 1688 further undermined his effectiveness. Yet it was not until November 1688, when Berwick went to serve with the army, that the king thought to break up the massive accumulation of power and patronage which was so unsuitable to the new political circumstances and to the person who had been called upon to wield them. Then John, the new Lord De la Warr, briefly acceded to the office of lord lieutenant.[8]

Another tendency in the central control of local office-holding and patronage which the Exclusion Crisis helped to stimulate lay in the purging of

[5] *Cal.S.P.Dom.*, 1682, pp. 81, 319, 471, 473; *Cal.S.P.Dom.*, Jan.–June 1683, pp. 99, 155; *Cal.S.P.Dom.*, 1683–4, pp. 164, 255; *Cal.S.P.Dom.*, 1684–5, p. 207.

[6] *Cal.S.P.Dom.*, 1685, no. 343, p. 80; *Cal.S.P.Dom.*, 1687–9, no. 487, p. 96; Brit. Lib., Addit. MS 34510 (MacIntosh Collection), fol. 65.

[7] For the content of aristocratic opposition see D. H. Hosford, *Nottingham, Nobles and the North, Aspects of the Revolution of 1688* (Hamden, Conn., 1976), ch. II, pp. 9–26.

[8] *Cal.S.P.Dom.*, 1687–9, no. 582, p. 112; N. Luttrell, *A Brief Historical Relation of State Affairs from September 1678 to April 1714* (6 vols., Oxford, 1857), i. 422, 429, 435; *Penal Laws and the Test Act: questions touching their repeal propounded in 1687–88 by James II*, ed. G. F. Duckett (2 vols., London (privately printed) 1882–3), i. 423n.

known opponents of the government from the commissions of the peace. Before the Popish Plot scare, the government had been aware that there were disaffected elements in Hampshire's commission, but had made only a piecemeal effort to rectify the situation.[9]

At the national level, it was the exclusionists who first proposed to purge the commissions of the peace systematically. Membership of the local bench had no direct electoral significance, since ejected justices could still vote, but purging was an easy way of humiliating opponents, as well as attuning local government to the views and policies of those in power at the centre. In May 1679, the exclusionists hoped to use their influence on the remodelled Privy Council to purge opponents from the commissions on the spurious grounds of inactivity. The marquis of Winchester and Lord Russell were the councillors ordered to consult the lord chancellor, the circuit judges, the diocesan bishop, lord lieutenant and the *custos rotulorum* with a view to purging Hampshire's commission.[10] Such consultations, if they took place at all, can hardly have been very fruitful, considering the political diversity of the participants. In any case, the whole plan was foiled by the king's insistence on striking out the names of undesirable justices personally, and reprieving them for frivolous reasons.

When the remodelling of the commissions took place early in 1680, in Hampshire as in other counties, the changes favoured the opponents rather than the supporters of exclusion, though the purge of the latter was somewhat haphazard and incomplete.[11] On 21 February 1680, the duke of Buckingham and two exclusionist MPs were removed from the Hampshire commission. At the same time, eleven men were admitted to the Hampshire commission, who would mostly prove to be staunch Tories. Then on 10 April, another seven JPs were excluded from the Hampshire bench, though at least two of these removals were for non-political reasons.[12] But two exclusionist MPs, Oliver St John and Henry Tulse, managed to remain on the commission of the peace at least until 1682. Oliver St John was joined by thirteen other Hampshire justices in voting for exclusionist candidates in the election for the Oxford Parliament, of whom only three besides St John were removed from the commission of the peace during Charles II's reign. In fact,

---

[9]   See above, p. 154; the Privy Council was aware that it had not removed all the disaffected as in April 1678 it referred the investigation of a local riot to 'some of the active and well affected Justices of the Peace' in Hampshire, P.R.O., P.C. 2/66, p. 301.

[10]   P.R.O., P.C. 2/68, pp. 47–8.

[11]   L. K. J. Glassey, *Politics and the Appointment of Justices of the Peace 1675–1720* (Oxford, 1979), pp. 42–3, 45–52.

[12]   Thomas Neale and John Stewkeley had both recently sold their Hampshire properties, *Hist. MSS Comm. Eleventh Report App. pt. II House of Lords MSS 1678–88*, pp. 177, 189; *H.C.,* iii. 129–31; *Verney Memoirs*, iv. 273; nationally 272 out of 2559 JPs were removed at this time, N. Landau, *The Justices of the Peace 1679–1760* (Berkeley, 1984), p. 74.

two other gentlemen who had voted for the exclusionists were only admitted to the bench in 1682.[13] The earl of Gainsborough, who had an important influence over the composition of the commission, was keen to win over moderate men, so only the irreconcilable were purged and kept out of the commission of the peace. But the Hampshire bench was nevertheless dominated by those who had supported Gainsborough and opposed exclusion throughout. This did not satisfy extremists. Bernard Howard, a younger son of the earl of Arundel and a Catholic, who became increasingly involved in Winchester politics as the 1680s progressed, complained bitterly about Gainsborough's indulgence to former Whigs, at the time of the election of 1685. He tried to circumvent Gainsborough and to persuade Sunderland to initiate a purge, apparently without success. For his part, Sunderland must have shared Gainsborough's view that a brief flirtation with exclusion did not prevent a man becoming a loyal servant of the king.[14]

In the years after 1681, other institutions of county government were remodelled on party lines under the auspices of an increasingly confident central government. The shrievalty was of great importance, as much for the control which could be exercised through it over local juries, as for possible electoral influence. It was particularly crucial in the early 1680s, with the government seeking to stamp out dissent and disaffection as well as win the propaganda war against its opponents, to have reliable juries empanelled at the assizes and quarter sessions. During the Danby period the office of sheriff had been bestowed on a curious collection of men in Hampshire, at least one of whom, Henry Whitehead (1677–8) was openly hostile to the regime. He had just been removed from the commission of the peace on that account. Few of the other sheriffs in that period were JPs either. None enjoyed the rank above that of esquire.[15] This completely changed in the 1680s. Of the six sheriffs appointed between 1680 and 1685, four were already on the commission of the peace by the time of their appointment, one was also a deputy-lieutenant, and another was a militia colonel. One was a baronet and two were knights. Apart from Gabriel Whistler (1681–2), who had voted for exclusionist candidates in 1681, their loyalty was unimpeachable, and Whistler was by no means irreconcilable.[16]

The impact of this transformation was soon working its way through to the

---

13 P.R.O., C193/12/4, fol. 106; C231/8, pp. 51, 62; All Souls College, Oxford, MS 223 (not foliated throughout): list of JPs in commission ? May–June 1682; Glassey, *Politics and the Appointment of Justices of the Peace*, p. 50; H.C.R.O., 44M69 06 'The names of the pole taken the 21th [sic] of ffebruary' [1681].
14 *Cal.S.P.Dom.*, 1685, no. 392, pp. 96–7; Sunderland had voted for exclusion.
15 P.R.O. *Lists and Indexes No. ix: Sheriffs for England and Wales to 1831*, p. 57.
16 P.R.O. *Lists and Indexes No. ix: Sheriffs for England and Wales to 1831*, p. 57; P.R.O., C193/12/4; All Souls MS 223; fol. 2; H.C.R.O., 44M69 06 'The names of the pole taken the 21th of ffebruary'.

composition of juries at Hampshire assizes. The assize grand jury of July 1681 was evenly divided between promoters and opponents of a loyal address, thanking the king for his declaration after the dissolution of the Oxford Parliament. It was adopted by a narrow majority.[17] But the uncompromising opponents did not long survive on the assize grand jury.[18] In March 1682, the grand jury unanimously supported an abhorrence of Shaftesbury's association scheme, in the name of the county. Subsequent grand juries were quick to condemn the Rye House Plot, and to help the king over his plan to build a palace at Winchester.[19] In these gestures, they collaborated easily with the bench, and this was hardly surprising as an increasing number of JPs served as grand jurymen.[20] There were five JPs on the grand jury which put the county hall at the king's disposal to facilitate the building of the palace at Winchester.[21]

This is not to say that Hampshire juries in this period lacked any sort of independence. Despite their political complexion, they were capable of showing moderation. The grand jury at the summer assizes of 1682 refused to find a 'true bill' on an indictment for riot against some Andover Quakers despite strong pressure from Justice Raymond, and would only agree to find an indictment of unlawful assembly.[22] But such scruples posed no threat to the government or the successful enforcement of its policies.

The experience of the Exclusion Crisis produced in Hampshire, as in other counties, a Tory gentry, who were prepared to see central interference in, and manipulation of, local office-holding to guarantee themselves in power. A similar phenomenon is observable in several of the county's principal boroughs even before the dissolution of the Oxford Parliament.

Within the corporation of Andover there had long been apparent a willingness to exploit external, and especially royal, favour in the town's interest. During the 1670s, the corporation remained reasonably united. The resumption of persecution of dissenters in 1673 provoked no serious tension

---

[17] Luttrell, *A Brief Historical Relation*, i. 114–15; *Cal.S.P.Dom.*, 1680–1, p. 370; P.R.O. (Kew), Adm. 77/1, fol. 190.

[18] Because only one grand jury list survives for this period in Hampshire, it is not possible to establish exactly how many, if any, opponents were won over; it is clear from another source that three members of the minority on the grand jury remained unreconciled to the royal government, see below, p. 213; however, one of the minority, Francis Hanbury sought to distance himself from the protestation which his colleagues drew up against the loyal address and went so far as to formally disown it through the *London Gazette* (no. 1640, 4–8 August 1681).

[19] Luttrell, *A Brief Historical Relation*, i. 172–3, 275; *Cal.S.P.Dom.*, Jan–June 1683, p. 84; *Cal.S.P.Dom.*, 1683–4, p. 303.

[20] For this phenomenon elsewhere see Landau, *The Justices of the Peace*, p. 50.

[21] In July 1667, there had hardly been any JPs on the grand jury: Staffordshire County Record Office, Dartmouth MSS D (W) 1778 V, no. 120B; P.R.O., S.P. 29/422/108: L.D.R., B/144.

[22] H.C.R.O., 24M54/14, fol. 27.

amongst magistrates, though it was extremely unpopular in the town at large. In 1678, two court supporters competed for the votes of members of the corporation to take the place of another court supporter, Sir Kingsmill Lucy, in one of the town's seats in Parliament.[23] But with the Popish Plot and Exclusion Crisis, a determined opposition faction emerged on the corporation, which tried to take over the borough. Under the leadership of William Wimbleton (bailiff 1678–9), they tried to put all power and representation into the hands of like-minded men. They replaced the steward John Collins, whom Shaftesbury reckoned doubly vile, with William Wither, whom they also returned to the first Exclusion Parliament, by dubious means according to the petition of the defeated court candidate. When Wither died they replaced him as steward with William Guidott, and as MP with Sir Robert Henley, of the Grange, Northington, this time defeating the ousted steward John Collins for the seat.[24] It was only when the opposition faction sought to entrench themselves in power through sharp practice that the majority on the corporation seriously challenged their activities. At a common council meeting held on 5 September 1679, where the faction held a narrow majority of those present, they tried to ensure that the contest for the office of bailiff in the coming year would be between Joseph Hinxman, one of their number, and William Barwick, a moderate, who had only been elected one of the 'approved men' (equivalent of aldermen) under their auspices on 10 February that year. Thomas Westcombe, the leader of the persecution in 1673, was specifically ruled out of the contest. But on 7 September, the enemies of the faction turned out in strength and sought to elect Westcombe bailiff. Wimbleton and his faction compromised to the extent of opting for Barwick, but they were still out-voted by the majority of those present, whom they sought to over-rule. Faced with such blatant malpractice the embryonic Tory majority appealed to the king and Privy Council, their petition being raised on 17 September. Wimbleton and his allies played for time and had the hearing adjourned until 4 November, but to no avail, for when the case was heard, the Privy Council had no hesitation in deciding the case in Westcombe's favour. After this triumph, the loyalists increased in confidence and secured the return of two like-minded men in the contested election for the Oxford Parliament, despite an abortive attempt by the defeated candidates to get the franchise widened to include freemen. Meanwhile John Collins regained his stewardship and was knighted in 1681.[25] But there was still an opposition

---

23 *Don Quixote Redivivus, passim*; Lucy had retreated from his earlier country stance before his death, *H.C.*, i. 246.

24 *H.C.*, i. 246; ii. 108; H.C.R.O., 37M84, 4/MI/3; the other seat continued to be held by Francis Paulet.

25 H.C.R.O., 37M84, 4/EL/1; P.R.O., P.C. 2/68, pp. 206, 216, 269; *H.C.*, i. 246; ii. 108.

faction on the corporation, which would require further government interference to remove.

The hold of loyalists over the government and representation of
Southampton was more secure than at Andover, but was still too precarious
for the liking of zealots. One such, Dr John Speed, spoke of their worries in a
letter to Secretary Jenkins in May 1680, in connection with the royal order for
the Corporation Act to be strictly enforced. For Speed and his fellows on the
corporation, the act of 1661 did not go far enough, since it failed to affect
those burgesses, who, having once taken the oaths and sacrament, had no
obligation to do so again unless they held one of the corporation's executive
offices. This enabled 'disaffected' men to survive in the corporation who
might one day take control of it, and they, along with ejected burgesses and
dissenters, retained their votes as freemen in parliamentary elections. Speed
was clearly thinking that the government would be well advised to take the
initiative to control membership of the corporation more tightly and restrict
the franchise.[26]

But in formulating its policy towards the boroughs in the early 1680s, the
government had to do without the co-operation of Parliament, which had
proved so useful in the early 1660s. The implementation of the policy was
therefore less systematic and comprehensive than the initial enforcement of
the Corporation Act, and was incomplete by the time of Charles II's death in
February 1685. Dr Miller does not take sufficient account of these factors in
his recent discussion of the royal government's handling of the boroughs in
this period. The fact that ministers proceeded with caution and with a variety
of intentions and that their plans were not executed to the letter should not
be allowed to distract attention from the real increase in royal influence
which occurred in many boroughs.[27]

Between the summer of 1682 and February 1685, there were moves against
the charters of five of Hampshire's twelve parliamentary boroughs, resulting
in five surrenders and the granting of three new ones during Charles II's
reign.[28] Dr Miller suggests that the initiative for such moves usually came
from local Tories.[29] But in Hampshire this can only be said categorically of

---

[26] *Cal.S.P.Dom.*, 1679–80, pp. 479–80.

[27] Miller, 'The crown and the borough charters in the reign of Charles II', pp. 70–84.

[28] Andover, Newport, Portsmouth, Southampton and Winchester surrendered their charters;
Andover, Newport and Portsmouth received new ones, R. G. Pickavance, 'The English
boroughs and the king's government: a study of the Tory reaction 1681–5' (Oxford Univ.,
D.Phil. thesis, 1976), pp. 159, 163–5; the relatively small number of new charters for
Hampshire boroughs seems to have had more to do with the untimely death of Charles II
than the attitude of local Tories, contrary to Dr Miller's hypothesis, Miller, 'The crown and
borough charters in the reign of Charles II', p. 84.

[29] *Ibid.*, pp. 74–84.

one borough, Southampton, though in every case the compliant attitude of local Tories was certainly a help.

There was a borough policy which was being enforced upon the localities, but what were its objectives? Dr Pickavance is right to reject the view that its motivation was principally electoral. Two of the boroughs in Hampshire which remained unscathed continued to return opposition MPs.[30] Indeed, Lymington became more factious after 1681 than it had been before, admitting formerly ejected burgesses, and local dissenting and exclusionist gentry to the corporation. Finally, Thomas Dore, who was mayor between 1683 and 1685 was actually in arms for Monmouth.[31] And if the declarations and addresses of the early 1680s are anything to go by, the boroughs whose charters were surrendered were already strongly loyal by 1681–2.[32] However, electoral considerations were not entirely absent. There were electoral dividends for remodelling some charters. Wimbleton and his faction were neatly removed from the corporation of Andover, thus rendering it a safe Tory seat.[33] Andover was the only place in Hampshire where significant changes of personnel were really necessary. But at Portsmouth and Newport the Crown was given power to alter the electorate en bloc in future.[34]

Even from the limited evidence relating to Hampshire's boroughs, it is clear that there was a desire at the highest levels of government to obtain effective control over local law courts, and to eradicate the jurisdictional anomalies which obstructed justice and the enforcement of central policies. In the new Portsmouth charter, which was the first to be passed after the memorandum of May 1682 which effectively launched the borough policy, the Crown was given the right to approve all members of the corporation, which gave the government control over the borough sessions. The jurisdiction of this court was also extended to include Gosport, a centre of dissent and disorder near the town.[35] In the new charter for Newport, of 5 March 1684, resident Hampshire JPs of the quorum were empowered to act within the borough, thus giving the Crown ultimate control over its quarter sessions as well, if

---

[30] Lymington and Whitchurch: both were administratively insignificant, *H.C.*, i. 248–9, 257–8.

[31] St Barbe, *Lymington*, pp. 9–10, 18; one reason for Lymington's escape may have been the fact that it was a corporation by prescription and did not possess a royal charter which rendered proceedings against it problematical, see below, p. 175.

[32] Luttrell, *A Brief Historical Relation*, i. 85, 88, 100, 103, 177, 178, 182, 193.

[33] *H.C.*, i. 246; H.C.R.O., 37M84, 1/CH/13 (Contemporary copy of charter of Charles II); the Crown was given a veto over future appointments of the town clerk, steward and deputy-steward.

[34] Portsmouth's new charter which was partly directed against the 'restless party' also had the effect of radically reducing the size of the electorate, *H.C.*, i. 254; I.W.C.R.O., translated copy of Newport charter 1684.

[35] Pickavance, 'The English boroughs and the king's government', p. 159; *Portsmouth Sessions Papers*, ed. Hoad, pp. 97ff.

need arose.[36] The separate county status of certain boroughs came under particular criticism in the memorandum of May 1682, especially in those areas like Southampton where the borough was outside the jurisdiction of normal assize circuits. So when Southampton corporation sought to have its charter renewed, the king, on the advice of Lord Keeper Guilford, insisted that the separate county status be surrendered as it 'is a great trouble to the judges and a grievance to the people'.[37] He might have added that it had been a thorn in the side of successive governments for at least forty years and more.

The boroughs of Lymington, Stockbridge and Whitchurch were subject to the jurisdiction of the county quarter sessions court and hence offered no sanctuary to those accused of disloyalty. In 1683, Giles Wadlington, constable of Stockbridge, was briefly imprisoned for failing to report the dangerous words of one John Reeves, spoken in the borough. There were warrants out for the arrest of Thomas Dore, mayor of Lymington, in 1683 and 1685. And at the Michaelmas quarter sessions, 1684, another future rebel David Roberts, a gentleman from Brockenhurst, was indicted for seditious words spoken at Lymington.[38]

But it was not only amateur office-holders in county and borough who were subjected to greater central scrutiny during the early 1680s. The royal government began to assert its influence over its paid and professional servants in the localities, notably in the military and revenue establishments, though for reasons of administrative efficiency rather than political manipulation.

One area where a greater degree of central control was obviously desirable was the local military establishment. Since the Restoration, local garrison commanders and gunners holding their offices by patent had shown an increasing independence of central authority. Garrison commanders like Major Edward Strange, commander of Hurst castle, and Sir Robert Holmes had obstructed rather than assisted revenue collection in the areas under their control. And soldiers quartered at Titchfield in 1679 did the same.[39] In the garrisons, absenteeism and false musters undermined military efficiency. But in 1681 and afterwards, all these problems were tackled with some degree of success. In 1682, a royal warrant enhanced the control of the master general of the ordnance over gunners in outposts such as those on the Solent and in the Isle of Wight, with power to turn out the inefficient, despite their patent offices. The emoluments of garrison appointments were brought under

---

[36] *Cal.S.P.Dom.*, 1683–4, p. 166.
[37] Pickavance, 'The English boroughs and the king's government', p. 184; S.C.R.O., SC2/1/9, p. 74.
[38] *Cal.S.P.Dom.*, July–September 1683, p. 385; *Cal.S.P.Dom.*, 1685, no. 818, p. 186; H.C.R.O., QO 6, fol. 56; Sessions rolls, file 13, indictment of David Roberts.
[39] P.R.O., P.C. 2/63, p. 290; P.C. 2/66, p. 164; *C.J.*, ix. 367; *Cal.S.P.Dom.*, 1679–80, p. 124.

stricter control. Gunners were subjected to full military discipline and ordered to exercise regularly. On 16 April 1683, a royal order was issued for absentee officers to be cashiered, and a year later Lieutenant John Fry lost his commission in Portsmouth garrison upon this account, and was replaced.[40] Political undesirables were also weeded out. One Lock, a gunner at Yarmouth, was turned out when Sir Robert Holmes discovered he preached at conventicles.[41] Nor were the various forms of sharp practice carried on by garrison commanders exempt from scrutiny. Sir Robert and Sir John Holmes (commander of Hurst castle) were ordered to stop obstructing local revenue collection and were obliged to submit.[42] In the spring of 1684, allegations of false musters were made against Sir Robert Holmes, who tried to use his influence with William Blathwayt, the secretary at war, to avoid a court martial. But when Dr George Clarke, the judge advocate, reported the manoeuvres to the king, he disapproved of them 'in fairly harsh terms'. So a court martial went ahead on 27 May, and the charges against Holmes were substantiated. Holmes did not lose his command, but the court martial certainly put a stop to his false musters, and the Treasury kept a careful eye on his accounts.[43] The effect of martial law generally in this period was to increase central control over the military, and to make it more dependable.[44] In the event, Sir Robert Holmes was to prove one of the loyalest servants of James II.

Tighter control was also exercised over the local revenue establishments in this period. Indeed, under the auspices of the Treasury, there was a quite unprecedented and systematic attempt not only to make the revenue officials more professional and dependable, but also to detach them from the local communities in which they served. In 1675, the customs establishment based in Hampshire numbered thirty-two, besides the patent officers and clerks (a notable increase on the Interregnum figure). By 1679, a number of changes had taken place in its structure, but it remained much the same size.[45] But after 1679, officers appear to have become more mobile and increasingly liable to be dismissed, for incapacity or political unsuitability. Between 1679 and 1684, eight customs officers were dismissed at Portsmouth, Cowes,

---

[40] C. M. Clode, *The Military Forces of the Crown: Their Administration and Government* (2 vols., London, 1869), i. 8–9; J. R. Western, *Monarchy and Revolution: The English State in the 1680s* (London, 1972), p. 130; Staffordshire County Record Office, Dartmouth MSS D(W)1778 V. no. 42; *Cal.S.P.Dom.*, January–June 1683, p. 180; Dalton, *Army Lists*, i. 326.

[41] P.R.O., S.P. 29/428/146.

[42] P.R.O., P.C. 2/69, p. 413; *Cal.S.P.Dom.*. January–June 1683, p. 203; *Cal.Treas.Bks.*, vii. 1212–13.

[43] P.R.O. (Kew), War Office 89, no. 1, pp. 67–8, 73–7; *Hist. MSS Comm. Leyborne-Popham MSS*, p. 262; P.R.O., E101/612/72: muster rolls of Cowes, Portsmouth, Sandham and Carisbrooke 1686; *Cal.Treas.Bks.*, vii. 1517.

[44] Childs, *The Army, James II and the Glorious Revolution*, pp. 91–8.

[45] P.R.O. (Kew), Customs Establishments, CUST 18/1A, fols. 14–15; CUST 18/2, fols. 14–15, see above, p. 25.

Southampton and Lymington for incompetence, malpractice or disaffection.[46] In 1684, the Treasury ordered that all promotions should be on merit, and customs officers were subjected to increasing scrutiny by the Customs Commissioners who went on circuits of inspection and recommended changes in local customs administration.[47] As they were promoted customs officers moved from one part of the country to another, and strangers came to be posted in Hampshire ports.[48] But the links between the customs establishment and the local community could not be severed overnight.

The potential for such independence and central control was greater in the case of excise officers. When direct collection was resumed in 1683, a thoroughgoing reform was instituted which rendered the excise department in Professor Geoffrey Holmes' words 'by far the largest and most consciously professionalised government department yet seen in England'.[49] This reform was carried through into the provinces between then and the summer of 1685, by means of tours of inspection comparable to those carried out by the Customs Commissioners. Dr Charles Davenant, who according to Hughes undertook the survey in 1684, reached Hampshire on 12 April 1684. After close inspection he made detailed recommendations for changes in the structure and personnel of excise collection in the county. In general his judgement on officers in Hampshire was a harsh one 'The county has a great many ignorant officers & most of 'em have been there too long.'[50] However, most of the twenty officers to whom Davenant refers were experienced men. In 1683, the local machinery of the excise farms had been taken over en bloc.[51] And yet by April 1684, only two of the officers referred to by Davenant had been in the same place before Michaelmas 1683. Only one, Edward Rainsford, surveyor at Yarmouth and Cowes had been in place long enough to develop local roots. He had been appointed a burgess in the recent new charter for Newport, and in Davenant's view was 'to[o] well acquainted in the Island'. He urged that he be moved.[52] This was a very long way from the situation which had prevailed even in the Interregnum.[53] At its upper levels, the local excise establishment had throughout the 1670s been controlled by men who were outsiders to the

[46] Baxter, *Treasury*, p. 91; *Cal.Treas.Bks.*, vi, 98. 137, 201; *Cal.Treas.Bks.*, vii. 563, 602, 997, 1075, 1289.
[47] Western, *Monarchy and Revolution*, p. 101; *Cal.Treas.Bks.*, vii. 968; viii. 908, 1290.
[48] *Cal.Treas.Bks.*, vi. 201; *Cal.Treas.Bks.*, vii. 507, 810.
[49] G. Holmes, *Augustan England: Professions, State and Society, 1680–1730* (London, 1982), p. 242.
[50] Diaries of the survey are contained in Brit. Lib., MSS Harl. 5120–3; the main section on Hampshire is to be found in MS Harl. 5121, fols. 10–20; for attribution to Davenant, E. Hughes, *Studies in Administration and Finance 1558–1825* (Manchester, 1934), p. 160.
[51] Chandaman, *The English Public Revenue*, p. 72.
[52] Brit. Lib., MS Harl. 5121, fol. 13.   [53] See above, p. 25.

locality. Now at the end of Charles II's reign, the excisemen of all ranks were a professional caste almost entirely separate from local society.

By the end of Charles II's reign, all the significant institutions of local government in Hampshire were in the hands of men loyal to the central government and the legitimate successor. Central control had been enhanced, not only in the boroughs, but also over the locally stationed military and revenue establishments. By comparison with the last four years of Charles II's reign, in the first two years of James II's there was considerable stability in local office-holding. The actions against the charters of Winchester and Southampton were allowed to lapse, at least in the latter case for want of funds.[54] The commission of the peace remained fairly static. The lieutenancy remained unchanged. Even the rate of change in the revenue establishments appears to have slowed down.[55]

But from the autumn of 1686, James II embarked on his policy of promoting Catholics in local government. He also wanted to promote men who would support the repeal of the penal laws and Test Acts. A retrospective explanation of what the king intended to do was contained in the instructions to the assize judges in the summer of 1688:

his Majesty is unalterably resolved to place trust and confidence in and to reward all such of his subjects as shall zealously assist in his present measures, and to look upon all that shall oppose him herein as contemners of his royal will and pleasure and enemies of the common good of his Kingdom.[56]

This policy had been applied to local government.

But from the start the enforcement of the king's will was bedevilled by ignorance and incompetence. Hampshire, unlike some counties, had a substantial Catholic landed class from which local officials could be recruited. The Privy Council committee, appointed on 22 October 1686, recommended nine Catholic gentlemen to be included in a new Hampshire commission of the peace, which was issued at the same time as those for other counties the following spring. However, the new Catholic justices were unable to act because the commission contained no dispensation clause to free them from the statutory oaths and a new commission had to be issued on 1 July 1687. Catholics did not begin to participate in county government in Hampshire until Michaelmas sessions 1687, precisely a year after the king had launched the initiative to include them on the bench.[57] The other changes which were

[54] R. H. George, 'The charters granted to English parliamentary corporations in 1688', *E.H.R.*, lv. (1940), 49.

[55] P.R.O., C231/8, pp. 118–58; *Cal.Treas.Bks.*, viii. *passim*.

[56] *Collectanea Curiosa*, ed. J. Gutch (2 vols., Oxford, 1781), i. 392–3.

[57] P.R.O., P.C. 2/71, p. 363; C231/8, p. 183; Glassey, *Politics and the Appointment of Justices of the Peace*, p. 71; H.C.R.O., QO 6, fol. 106.

made in Hampshire's commission at this time were woefully misinformed. Apart from Lord Dartmouth, the Council committee included no one with any knowledge of the county. Of the six justices purged, one, George Bridges, would later assent to the Three Questions. Worse, out of the twelve Protestants appointed at the same time, seven would subsequently return a negative to the first two questions. Lacking reliable information about the attitudes of justices to the king's religious policy, the government had inadvertently increased the number of those on the bench who opposed it. Hitherto, the government had gained such information via the lord lieutenant, but Gainsborough himself was known to be unhappy about the king's policy.[58] In December 1687, he was displaced, and his successor Berwick was entrusted with putting the Three Questions to justices, about their attitudes to the Test Acts, and penal laws and to non-Anglican neighbours.

The Three Questions were put either in person at a meeting at Winchester, or subsequently by post to fifty-four magistrates in Hampshire. Forty-six made replies, of which forty were clearly for or against the royal policy. Twenty-seven deputy-lieutenants and justices of the peace returned negative answers to the first two questions, thirteen assented.[59] Many of the refusers laid down their commissions before the middle of February, without even waiting to be purged, a situation which not even the Commonwealth government had been faced with in Hampshire.[60] This resulted in another radical development, the drawing up of a new commission of the peace from scratch in April 1688. It included the thirteen assenters, the nine Catholics already in commission, eleven naval officers and others who were thought to support the royal policy, and eleven apparently new men, three of whom were Catholics.[61] Out of ninety-six JPs in commission in December 1687 (excluding peers and honorific appointees) twenty-seven were named in the new commission, twenty-eight per cent.[62] At the same time, the lieutenancy was remodelled. Gainsborough and his son Lord Campden had already been removed from the post of lord lieutenant. Now five out of their seven deputies

[58] Glassey, *Politics and the Appointment of Justices of the Peace*, p. 70; *Penal laws and the Test Act*, ed. Duckett, i. 423; K. H. D. Haley, 'A list of the English peers, c. May 1687', *E.H.R.*, lxix. (1954), 305.

[59] *Penal laws and the Test Act*, ed. Duckett, i. 413–14, 420–7.

[60] Brit. Lib., Addit. MS 34510, fol. 83.

[61] One of the apparently new names may be that of an existing JP, see n. 62, below; *Penal laws and the Test Act*, ed. Duckett, i. 419–20, checked against original Bodl. MS Rawl. A 139B, fol. 209; Miller, *Popery and Politics*, p. 271.

[62] This assumes that 'Whisper' or 'Whister' in Bodl. MS Rawl. A 139B, fol. 209, is to be identified with Gabriel Whistler as suggested by the evidence of P.R.O., E372/532 and E372/533; this removal rate of 72 per cent was considerably higher than the national average of 63 per cent calculated by Professor Landau, *The Justices of the Peace*, p. 78; P.R.O., C193/12/5, fols. 123–8; C231/8, pp. 146, 154; P.C. 2/71, p. 363.

were also removed. Lord De la Warr, who had assented to the Three Questions, and Richard Bishop, who had assented with some qualification, were the sole survivors. The lieutenancy was filled out with four Catholics and two Protestants who supported the royal policy.[63]

But despite the unprecedented scale of the turnover in county government, the intentions behind the policy seem to have been essentially limited. The king wanted prestigious offices to be confined to those who positively supported his controversial religious policy. In Hampshire, as in most other counties, this called for a massive purge. But Dr Childs has read more ambitious intentions into the royal policy. According to Childs, 'James stood for the extension of royal control and the centralization of government', and this attitude lay behind the appointment of army officers to positions in the local administration of 1688.[64]

But at least in the case of Hampshire, this development needs to be put in perspective. Here army officers and garrison commanders had long been named to and active in offices in local government. This continued during the early 1680s, when Colonel George Legge, as governor of Portsmouth, was appointed a deputy-lieutenant and commanded a regiment in the county militia.[65] Sir Charles Wyndham, a Guards officer, who owned property locally was appointed a JP in 1682, and deputy-lieutenant in 1683 and acted as such. At the same time, officers holding lesser commands in the Portsmouth, Hurst castle and Isle of Wight garrisons remained in or were appointed to the county commission of the peace. The commission of sewers in the Isle of Wight in 1684 contained five military officers.[66] Thus the six commissioned officers (apart from the earl of Gainsborough) in the Hampshire commission of the peace in October 1685 represented no unprecedented intrusion of the military into local government, especially since seldom more than one was active at any one time.[67] Nor were the six commissioned officers (apart from Sir Henry Tichborne, lieutenant of the ordnance) on the commission of the peace of April 1688 anything out of the ordinary. They owed their places less to the fact that they were officers than to the fact that they had assented to the Three Questions. What had changed was the fact that most of their civilian colleagues had resigned or been removed from the bench for their rejection of the Three Questions. The mili-

[63] *Penal laws and the Test Act*, ed. Duckett, i. 419, 423: *Cal.S.P.Dom.*, 1687–9, no. 1032, p. 189.

[64] Childs, *The Army, James II and the Glorious Revolution*, pp. 104, 109.

[65] Staffordshire County Record Office, Dartmouth MSS, D (W) 1778, V., no. 766; All Souls, MS 223, fol. 29.

[66] P.R.O., C193/12/4, fols. 103–7; C231/8, pp. 49, 59, 62, 89; H.C.R.O., QO 6, *passim; H.C.*, iii. 772; *Cal.S.P.Dom.*, January–June 1683, p. 99: Dalton, *Army Lists*, i. 284, 293, 298; I.W.C.R.O., Car/D.274.

[67] P.R.O., C193/12/5, fols. 123–8.

tary officers and naval officials now amounted to more than a third of the entire commission of the peace, apart from the peers who continued to be named regardless.[68] But this did not produce any significant increase in central control, not least because so few of them were ready to act.

James II might talk of reforming poor law administration,[69] but the purges which he initiated disrupted county government in Hampshire, and undermined rather than enhanced central control over it. The quarter sessions order book contains no evidence of quarter sessions taking place in the county between Easter 1688 and January 1689.[70] However, attendance allowances listed in the Pipe rolls for 1688–9 suggest that some sort of sessions may have been maintained by a skeletal bench.[71] In other counties, a complete breakdown in county government seems to have taken place, though in some cases not until after the king's flight.[72]

In Hampshire, other institutions of county government, while continuing to function, ceased to be controlled by central government. Sir Hele Hooke, the sheriff appointed in December 1687, was a Protestant and headed the list of local officials taking the declaration against transubstantiation at Easter quarter sessions 1688. The grand jury which he empanelled at the summer assizes came close to presenting Catholics for holding local offices without taking the statutory oaths, which would have been a blatant act of defiance against government policy.[73]

The government's campaign against the boroughs in 1687–8 showed many of the characteristics of the purge of county government. Initially those in charge at the centre displayed utter ignorance of local conditions. This was partly remedied by detailed local research carried out by the electoral agents and was followed by ruthless purges of personnel. Like the campaign of 1682–5, it was incomplete when brought to a premature end in October 1688, but unlike the earlier policy its aim seems to have been mainly electoral. Indeed, as with county government those in power at the centre displayed a

---

[68] *Penal laws and the Test Act*, ed. Duckett, pp. 419–20; Glassey, *Politics and the Appointment of Justices of the Peace*, p. 85.

[69] Miller, *James II*, p. 161.

[70] H.C.R.O., QO 6, fols. 109, 114.

[71] P.R.O., E372/532 and 533; nine justices were paid for eight days attendance, the usual annual total, for the period up to and including July 1688, though at least three of them had been removed from the commission of the peace by then; six justices, at least five of whom were Catholics, were paid for nine days for the period from October 1688 to July 1689, though all Catholic justices had ceased to act by January 1689; it is hard to know what these attendances amounted to in terms of the holding of the quarter sessions in Hampshire.

[72] Forster, 'Government in provincial England under the later Stuarts', p. 47.

[73] H.C.R.O., Q.S. File, declarations against transubstantiation 1679–88, fol. 13; *The Ellis Correspondence: Letters written during the years 1686, 1687, 1688 and addressed to John Ellis Esq.*, ed. G. A. Ellis (2 vols., London, 1829), ii. 108–9.

marked lack of interest towards both the smooth-running of local administration and the exercise of control over it.[74]

In the case of Hampshire, the campaign began with three *quo warranto* writs being issued, against the corporations of Lymington, Southampton and Winchester, which were served in January 1688. But the latter two were not strictly necessary, for both Southampton and Winchester corporations had sealed deeds of surrender of their charters in Charles II's reign. Southampton corporation politely reminded the government of this fact in a letter to the attorney-general, in which it signified its intention not to contest the *quo warranto*.[75] But both Lymington and Winchester corporations resolved to contest theirs, the former incurring the cost of £47 in the process, before the Crown abandoned the case.[76] The only other action taken against Hampshire boroughs at this time had little electoral significance. On 10 February 1688, five members of Basingstoke corporation were removed by order of the Privy Council, though the town had no parliamentary representation. And the town clerk of Andover was removed on 25 March 1688, presumably in order to persuade the other members of the corporation to support the royal policy.[77]

The pressure was maintained against Winchester corporation. The former surrender was discovered and enrolled, and a judgement obtained in King's Bench upon the recent *quo warranto*. But the corporation continued to resist the attack on its privileges, and it was apparently necessary for Bernard Howard, now a lieutenant-colonel in the army, to billet a large number of soldiers on the city before the corporation would submit. Finally, the king displaced the corporation altogether and installed commissioners to run the city, while a writ of seizure under the *quo warranto* was issued from King's Bench on 4 July.[78]

By the end of April, electoral agents were active in the county and their report gave central government its first solid information about the local situation for some months.[79] They recommended thorough purges of the corporations of Andover, Southampton and Winchester. No action was taken against the former, but the latter two received new charters in

---

[74] As Forster has aptly put it 'it meant interference not with measures but with men', 'Government in provincial England under the later Stuarts', p. 47.

[75] George, 'The charters granted to English parliamentary corporations in 1688', p. 49 and note; H.C.R.O., W/B1/7, fol. 36; 27M74A DBC/2, fol. 107; S.C.R.O., 2/1/9, pp. 134–5.

[76] *Penal laws and the Test Act*, ed. Duckett, i. 429, 433; H.C.R.O., 27M74A, DBC/2, fol. 109; St Barbe, *Lymington*, p. 25.

[77] P.R.O., P.C. 2/72, pp. 608, 640.

[78] George, 'The charters granted to English parliamentary corporations in 1688', p. 49; Childs, *The Army, James II and the Glorious Revolution*, p. 111.

[79] The identity of the agent who operated in Hampshire is not known, *Penal laws and the Test Act*, ed. Duckett, i. 427–31.

September, at the Crown's expense in accordance with a recommendation from the central committee regulating corporations.[80]

The purges of Southampton and Winchester corporations which were enacted in the new charters were massive. Of the ten senior members of Southampton's corporation who had agreed not to contest the *quo warranto* in January 1688, five at most were named in the new corporation. No more than a dozen of the twenty-seven members of the new corporation had been in the old one, the new men included dissenters and formerly ejected burgesses like Richard Hunt and William Braxton.[81] At Winchester, the purge was even more extreme. In 1685, the corporation had included a few Catholic gentlemen, and apart from Protestant supporters of the royal policy, like Sir Thomas Higgons and Sir Roger L'Estrange, these were virtually the only survivors from the old corporation to be named to the new. Bernard Howard became recorder.[82] Both charters contained clauses dispensing those appointed from statutory oaths. But these corporations existed even on paper for barely a month, for on 17 October, James II annulled all proceedings against borough charters since 1679, and all ejections were reversed. As Winchester's surrender had been enrolled it was necessary in effect to make a re-grant of the old charter in order to restore the old corporation, which took place in early November.[83]

The campaign of 1687–8 had been primarily electoral in its purpose: the election of a Parliament which would repeal the penal laws and Test Acts. Southampton's new charter had confined the electorate to the mayor, aldermen and burgesses named in the charter, and a similar clause appeared in the Winchester charter. Other boroughs escaped remodelling either because the agents held out the hope of getting 'right' candidates returned, or as in the case of the corrupt borough of Stockbridge, they regarded the situation as hopeless.[84]

Neither the agents nor the government which employed them showed the least interest in the functioning of local administration, or enhancing central control over it. There was none of the concern, so apparent in the case of Hampshire between 1682 and 1685, to undermine the judicial independence

---

[80] *Cal.S.P.Dom.*, 1687–9, nos. 1427, 1439, pp. 261, 263; on the committee for regulating corporations, see Western, *Monarchy and Revolution*, p. 222.

[81] Eight out of a total membership of twenty-seven had been prosecuted for conventicling or absence from church, and the wife of another had been convicted for attending a conventicle in 1673, *Cal.S.P.Dom.*, 1687–9, no. 1439, p. 263; *Hist. MSS Comm. Eleventh Report App. pt III Southampton MSS*, p. 55; S.C.R.O., SC2/1/9, p. 135; SC9/1/11, 16, 17, 31.

[82] *Cal.S.P.Dom.*, 1687–9, no. 1407, p. 257; H.C.R.O., W/B1/7, fol. 14; Winchester City Charter, 15 September 1688.

[83] P.R.O., P.C. 2/72, pp. 748–51, 786; H.C.R.O., Winchester City Charter, 6 November 1688.

[84] *Cal.S.P.Dom.*, 1687–9, no. 1407, 1439, pp. 257, 263; *Penal laws and the Test Act*, ed. Duckett, i. 432.

of the boroughs. Southampton's county status with all the evils which that entailed was restored in its charter of 1688.[85] The use of the military to coerce Winchester was shortlived and although men connected with the military were named or continued in offices in some corporations in 1688, there was no significant increase in the role of the military in borough government. Sir Robert Holmes had been involved in the corporation of Newtown since the 1670s and by 1686, he had become mayor of Yarmouth also, with his subordinate Captain William Roch acting as his deputy mayor. His deputy-governor Sir Edward Worsley was one of the chief burgesses.[86] Lieutenant-Colonel Bernard Howard had been on the roll of Winchester's corporation since 1677, before holding the office of recorder there for barely a month in the autumn of 1688.[87] No army officer acted as a justice of the peace at Portsmouth during 1688, although Richard Ridge, a local ordnance store-keeper did act as one, as he had done for the past three years, having been elected mayor in mid-term in February 1685, in succession to William Legge who was an army officer. John Grundy, who was surgeon to the Portsmouth garrison was continued as mayor for a second term by royal warrant dated 27 August 1688, but this appointment was effectively nullified on 17 October.[88] The borough campaign of 1687–8, far from enhancing central government control over them had a detrimental effect on the running of the corporations. Record-keeping broke down at Winchester between January and November 1688 and at Southampton between 18 May and 24 October.[89]

In the area of local office-holding, the 1680s seem to fall into two unequal phases. The period 1680–6 in Hampshire saw moderate but effective purges of office-holders in county and borough to remove those who persisted in opposition to the legitimate succession. This was combined with a tightening of control over military and revenue establishments to make them more efficient and dependable, and in the case of excise officers to separate them to a totally unprecedented degree from the local communities amongst which they served. Significant steps were taken to streamline local administration so that it would be less obstructive to royal policies and the uniform exercise of the law. It is fair to say nationally that Charles II bequeathed a more central-

[85] E. Welch, *Southampton City Charters* (Southampton, 1966), p. 22.
[86] For Holmes' role at Newtown, see above, pp. 102, 151; on Yarmouth, College of Arms, original Hampshire visitation of 1686, p. 217.
[87] H.C.R.O., W/B1/6, fol. 104; for Howard, see above, pp. 163, 175.
[88] Dr Childs' suggestion on the basis of Portsmouth City Record Office, S3/B/47 that field officers served as justices in the town and were succeeded by their reliefs seems to be a bit of an exaggeration, *The Army, James II and the Glorious Revolution*, p. 108; *Portsmouth Sessions Papers*, ed. Hoad, appendix V, p. 177; East, *Portsmouth*, p. 316; Dalton, *Army Lists*, ii. 50, 123.
[89] H.C.R.O., W/B1/7, fols. 36–7; S.C.R.O., 2/1/9, pp. 137–8.

ized state to his brother. Once James began to change government policies in 1686–7 there followed a new, radical and accelerating round of purges in local government, which did little to increase central control over local office-holders and institutions and which in certain respects actually weakened the government's hold over Hampshire. The obsession with electoral politics which overtook the increasingly isolated regime left very little room for anything else. Indeed, if the Hampshire evidence is anything to go by, the advance of truly stronger government was checked rather than championed by James II.

8

The enforcement of policy 1679–88

DEFENCE AND INTERNAL SECURITY

The atmosphere of conspiracy between 1678 and 1683, followed by the rebellions of 1685, and their suppression, and the Dutch invasion of 1688 gave central government ample cause to be involved in managing defence and security arrangements at local, especially in strategically vital areas like the Solent. Though the means changed over the period, both Charles II and James II insisted on keeping these arrangements under their own control. On 30 November 1678, Charles rejected a militia bill on the grounds that it would take the militia out of his control, which he would not tolerate even for half an hour.[1] Over the next seven years, control over the personnel and activities of local lieutenancies remained strong. J. H. Plumb has written about the country gentry that 'in the last resort they controlled the militia'.[2] During the 1680s, many gentry had cause to wish that this were true. In fact, ultimate control over the militia lay with the Crown. The gentry were power-less to prevent James II's move to reliance on a standing army to meet defence and security needs, indeed, Professor Schwoerer has written of the majority of the gentry in the 1685 Parliament: 'It may be argued that if James had asked for a standing army officered by Protestants, he could probably have won it from this Parliament.'[3] There is no doubting the radicalism of James' policy; his was the first regime in seventeenth-century England actually to dis-countenance local participation in defence and security and to attempt to rely exclusively on its own troops. Lieutenancies in effect became redundant, and there was nothing the gentry could do about it. All that lay open to them was to sabotage James' efforts to revive the militia when he reversed his policy in 1688.[4] In the Isle of Wight, the militia was not undermined by the disaffection

[1] D. Ogg, *England in the Reign of Charles II* (2nd edn, Oxford, 1955), ii. 574.
[2] J. H. Plumb, *The Growth of Political Stability in England 1675–1725* (reprint, London, 1977), p. 20.
[3] Schwoerer, *No Standing Armies!*, p. 144.
[4] J. Miller, 'The militia and the army in the reign of James II', *H.J.*, 16 (1973), 667–71.

of the gentry officers, who seem to have remained loyal, but by the mutinies of the rank and file, who were drawn from the humblest inhabitants of the island.[5] Only when the hold of central government had virtually collapsed in late November 1688, did the nobility and gentry in certain areas assert independent control over the county militia in defiance of James II, and their success in this regard is at least partly due to the presence of a rival focus of loyalty in the person of Princess Anne.[6] In normal times, defence and security policy was to a large extent centralized on the king and his close advisers. Complacency on the part of the king, notably in 1685 and 1688, when James was slow to recognize the seriousness of the threat facing him, could have a disastrous effect on arrangements at local level.[7]

The defence and security of Hampshire were kept firmly under central control in the 1678–88 period. On 30 September 1678, in response to recent revelations of the Popish Plot, local lords lieutenant, including Edward Noel, were ordered by the Privy Council to search the houses of Catholics for arms. This was certainly carried out at Southampton.[8] On 15 November, the Council sent a personal letter to Noel ordering him to investigate a knocking sound heard in Tichborne church at the time when the plot broke, and to search the church, and particularly the aisle belonging to the Catholic Tichborne family, for arms. On 20 December, all magistrates were ordered to disarm Catholics.[9]

There were also local initiatives during the initial panic of the Popish Plot. An armed vigilante group commanded by Dr William Harrison, rector of nearby Cheriton, chased guests as they left a dinner party at the Tichbornes' house with intent to kill any they caught, soon after the news of the Popish Plot broke.[10] More orderly was the special twelve-man watch (six of them armed) which was posted at Southampton between 15 November 1978 and 10 January 1679.[11]

But the central authorities were quick to assert control over defence and security arrangements. On 24 November 1678, the duke of Monmouth, as captain-general of the army, ordered a troop of dragoons to the Isle of Wight to help defend the landing places there. Sir Robert Holmes ordered that they

---

[5] See below, p. 188.
[6] Hosford, *Nottingham, Nobles and the North*, pp. 109–11.
[7] R. Clifton, *The Last Popular Rebellion: The Western Rising of 1685* (Hounslow, 1984), pp. 156–8; see below, pp. 183, 185.
[8] P.R.O., P.C. 2/66, pp. 409–10; S.C.R.O., SC2/1/8, fol. 345.
[9] P.R.O., P.C. 2/66, p. 446; Miller, *Popery and Politics*, p. 166.
[10] *Private Memoirs of John Potenger, Esq, Comptroller of the Pipe etc in the reigns of Charles II, James II with a letter to his Grandson going to the University*, ed. C. W. Bingham (London, 1841), p. 54.
[11] S.C.R.O., SC2/1/8, fol. 347.

be deployed at Ryde and Bembridge.[12] On 12 January 1679, the militia of the western coastal counties was put on alert against foreign attack. In the case of an alarm, Hampshire's militia was to march to Southampton and Portsmouth. Lords lieutenant were ordered to be down in their counties by the end of the month. Secretary of State Williamson also inquired into how the militia had been deployed in 1672, 1673 and 1675. He followed up his inquiries with a circular letter to lords lieutenant calling for an account of the size and structure of the militia in each county. Edward Noel soon obliged, giving exact figures under the name of the commander of each unit. Monmouth backed up the militia's coastal defence role, in April 1679, by ordering the substantial regular forces stationed in Hampshire and Sussex to defend Portsmouth and other vulnerable places in case of emergency.[13] The next month, a contract was signed for the improvement of Portsmouth's fortifications, upon which work continued throughout the Exclusion Crisis, under the auspices of the Ordnance Office, though shortage of money proved a problem.[14]

With Guards, garrisons, magazines (like Portsmouth) and county lieutenancies firmly under government control, Charles II had little to fear from the Whigs. Neither he, nor his ministers, thought it necessary to take extraordinary steps to safeguard local security. The Hampshire militia was fully operational in 1681–2. A fire and riot at Portsmouth in the autumn of 1682, made Gainsborough fear for the safety of the garrison, and he reported the matter to the king, but the crisis soon blew over.[15]

But the revelation of the Rye House Plot the following summer, caused more concern at Whitehall, and a greater interest in local security arrangements. Portsmouth had actually been one of the targets of the wider insurrection planned for that year.[16] On receiving a letter from Secretary Jenkins in late June 1683, Gainsborough sent orders for the guard to be doubled there, and for soldiers to search the houses of the disaffected for arms, with the help of local constables. He alerted militia officers at Southampton and at other parts of the county to do the same.[17] The magistrates and militia officers of Southampton responded very rapidly, searched all suspects, restricted movement overseas, disarmed all dissenters and arrested Nathaniel Robinson, a

---

[12] *Cal.S.P.Dom.*, 1678 and *Addenda* 1674–9, p. 538; I.W.C.R.O., DOI/22.
[13] *Cal.S.P.Dom.*, 1679–80, pp. 18, 28, 60–1, 130.
[14] Brit. Lib., Addit. Ch. 32751; Staffordshire County Record Office, Dartmouth MSS, D (W) 1778 I i. nos. 512, 514, 516, 519, 561, 565, 568, 571, 573, 575, 577, 578–581, 583, 585, 587, 590, 597–8, 601, 603, 605, 609, 616, 619, 621, 626; *Cal.S.P.Dom.*, 1679–80, pp. 18, 37–8, 128, 138, 366, 467, 620–1; *Cal.S.P.Dom.*, 1680–1, pp. 71, 241, 297–8.
[15] P.R.O., S.P. 30, Case G: Account of R. Cobbe and Thomas Colnett; *Cal.S.P.Dom.*, 1682, pp. 451, 464–5, 473.
[16] Brit. Lib., Addit. MS 38847 (Hodgkin Papers), fol. 95.
[17] *Cal.S.P.Dom.*, January–June 1683, p. 344.

nonconformist minister. Dr John Speed reported back on their behalf to Secretary Jenkins on 28 June.[18] The search for arms in Hampshire revealed little. Nevertheless, Gainsborough on the advice of his deputies, decided to mount a standing militia guard at Winchester, consisting of three companies of foot and a troop of horse, to be relieved weekly: perhaps 300 men. This was to continue until Gainsborough received further orders to the contrary. But the king, while thanking Gainsborough profusely for his diligence, did not see the necessity for this guard to continue, and being 'very tender of putting the country to charge' ordered it to be disbanded.[19] This caveat against putting the country to any charge was reiterated by Secretary Jenkins' circular letter to lords lieutenant on 10 July 1683. It was left to them and their deputies to decide who were to be counted as suspects, but fowling pieces and formal dress swords were not to be taken, and inventories of arms taken were to be returned to one of the secretaries of state.[20] Gainsborough dutifully initiated another search for arms, which yielded as little as before. Nevertheless, he returned a full account of them to Secretary Jenkins in the autumn, after he had had an opportunity at the assizes to get reports from his deputies and militia officers. Many of the arms concerned were those provided by their owners for the militia. Ultimately, the royal government ordered that those which belonged to or were suitable for the militia were to be kept apart somewhere, whilst those that were not should be sent to the magazine at Portsmouth.[21]

In response to the letter of 10 July 1683, Sir Robert Holmes reported on his activities since receiving a letter from Secretary Jenkins late in June, such as searching for dissenting ministers and removing Whigs like Henry Whitehead from the island. Here too the arms discovered had not been spectacular, consisting of twenty-eight muskets, five pistols, four birding pieces, a carbine, two pikes and twenty-four swords in the entire island. For good measure, Holmes had also gathered the twenty pieces of field artillery from the island's parishes into Carisbrooke castle, in the teeth of local opposition. The Isle of Wight militia continued to be active in 1684–5.[22]

But the government did not rely solely on the local lieutenancy and the militia to hunt down suspects and disarm them. It continued to depend on ordinary local justices to investigate the activities of conspirators and to provide it with intelligence.[23] Other agencies were also used. Assize judges and

---

[18] *Cal.S.P.Dom.*, January–June 1683, p. 361.
[19] *Cal.S.P.Dom.*, July–September 1683, p. 27; P.R.O., S.P. 44/68, p. 322.
[20] *Cal.S.P.Dom.*, July–September 1683, pp. 93–4.
[21] *Cal.S.P.Dom.*, 1683–4, p. 16; *Cal.S.P.Dom.*, 1684–5, p. 27.
[22] P.R.O., S.P. 29/428/146; Carisbrooke Castle Museum, MS Serle, no. 16; the Brightstone field piece may have remained in Carisbrooke castle until 1686, I.W.C.R.O., BRX/PR/2; H.C., iii. 483.
[23] *Cal.S.P.Dom.*, July–September 1683, p. 378; *Cal.S.P.Dom.*, 1684–5, pp. 118–19.

king's messengers were involved in investigating and apprehending those thought to be disaffected. In one way or another, Whitehall was kept informed of the demeanour and activities of its local enemies.[24]

When Charles II's last illness struck, the Privy Council put all the county lieutenancies on a twenty-four hour stand-by and alerted the mayors of the major ports, but in the event there was no disturbance at the passing of the king and the accession of James II. His peaceful accession bred a near fatal complacency in the new king and his ministers. Little was done to thwart Monmouth's rising before he landed. Two days before this landing at Lyme, an order was dispatched to Gainsborough to arrest Thomas Dore, the mayor of Lymington, but there was no time to carry it out before Dore rose in arms. On 13 June 1685, an order was issued to Gainsborough, as to other lords lieutenant to raise the militia, or such part of it as he thought fit: another sign that central government had not yet realized the scale of the problem which confronted it.[25]

Despite the poor lead from the centre, Hampshire's lieutenancy responded excellently. Gainsborough replied to the king's order on the 14 June, and by the 16th was able to write to Lord Dartmouth that he had raised the militia, who he hoped would now be marching to their quarters. 'Finders' were ordered to supply fourteen days pay and money for powder and bullets.[26] Some failed to send their horses, arms and riders in time. Thomas Brocas' troop from the eastern part of the county lacked fourteen of its horses. But fifty-seven men were fully provided for the march with their captain.[27]

But it was not until 17 June that the king sent any order as to where the Hampshire militia should go, when at last they were directed to Salisbury. Then on 19 June, they were ordered to Chippenham. At last, the central government had begun to take the rebellion seriously. On 18 June, Sir Edmund Andros was sent down to assist Gainsborough (though in his case, unlike some other lords lieutenant to whom professionals were sent, this was not really necessary) and to raise a troop of regular horse in Hampshire.[28] On 20 June, lords lieutenant were authorized to make sweeping arrests of disaffected persons, nonconformist ministers, and even former parliamentarians. By this time the Hampshire militia appears to have left the county, fully supplied with ammunition and pay for a full-scale campaign.[29] It was

[24] *Cal.S.P.Dom.*, July–September 1683, pp. 385, 386; *Cal.S.P.Dom.*, 1683–4, pp. 295–6, 303.

[25] *Cal.S.P.Dom.*, 1684–5, p. 308; *Cal.S.P.Dom.*, 1685, nos. 818, 852, pp. 186, 193.

[26] *Hist. MSS Comm. Eleventh Report App. pt V. Dartmouth MSS*, i. 124–5; H.C.R.O., 37M84, 4/AC/13.

[27] H.C.R.O., 44M69 029, 'A list of the troop of horse in the east division'.

[28] *Cal.S.P.Dom.*, 1685, nos. 908, 944, pp. 204, 210; P.R.O., S.P. 31/2, fol. 7; S.P. 44/56, p. 227.

[29] *Cal.S.P.Dom.*, 1685, no. 957, pp. 212–13; H.C.R.O., 37M84, 4/AC/13.

left to the Sussex militia following on behind to deal with the localized rising of Dore and eighty henchmen around Lymington.[30]

Unfortunately, despite this rapid and efficient mobilization, at least part of the Hampshire militia failed to live up to the expectations of its leaders and commanders. By the end of June, Feversham, now supreme commander of the royal forces, had ordered two of the Hampshire foot regiments back to Salisbury and another back to Devizes, because they had proved disorderly.[31] Whether this was because of disaffection or simple indiscipline is not clear. But the rest of the county's militia which proved more reliable was used to escort the artillery.

After Sedgemoor, the central government used the local lieutenancies to search for and seize rebel fugitives, or any other suspicious persons. As ever, Gainsborough performed this task with alacrity. Based at Portsmouth during the rebellion, he wrote to Lord Middleton that he had already sent the 'Merlin' yacht to cruise off the coast near Lymington and the New Forest searching creeks to prevent rebels escaping.[32]

Because of the poor performance of parts of the militia during the Sedgemoor campaign, and notwithstanding the good conduct of most of it, James II decided to rely both for defence and internal security entirely upon standing forces. There are hints that James actually intended to dismantle the militia. Lords lieutenant were asked the cost of keeping up the militia for the maximum period each year, with a view to making alternative arrangements. There were later plans to take over the weapons. Some lords lieutenant were positively discouraged from holding musters.[33] For the rest of the country including Hampshire, central government just neglected the militia. There is no evidence of musters being held in mainland Hampshire between 1685 and 1689, and in the Isle of Wight there is a gap between 1685 and the autumn of 1688.[34] This was followed by the purges of 1687–8 and corresponding influx of inexperienced deputy-lieutenants, which completed the eclipse of the militia.

At the same time the regular military arms was built up systematically. In 1686, the survey of inns was carried out so that necessary accommodation could be found for troops stationed all over the country rather than just in garrisons. Strongholds like Portsmouth were also built up. Work on the fortifications at Portsmouth had continued during Charles II's last years. In

---

[30] *Cal.S.P.Dom.*, 1685, nos. 958, 960, pp. 213–14.

[31] *Hist. MSS Comm. Stopford-Sackville MSS*, i. 11.

[32] *Cal.S.P.Dom.*, 1685, nos. 1169, 1177, pp. 252–3; Brit. Lib., Addit. MS 41804 (Middleton Papers), fol. 12.

[33] Miller, 'The militia and the army', p. 622; Carter, 'The Lancashire lieutenancy 1660–88', pp. 73, 174.

[34] I.W.C.R.O., BRX/PR/2.

July 1686, Dartmouth was given a warrant as master general of the ordnance, to execute plans for the further defence and security of Portsmouth.[35] By the summer of 1686, Portsmouth's garrison establishment had been reduced to two companies. One of these companies, consisting of grenadiers numbered fifty-eight officers and men. There were also thirty gunners.[36] But it was usual for this to be augmented by field units temporarily stationed in the garrison. In June 1686, there were ten other such companies, and by the winter of 1686–7 this had doubled to twenty. From August 1687, Princess Anne's regiment of foot was stationed there, and this was soon joined by Colonel Trelawney's regiment of foot.[37]

The crisis of 1688 showed up the deficiencies of the defence and security system which James II had developed. The first was that it was so centralized on himself that his complacency could seriously undermine it. James refused to believe until it was almost too late that the Dutch preparations were meant against him. On 3 September 1688, Sir Robert Holmes wrote to Pepys from the Isle of Wight, 'I was never soe afraid as I am at presente for feare of those devils [i.e. the Dutch] falling upon me in this sad Condiston this place is . . . if I have any helpe from the king they shall not have this Island soe easily as they may expect.' But Holmes' letter to the king of 1 September drawing attention to the Dutch threat went unanswered by Sunderland for a week. And when it was answered, the word from Whitehall was simply that the king did not believe the preparations were intended against himself.[38] The confidence of some members of the government in this line of argument had already begun to crack.[39] But it was nearly the end of the month before the king officially recognized that there was any threat at all, by the issue of the proclamation of 28 September 1688.[40] In these circumstances there were limits to what commanders on the ground could achieve. Holmes busied himself strengthening Yarmouth and Hurst castles and drawing 200 men out of the militia to act as dragoons.[41]

But even when the king and his government were fully awake to the danger, the problem with a defence and security policy that depended so heavily on regular forces was the same in the 1680s as it had been in the 1650s: there were not enough troops to go round. Holmes persistently appealed for

[35] P.R.O. (Kew), W.O. 30/48; *Hist. MSS Comm. Eleventh Report App. pt V. Dartmouth MSS*, i. 120; *Cal.S.P.Dom.*, 1686–7, no. 816, p. 212.
[36] P.R.O., E101/612/72.
[37] Brit. Lib., Addit. MS 15897, fols. 79–80, 84; E. J. Priestley, 'The Portsmouth captains', *Journal of the Society for Army Research*, 55 (1977), 155; P.R.O. (Kew) W.O. 4/1, p. 74.
[38] Bodl., MS Rawl. A 179, fol. 44; *Cal.S.P.Dom.*, 1687–9, no. 1459, p. 267.
[39] On 25 August, the horse quartered in Sussex and at Petersfield was ordered to march to Portsmouth in case a Dutch fleet approached, P.R.O. (Kew), W. O. 5/3, pp. 227–8.
[40] Steele, *Proclamations*, i. no. 3878, p. 469.
[41] Bodl., MS Rawl. A 179, fols. 44–5.

regular support for the exposed Isle of Wight, yet none was forthcoming.[42] Shortage of men forced James II and local commanders like Holmes to deploy the local militia whose effectiveness was necessarily undermined by disuse and worse by disaffection.

But disaffection towards royal policies was by no means confined to the militia: the very regular forces upon which James II relied for his survival had been touched by it. A warning signal came in February 1688, when the majority of army officers stationed at Portsmouth refused to accept the Three Questions unamended which Berwick was trying to tender to them. They would only give an answer when the first two politically significant questions had been struck out, despite the threat of being cashiered for refusal. This was bolder resistance than Hampshire's deputy-lieutenants and JPs had offered. But it succeeded and the obnoxious questions were withdrawn.[43] Worse was to follow when, early in September 1688, Berwick tried to draft forty-five or fifty supernumerary Irishmen from MacElligott's regiment into Princess Anne's regiment of foot, of which he was colonel; Lieutenant-Colonel Beaumont and five captains protested. They objected to having the 'foreigners' foisted on them. As the Irish were Catholics there were also clear religious overtones to the officers' stand. But although Beaumont was involved in the growing conspiracy against James II in the army, this was an entirely independent gesture. James reacted strongly, having the officers brought up to Windsor where they were court martialled and cashiered. Three lieutenants and four ensigns in the same regiment resigned their commissions in sympathy, and as many as a hundred private soldiers may have taken the opportunity to desert.[44] This eliminated the opposition within the regular forces on the Solent for the meantime, but there were other problems concerned with their management.

The Irish troops, loyal as they were, were hardly an asset towards keeping the peace.[45] They were difficult to control. By October, they had taken to committing robberies and acts of violence against civilians. On one occasion, when some English officers tried to restrain them from breaking into an alehouse, they reacted violently and in the ensuing brawl with some English soldiers, four or five were killed and several wounded. Two officers were said to have been run through the body.[46] Another riot took place between English and Irish soldiers shortly before the Dutch invasion, in which there were

---

[42] I.W.C.R.O., GW/10.

[43] Brit. Lib., Addit. MS 34510, fol. 82.

[44] Brit. Lib., Addit. MS 34512, fol. 98; Childs, *The Army, James II and the Glorious Revolution*, pp. 151–4.

[45] MacElligott's regiment was concentrated at Portsmouth towards the end of September; P.R.O. (Kew), W.O. 5/3, pp. 255–6.

[46] *Hist. MSS Comm. Twelfth Report App. pt VII Le Fleming MSS*, pp. 213–15.

serious casualties on both sides. It had apparently been sparked off by an Irish soldier firing a bullet into a Protestant place of worship. It was on foundations as shaky and discordant as these that royal government in Hampshire depended on the eve of William's landing.[47]

Despite these problems, James continued to entrust the defence of the Solent largely to the regular forces. There is no mention of the Hampshire militia in this period. Sir Robert Holmes only drafted 400 Isle of Wight militiamen into Yarmouth and Hurst castles subject to royal permission, on 20 October, as a last resort, because, according to the reports he was receiving and relaying to the government, the Dutch invasion was imminent. He reckoned he could not hold out for more than forty-eight hours if attacked. Yet he continued to be starved of regular re-inforcements because, at least before the end of October, the central government did not believe that the Solent was a likely target for the invasion.[48] However, when in early November, James became convinced that the Solent was indeed the destination of William's expedition, orders were given for the rapid deployment of a large part of the field army there, but still no re-inforcements were sent to the Isle of Wight, though it was an obvious springboard for an invasion up Southampton water.[49] It is not clear how many units reached their assigned positions before the orders were countermanded and they were commanded to march to the west. Detachments of horse grenadiers and of the queen dowager's regiment of horse continued to be quartered around Portsmouth. MacElligott's foot and Princess Anne's regiment of foot remained in situ throughout the invasion.[50]

As he marched to the west, James II was relying on his army to save his monarchy, a policy which appeared prudent in the light of Sir Robert Holmes' experience with the militia in the Isle of Wight. At the end of August, Holmes had stationed Major Thomas Knight on the eastern tip of the island to observe shipping movements and to raise his company of militia in case the Dutch appeared. The whole militia seems to have been raised when the Dutch fleet was seen approaching on 4 November, and spent the whole of 5 November out on the hills after it had sailed by. The two companies of dragoons under Captain James Serle and Captain Holmes proved sufficiently loyal to chase away a small Dutch landing party which came ashore at the

---

[47] *Hist. MSS Comm. Twelfth Report App. pt VII Le Fleming MSS*, p. 218; the figure of fifty killed on each side in this report is certainly an exaggeration, but gives some indication of the scale of the violence; Van Citters heard a report that a total of forty had been killed, Brit. Lib., Addit. MS 34510, fol. 152.

[48] *Cal.S.P.Dom.*, 1687–9, nos. 1763, 1795, pp. 324–5, 330; *Hist. MSS Comm. Eleventh Report App. pt V Dartmouth MSS*, i. 163.

[49] P.R.O. (Kew), W.O. 5/3, 31 October–6 November 1688.

[50] P.R.O. (Kew), W.O. 5/3, 31 October–6 November 1688.

eastern end of the island on 5 November.[51] But thereafter the situation began to deteriorate. Writing to Lord Preston from Yarmouth in the early hours of 6 November, Holmes reported: 'Part of the militia is grown mutinous already and refuses to follow their commanders' orders, as I am afraid they will do everywhere where his Majesty has occasion to call for them.' Holmes begged for a troop of regular horse to keep them in awe, adding desperately 'God knows how I shall be dealt with by this militia I have drawn in Yarmouth and Hurst for want of 100 men to keep them in awe.' No help arrived. But the combined influence of the regular foot company under Holmes' command, and the militia officers who all remained loyal, seem to have had a stabilizing effect. Holmes was confident enough on 12 November to issue orders to his lieutenant-governor, Sir Edward Worsley, for the deployment of the militia along the vulnerable north coast of the island to beat off any Dutch attack.[52] Holmes' position was further bolstered by the arrival of the English fleet in St Helen's roads on 20 November. It anchored at Spithead on 22 November and made any idea of a rising by the people of the Isle of Wight unrealistic.[53]

James II gambled everything on the complete loyalty and effectiveness of his professional forces, and lost. Some parts of them were disaffected, but the rest simply fell into disorder while genuinely trying to carry out the king's orders. Defections in the army totally undermined James' will to resist. On 25 November, he was at Andover on the retreat from Salisbury and sent Lord Dover to take command at Portsmouth, with verbal orders to send the prince of Wales to France. This plan was checked by Dartmouth's refusal to carry it out early in December.[54]

Control of the Solent and Hampshire in general now depended entirely on the attitudes adopted by the garrisons and the fleet. William of Orange did not pursue James II's retreating army through northern Hampshire, but rather moved north marching towards London through Berkshire. However, detachments of horse were sent by William to Ringwood and to Bere Forest, north of Portsmouth, the former to encourage the betrayal of Hurst castle, the latter to intercept the prince of Wales on the way back to London, though neither was successful.[55]

But disaffection was growing within the garrisons, making it increasingly difficult to hold down the population. On the night of 8 December, while

[51] Carisbrooke Castle, MS Serle no. 24; J. D. Jones, 'The Isle of Wight and the Revolution of 1688', *Proceedings of the Isle of Wight Natural History and Archaeological Society*, v. (1965), app. B, 481; *Hist. MSS Comm. Seventh Report App. pt I Graham MSS*, p. 413.

[52] *Hist. MSS Comm. Seventh Report App. pt I Graham MSS*, p. 414; Carisbrooke Castle, MS Serle no. 20; J. D. Jones, 'The Isle of Wight and the Revolution of 1688', app. C, 482.

[53] E. B. Powley, *The English Navy in the Revolution of 1688* (Cambridge, 1928), pp. 110–11.

[54] Powley, *The English Navy in the Revolution of 1688*, pp. 124–40.

[55] Childs, *The Army, James II and the Glorious Revolution*, pp. 193–4; *Hist. MSS Comm. Eleventh Report App. pt V. Dartmouth MSS*, i. 225.

Holmes' regular lieutenant was away from Yarmouth foraging, a junior officer, apparently the ensign William Hook, in what may have been a pre-arranged move, took about thirty men from his company by boat over to Hurst castle and tried to trick its commander into surrendering it on behalf of William of Orange. But the attempt was not successful. However, Holmes, who had lost a substantial proportion of his regular manpower, was devastated by the blow and begged Dartmouth for some naval support, claiming he had no one to stand by him. The population of Yarmouth was ready to declare for William of Orange. By the time Holmes wrote to Blathwayt and Dartmouth on 12 December, he had greatly recovered his confidence and purported to be glad to be rid of the 'villaines and rogues' from the company who might have done him worse harm. He hoped to recruit more loyal men to fill up the company, and to this end he sought a blank ensign's commission from Blathwayt. At the same time, Sir Edward Scott, deputy-governor of Portsmouth, was having difficulty in holding down the local population and the town's magistrates. He feared a conspiracy between the latter and some of the garrison officers.[56]

But it was the flight of the king on 11 December and the surrender of the fleet on the 12th which effectively ended resistance to William of Orange on the Solent. Dartmouth and other naval commanders and officials had difficulty controlling the excesses of Portsmouth garrison, but after the 12th there was no serious prospect of it holding out against the Dutch. Those in command of the garrison were confused by the new situation and increasingly deferred to Dartmouth. Berwick sought his advice. On 17 December, Sir Edward Scott, the deputy-governor resigned his commission to Dartmouth on an order from the Prince of Orange and the Lords at the Guildhall. On that day also a surrender of the Isle of Wight and Hurst castle was signed in the name of the governor, lieutenant-governor and others.[57]

The breakdown of discipline in the army which followed the king's flight helped to spark off the famous Irish 'scares'. These were an almost nation-wide phenomenon but they had good cause in Hampshire where a large number of unruly Irish soldiers were still stationed. Indeed, James had added to the problem shortly before his flight by sending Colonel John Butler's Irish dragoons to Portsmouth. But they were not admitted to the garrison and so had to be quartered in the surrounding countryside.[58] Partly as a result of this, people in Hampshire began to look to their own security for the first time in

---

[56] *Hist. MSS Comm. Eleventh Report App. pt V Dartmouth MSS*, i. 225, 231; I.W.C.R.O., GW/11.

[57] Staffordshire County Record Office, Dartmouth MSS D (W) 1778 I i. no. 1678; *Hist. MSS Comm. Eleventh Report App. pt V Dartmouth MSS*, i. 236; I.W.C.R.O., GW/14.

[58] G. H. Jones, 'The Irish fright of 1688: real violence and imagined massacre', *B.I.H.R.*, 55 (1982), 148.

a decade. On Thursday, 13 December, Richard Norton raised the country for ten miles around his home at Southwick to guard against the depredations of the Irish soldiery. The next day, he marched at the head of the men who had turned out, to Portsdown, overlooking Portsmouth. There he mustered 1,000 effectives, horse and foot, whom he fed and exercised. Gentlemen and militia officers from elsewhere in the county rallied to Norton, promising to send him a thousand horse if necessary. Berwick thought it wise to negotiate with Norton, who also made contact with Dartmouth and tried to arrange a meeting with him. On a solemn promise from Berwick not to allow any atrocities against civilians or disbandment of Irish soldiers to take place, Norton dismissed his hastily raised force, but ordered them to be ready at an hour's notice. But those who had been witnesses to the misbehaviour of the soldiers in Portsmouth were not so easily pacified. On 14 December, some seamen, presumably from the fleet, took Gosport castle by surprise and ejected the soldiers from it and from Gosport itself. The local inhabitants rose to assist them. Despite threats from Berwick that he would beat the castle down about their ears, the seamen and inhabitants were only ready to surrender it to a wholly Protestant garrison, and they seem to have remained in control until Portsmouth was handed over to William of Orange.[59]

There were 'Irish scares' in other parts of the county apart from Portsmouth and Gosport. At Romsey, £1 1s 7d was spent on powder, ammunition and pay for a watch 'when the uproar was concerning the Irish'.[60] The burning of Andover was rumoured but no similar defence measures appear to have been taken there, although a man and a horse were sent to Newbury in response to a message brought by a soldier, who subsequently became drunk, made a disturbance and had to be packed off to Kingsclere the next day.[61] Such were the bizarre goings-on that accompanied the passing of the regime. But only with the extinction of central government had significant local security initiatives taken place in Hampshire.

During the early 1680s, while keeping local defence and security firmly in its own control, central government had been able to deploy a wide range of agencies to see that its will was carried out and its enemies neutralized. The local lieutenancy had collaborated with regular military units and ordinary magistrates in almost totally eliminating the Whig threat. Despite royal complacency and mismanagement, these forces were quick to respond to the challenge of Monmouth's rebellion, and prevent it from spreading on any significant scale to Hampshire. Nevertheless, on the pretext of the poor

---

[59] *The English Currant*, no. 4, 19–21 December 1688; *Hist. MSS Comm. Eleventh Report App. pt V Dartmouth MSS*, i. 237; *Hist. MSS Comm. Fifteenth Report App. pt I, Dartmouth MSS*, iii. 135.

[60] Brit. Lib., Addit. MS 26774, p. 188.   [61] H.C.R.O., 37M84, 4/AC/14.

performance of some militia units, James II embarked on a totally one-sided policy effectively writing off the lieutenancy as an instrument of his government in the localities and relying instead on the regular forces. This foolhardy and unprecedented attitude led to a recurrence of the problems which had beset Interregnum regimes, such as the difficulty of housing and controlling large numbers of regular soldiers in the localities, and the fact that even a substantial standing army would be overstretched if called upon to police and defend the whole of England. These problems, coupled with another bout of royal complacency and the disaffection of significant elements within the regular officer corps, paved the way for the disaster of November–December 1688, when James II's government failed to crush an easily containable Dutch invasion.

FINANCE

It is well known that in this period, central government achieved an almost unprecedented degree of financial solvency and independence. This was no mere windfall resulting from French subsidies or trade booms, though these were contributing factors.[62] It was a direct consequence of administrative centralization and good management which had an impact on the provinces as well. But though central government developed the most effective fiscal system which England had yet seen, it provoked less opposition in the provinces to its fiscal measures than virtually any previous regime. The landed classes were placated by the temporary demise of direct taxation and the rest of the population were appeased by the growing professionalism of the revenue departments and the central control which was enforced on their personnel.

But the government had to overcome serious problems before it reached this happy state. During the Popish Plot and Exclusion Crisis, Parliament passed a number of measures which threatened Charles II's financial independence. There were only short term grants of direct taxation, to enable Charles to pay off the army. To one of these, the poll bill, was tacked a three year ban on the import of French goods which threatened customs revenue.[63] Then, having refused to vote further funds until the exclusion bill was passed, the Commons in the second Exclusion Parliament threatened anyone who lent money on the basis of the king's hereditary revenue.[64] The object of this section is to examine the impact of the government's difficulties and its measures

[62] Chandaman, *The English Public Revenue*, pp. 252ff; Western, *Monarchy and Revolution*, pp. 100–5.

[63] 29 & 30 Car. II c.1; 30 Car. II c.1; 31 Car. II c.1 – *S.R.*, v. 852–934.

[64] Ogg, *England in the Reign of Charles II*, ii. 605.

to overcome them in Hampshire, to show how greater central control was achieved and what local reactions to this were.

If the case of the Solent is anything to go by, the impact of the embargo against France was simply to deprive the Crown of the customs revenue on French trade. Smuggling became big business and was carried on by growing numbers with increasing confidence. Bands of smugglers armed with swords and pistols were active in broad daylight, as is clear from Richard Norton's letter to Secretary Coventry of 20 September 1679. Attempts to suppress the traffic and seize contraband provoked riots and violent resistance along the Hampshire and Dorset coasts and as far inland as Salisbury. Smugglers clearly enjoyed some popular sympathy. This is hardly surprising as the embargo seriously threatened the trade of towns like Southampton, which was already poor enough.[65] Things were not improved by the attitude of some of the military stationed locally. In April 1679, some soldiers of Captain Kirby's company of Sir Charles Wheeler's regiment stationed at Titchfield beat up three Southampton-based customs officers and seized the French wine in their possession.[66]

But Parliament as well as curtailing the Crown's revenue from indirect taxation had also made substantial grants of direct taxation which had to be collected. The poll tax of 1678 was paid fairly rapidly for Hampshire. The act had called for it to be paid in by 12 June, and just over three months after this deadline 77 per cent of the sum due from the county had been paid into the Exchequer. Thereafter, however, the money took longer to come in, and subsequent assessments were not paid in so rapidly.[67] In Hampshire this did not arise from the recalcitrance of the tax-payers or the negligence of assessment commissioners.[68] Rather there was a hiatus in the central management of the revenue. At Danby's fall the Treasury was put into commission, which was at first a politically mixed body. The Tax Office was not reconstituted and operational again until December 1679. It took time for the central authorities to re-assert their control over taxation in the localities. Between 15 April 1679 and 20 February 1680, Samuel Williams, receiver-general for Hampshire, paid only £408 12s 7d into the Exchequer, which consisted entirely of arrears for the previous year's poll tax.[69] Meanwhile Williams, apparently without

---

[65] *Cal.Treas.Bks.*, vi. 239–40, 534, 687–8; Brit. Lib., MS Harl. 5121, fol. 15.

[66] *Cal.S.P.Dom.*, 1679–80, p. 124.

[67] *S.R.*, v. 855; P.R.O., E360/145: Accounts of Samuel Williams; Chandaman, *The English Public Revenue*, pp. 188–9.

[68] The commissioners in several parts of Hampshire were inquiring of Samuel Williams as early as the beginning of October 1678 what days he would set for the receipt of the six months' assessment so that the first instalment could be paid in well within the 24 November deadline; Staffordshire County Record Office, Dartmouth MSS D (W) 1778 V. no. 17, S. Williams to Mr Grahame, 5 Oct. 1678.

[69] Ogg, *England in the Reign of Charles II*, ii. 585, 592, 641; Ward, 'The Office of Taxes', p. 205; P.R.O., E360/145: Accounts of Samuel Williams.

the knowledge of the Treasury, advanced £4,857 11s 4d of the money in his hands to the deputy commissioners for disbanding, who were then active at Portsmouth, paying off soldiers and quarters.[70]

The Treasury did what it could to hasten payment. Henry Guy, secretary to the Treasury and the tax agents continued to badger Williams throughout 1679–81, to send money to the Exchequer. Guy tried to deploy the influence of Colonel George Legge, Williams' surety, over him, but to no immediate effect. By December 1680, Guy and the Treasury Lords had got wind of the fact that Williams had £1,785 18s 0d in his hands. He was ordered to pay it into the Exchequer by Christmas. In fact, his next payment was for only £1,000 and was not made until 28 May 1681 following. The last, mostly small sums, were not paid in or accounted for until early in James II's reign and Williams' account was not declared until 10 February 1687, though this was largely due to the incompetence of some of Williams' subordinates and the tangled nature of his dealings with the money.[71] The situation in regard to direct taxation which Dr Brooks has observed after 1688 seems to have been equally true ten years earlier: 'The problems of tax collection were less those of extracting the money from the taxpayers themselves, than of squeezing it out of the Receivers and their agents, getting it to London and lodging it safely in the Exchequer.'[72]

But such problems were not insuperable. The Treasury realised its mistake in appointing Williams to receive both the poll tax and the subsequent assessments. William Taylor, a member of Winchester's corporation was appointed to succeed him as receiver-general for the last six months' assessment which was due to be paid into the Exchequer in two instalments by 8 June and 8 September 1680. Receiving full co-operation from the active assessment commissioners, Taylor was able to collect the money very rapidly, and paid the bulk of both instalments into the Exchequer within three weeks of the respective deadlines. In March 1681, the Treasury Lords were able to write to the assessment commissioners in Hampshire to report that Taylor had already obtained his *quietus est*, having paid the full sum into the Exchequer.[73]

In the wake of the Exclusion Crisis, with the need to mobilize all possible funds, the Treasury re-asserted its control over money which had been raised in the localities on the government's behalf. Guy and his colleagues were not only keen to investigate recently incurred arrears of taxes. A fresh investi-

---

[70] *Cal.Treas.Bks.*, vii. 211, 378–9.
[71] *Cal.Treas.Bks.*, vi. 150, 272, 691, 713, 740; *Cal.Treas.Bks.*, vii. 124, 335; viii. 578, 753; P.R.O., E360/145.
[72] Brooks, 'Public finance and political stability: the administration of the Land Tax 1688–1720', p. 285.
[73] P.R.O., E179/176/572; E401/1965, pp. 123, 263; *Cal.Treas.Bks.*, vii. 80–1.

gation into arrears of Commonwealth assessments was commissioned in July 1682. By a Treasury estimate, £4,143 15s 0d was outstanding for Hampshire.[74] By the end of 1682, an inquiry was under way, in conjunction with the secretary of state's office, into the three months' £70,000 militia tax which had been raised in the counties in the early 1660s. Richard Norton, the then treasurer of the militia in Hampshire, was questioned about the disposal of the money. Through him the government was reminded that £1,684 8s 0d had been paid to Sir Philip Honeywood for Portsmouth's fortifications. The government had also discovered that only two instalments of the tax had been assessed and collected in Hampshire and that it had been under-assessed by £530 0s 6d in the years in which it had been raised. But this still left £1,830 8s 2d unaccounted for. So further investigation was referred to the lord lieutenant in Hampshire, as in other counties at the same time. Gainsborough referred the whole matter to his deputies, and then replied to the Treasury, though the contents of his reply are not known.[75] At the same time, there was an inquiry into current militia accounts with a view to appropriating the week's tax. A copy of the sworn militia account for Hampshire for 1681–3 which is amongst the State Papers showed a surplus on 5 September 1683 of £207 15s 11¼d.[76] The Treasury Lords even launched an attempt in March 1684 to hasten the government's share of fines on conventicles into the Exchequer, by appealing to JPs.[77]

More realistically in the early 1680s, the main categories of indirect taxation were brought under firmer control, in order to enhance their yield. The prohibition of trade with France ended on 20 March 1681.[78] If the government could clamp down on smuggling, it stood to profit by the resurgence of legitimate trade. So the Treasury authorized the Customs Commissioners to employ more staff on the coasts which had hitherto proved so difficult to police. Captain Gregory Alford was hired in June 1681 to act as a special surveyor in Hampshire, Dorset and Devon, on a salary of £250. And in November, Samuel Ellyott was commissioned to seize uncustomed and prohibited goods in Wiltshire, Hampshire and Dorset. Alford clearly earned his salary, as he was continued for another year for his good services in June 1682. At about the same time, the Treasury Lords insisted that one of the Customs Commissioners go on circuit and begin with the ports of Southampton, Poole, Weymouth, Lyme, Dartmouth and Exeter and their members. Subsequent circuits produced modifications in the local customs

[74] *Cal.Treas.Bks.*, vii. 520, 525.
[75] *Cal.S.P.Dom.*, 1682, p. 566; *Cal.Treas.Bks.*, vii. 812, 826–7, 927.
[76] Western, *The English Militia*, p. 48; P.R.O., S.P. 30, Case G: Account of R. Cobbe and T. Colnett.
[77] *Cal.Treas.Bks.*, vii. 1069.
[78] Chandaman, *The English Public Revenue*, p. 253.

administration. If customs officers met with difficulties, the Treasury was capable of intervening directly to help them. When in August 1687, the Treasury received reports from customs officers at Southampton and Christchurch of smugglers recovering seized contraband, it called for sworn testimony and then dispatched Philip Reyny, sergeant at arms, to arrest the three culprits. Revenue was not allowed to remain long in the hands of the officers who collected it. When it came to the notice of Henry Guy in August 1686, that £1,500 or so remained in the hands of the collector at Southampton, a letter was immediately dispatched for it to be returned by bills to London, as there was no need for money in the country.[79] But the customs administration was already under direct Treasury control through the Customs Commissioners, and there was a limit to what fresh centralizing initiatives could achieve.

In Charles II's last years the other principal indirect taxes, the excise and the hearth tax, were brought out of farm into direct collection. This happened to the excise in 1683. Immediately steps were taken to enhance central control over local administration. The country was divided into four districts, in each of which was appointed a general rider to carry out surveys on behalf of the Commissioners and two general supervisors to oversee local officers, and the Commissioners themselves conducted circuits of inspection. In all, scrutiny of local administration was very close. The survey of Hampshire, carried out in April 1684, revealed some serious evasions, and a general under-exploitation of the revenue by local officers. Partly as a result of the reforms recommended in the surveys of 1684–5, excise revenue rose to £725,000 p.a. in 1686–8.[80]

Similar progress was made when the hearth tax came under direct exploitation from March 1684. The central administration was combined with that for the excise. Two receivers-general were appointed to keep a close check on the local collectors' entry books and to hasten payments into the treasurer's office and the central excise officials were ordered to scrutinize hearth-tax administration on their circuits.[81] This, combined with a new survey of hearths, enhanced the yield of the hearth tax within a year. The increase of 0.88 per cent in Dorset, Hampshire and Sussex was not very large compared with the Welsh increase of 16.46 per cent or the four northern shires' rise of 30.12 per cent, but this is also evidence that under-exploitation had been less of a problem in the south than in further flung areas.[82]

In the crisis of 1688, the centralized revenue system began to falter. When

---

[79] *Cal.Treas.Bks.*, vii. 198, 292, 553, 968; viii. 888, 908, 1507, 1569.
[80] Chandaman, *The English Public Revenue*, pp. 73, 75; Brit. Lib., MS Harl., 5121, fols. 10–20.
[81] Chandaman, *The English Public Revenue*, pp. 105–6.　　　　　[82] *Ibid.*, pp. 108–9.

the news of William of Orange's landing reached London, James II ordered the Excise and Hearth Tax Commissioners to instruct their local collectors not to dispatch the weekly monies to London, but to retain them in principal towns. And on 29 November 1688, the Treasury ordered them to instruct the collectors near Portsmouth and Southampton to pay all their ready money to Lord Dover. Meanwhile, central departments of state like the Ordnance Office, found it virtually impossible to pay their way.[83]

But while it was functioning properly, the most remarkable thing about the more effective, more centralized revenue system was the lack of local opposition to it. Smuggling persisted on the Solent, but after 1681, it had a lower profile. There was occasionally tension between revenue officers and borough magistrates. In 1682 and 1687, informations were taken against hearth-tax collectors at Portsmouth for speaking ill of the mayor of the borough.[84] A complaint by excise officers against the mayor and recorder of Romsey for refusing to re-open the case of a local innkeeper was referred to the attorney-general in 1684 but nothing came of it.[85] But these were the only cases of their kind in Hampshire. Even magistrates in the county who had Whiggish inclinations seem to have been fully behind the revenue officers. Richard Norton was clearly concerned for the Crown's revenue and in his letter to Coventry in 1679 lamented the fact that the import of other wines had not been encouraged to supply the shortfall caused by the loss of duties on French wines.[86] On 19 September 1680, Henry Tulse, one of the exclusionists who had been left on the commission of the peace, joined Roger Clavell in committing John Deale to the county gaol for not paying the excise.[87] The Whigs were not the first parliamentary opposition to be more radical at Westminster over fiscal matters than they were in the provinces.

RELIGIOUS POLICY

The decade between the Popish Plot and the Revolution of 1688 certainly saw some dramatic reversals of policy in the area of religion. First, the Popish Plot brought an end to Danby's policy of the equal repression of Protestant dissenters and Catholics, which was replaced by attempts to preserve Protestant unity whilst vigorously suppressing popery. Then in 1681, there was a reversion to Danby's policy, which lasted until 1686–7 when James II

---

[83] Hughes, *Studies in Administration and Finance*, p. 165; *Cal.Treas.Bks.*, viii. 2137; *Hist. MSS Comm. Eleventh Report App. pt V Dartmouth MSS*, i. 222; H. C. Tomlinson, 'The Ordnance Office and the Navy 1660–1714', *E.H.R.*, xc (1975), 37.
[84] *Portsmouth Sessions Papers*, ed. Hoad, pp. 94, 137.
[85] *Cal.Treas.Bks.*, vii. 1269, 1323.
[86] *Cal.Treas.Bks.*, vi. 239.
[87] H.C.R.O., Sessions rolls, file 19: Gaol Calendar, 11 January 1680/1.

began seriously promoting Catholicism and giving toleration to Protestant dissenters, through his Declaration of Indulgence. This section will be devoted to exploring the impact of these changes and the respective policies at local level, in Hampshire, to discover the extent of control exercised by central government, the level of local obstruction and the success with which it was overcome.

Accounts of the enforcement of religious policy during the period of the Popish Plot and Exclusion Crisis generally place heavy stress on provincial obstruction in thwarting the will of central authorities. Professor Kenyon has written 'Local magnates and justices were reluctant to proceed against their neighbours, and in counties with large recusant minorities their reluctance was greater not less.'[88] But in Hampshire at least, factors such as neighbourliness and kinship did not necessarily work to the advantage of the large Catholic community in softening magisterial attitudes. The marquis of Winchester, despite, or perhaps because of, his Catholic roots and relations, was an active member of the Lords Committee for Examinations during the first six months of its existence, though he was not above doing favours to individual Catholics.[89] Dr William Harrison, who soon afterwards became an active JP, led a mob of villagers which besieged the house of his neighbours the Tichbornes at the beginning of the Popish Plot scare. By then, Sir Henry Tichborne had become isolated from his Protestant neighbours of all sorts, for the guests at the dinner which he gave that night consisted entirely of Catholics except for John Potenger, a London-based government official.[90] Tichborne's alleged implication in the Popish Plot soon afterwards can have done little for his local reputation. Justices at Hampshire's Epiphany quarter sessions in January 1679 showed no reluctance whatever to proceed against their Catholic neighbours. In response to the recent royal proclamations for disarming and securing Papists, JPs in each division were ordered to issue warrants to hundred constables to bring reputed Papists before two of their number to enter into recognizances to appear at the next quarter sessions to be proceeded against. Divisional meetings were planned for the beginning of February to carry this out.[91] But the attitude of lesser officials was another matter. The keeper of the county gaol at Winchester, though he had managed

[88] J. Kenyon, *The Popish Plot* (London, 1972), p. 227; Miller, *Popery and Politics*, pp. 162–9.
[89] For a full treatment of the paradox of keen priest-hunters from Catholic backgrounds, see P. Jenkins, 'Anti-popery on the Welsh Marches in the Seventeenth Century', *H.J.*, 23 (1980), 275–91; Bodl., MS Rawl. A 136, pp. 234, 390; *Hist. MSS Comm. Eleventh Report App. pt II House of Lords MSS 1678–1688*, pp. 1, 14, 46, 48–9, 75–6.
[90] P.R.O., C231/8, p. 5; H.C.R.O., QO 6 *passim*; Potenger, *Memoirs*, ed. Bingham, pp. 52–4.
[91] H.C.R.O., QO 5, p. 184; unfortunately the records do not provide evidence about the enforcement of this order, but there were 259 convictions for recusancy at the Hampshire summer assizes of 1679, and after a dip in 1680, convictions peaked at 752 in 1681, though these may have included some Protestant dissenters; P.R.O., E377/74, 75, 76.

to keep Sir Henry Tichborne in custody until he was transferred to the Tower, allowed a priest called Hill to escape. His negligence was reported to the king and Council by the zealous mayor of Winchester.[92]

But the main problem with the enforcement of religious policy in Hampshire between 1679 and 1681 seems to have consisted less in local obstruction than in the inherent contradictions and inconsistencies in the policy itself. It was no simple matter to preserve unity amongst Protestants of all sorts, while attempting to suppress popery. The simple application of laws against Catholics was likely to hit Quakers harder than it hit Papists. A petition from Hampshire Quakers to the county's MPs in November 1680 lamented the sufferings of their co-religionists under 'divers Laws . . . some of which were made against the Papists though we who are true Protestants have suffered much by th[e]m'.[93] Church attendance had been the traditional means of discovering and dealing with Catholics, but the simple application of the recusancy laws would hit Protestant as well as Catholic separatists. Instead, law enforcers had to resort to the uncertain category of the 'reputed Papist', to whom relevant oaths could be applied. But even local estimates of 'reputed Papists' might vary widely. The ministers and churchwardens in Hampshire in the Compton census of 1676 produced an estimate of the adult Catholic population of the county as 846. Yet constables and churchwardens just two years later in lists initially ordered to be drawn up by the king, which subsequently provided the basis of the Papists (removal and disarming) bill came up with a figure of 588.[94]

Nor did such estimates prove that anyone was a Catholic. The oaths of supremacy and allegiance had to be tendered to prove it. But Catholics were increasingly prepared to take the latter and oaths in general proved more of a stumbling block for Quakers. This difficulty is amply demonstrated in the case of Winchester. Here, the mayor enthusiastically applied the oaths in January 1679, only to see forty reputed Papists led by a priest come into the sessions to swear the oath of allegiance.[95] Meanwhile Stephen Whitland, a Quaker of Winchester, was imprisoned for refusing to swear.[96] Reputed Papists were sometimes prepared to take both the oath of supremacy and the oath of allegiance, as was John Heycock at Newport in December 1678.[97]

[92] *Hist. MSS Comm. Eleventh Report App. pt II House of Lords MSS 1678–88*, p. 79; *Cal.S.P.Dom.*, 1678 and *Add.*, 1674–9, p. 579.

[93] H.C.R.O., 44M69 07, 'The Quakers' petition of Hampshire to the members of the County at Parliament, 1680'.

[94] *The Compton Census*, ed. Whiteman, p. 96; *Hist. MSS Comm. Eleventh Report App. pt II House of Lords MSS 1678–1688*, p. 226.

[95] *Cal.S.P.Dom.*, 1679–80, p. 14; H. Aveling, *Northern Catholics: The Catholic Recusants of the North Riding of Yorkshire 1558–1790* (London, 1966), p. 329; the incident was related in the correspondence of some Yorkshire Catholics.

[96] H.C.R.O., 24M54/14, fol. 25.   [97] I.W.C.R.O., 45/16b, p. 179.

Central initiatives might be taken to alleviate the lot of Quakers caught up in the persecution, but the government was still no nearer to getting at the Catholics, for there was genuine uncertainty about how to deal with those prepared to take the oath of allegiance but not the oath of supremacy.[98]

The government's incoherent policy could only really be clarified through legislation, either to provide new and more effective procedures against Catholics, or take Protestant dissenters out of the scope of the penal laws. But no new anti-Catholic legislation, apart from the second Test Act, found its way on to the statute book between 1678 and 1681. And measures to comprehend or tolerate dissenters, promoted by Daniel Finch, did not succeed either.[99]

But before the end of the Exclusion Crisis, the prevalent attitude at Whitehall had begun to change. The king and his ministers came to regard the exclusionists and their nonconformist allies as greater enemies of the government than Catholic gentlemen. An early symptom of this change was the release on bail in May 1680 of Sir Henry Tichborne and others who had been accused of implication in the plot.[100] At the same time, orders were issued to check on the enforcement of the Corporation Act in the boroughs. By this time too, changes had been made in the county commissions of the peace, by which many who sympathized with dissent had lost office. By October 1681, Hampshire's bench was dominated by men who were keen to defend the Church of England from its enemies. At that sessions, Thomas Lamb, a blacksmith from Fareham, was ordered to publish his recantation of scandalous words against Lord Noel and the church, on a market day in Fareham and Titchfield.[101]

The government of the county's principal boroughs also came to be dominated by those who were unsympathetic to Protestant dissent. Thomas Westcombe and his allies had won control of Andover with the blessing of king and Council.[102] Dr John Speed, who complained to Secretary Jenkins in May 1680 about ejected burgesses at Southampton, harbouring nonconformists and dispensers of seditious news, was elected mayor of the borough in September 1681.[103] But such men as Westcombe and Speed were waiting for a firm lead from the centre before launching a fresh persecution of dissent.[104]

---

[98] Kenyon, *The Popish Plot*, p. 234.
[99] A 'Bill for distinguishing Protestant dissenters from Popish recusants' was lost through lack of time in the second Exclusion Parliament, R. Thomas, 'Comprehension and Indulgence', *From Uniformity to Unity 1662–1962*, ed. G. F. Nuttall and O. Chadwick (London, 1962), pp. 222–30; H. Horwitz, *Revolution Politicks* (Cambridge, 1968), p. 29.
[100] Kenyon, *The Popish Plot*, p. 201.
[101] H.C.R.O., QO 6, fol. 35.   [102] See above, p. 165.
[103] *Cal.S.P.Dom.*, 1679–80, pp. 479–80; S.C.R.O., SC2/1/9, p. 41.
[104] In 1673, Westcombe and those like him had followed the lead of Parliament in defying the Declaration of Indulgence, see above, p. 149.

This is precisely what they got in 1681 and after. Before the end of 1681, Charles II issued orders in Council for conventicles to be suppressed, and the penal laws to be put into effect against Catholics and dissenters. But at the same time, the execution of priests was stopped.[105] The government's campaign against nonconformity was given an added stimulus two years later by the revelation of the Rye House Plot, which only underlined the government's view, shared by many provincial Tories, that the Whigs and 'fanatics' posed the biggest danger to the regime. Central authorities took a definite lead in the campaign against nonconformity. Those failing to attend Anglican worship were ordered to be removed from the revenue establishments.[106] The result of these various initiatives was the most systematic campaign against Protestant nonconformity which the seventeenth century was to witness, in Hampshire as in many other counties.[107]

There is once again a problem of evidence in estimating the full extent of persecution, but something of its pattern may be discerned.[108] In 1682, there was a widespread campaign against conventicles and the leaders of dissent. In April 1682, Nathaniel Robinson and two nonconformist schoolmasters were prosecuted at Southampton.[109] By May, Quaker meetings were being suppressed in Andover. Several Quakers were imprisoned and others who came to visit soon joined them in gaol. In June, five of them were put in a cage for meeting together, and at the end of the month and at the beginning of July, Quaker meetings were violently broken up by constables. It was small comfort to the twelve Quakers by now imprisoned at Andover that neither a town jury nor the assize grand jury would find them guilty of riot. They were indicted instead for unlawful assembly and stayed in prison.[110] Before the end of 1682, the campaign against conventicles had spread to other boroughs like Portsmouth and Newport and was also being carried out in some rural areas. By the summer of 1683, there were said to be many Quakers in prison in the county.[111]

[105] Ogg, *England in the Reign of Charles II*, ii. 624; Miller, *Popery and Politics*, p. 190.
[106] Baxter, *Treasury*, p. 91; *Cal.Treas.Bks.*, vii. 602; there was even a move to suspend from duty those dockyard officials and employees at Portsmouth who failed to conform or who attended conventicles, though this was shortlived, Brit. Lib., Addit. MS 33283, fol. 145 (transcript of excerpt from *The Protestant Mercury*, no. 124).
[107] G. V. Bennett, 'The Seven Bishops: a reconsideration', *Studies in Church History*, 15, ed. D. Baker (Oxford, 1978), pp. 269–70; my own discussion is based on the evidence of secular courts, but it appears, for example, in neighbouring Chichester diocese amongst others, that the ecclesiastical courts played their full part in the campaign against nonconformity, E. Davies, 'The enforcement of religious uniformity in England 1668–1700, with special reference to the dioceses of Chichester and Worcester' (Oxford Univ., D.Phil. thesis, 1982), pp. 287–301.
[108] See above, pp. 133–4.
[109] S.C.R.O., SC9/1/26, nos. 7 and 13; H.C.R.O., 24M54/14, fol. 26.
[110] H.C.R.O., 24M54/14, fols. 26–7.
[111] *Portsmouth Sessions Papers*, ed. Hoad, p. 97; I.W.C.R.O., 45/59, November 1682; H.C.R.O., QO 6, fol. 48; *Cal.S.P.Dom.*, January–June 1683, p. 133.

It was one thing to suppress conventicles, but quite another to enforce church attendance, which magistrates increasingly tried to do. The first presentments for recusancy under this new campaign were made at Newport in July 1682.[112] By 1683, Quakers at Yately and Hartley Wintney in the north-east of the county were being presented for failure to attend church.[113] At Southampton, beadles were ordered to present everybody within their wards who did not attend church on Sundays.

The persecution of all varieties of nonconformity intensified with the discovery of the Rye House Plot in June 1683. At the end of that month, all nonconformists at Southampton were disarmed, and Nathaniel Robinson was committed to prison under the Five Mile Act.[114] Early in July, fifty people were convicted of holding or attending conventicles in the town. William Herne, a dissenting schoolmaster from the Isle of Wight was sent to the county gaol for six months by justices there.[115] At the first county quarter sessions after the news of the plot, an order was made that hundred constables confer with churchwardens to discover how many people were absent from church in each parish. The following April (1684), tithingmen were ordered to make sworn presentments before JPs of all absentees from church within their tithings. This resulted in a stream of indictments before quarter sessions, which were almost all found 'true bills' by the grand jury. At least 376 people were indicted in this way, for varying periods of recusancy, some being indicted two or three times in successive sessions. Though they suffered under the recusancy laws, there is little doubt that Protestant dissenters were the main targets and the main victims of the persecution. The original order which launched it was revealingly prefixed as follows:

This court being satisfied th[a]t the Daingerous designes of such p[er]sons as are Dissenters from the Church of England against his Ma[jes]ties p[er]son & the Gov[ern]m[en]t both in Church and State . . .[116]

Comparatively few Catholics were caught up in it. Only nineteen of those indicted had been listed as Catholics in 1678–80, though this had not been a comprehensive listing.[117] The Catholic gentry were conspicuously absent from the indictments.[118] The Quakers suffered greatly under this campaign.

---

112 I.W.C.R.O., 45/59, under date.
113 H.C.R.O., 24M54/14, fol. 27.
114 *Cal.S.P.Dom.*, January–June 1683, p. 361; for Robinson's previous sufferings, see above, pp. 135, 137, 138.
115 S.C.R.O., SC9/1/30; H.C.R.O., Sessions rolls, file 9, gaol calendar, 2 October 1683.
116 H.C.R.O., QO 6, fols. 54, 63; Sessions rolls, files 10, 11, 12 and 18; these indictments do not cover the principal boroughs which had their own sessions.
117 See above, p. 198; H.L.R.O., Main Papers (no. 321), 3 December 1680, fols. 36–42.
118 This was not a universal phenomenon: the Catholic gentry of Cheshire continued to suffer persecution in this period, P. J. Challinor, 'The structure of politics in Cheshire 1660–1715' (Wolverhampton Polytechnic, Ph.D. thesis, 1983), pp. 95–6.

Some had their goods distrained to pay fines and seven Quakers from rural parishes were imprisoned as a result of it.[119]

There was an independent initiative to enforce church attendance at Southampton, where there were few known Catholics. In September 1683, the grand jury at the quarter sessions presented eighty people for absence from church for three Sundays. Two Quakers, who were amongst those presented, were ultimately fined and imprisoned for their recalcitrance. In July 1684, the order for beadles to present recusants in their wards was reiterated, while fourteen dissenters were indicted for absence from church.[120]

The persecution does seem to have made inroads into local nonconformity. As early as January 1683, all but one of a group of Muggletonians at Southampton had conformed.[121] Isaac Watts, a Congregationalist and father of the hymn-writer, having once again been presented for unlawfully keeping a school, in September 1683, fled the town for two years.[122] Other dissenters at Southampton resorted to the Walloon church, a Calvinist congregation established under royal protection in the reign of Elizabeth. This provoked appeals to the government and ecclesiastical authorities from some of the magistrates that this church's liberties be curtailed, though such an extreme policy was not adopted.[123]

Persecution did not cease in Hampshire at the end of Charles II's reign, but continued into James II's reign. Four Quakers from various places within the county were imprisoned for absence from church in March 1685, so that by June of that year, eleven Quakers were still in the county gaol.[124] The persecution of Protestant dissenters continued with the government's blessing until 1686. In December 1685, Lord Treasurer Rochester signed a warrant to the clerk of the Pipe to issue summons of the Pipe (which should have been issued the previous Trinity term) against convicted recusants at Bristol and the town of Southampton and deliver them to the respective sheriffs.[125] On 17 February 1686, fifteen Quakers were convicted for attending a conventicle at Southampton.[126]

The main obstruction to persecution in Hampshire had hitherto been the recalcitrance of some lesser officials and local officers, such as constables.

---

[119] H.C.R.O., 24M54/14, fol. 28.
[120] S.C.R.O., SC9/1/31; SC9/1/33; H.C.R.O., 24M54/14, fol. 28; Mildon, 'Puritanism in Hampshire', p. 419.
[121] *A Volume of Spiritual Epistles being the Copies of several Letters written by the last Prophets and Messengers of God John Reeve and Lodowicke Muggleton*, ed. Alexander Delamaine (London, reprint 1820), pp. 518–21.
[122] S.C.R.O., SC9/1/31; Mildon, 'Puritanism in Hampshire', p. 418.
[123] Bodl., MS Rawl. C 894, fol. 48; *Cal.S.P.Dom.*, 1684–4, p. 177.
[124] H.C.R.O., 24M54/14, fol. 28.
[125] *Cal.Treas.Bks.*, viii. 493.   [126] S.C.R.O., SC9/4/20.

Now in the early 1680s, central government and local justices co-operated in seeking to overcome this problem. Portsmouth's new charter in 1682, gave the borough jurisdiction over Gosport, hitherto a haven for dissent. In September 1682, Theophilus Lloyd was fined £20 by Portsmouth magistrates for teaching at a conventicle of fifty persons at the house of Stephen Locke in Gosport. In November, Humphrey Scott, constable of Gosport, co-operated in a fresh initiative to suppress this conventicle, with the help of some local inhabitants and soldiers.[127] Constables at Andover in the 1680s showed none of the reluctance of their predecessors about the suppression of local conventicles, but did it ruthlessly.[128] JPs in the county were ready to deal vigorously with negligent local officials. When the constables of the hundred of Evingar failed to distrain for the fines imposed by John Fawkenor, JP, on conventicles in 1682, they were ordered to do so by Epiphany quarter sessions in 1683, or face a £5 fine. When the justices launched their campaign against recusancy in 1683–4, they took steps to deal with obstruction by petty constables or tithingmen. In July 1684, hundred constables were ordered to return the names of any tithingmen who refused or neglected to make presentments.[129] Hampshire justices acted in concert with those of neighbouring shires to crush dissent. When John Kilburne was fined £20 for teaching at a Quaker meeting at Reading, the mayor sent word to Richard Bishop of South Warnborough, JP, who duly issued a warrant to the constabales of Alton hundred, who seized £23 10s 0d of Kilburne's property at Holybourne.[130] Jurisdictional boundaries, it would seem, no longer provided much protection to dissenters.

But there were some constraints on the complete suppression of non-conformity. Some people who were involved in implementing the persecution were more moderate than others. Richard Norton, retaining a residual sympathy for dissent, used his influence as a JP to mitigate the persecution to some extent. One recusancy indictment reveals that he was responsible for the discharge of Hester Ham, widow, presumably on humanitarian grounds.[131] Indictments from other parts of the county have clearly been doctored at some stage to change the stated period of recusancy from a month or more to three weeks, thus lowering the possible fine from a ruinous £20, which it would have been quite impossible for most of those indicted to pay, to a mere three shillings.[132] But then a reluctance to ruin people should not

[127] *Portsmouth Sessions Papers*, ed. Hoad, pp. 97, 99.
[128] H.C.R.O., 24M54/14, fols. 26–7.
[129] H.C.R.O., QO 6, fols. 48, 67; for a similar tightening up of procedure in neighbouring Sussex see Fletcher, *Reform in the Provinces*, p. 353.
[130] H.C.R.O., 24M54/14, fol. 29.
[131] H.C.R.O., Sessions rolls, file 10: indictment of Hester Ham, widow.
[132] H.C.R.O., Sessions rolls, files 10, 11, 12 and 18.

necessarily be interpreted as a sign of sympathy for their plight. It made far more sense to impose a realistic fine upon nonconformists than to destroy their livelihoods through impossible fines and distraint. Lodowicke Muggleton comforted his beleaguered follower William Sedley of Southampton in January 1683 with the thought that as he was a poor man with a large family, even the relentless persecution of the Southampton magistrates would be restrained by the fact that his flight or total ruin would leave his children on the parish.[133]

It was difficult for central government to obtain control over the revenue raised through prosecution. Simon Smith had been appointed as receiver-general of recusant revenue in Wiltshire and Hampshire in 1680. But though he expended £71 on writs of inquiry and other instruments issued through sheriffs during the four years he served, he paid only £48 10s 0d into the Exchequer. A bid to bring conventicle fines in, in March 1684, seems to have been no more successful.[134] Much later, on 30 July 1688, a commission was issued to certain London-based lawyers, and local Catholic gentlemen and government servants in Kent and Hampshire to inquire into money raised from dissenters and Catholics since 29 September 1677. This was the product of James II's policy of investigating past persecution. But though this investigation produced results in some counties like Essex and Devon, there is no evidence that the Hampshire–Kent commission ever operated.[135]

But the persecution of religious minorities in the localities was subject to royal control and direction, though the exact rhythm of persecution varied from area to area. The government had launched the campaign against dissent in 1681 and could modify or prevent it whenever it chose. For his first year or more on the throne, James II was content to direct the persecution away from Catholics, a tendency which had been apparent in the persecution in Hampshire since 1681. The Treasury, assize judges and ecclesiastical authorities were duly briefed, and persecution was confined to Protestant nonconformists.[136]

As his relationship with the Tories went sour, James II gradually changed his policy. In March 1686, he ordered the pardon and release of imprisoned Quakers. This was implemented at the Easter quarter sessions in Hampshire on 13 April 1686.[137] James seems to have inclined initially to a policy of limited and controlled toleration, with dispensations being given to particu-

133   *A Volume of Spiritual Epistles*, ed. Delamaine, p. 521.
134   P.R.O., E377/75; E401/1969, p. 54; *Cal.Treas.Bks.*, vii. 1069.
135   *Cal.Treas.Bks.*, viii. 2028; Miller, *Popery and Politics*, p. 216.
136   Miller, *Popery and Politics*, pp. 190–3, 195, 204; Kenyon, *The Popish Plot*, p. 237; it took time for the change of policy to filter down to the lowest level of administration, for example in Cheshire where the pressure did not come off Catholics until 1686, Challinor, 'The structure of politics in Cheshire', p. 140.
137   Miller, *Popery and Politics*, p. 210; H.C.R.O., QO 6, fol. 90.

lar dissenting congregations in various parts of the country.[138] Such a policy would have enabled him if he had pursued it to put considerable pressure on the beleaguered dissenters to show active support for his wider policy of abolishing the tests and penal laws. But this opportunity was missed as the king adopted a more generous and less controlled toleration for Protestant dissenters as for Catholics, which was enshrined in the Declaration of Indulgence of April 1687.

The king's policy was generally complied with in Hampshire. The Quakers continued to suffer, as in other counties, but not for absence from church or attending conventicles of their own. Their refusal to pay tithes inevitably brought distraint and even imprisonment in their wake, and though civil magistrates were involved in inflicting these penalties this did not represent any conscious defiance of government policy.[139] James II's government, keen to counter accusations of a conspiracy against the established church, did nothing to undermine the tithe system or to exempt Quakers from lawful payments. Some local officials were only too glad to be freed from the obligation of routine persecution. In 1684, the churchwardens of Compton had finally given up presenting the Catholic school at Silkstead. With James II's policy towards Catholics there were no constraints on them to do so.[140]

The only serious obstruction to James' policy in Hampshire or elsewhere came, belatedly, from within the ranks of the ecclesiastical hierarchy. Bishop Peter Mews, who was translated from Bath and Wells to Winchester diocese in succession to Morley in 1684, had been a strong supporter of the Crown's policies in Charles II's last years, and sought to maintain the good relationship between Crown and church in James II's reign. But he soon found himself at odds with the king's new policy. By June 1687, he was desperately fighting off an attempt by Lord De la Warr to have his non-clerical son made a prebendary at Winchester, by means of a royal dispensation.[141] Mews supported the stand of the Seven Bishops and when, in 1688, Sunderland (the secretary of state) had the temerity to issue an order direct to the clergy in his diocese to read the Declaration of Indulgence as the king had directed, he had no hesitation in countermanding it, 'conceiving that no one had anything to say in his Diocese'.[142] The bold stand by the bishops prompted some laymen locally to find their voices. The assize grand jury in the summer of 1688 in Hampshire not only refused to endorse an abhorrence of the bishops' petition promoted by Bernard Howard, but threatened to present all office-holders

[138] Miller, *Popery and Politics*, pp. 210–11.
[139] H.C.R.O., 24M54/14, fols. 29–30; 24M54/76, pp. 1–3; 24M54/151, p. 1.
[140] A. C. F. Beales, *Education Under Penalty: English Catholic Education from the Reformation to the Fall of James II 1547–1689* (London, 1963), p. 220.
[141] Bodl., MS Tanner, 29, fol. 38.
[142] *Collectanea Curiosa*, ed. Gutch, i. 337; Brit. Lib., Addit. MS 34510, fol. 133.

serving locally who had not taken the statutory oaths.[143] But in fact the king's Declaration of Indulgence continued to operate in Hampshire during 1688, whatever the local clergy or jurymen thought of it.

Between 1679 and 1688, religious policy was made by central government, though the considerations which shaped it varied widely from one part of the decade to another. There were constraints in the provinces on the uniform enforcement of any policy, notably local negligence and obstruction. But in the 1679–81 period, the principal problem lay in the contradictory nature of the policy itself, and in the period 1681–6, more progress was made than ever before towards reducing obstruction to the persecution of nonconformity by local jurisdictions and officials. James II abandoned not only the policy of persecution of recent years but also the strong central control over local religious life which had characterized even the toleration granted by his brother in 1672–3. He only briefly reverted to the policy of licensed and limited toleration for dissenters, and soon moved on to a more generous and less controlled policy. Worse, James, through insensitivity and intransigence, turned the Anglican episcopate, which had been a strong prop of his brother's government in the localities, into the co-ordinator and mouthpiece of provincial opposition, which succeeded in humiliating him in the summer of 1688, though his toleration survived until the fall of his regime.

[143]   *Ellis Correspondence*, ii. 108–9.

9

Court and county 1679–88

English politics in the decade which followed the revelation of the Popish Plot in the autumn of 1678 were characterized by confusion and crisis. These hectic years saw the break-up of one opposition, the country coalition of the 1670s, a rallying to the Crown in the early 1680s and the dissipation of this support and the creation of a new opposition by James II, in the latter part of the decade. The stronger central government became under Charles II, the more positive support it obtained in the localities, and conversely the weakness and unpopularity of James' regime grew simultaneously. More centralized and authoritarian government was not necessarily unpopular in the provinces of England and independence of provincial opinion as enjoyed by James II, far from being an asset, was merely a symptom of the decadence of his regime.

The revelation of the Popish Plot seems to have caused genuine panic in some parts of Hampshire, and in the winter of 1678–9 the country coalition looked formidable.[1] In the attack on Danby, the opposition could deploy the accumulated local and personal resentments against his ministry. Indeed, some office-holders connected with Hampshire such as Sir Robert Howard and Sir Robert and Sir John Holmes voted for Danby's impeachment in the last days of the Cavalier Parliament.[2]

As the old Parliament gave way to a general election early in 1679, several opposition leaders were involved in promoting like-minded candidates in Hampshire. Early in February, the marquis of Winchester was holding meetings of gentry as Basing, with a view of having Lord Russell returned for the county.[3] The earl of Clarendon making his first nominations to the corporation, as lord of the manor of Christchurch, recommended Sir Thomas Clarges and Henry Tulse as worthy persons having 'given soe good evidence of their

---

[1] See above, p. 180.

[2] Oliver, *Sir Robert Howard*, pp. 219–20.

[3] Lord Russell, who had inherited the Stratton estate from his father-in-law, the earl of Southampton, had spent several summers there with his wife, *Letters of Rachel, Lady Russell*, ed. Lord J. Russell (2 vols., London, 1853), i. 5n, 44–8.

being good Patriotts in the last Parliament, by their stedy adhering to the true Interest of their Countrey & the Protestant Religion'.[4]

Nevertheless, the opposition by no means swept the board in the elections to the first Exclusion Parliament. In the county election, Edward Noel, the lord lieutenant and supporter of Danby was returned, along with Richard Norton, a moderate opposition supporter, who nevertheless had the recommendation of the duke of York. Noel would subsequently vote against York's exclusion from the throne and Norton was absent from the division. Of the twenty-four MPs returned for Hampshire's boroughs, Shaftesbury reckoned that twelve were 'worthy' or 'honest' (i.e. his supporters), while he described eleven as 'base' or 'vile' (i.e. supporters of the court). He was doubtful about Bartholemew Bulkeley (MP for Lymington).[5]

The broad country coalition however soon broke up over the issue of exclusion, for which only six of Hampshire's MPs were prepared to vote. Seven (or possibly eight) voted against and the rest were absent. It is notable that all the exclusionists were native gentry, while their opponents were all outsiders with the exception of Edward Noel, whose connections with the county were comparatively recent.[6]

The aristocratic leadership of the opposition in Hampshire rapidly defected from the cause of exclusion. The marquis of Winchester was a member of the remodelled Privy Council and unlike his exclusionist colleagues he neither resigned nor was removed. He appears to have left England for France before the meeting of the second Exclusion Parliament and was seldom in England again before August 1682.[7] The earl of Clarendon was opposed to exclusion. His client Clarges had voted against it, and Henry Tulse, the other Christchurch MP, who had voted for it was summarily de-selected by Clarendon at the next election. In 1681, Clarendon would be called 'a maintainer and upholder of popery, and an enemy to the king and kingdom' by an exclusionist candidate who was challenging his interest in the borough.[8]

---

[4] Christchurch Civic Offices, volume of correspondence relating to elections, p. 49, earl of Clarendon to the mayor [1679].

[5] *H.C.*, i. 244–5; iii. 145, 161; J. R. Jones, 'Shaftesbury's "Worthy Men": a Whig view of the Parliament of 1679', *B.I.H.R.*, 30 (1957), 239.

[6] Henry Tulse (Christchurch), Sir Robert Dillington (Newport), Henry Whitehead, Oliver St John (Stockbridge), Richard Ayliffe and Henry Wallop (Whitchurch) voted for the bill: William Wither (Andover) though listed as a supporter was in fact dead by the time the vote was taken; Edward Noel (county), Sir Thomas Clarges (Christchurch), Sir Robert Holmes (Newport), Sir John Holmes, John Churchill (Newtown), George Legge (Portsmouth), Sir Richard Mason and possibly also Thomas Lucy (Yarmouth) voted against the bill, A. Browning and D. J. Milne, 'An Exclusion Bill division list', *B.I.H.R.*, 23 (1950), 218–19.

[7] *H.C.*, iii. 276–8; P.R.O., P.C. 2/70: list of privy councillors in 1683; Luttrell, *A Brief Historical Relation*, i. 211, 214; Winchester's discarded mantle of opposition to the government fell in 1681 to his son, Lord Wiltshire.

[8] Luttrell, *A Brief Historical Relation*, i. 198; *H.C.*, i. 247.

By the late summer of 1679, when the second general election of the year was held, the opposition appeared to be a spent force in Hampshire. All the JPs who attended the summer assizes in 1679 promised to support Noel again for the county, and supporters of exclusion stood to make little headway in the boroughs.[9] However, the exclusionist gentry managed at the last minute to pull off an amazing coup in the county election. Sir Francis Rolle, former knight of the shire in the closing years of the Cavalier Parliament, stood again and enjoyed wide support with the freeholders gathered at Winchester castle on 28 August. Noel still seemed likely to take the other seat, while Sir Richard Knight, another court candidate trailed a poor third. But then, somebody pursued the plan which the marquis of Winchester had been contemplating in February and put forward Lord Russell's name as another candidate. At this, the freeholders who supported Rolle switched their second votes to Russell, so that Noel and Knight faced defeat. Noel was ill and unable to attend, but Frederick Tilney, who had been acting as Knight's election agent desperately tried to stave off disaster by demanding a poll and belatedly entered the election himself. But this did not save the court side from humiliation. Lord Russell and Sir Francis Rolle carried the day by a massive majority (estimated by a sympathetic source at five to one). Tilney polled a derisory sixteen votes. In the subsequent by-election, arising from Lord Russell's decision to sit for Bedfordshire, Thomas Jervoise, another supporter of exclusion was returned.[10]

The Hampshire county election for the second Exclusion Parliament seems to bear all the marks of a conspiracy by dissident gentry to get as many uncompromising exclusionists returned to the House of Commons as possible, regardless of localist sentiments. Certainly the result promised to sour relations amongst the gentry, as Cary Gardiner wrote to Sir Ralph Verney 'thir has been very foul play . . . so thir is like to be great differences in hampshir amongst the gentlemen'.[11] A minority of the gentry had triumphed by mobilizing the ordinary freeholders. The motivation of the latter is hard to gauge, but they refused to let Sir Francis Rolle spend any money on them. Lord Russell had been absent on election day, and both he and Rolle denied any part in the vote shifting ploy which had won them the election.[12]

But the triumph of the exclusionists in the county election of August 1679 was exceptional in several respects. First, it was one of their very few recorded victories at the expense of court candidates at elections in Hampshire during

[9] Brit. Lib., Verney MSS microfilm, M/636, reel no. 33, Cary Gardiner to Sir Ralph Verney, 3 September 1679.
[10] *Domestick Intelligence or News both from City and Country*, no. 18, 5 September 1679.
[11] Brit. Lib., Verney MSS microfilm, M/636, reel no. 33, Cary Gardiner to Sir Ralph Verney, 3 September 1679.
[12] *Domestick Intelligence*, no. 18, 5 September 1679.

the Exclusion Crisis. In the boroughs, the trend was running in quite the opposite direction, with the control of Andover soon to be lost to a pro-court faction, thanks to an intervention by the Privy Council.[13] Secondly, the supporters of exclusion showed a remarkable degree of organization and even party discipline. At Stockbridge in the same general election and in the subsequent election for the Oxford Parliament, several ambitious exclusionist gentry competed bitterly to represent this increasingly corrupt borough.[14] In the county election for the Oxford Parliament in February 1681, personal ambition was again to the fore with Lord Wiltshire, son and heir of the marquis of Winchester, competing with the two sitting MPs, Rolle and Jervoise for the prestigious seats. Rolle topped the poll with 752 votes, Lord Wiltshire came second with 511, and Jervoise trailed behind with 372.[15]

Since the researches of Professor J. R. Jones on the subject, it has been known that the exclusionists, or Whigs as they increasingly came to be called, were a loose alliance of disaffected elements united only by their commitment to a policy.[16] These first Whigs are also widely held to have been a party which relied on wide popular support, and upon Protestant nonconformity in particular for their power-base. There is some evidence to support this view in Hampshire, especially in the elections to the Oxford Parliament. Sir Richard Stephens tried unsuccessfully to revive the inhabitant franchise at Portsmouth, against the traditional franchise which lay with the free burgesses of the corporation. He won the votes of only four of the latter but was supported by 171 of the inhabitants.[17] Sir Robert Henley and Francis Paulet, having been ousted as MPs for Andover, sought to widen the franchise to include freemen, though without success.[18] Several Whig peers and Lord Wiltshire were involved in an abortive attempt to persuade Christchurch corporation to throw off the patronage of the earl of Clarendon and displace his nominees with two hardline exclusionists.[19]

But all these attempts failed and on closer inspection, Whig populism looks more like electoral opportunism. No one thought of enfranchising the freemen at Andover until the change of leadership in the corporation made it the Whigs' only hope. Elsewhere, notably at Newport and Whitchurch, they were quite happy to be returned by small, oligarchical electorates.[20] Even the county election of 1681 witnessed a comparatively low poll.[21]

[13] See above, p. 165.
[14] *Cal.S.P.Dom.*, 1679–80, pp. 222, 234, 281; *H.C.*, i. 257.
[15] H.C.R.O., 44M69 06: 'The names of the pole taken the 21th of ffebruary [1681]'.
[16] J. R. Jones, *The First Whigs* (London, 1961), pp. 1–19.
[17] *H.C.*, i. 254; H.C.R.O., 5M50, no. 1610: 'Portsmouth Election'.
[18] *H.C.*, i. 246.
[19] P.R.O., S.P. 29/145, fols. 64–5.   [20] *H.C.*, i. 250, 259.
[21] H.C.R.O., 44M69 06: 'The names of the pole taken the 21th of ffebruary', the total number of votes cast (1,635) was low compared with the election of 1614 (4,358) and with that of

Local court supporters were understandably wary of popular politics. Portsmouth corporation, in a submission to the Committee of Privileges and Elections to counter an earlier attempt to introduce an inhabitant franchise in 1679, argued that it was more reasonable for those who had a share in the government of a borough to choose its representatives than for freeholders in the county.[22] Yet it was not only Whigs who stood to gain from the introduction of popular politics into the borough. In both 1679 and 1681, the devoted Yorkist, Colonel George Legge did well in the unofficial polls of inhabitants. In the poll for the Oxford Parliament he came top with 251 votes.[23]

The relationship between the cause of exclusion and nonconformity was a complex one too. Concern for dissenters was by no means confined to supporters of exclusion.[24] In Hampshire, as in Cheshire, several exclusionists had no connection with nonconformity.[25] The Quakers had their own independent national lobbying network, and a number of leading Hampshire Quakers petitioned all the MPs who sat for constituencies within the county on behalf of their co-religionists.[26] There is evidence of nonconformist support for some, but not all, exclusionist candidates in the general election of 1681. Sixteen Quakers, each designated by a 'q' beside their names in the poll book of the county election, gave their votes to Sir Francis Rolle or Thomas Jervoise or both. Four nonconformist ministers who had been licensed to preach in 1672 voted for Rolle and Jervoise.[27] And Sir Richard Stephens, the unsuccessful candidate at Portsmouth was said to enjoy 'a great interest with the fanatic party'.[28]

By 1681, the Whigs needed whatever support they could muster in Hampshire. Of the county's twenty-six MPs returned to the Oxford Parlia-

---

1710 (9,590), Richmond, 'The work of the justices of the peace in Hampshire', p. 551; W. A. Speck and W. A. Gray, 'Computer analysis of poll books: an initial report', *B.I.H.R.*, 43 (1970), 106; this discrepancy is only partly explained by the large proportion of 'plumpers', who used only one of their votes in 1681.

[22] H.C.R.O., 5M50, no. 1609: 'brieff Election of Portsmouth'.

[23] P.R.O. (Kew), Adm. 106/343, fol. 398; H.C.R.O., 5M50, no. 1610; the figures in 1681 were, Colonel Legge: 79 burgess votes, 251 popular votes; Richard Norton: 81 burgess votes, 137 popular votes; Sir Richard Stephens: 4 burgess votes, 171 popular votes.

[24] H. Horwitz, 'Protestant reconciliation in the Exclusion Crisis', *Journal of Ecclesiastical History*, xv (1964), 201–17.

[25] Challinor, 'The structure of politics in Cheshire', p. 92.

[26] D. R. Lacey, *Dissent and Parliamentary Politics in England, 1661–1689* (New Brunswick, 1969), pp. 109, 113; Reay, *The Quakers and the English Revolution*, p. 108; H.C.R.O., 44M69 07: 'The Quakers' Petition of Hampshire to the Members of the County at Parliament, 1680'.

[27] H.C.R.O., 44M69 06: 'The names of the pole taken the 21th of ffebruary'; Bate, *The Declaration of Indulgence*, pp. xxix–xxx: William Houghton, Thomas Warren, Humphrey Weaver and James Wise were the ministers.

[28] *H.C.*, i. 254.

ment, only six appear to have favoured exclusion. They provided a much less impressive opposition to the royal government than the parliamentarians had done to that of Charles I in 1642. Even so, the court's position in the county might have been stronger, if it had given a more vigorous lead. Ministers failed to give consistent support to borough managers who were doing their best to return loyal candidates in the face of Whig challenges. Lord Chancellor Finch was prevailed upon to entrust the writ for the Christchurch election of 1681 to Lord Wiltshire, thus giving him control over the timing of the poll, to the fury of the earl of Clarendon. Clarendon also found that there were several loyal gentry in Hampshire who were genuinely confused as to how they should vote and act in order to serve the king as they wished to do. They expected a royal declaration to set out clearly the Crown's policy and give them guidance as to how they should vote.[29] The exclusionists certainly picked up some surprising votes at the county election, such as those of the two Winchester MPs, Lord Annesley and Sir John Clobery, whom Shaftesbury had considered 'base' as long ago as 1679. They may have voted out of personal regard for the candidates, as may have the eighteen members of Winchester's corporation who also voted.[30]

After the dissolution of the Oxford Parliament, Charles II and his ministers, in Dr Beddard's words 'husbanded the genuine strength of their support in the localities'.[31] A declaration was issued, penned by Sir Francis North (soon to be lord keeper), which was ordered to be read in every parish church. The king was shown to be the innocent victim of Whig intransigence. He expressed his commitment to Parliament, the legitimate succession, the suppression of popery, and governing according to law. The king's enemies were smeared as men of Commonwealth principles, or as having no principles at all, and finally the experience of the Civil War and republican government were revived and depicted as the greatest dangers to religion and property.[32]

It would be hard to over-estimate the psychological impact of this document in the localities in England. It rallied despondent loyalists, won over neuters and waverers and isolated uncompromising Whigs. It elicited

[29] P.R.O., S.P. 29/145, fol. 65.

[30] H.C.R.O., 44M69 06: 'The names of the pole taken the 21th of ffebruary'; Jones, 'Shaftesbury's "Worthy Men" ', p. 239; ten of the members of Winchester corporation who voted for the exclusionists in February were present at a meeting on 20 May which approved a loyal address of thanks to the king for his declaration on the dissolution of the Oxford Parliament, H.C.R.O., W/B1/6, fol. 132.

[31] R. A. Beddard, 'The retreat on Toryism: Lionel Ducket, Member for Calne, and the politics of conservatism', *Wiltshire Archaeological Magazine*, 72–3 (1977–8), 102.

[32] The text can be found in L. Echard, *The History of England from the first entrance of Julius Caesar and the Romans to the establishment of King William and Queen Mary upon the throne* (3 vols., London, 1707–18), iii. 624–6.

addresses of thanks from several local bodies. The Hampshire assize grand jury was fairly evenly divided on the subject of how to respond to the king's declaration. A large minority objected to the proposed loyal address introduced by ten of their colleagues, both on technical grounds that it required twelve proposers 'as the Act of the County' and because it 'Tended to bring one part of the Constitution into contempt, and for that they apprehended the proceedings of the 2 last Parliaments deserved not an aspersion'. The address was nevertheless adopted.[33] Amongst the boroughs, Newport, which had returned the exclusionist Sir Robert Dillington to the Oxford Parliament was one of the first to respond. More predictable were the addresses from loyal strongholds like the corporations of Southampton and Portsmouth. In general, the addresses simply reiterated the themes of the royal declaration in warmly loyal terms, adding little local comment of their own. Subsequent revelations against the Whigs such as Shaftesbury's association plan, and the Rye House Plot produced a fresh crop of addresses, from a now unanimous assize grand jury, the Hampshire bench and lieutenancy, the governor, deputy-governor and militia officers of the Isle of Wight and nine out of the county's twelve parliamentary boroughs.[34]

Central government and local ruling elites were in complete harmony on the basis of shared commitments to the prerogative, legitimate succession, the Church of England and the rule of law. Addresses also provided a convenient means of isolating opponents, such as the minority on the grand jury in 1681. Three of them, John Lamport, Thomas Wansey and Thomas Dore who continued to be politically active, were marked men from then onwards. Robert Hulton, who was schoolmaster at Newport, put his job in jeopardy by refusing to subscribe a loyal address there in July 1683.[35]

After 1681, Whiggery was simultaneously marginalized and stigmatized in Hampshire as elsewhere in the country. It survived in clearly identified pockets, in and around Lymington and Portsmouth in the south, or in a few scattered manor houses near Andover in the north of the county.[36] Lord Wiltshire and Sir Francis Rolle were seen as leading figures in the 'Whiggish' or 'disaffected' party in other counties in 1682–3.[37]

Meanwhile, local Toryism, enjoying several fruitful links with the court,

[33] P.R.O. (Kew), Adm. 77/1, fol. 190; Luttrell, *A Brief Historical Relation*, i. 114–15.
[34] The exceptions were Lymington, Petersfield and Whitchurch; *The London Gazette*, no. 1615, 9–12 May 1681; H.C.R.O., W/B1/6, fols. 132, 136, 153; S.C.R.O., SC2/1/9, pp. 35, 66; Luttrell, *A Brief Historical Relation*, i. 88, 100, 103, 173, 177, 178, 182, 270, 273, 275–6, 283.
[35] *Cal.S.P.Dom.*, July–September 1683, p. 392; I.W.C.R.O., 45/16b, p. 235.
[36] *Cal.S.P.Dom.*, 1682, p. 465; *Cal.S.P.Dom.*, July–September 1683, 391–2; *Cal.S.P.Dom.*, 1683–4, pp. 295–6; H.C.R.O., Sessions rolls, file 13: indictment of David Roberts gent.
[37] Rolle in Somerset, *H.C.*, iii. 348; Lord Wiltshire in Yorkshire; I am very grateful to Cheryl Keen for information about him.

flourished. One such link consisted in the assize judges. A good rapport developed between the judges on the western circuit and the loyal gentry of the counties through which they passed. Lord Chief Justice North was particularly popular 'because he was the first clear loyalist of a judge that had come amongst them since the wars'.[38] Going on circuit in February 1684, Lord Chief Justice Jeffreys was encouraged in Hampshire by 'the Conversacon of a numerous Train of Loyal Gentlemen in this County who declare their stedfast resolucons of useing their utmost endeavers in his Ma[jes]ties Service'.[39]

But the Hampshire Tories did not have to satisfy themselves with impressing the assize judges with their loyalty, because during the last years of Charles' life, they had the privilege of his presence in person, as he attended the races at Winchester and planned to build a palace for himself there. The corporation of Winchester and the county bench and grand jury did their best to encourage these developments, and the presence of the king and court gave ample opportunity for loyal demonstrations. The local nobility and gentry and 'great numbers of all sorts of People' flocked to see the king, 'and to express their joy and gratitude for the Honour he has vouchsafed to do them in favouring them with his Royal presence'.[40] The king's presence also provided an opportunity for serious political business to be transacted, such as the formal surrender of Southampton's charter.[41]

Other links between Hampshire's ruling elites and the court also flourished. Several leading men and families had personal contacts there ensuring that patronage was widely spread. Edward Noel looked to Colonel George Legge to obtain an earldom for his father, but in the event received one himself, and many other grants.[42] Sir Robert Holmes broke off his embarrassing connection with the duke of Monmouth and looked to William Blathwayt to represent him at court.[43] Holmes played host to the king and several courtiers in the Isle of Wight in 1684.[44] Even the marquis of

---

[38] *The Lives of Rt. Hon. Francis North, Baron Guildford; the Hon. Sir Dudley North and Rev. Dr John North by Roger North*, ed. A. Jessopp (3 vols., London, 1890), iii. 133.

[39] P.R.O., S.P. 29/436, fol. 218.

[40] J. P. Hore, *The History of Newmarket and the Annals of the Turf* (3 vols., London, 1885–6), iii. 154–8, 184–7; Rosen, 'Winchester in transition' in Clark, *Country Towns in Pre-Industrial England*, pp. 180–1; *Cal.S.P.Dom.*, January–June 1683, pp. 22, 84.

[41] Brit. Lib., Addit. MS 41803 (Middleton papers), fol. 100.

[42] *Hist. MSS Comm. Eleventh Report App. pt V. Dartmouth MSS*, i. 76–7; *Cal.S.P.Dom.*, 1684–5, pp. 77, 111; see above, p. 160.

[43] Holmes' last gesture in favour of Monmouth was an abortive attempt to act as intermediary between him and the king in May 1682, Bodl., MS Carte 216, fol. 53; Dr Clifton is wrong to attribute this mission to Major Abraham Holmes, the rebel, *The Last Popular Rebellion*, p. 135; *Hist. MSS Comm. Leyborne-Popham MSS*, p. 262; R. Ollard, *Man of War: Sir Robert Holmes and the Restoration Navy* (London, 1969), pp. 193–4.

[44] I.W.C.R.O., Northwood parish register 1539–1660, p. 78: chronicle of events 1684–8.

Winchester, who had now made his peace with the regime, used the earl of Sunderland to obtain favours for him.[45] Several Hampshire families now had relations at court. Edward Chute, heir to the Vyne estate, was a clerk in the secretary of state's office.[46] Sir John St Barbe of Broadlands, now head of this Hampshire/Somerset family, was a gentleman of the Privy Chamber.[47] Sir William Kingsmill of Sydmonton (son of the royalist poet) had a sister who was a lady-in-waiting to Mary of Modena, and through her he managed to obtain a pardon for manslaughter when he killed his cousin Haslewood.[48]

Such court contacts were by no means confined to the gentry. Partly as a result of the borough campaign an increasing number of courtiers found their way onto the rolls of local corporations. By 1682, the marquis of Worcester had become high steward of Andover and was instrumental in bringing about the surrender of its charter. Under Portsmouth's new charter, many courtiers including the duke of York, were named as aldermen. Winchester corporation went one better and actually elected the king as well as the duke of York as freemen.[49]

It is easy to be cynical about the reasons why these local elites supported the regime. The presence of the king and court in Winchester were very good for business, and it was clearly in the city's interests to make this an annual phenomenon.[50] The corporation of Andover stampeded the Crown into granting a new charter which would give it the long-coveted control over Weyhill fair, and similar attitudes no doubt underlay the surrender of other charters.[51] The promise of a new charter for no extra cost was certainly very attractive to the corporation of impoverished Southampton. However, it is clear that before the possibility of such patronage became apparent, the leading figures of all these corporations were in favour of the policies of the Crown as outlined in the April 1681 declaration and the intolerant Anglicanism which it was now championing.[52] Ideology and local interest could go hand in hand.

---

[45] *Cal.S.P.Dom.*, 1684–5, pp. 141, 251–2.
[46] J. C. Sainty, *Officials of the Secretaries of State 1660–1782* (London, 1973), p. 71; H.C.R.O., 31M57 (Chute papers), no. 894.
[47] M. Urquhart, *Sir John St Barbe Bt of Broadlands* (Southampton, 1983), pp. 35–6.
[48] Brit. Lib., Verney MSS microfilm M/636, reel no. 38, A. Nicholas to John Verney, 7 November 1683; Lady Hobart to Sir Ralph Verney, 18 November 1683; *Cal.S.P.Dom.*, 1684–5, pp. 26, 47, 53.
[49] *Cal.S.P.Dom.*, 1682, p. 514; H. A. Mereweather and A. J. Stephens, *The History of the Boroughs and Municipal Corporations of the United Kingdom* (3 vols., 1935; Harvester Press Reprint, Brighton, 1972), iii. 1719; H.C.R.O., W/B1/6, fol. 140.
[50] The Crown alone expended £1,755 19s 10¼d on the visit to Winchester in September 1683, though the corporation pegged prices to prevent excessive profiteering, Hore, *The History of Newmarket*, iii. 179; H.C.R.O., W/B1/6, fols. 154–5.
[51] *Cal.S.P.Dom.*, 1682, p. 525.
[52] See above, pp. 165–6; as their address of May 1681 makes clear, the leading men of Winchester corporation were particularly keen to defend the king 'against all popish and

The loyalty of some Tories caused them to put narrow local interests second to wider concerns. The JPs and grand jury of Hampshire were prepared to donate their county hall at Winchester, on which much care and money had been spent over the years, to the king simply to facilitate the building of his palace there. In July 1683, when news of the Rye House Plot broke, the deputy-lieutenants insisted that Gainsborough establish a standing militia guard at Winchester at great cost to the county. It was left to the royal government, more sensitive of alienating moderate opinion, to order Gainsborough to disband it.[53] Commitment to the regime could distract men from merely local interests. Some local interests suffered.

In these circumstances, it is hardly surprising to find localist opposition breaking out against some of the measures of the early 1680s. The over-hasty granting of control over Weyhill fair to Andover corporation antagonized several market towns as far away as Blandford in Dorset (including Winchester, Romsey and Fordingbridge in Hampshire) as well as parties like Queen's College, Oxford, whose interests had formerly been championed by Secretary Williamson, who lost office in the Exclusion Crisis. At first, the Crown tried to mediate but then left it to litigation.[54] Some people in Gosport objected to being incorporated within the jurisdiction of Portsmouth under the new charter, and sixty-one of them petitioned Bishop Morley, who was lord of the manor, against it, though in vain.[55] There was some opposition from within the corporation of Southampton to the surrender of the borough's county status. Only a majority of those present on 7 November 1683 agreed to the appointment of a committee to consider the old charter, and when it came to subscribing the instrument for its surrender on 8 September 1684, four of the members of the corporation refused.[56] But considering the momentous step that was being taken, and the loss of local independence involved, it is rather the lack of stronger opposition which is surprising. Other surrenders went through with little or no opposition, though Winchester corporation had been disturbed in 1682 by an argument over the king's nomination of Edward Harfell as a freeman. However, it soon became clear that the conflict was one of personalities and none of the protagonists objected in principle to royal interference. The addresses, which the corporation was simultaneously agreeing to, put the political loyalty of the bulk of its members beyond doubt, and the conflict soon blew over.[57]

Some of the security measures of the early 1680s provoked a strictly localist

Phanatical persons whatsoever', C. Bailey (ed.), *Transcripts from the Municipal Archives of Winchester and other Documents* (Winchester, 1856), p. 158.

[53] *Cal.S.P.Dom.*, January–June 1683, pp. 22, 84; *Cal.S.P.Dom.*, July–September 1683, pp. 27, 68.

[54] P.R.O., P.C. 2/69, pp. 559, 563, 574.

[55] Brit. Lib., Addit. MS 33278, fol. 54.

[56] S.C.R.O., SC2/1/9, pp. 71, 86.

[57] H.C.R.O., W/B1/6, fols. 144–9.

opposition. When a fire broke out at Portsmouth in October 1682, the gates of the garrison were closed in accordance with orders from Gainsborough, lest disaffected elements take advantage of such a situation. But this prevented those outside the walls from aiding their neighbours to extinguish the fire, so some 300 to 400 of them assembled at the Point gate demanding to be let in, but were kept back by the guards on it.[58] Sir Robert Holmes' gathering of the parochial artillery into Carisbrooke castle in the Isle of Wight, provoked bitter local opposition. But though the Whigs hoped to capitalize on these resentments they failed to do so.[59]

The central government made every effort to ensure that the inconvenience caused to civilians by the military presence was kept to a minimum. Barracks and a garrison hospital were constructed at Portsmouth, thus reducing the need for quartering upon civilians. Ministers tried to ensure that criminous soldiers were liable to the penalties of civilian as well as military justice, and generally speaking they were.[60] It is fair to say that by the end of Charles II's reign, the people of Hampshire had fewer material grievances against central government than they had had for forty years.

But by the end of Charles II's reign, the central government had reached the zenith of its power in the seventeenth century. Charles was able to rule without Parliament for the last four years of his reign, despite the toothless Triennial Act of 1664. The king's death and the accession of his Catholic brother James left Tory enthusiasm for the regime undiminished as would soon be shown in the return of a strongly loyal House of Commons in the general election of 1685. Monmouth's rebellion and its aftermath merely completed the crushing of the opposition.

The ruling elites of Hampshire almost all welcomed the peaceful accession of James II. Congratulatory addresses flooded in from the corporations of Portsmouth, Winchester, Southampton, Andover, Basingstoke and Christchurch. There were also addresses from the county assizes and a separate address from the bishop and clergy.[61] Henry Anderson, vicar of Kings Somborne, welcomed the peaceful accession of 'the Great and Good King James'.[62] Lavish celebrations were laid on at the proclamation of James II as

[58] *Cal.S.P.Dom.*, 1682, pp. 451, 464–5.
[59] P.R.O., S.P.O. 29/428/146; there were hopes of deploying the disaffection of the townsmen of Portsmouth under the 'Insolencyes of the Garrison' to capture the town as part of the wider Rye House conspiracy, Brit. Lib., Addit. MS 38847 (Hodgkin papers), fol. 95.
[60] C. G. T. Dean, 'Charles II's Garrison Hospital, Portsmouth', *Proceedings of the Hampshire Field Club*, xvi. (1947), 280–3; *Cal.S.P.Dom.*, 1680–1, pp. 182–3; *Cal.S.P.Dom.*, 1683–4, pp. 251–2; *Cal.S.P.Dom.*, 1684–5, p. 238; *Portsmouth Sessions Papers*, ed. Hoad, pp. 114–15.
[61] Luttrell, *A Brief Historical Relation*, i. 331, 333, 334, 336, 337.
[62] H. Anderson, *A Loyal Tear Dropt on the Vault of the High and Mighty Prince Charles II of Glorious and Happy Memory* (London, 1685), p. 25.

king. The town of Romsey, where Gainsborough was high steward and Sir John St Barbe was influential spent £18 11s 2d on it. James was proclaimed with great solemnity at Southampton, 'w[i]th such generall Rejoicing as hath not beene seene'.[63]

The local elites were able to secure the return of loyal members in most of Hampshire's parliamentary constituencies, in the ensuing general election of 1685. The marquis of Winchester promised to deploy his interest to return loyal candidates. Wriothesley Baptist Noel, Lord Campden, son of Gainsborough and his co-lord lieutenant, of whose loyalty his father had boasted to Dartmouth, took one of the county seats, the other being conceded to Lord Wiltshire to avoid a contest. Courtiers or local Tories were returned for eighteen out of twenty-four of Hampshire's borough seats. Two obscure neuters managed to win the seats at Stockbridge, keeping out the exclusionist Oliver St John in a contest. Some people who wanted to contest the election of two Tories at Andover by appealing to a wider franchise were deterred by a threat of prosecution for riot from Walter Robinson, the town clerk. John Deane, a Tory deputy-lieutenant, tried to challenge the Whig hold over the borough of Whitchurch, though without success. Only at Lymington were two Whigs returned without a contest.[64]

Nevertheless, the election campaign witnessed some misunderstandings and bad feelings between the court and its electoral managers on the ground, over the selection of candidates. By 1685, Sir Robert Holmes was able to put both seats in all three Isle of Wight boroughs at the court's disposal, but he refused to reserve a seat for Solicitor-General Heneage Finch, despite a clear order from Sunderland that he should do so, preferring to give the spare seat at Newtown to Thomas Done, an Exchequer official.[65]

There was worse trouble at Winchester, involving the earl of Gainsborough. By the beginning of March, it had been agreed between him and the corporation that the candidates should be two local men, Sir John Clobery and Francis Morley, who, whatever the past record of the former, were now totally loyal to the regime. But at this point, Bernard Howard, who was beginning to assert himself in the city's politics, upset the apple-cart by obtaining a royal nomination for Roger L'Estrange, the hardline Tory journalist and surveyor of the press and Charles Hanses, a client of Judge Jeffreys, to be candidates instead. The king's nomination was delivered to the corporation by Justice Levinz, during his Lent assize circuit. It provoked considerable division and controversy locally. An anonymous letter was sent to the mayor, accusing L'Estrange of being a Papist, a letter which L'Estrange

63 Brit. Lib., Addit. MS 26774, p. 187; Addit. MS 41803, fol. 138.
64 *Cal.S.P.Dom.*, 1685, no. 391, p. 96; *Hist. MSS Comm. Eleventh Report App. pt V. Dartmouth MSS,* i. 76; *H.C.,* i. 245–61.
65 *Cal.S.P.Dom.*, 1685, nos. 393, 410, 589, 620, pp. 97, 100, 118, 125.

promptly printed and refuted in *The Observator*.[66] Strenuous efforts were made to persuade Clobery and Morley to accept the loss of face of being deselected, efforts which eventually succeeded, though not before Gainsborough had washed his hands of the whole business, and Howard had furiously denounced him to Sunderland. In the event, L'Estrange and Hanses were returned without a contest.[67]

The row soon blew over and certainly did not sour the relationship between Gainsborough and the king. Nor did it dent the loyalty of Winchester corporation, the majority of whose members were only too keen to do the king's will, once they had established what this was. But the incident contained clear warnings for the future about the dangers of ham-handed electoral management by the court. Bernard Howard, through his tactlessness and extremism had also shown himself to be something of a political liability.

After the general election was over, there were some expressions of popular disaffection in various parts of the county. At Bishops Waltham on 23 April, Mary Kemp recounted that the ghost of Charles II had appeared to his brother saying 'Dost thou think to be king that has murthered me', had gone upstairs, lain on his bed and frightened the queen to death.[68] In May, Ann Wood of Portsmouth was heard to say that 'for aught she knew the Duke of Monmouth was no more a bastard than she was'. After Monmouth's landing William Reynolds of Portsmouth was accused by a soldier of saying that 'the Duke of Monmouth had a great force and would have a bigger straight, and that he was a true Protestant'. More subtle was the gesture of 200 to 300 inhabitants of Portsmouth who pointedly held a pope-burning on 1 May, hardly the traditional occasion for such a demonstration.[69] It is hard to interpret such fleeting insights into the popular mind, but it would seem that some very ordinary people were unhappy about having a Catholic king. This disaffection may help to explain the poor performance of some elements in the militia during Monmouth's rebellion.

But there was little active support for Monmouth in Hampshire. Eighty men were said to have risen under the leadership of Thomas Dore, the mayor of Lymington and David Roberts of Brockenhurst, though their isolation soon demoralized them. They failed to join up with the main body of rebels and were ready to come to terms by 27 June, nine days before Sedgemoor.[70] Rumours of wider elite support for the rebels in Hampshire abounded. But contrary to expectations, Lord Wiltshire did not appear for them, and Sir

[66] *The Observator*, vol. 3, no. 16, 12 March 1685.
[67] *Cal.S.P.Dom.*, 1685, nos. 290, 329, 366, 375, 392, 394, pp. 63, 75, 88, 93, 96–7.
[68] *Cal.S.P.Dom.*, 1685, no. 584, pp. 137–8.
[69] *Portsmouth Sessions Papers*, ed. Hoad, pp. 123, 124, 129.
[70] *Cal.S.P.Dom.*, 1685, nos. 938, 1054, pp. 213, 230.

Francis Rolle was imprisoned and thus prevented from participating even if he had wanted to.[71] Richard Norton felt it necessary to write to the king personally to counteract gossip that he was implicated in the rebellion.[72] In the event, it was only poor old Alice Lisle who was caught giving succour to the rebels and that after their defeat, but it cost her her life.[73]

The harmonious relationship between the court and the ruling elites of Hampshire survived for at least another year after the suppression of Monmouth's rebellion. Though the work ceased on the palace at Winchester, James continued to make regular visits to the county and was met with loyal demonstrations wherever he went, notably at Portsmouth and Winchester. In 1686, he stayed with Gainsborough at Titchfield.[74]

But it was not simply unthinking loyalism or self-interest which bound local Tories to the court. There were principles involved. First, and perhaps most important amongst these, was a commitment to Protestantism as practised in the established church. It was their fervent Anglicanism that had won men like Sir John Norton over to the support of the court after 1681.[75] Preaching the assize sermon at Winchester in July 1686, Edward Young, a fellow of Winchester College, told the assembled company: 'It would trouble me to doubt of any of your Zeal for that Religion, which You and the Laws profess: Look where you will, you will never find any constituted of a more saving wisdom than it is.' Tories were equally committed to the rule of law. Thinking perhaps of the recent judgement in Godden *v.* Hales the month before, Young declared:

Torturing the laws to make them speak Contrary to the Intention of the Makers is a Solemn Evil; It is the Extremest Violation and Contempt of the Governing and Legislative Power, which if not held sacred in one Point, it has no security of being so in any.[76]

Thomas Manningham, rector of East Tisted, boasted of Sir John Norton at

[71] *The Secret History of the Rye House Plot and of Monmouth's Rebellion, written by Ford, Lord Grey in 1685* (London, 1754), pp. 121–2.

[72] He received a reassuring answer from Lord Middleton, Brit. Lib., Addit. MS 41823, fol. 116.

[73] After some hesitation a trial jury at Winchester found her guilty of knowingly helping the two rebels Hickes and Nelthorpe after Sedgemoor, for which Jeffreys condemned her to death, she was executed at Winchester on 2 September, T. B. Howell (ed.), *A Complete Collection of State Trials and Proceedings for High Treason and other Crimes and Misdemeanours from the Earliest Period to the present time* (23 vols., London, 1809–26), xi. columns 297–382.

[74] *The Diary of John Evelyn*, ed. E. S. De Beer (London, 1959), pp. 824–5; Hore, *The History of Newmarket*, iii. 239–40; H.C., iii. 145.

[75] T. Mannyngham, *A Sermon at the Funeral of Sir John Norton Bart, lately deceased Preached in the Parish Church of East Tysted in Hantshire* (London, 1687), pp. 1–31.

[76] E. Young, *Two assize sermons preached at Winchester. The first February 26 1694 James Hunt of Popham Esq being Sheriff of the County of Southampton. The second July 14 1686, Charles Wither of Hall Esq being Sheriff* (London, 1695); Young did not publish this sermon until after the Revolution for fear of incurring government displeasure.

his funeral early in 1687, 'he would have bravely serv'd his Prince to the utmost extent of what is lawful; and had there been more requir'd, he would have humbly and mildly suffered for the testimony of a good conscience'.[77]

With the adoption of his Catholicizing policies, his Declaration of Indulgence and his campaign against the Test Acts and penal laws, James II threatened to ride roughshod over all that the Tories held dear. But unlike his brother, James refused to compromise with the religious prejudices of his most zealous supporters in the localities, and so encountered a rising tide of opposition. Gainsborough refused to agree to the king's policy, even at the cost of losing all his offices. It soon became clear that Gainsborough was typical of the majority of county office-holders in Hampshire. No person of quality bothered to meet the duke of Berwick in the traditional manner when he came into his new lieutenancy early in 1688.[78] Only a minority of JPs attended him at Winchester to register their answers to the Three Questions. Twenty had the questions posted to them, but most of those who sent returns gave evasive answers to the first two. George Coldham replied that 'having been raised in the Church of England, he hopes he shall never do anything in derogation thereof, but he shall vote for the Election of such members as have demonstrated their loyalty to the King'. Others replied similarly, but Richard Chaundler was more forthright, saying he 'cannot be for the taking off any Law, that tends to the support of his religion, neither shall he vote for any man, that shall act contrary to this principle'.[79] From those who attended and refused the first two questions, Berwick faced mass resignations. Some clearly resented this novel form of canvassing. Nevertheless, James extended his election campaign into the boroughs through the agents, meeting stiff resistance from the previously loyal corporation of Winchester.[80]

Professor J. R. Jones has seen this election campaign as 'an invasion of the life and autonomy of local communities by professional agents of the central administration', to which there are parallels in the 1630s and 1650s.[81] In the light of this local study, it is possible to point up these parallels rather more specifically. In all these periods, there was a refusal on the part of central government to listen to local views,either through not having a Parliament at all, as in the 1630s or through only having a purged Parliament or managed elections as in the 1650s. In both the 1650s and in 1687–8, there were attempts to make Parliament into a cipher of court policy rather than seeking the free consent of local communities. In the 1630s, the assize judges had been used to impose the royal will, for example over ship money, in an authoritarian manner, without local consultation. So in 1688, the judges were

---

[77] Mannyngham, *A Sermon at the Funeral of Sir John Norton Bart*, p. 27.
[78] See above, p. 172; Brit. Lib., Addit. MS 34510, fol. 83.
[79] *Penal Laws and the Test Act*, ed. Duckett, i. 421–6.
[80] See above, p. 175.   [81] Jones, *The Revolution of 1688 in England*, p. 130.

instructed in their charges to justify the king's policy and to state that 'his Majesty is unalterably resolved' to make changes in local office-holding accordingly.[82] James was not prepared to listen to local views as articulated through the assize grand jury, he rejected the warnings of men like Gainsborough and the bishops. Gradually all the channels to the centre were blocked off, as the court became narrower in its political complexion.[83] Sir John St Barbe took an extended holiday in France, supposedly on health grounds, from the winter of 1687–8.[84] Sir William Kingsmill, having given negative replies to the first two questions, lost all his influence at court.[85] The paradoxical consequence of these developments was that in the summer of 1688, when the election campaign was at its height, James was profoundly ignorant of provincial events and feelings.[86] Centre and localities were drifting apart.

Professor Jones, working from central sources, has been impressed by James II's election campaign and has suggested that if it had been continued, the king might even have obtained the Parliament he was looking for.[87] But what minimal research has been done into the campaign's impact at local level generally points to a less sanguine conclusion.[88]

On the basis of the Hampshire evidence, it would appear that there is a danger of exaggerating the novelty and effectiveness of the electoral agents. The agents merely represented the application of well-tried Treasury techniques to electoral problems.[89] By 1688, counties like Hampshire were used to tours of inspection by professional salaried officials who had no roots in the local community. The surveys of the excise administration in 1684–5 are a case in point. Local people were not afraid to lobby such officials, as the people of the Isle of Wight did in their dispute with Trinity House over light-house dues, which were adversely affecting the island's trade in 1684.[90] However, no such 'give and take' between officialdom and local communities was possible in the election campaign of 1688, hence the unpopularity of the agents.

---

[82] *Collectanea Curiosa*, ed. Gutch, i. 391–3.
[83] Jones, *The Revolution of 1688 in England*, pp. 31–3.
[84] Urquhart, *Sir John St Barbe Bt of Broadlands*, p. 37.
[85] *Penal laws and the Test Act*, ed. Duckett, i. 423.
[86] Miller, *James II*, pp. 174, 201.
[87] Jones, *The Revolution of 1688 in England*, chapter 6, pp. 128–75.
[88] Hosford, *Nottingham, Nobles and the North*, pp. 10–11, 56–8, 77; P. E. Murrell, 'Bury St Edmunds and the campaign to pack Parliament, 1687–8', *B.I.H.R.*, 54 (1981), 188–206; J. T. Evans, *Seventeenth-Century Norwich: Politics, Religion and Government, 1620–1690* (Oxford, 1979), pp. 305–15: even after extensive royal intervention, Bishop Lloyd was still confident in late September 1688 that Norwich would return MPs loyal to the Anglican church.
[89] Robert Brent, leader of the agents, had been connected with the Treasury for some time, J. R. Jones, 'James II's Whig Collaborators', *H.J.*, 3 (1960), 67–8.
[90] Brit. Lib., MS Harl. 5121, fol. 14.

But it should not be assumed that they were necessarily ruthless or particularly effective. The Hampshire evidence suggests that they were not. They were wary of encroaching upon existing borough managers, even when it was uncertain whether they would return 'right' candidates or not. They made no visit to the Isle of Wight, leaving the management of the boroughs there to Sir Robert Holmes, despite the difficulties which he had made in 1685. He still regarded the seats as in his personal gift, promising one to his friend Samuel Pepys, without reference to the court. Worse, he now faced a formidable opposition in the staunchly Anglican borough of Newport, which put the return of court supporters in doubt.[91] The agents left the management of Winchester in the capable if ruthless hands of Lieutenant-Colonel Bernard Howard, a long-standing member of the corporation, after he had resisted their interference. More surprisingly, nothing was done about Christchurch, where the earl of Clarendon nominated to both seats. Clarendon had fallen from favour more than a year before and was known to be opposed to the repeal of the Test Acts. Yet no attempt was made to challenge his interest, though the mayor John Blake was known to support the king's policies. In this case, the agent rather lamely suggested that the court apply to Clarendon for his support for two apparently 'right' candidates.[92]

But the agents were not only circumspect, they were also incompetent, relaying erroneous information to their masters in Whitehall. In April 1688, it was reported that the candidates likely to be chosen at Lymington did not favour the king's policies; only after the abortive *quo warranto* proceedings did the Crown learn in September, that the same two candidates had declared for the king's interest. The king was also assured erroneously that the position of bailiff of Andover depended on him, whereas in fact under the 1682 charter, the Crown only controlled the appointment of town clerk, steward and deputy-steward.[93] The Hampshire evidence does not support Professor Jones' contention about the agents that their 'efficiency was in sharp contrast with the ineffectiveness of the traditional instruments of royal policy'.[94]

In fairness to the agents, it can be said that they faced a truly daunting task in Hampshire. There was little support for the king's policy among the landed classes apart from the Catholic gentry, for whom James' reign provided a

---

[91] *Penal laws and the Test Act*, ed. Duckett, i. 432–3; Bodl., MS Rawl. A 179, fol. 44; in September 1688, the corporation of Newport for the first time introduced a full Anglican service in the procedure for mayor-making, doubtless to signify their solidarity with the church, Medina Borough Council Offices, Newport, Newport 'Old Leidger' or 'Ligger Book', fol. 140.

[92] *Penal laws and the Test Act*, ed. Duckett, i. 430–3; D. H. Hosford, 'The peerage and the Test Ace: a list c. Nov. 1687', *B.I.H.R.*, 42 (1969), 118.

[93] *Penal laws and the Test Act*, ed. Duckett, i. 429, 433; St Barbe, *Lymington*, p. 25; H.C.R.O., 37M84, 1/CH/13 (copy of charter of 1682).

[94] Jones, *The Revolution of 1688 in England*, p. 131.

fleeting opportunity of holding public office in central and local government.[95] Several of the Protestant gentry who supported the court were
dependants of the Crown or hoping to reap family benefits from their
support. Sir Edward Worsley and Sir Charles Wyndham had commands in
the garrisons or Guards.[96] Lord De la Warr had been seeking to have his son
made a prebendary of Winchester using a royal dispensation and so settle it
in his family in perpetuity.[97] A son of Sir Thomas Higgons of Greywell was
one of those prepared to accept a fellowship at Magdalen College in place of
the ejected fellows, to the consternation of Anglican observers at Oxford and
no doubt in Hampshire as well.[98] Such self-seekers were isolated in local
society and the county electorate was set on returning Lord Campden and
Lord Wiltshire to Parliament, who were both opposed to royal policies.

The king's election campaign was based on winning over the old Whig
interest, yet in Hampshire few former Whigs were amenable and those who
were often proved to be broken reeds. The agents were hopeful in the spring
of 1688 of seeing Oliver St John, who seemed to support the king's policy,
returned for Stockbridge, but by September this hope had apparently been
abandoned, though by then Lymington seemed more promising.[99] But
Thomas Dore, the former mayor and pardoned Monmouth rebel, who might
have been coerced into supporting the royal cause, never seems to have done
so.[100] Henry Wallop was opposed to the Crown policy and of the other five
MPs for Hampshire seats, who had voted for the exclusion bill back in 1679,
three were dead by 1688.[101] It is hard to know exactly what attitude Thomas
Jervoise and his son Thomas took to royal policies, but if they shared the
attitude of their correspondents in France and Oxford, as it seems likely that
they did, then they were strongly opposed to them. They had also been taking
note of royal measures in favour of Catholics since 1686.[102] The marquis of
Winchester had long since given up opposition politics, and halving his time
between Yorkshire and Hampshire shrouded his feelings in apparent
insanity. But by February 1688, he was in touch with William of Orange and

[95] Sir Henry Tichborne obtained a post in the Ordnance Office, H. C. Tomlinson, *Guns and
Government* (London, 1979), p. 63.
[96] *H.C.*, iii. 772; I.W.C.R.O., Ward Collection, no. 906.
[97] Bodl., MS Tanner 29, fol. 38.
[98] H.C.R.O., 44M69 012, Thomas Hinton to Thomas Jervoise, 21 December 1687.
[99] *Penal laws and the Test Act*, ed. Duckett, i. 430, 433.
[100] He supported the decision to contest the *quo warranto*, H.C.R.O., 27M74A DBC/2, fol. 107
and is not mentioned in the agent's report.
[101] Browning, *Danby*, iii. 160; Richard Ayliffe, Sir Robert Dillington and Henry Whitehead
were dead.
[102] H.C.R.O., 44M69, E77 Honor St Barbe to Thomas Jervoise junior, 8 April 1688; 1 July
1688; 07, copies of royal dispensations for converted Catholics to continue to hold livings
in the universities and parishes, 1686; 012, Hinton letters.

by April, was preparing to send his sons Lord Wiltshire and Lord William Paulet over to pay their respects in person.[103]

Support from local dissenters was equally unimpressive. Addresses of thanks for the Declaration of Indulgence had been obtained from dissenters in Romsey, Ringwood, Fordingbridge, Christchurch, Andover, Whitchurch, Clatford and Portsmouth in late summer and autumn of 1687, but nothing more was heard from them as the election campaign got under way and the Declaration was reissued. Dissenters elsewhere in the county were apparently silent.[104] More conservative dissenters were far from happy with the course that royal policy now took. One 'strong Presbyterian' at Portsmouth was actually consulted by the military officers stationed locally who were unhappy about the Three Questions which Berwick was trying to tender to them. This particular dissenter managed to persuade Berwick to omit the first two, politically significant, questions altogether.[105]

Having broken with most of the Tories and failed to win over significant numbers of Whigs or dissenters, James' government showed an impressive ability to alienate moderate opinion as well. Richard Norton and Richard Cobbe agreed to the repeal of the penal laws but not to the taking away of the Test Acts. But the government was not prepared to meet them halfway and they were removed from the commission of the peace along with total refusers. Then Major John Braman, who canvassed Norton on behalf of the agents, found he was 'right', though by this time the damage had been done and Norton's removal from the bench (for the first time for forty-six years!) was said to be 'a trouble to many'.[106] Any non-aligned citizens of Winchester can hardly have been encouraged to support the government or its policies by the sanctioning of massive billeting used against them to coerce the corporation.[107]

Under the threat of a Dutch invasion, James II began to make grudging concessions to those who opposed his policies. But they were too limited to reconcile many people to him. The election campaign was shelved and in October all new charters and borough appointments since 1679 revoked. In Hampshire, this resulted in the restoration of the old corporation of Southampton (special steps had to be taken to restore the corporation at Winchester). But it also stripped Andover, Newport and Portsmouth of their new charters and the privileges which they contained.[108]

---

[103] *The Memoirs of Sir John Reresby*, ed. A. Browning (Glasgow, 1936), pp. 466–7; Sir John Dalrymple, *Memoirs of Great Britain and Ireland* (3 vols., London and Edinburgh, 1771–8), appendix part 1, vol. ii. 213–14, 215–16.
[104] Luttrell, *A Brief Historical Relation*, i. 412, 415–16; no county address was obtained from Hampshire, despite the efforts of Bernard Howard, see above, pp. 205–6.
[105] Brit. Lib., Addit. MS 34510, fol. 82.
[106] *Penal laws and the Test Act*, ed. Duckett, i. 431–2.
[107] See above, p. 175.   [108] Jones, *The Revolution of 1688 in England*, pp. 263–4.

Other concessions were too limited to change many minds. Word of the king's surrender over Magdalen College soon spread to Hampshire.[109] But other aspects of the religious policy, like the Declaration of Indulgence, remained in force. Just before the concessions to the corporations, the prince of Wales was baptized at court, with the papal nuncio acting as godfather, a fact that was noted and deplored by Samuel Smith, vicar of Carisbrooke and Northwood in the Isle of Wight.[110] Sir Henry Tichborne retained his post in the Ordnance Office. At local level too, Catholic officers continued to serve. The duke of Berwick remained as lord lieutenant and *custos rotulorum* in Hampshire as well as governor of Portsmouth until the actual invasion by William of Orange. He was then replaced as lord lieutenant by the Protestant, John, lord De la Warr, but as acting governor of Portsmouth by the Catholic Lord Dover. Meanwhile his deputy, Henry Slingsby, a firm Protestant had obtained a command in the field army, and had been replaced by the intemperate Irishman, Sir Edward Scott.[111] Catholics continued to be protected in their worship. There were six priests attached to a chapel which had been established at Portsmouth, until the end of the regime.[112]

As the crisis of the regime loomed in the autumn of 1688, loyalists found themselves increasingly isolated in their support for James. The corporation of Portsmouth had long been a bastion of loyalty to the government, sending addresses of support to the king, and promising to return complaint MPs. An address, purporting to come from the mayor, aldermen and burgesses of Portsmouth, even appeared after William of Orange had landed, expressing the hope that 'your Rash and Unjust Enemies may be cloathed with Shame, and that upon your Royal Head the Imperial Crown may for ever Flourish'.[113] But the loyal magistrates of Portsmouth were isolated amidst an increasingly disaffected population. Since September, large numbers of soldiers, many of them Catholics, had been drafted into the town. Because of a shortage of bedding, the barrack space available could not be used to the full so that many had to be quartered on civilians. But insufficient funds were provided to pay for the quarters. On 22 October, an ordnance officer observed 'the towne is soe much oprest with the solgiers quartering upon them . . . that there is noe rest for the governor of the place for the Continuall

---

[109] H.C.R.O., 44M69 012, Thomas Hinton to Thomas Jervoise junior, 28 October 1688; Bishop Mews of Winchester as visitor of Magdalen was entrusted with the reinstatement of the fellows.

[110] I.W.C.R.O., Northwood parish register, 1539–1660, p. 78.

[111] *Hist. MSS Comm. Eleventh Report App. pt V. Dartmouth MSS* i. 222, 230; *Penal laws and the Test Act*, ed. Duckett, i. 324n; Brit. Lib., Addit. MS 34512, fol. 110.

[112] *The English Currant*, no. 4, 19–21 December 1688.

[113] Luttrell, *A Brief Historical Relation*, i. 446; *Penal laws and the Test Act*, ed. Duckett, i. 432; *The London Gazette*, no. 2398, 8–12 November 1688.

Clamours of the People'.[114] They put the blame on Berwick and the king whom he served. Margaret Bee, landlady of a lodging house, refused to give a soldier another flagon of beer and remarked 'the Duke was a rogue and the King was a fool sending such fellows hither'.[115] The growing lawlessness and intimidation practised by the soldiery only made matters worse, and alienated even the previously loyal mayor and magistrates of the town. By the time of the king's flight in December, Sir Edward Scott had reason to fear a conspiracy between certain officers of the garrison and members of the corporation to betray the town.[116]

Finally at the time of James' flight, the outrages of the soldiers pushed the people of Portsmouth area into revolt. Many in the Portsdown division rose under Richard Norton's leadership to defend themselves and the citizens of Portsmouth against the soldiery. Then the citizens of Gosport rose in support of some seamen in driving the soldiers from the castle and declared that they would only let Protestants back in.[117]

Sir Robert Holmes had meanwhile found himself increasingly isolated in his support for the king in the Isle of Wight, despite an absence of material grievances comparable to those experienced at Portsmouth. A small landing party which came ashore from the Dutch fleet as it sailed past was not resisted by the local inhabitants, apart from the dragoons of the militia. Simultaneously part of the rank and file of the foot militia became mutinous and Thomas Newnham, preaching to dissenters at Chale on that Sunday, changed the subject of his sermon to a providential theme appropriate to the occasion.[118] By 9 December, Holmes was convinced that the citizens of Yarmouth were ready to declare for William of Orange. But in fact it was not until 17 December that a declaration was signed in the name of the governor, lieutenant-governor, JPs, gentry, clergy, militia officers, soldiers and inhabitants of the island, in support of William of Orange and a free Parliament.[119]

During the previous decade, support for the Crown and its policies had fluctuated wildly in Hampshire as in the rest of the country. Charles II's government had successfully seen off the Whig challenge and won over the elites of Hampshire to support its rule and the legitimate succession. James II came to the throne peacefully and popular disaffection in Hampshire, as in most of the rest of the country, was easily contained. But James frittered away

[114] See above, pp. 186, 187; Staffordshire County Record Office, Dartmouth MSS, D (W) 1788, I. i, no. 1455a (Thomas Phillips to Dartmouth, 22 October 1688).
[115] *Portsmouth Sessions Papers*, ed. Hoad, p. 143.
[116] See above, p. 189; *Hist. MSS Comm. Eleventh Report App. pt V. Dartmouth MSS*, i. 230–1.
[117] See above, p. 190; *The English Currant*, no. 4, 19–21 December 1688.
[118] See above, pp. 187–8; J. D. Jones, 'The Isle of Wight and the Revolution of 1688', pp. 473–4.
[119] *Hist. MSS Comm Eleventh Report App. pt V. Dartmouth MSS*, i. 225; I.W.C.R.O., GW/12.

the strong support which he enjoyed, through the insensitive promotion of Catholics and his abortive election campaign. Finally, in his belated concessions and ultimate flight he threw English politics once again into a state of panic and confusion such as it had experienced exactly ten years before.

EPILOGUE AND CONCLUSION

The king's flight and its aftermath provoked confusion rather than consensus amongst the ruling elites of Hampshire. Richard Norton probably spoke for many when he wrote to the earl of Dartmouth in amazement soon after the king's first departure: 'Oh, unhappy man to follow such counsel, the like was never or will be in story, a king with a great army driven out of his kingdom by a lesser army without fighting.'[1] The Convention Parliament of 1689 would settle James' fate.

But the Revolution of 1688–9 far from uniting Hampshire's elites, merely contributed further to their political fragmentation, as different groups and interests reacted to central events. Personal ambition and rivalry were very apparent in the elections to the Convention, in which four of the county's boroughs experienced contests, and three gentlemen competed for one of the county seats in February 1689 after Lord William Paulet, who had been elected with his elder brother Lord Wiltshire, took the unusual step of deciding to sit for Winchester, where he had also been elected.[2] Sir Robert Holmes was able to use his position as coroner of the Isle of Wight to defend his interest there, in the face of strong opposition. He lost control of Newport to the local gentry, but retained the nomination in the other two boroughs, having himself returned for Yarmouth and two officials Lord Ranelagh and Thomas Done for Newtown. Holmes seems to have conceded the other seat at Yarmouth to Fitton Gerard, son of the earl of Macclesfield, perhaps as an insurance policy to influence the prince of Orange in his favour.[3] William in due course continued Holmes as governor.

On the mainland, the dynastic issue was totally bound up with the interests of one family: the Paulets, who now broke back into the county's politics in a big way. They astutely committed themselves to the cause of the prince of

---

[1] *Hist. MSS Comm. Fifteenth Report, App. pt I, Dartmouth MSS,* iii. 135.
[2] H.C., i. 245, 252, 255; I.W.C.R.O., 45/16b, p. 250.
[3] As coroner, Holmes was entrusted with the supervision of the Isle of Wight elections; *H.C.,* i. 252, 261; I.W.C.R.O., GW/14 and 15.

Orange, gambling on his triumph. Both the marquis of Winchester and his son Lord Wiltshire were amongst the first to advocate the offer of the throne to William and Mary jointly, and both featured prominently in the framing of the Declaration of Rights.[4]

The settlement must have pleased the Paulets, but it was hardly what the majority of the political nation had in mind.[5] It was opposed by ten of Hampshire's MPs, who voted against the vacancy of the throne.[6] Actual non-jurors were rare in Hampshire, as they were elsewhere. The Hampshire part of Winchester diocese produced only two clergymen, who resolutely refused to take the oath of allegiance to William and Mary.[7] The surviving records reveal only two borough magistrates who refused to swear, Nicholas Chestle and Nicholas Odar, aldermen of Newport. They were removed in September 1689.[8] But one wonders how many swore with reservations or qualifications.

The Paulets duly reaped their rewards for supporting the prince of Orange. The marquis of Winchester was made duke of Bolton and a colonel of a regi-ment in the army, as well as being restored to his former offices as privy councillor, lord lieutenant and *custos rotulorum* of Hampshire and lord warden of the New Forest. Lord Wiltshire became lord chamberlain to Queen Mary.[9] Their political dominance in Hampshire was now unchallenged. Patronage in the county depended heavily upon them as King William made little attempt to control county office-holding at this stage.[10]

But the Paulets were not satisfied with their spoil. The new duke of Bolton wanted a place on the Treasury commission. Lord Wiltshire, now known by the courtesy title of marquis of Winchester, wanted a peerage for himself. But William seems to have taken a perverse pleasure in thwarting their ambitions.[11] Bolton responded by flirting with radical politics, but to no

---

[4] L. G. Schwoerer, *The Declaration of Rights of 1689* (Baltimore, 1981), pp. 171, 223, 232, 304–7.

[5] Kenyon, *The Stuart Constitution*, p. 1.

[6] Richard Brett (Southampton), Thomas Done (Newtown), William Ettrick (Christchurch), Francis Gwyn (Christchurch), Sir Robert Holmes (Yarmouth), Francis Morley (Winchester), Sir Benjamin Newland (Southampton), John Pollen (Andover), Richard, earl of Ranelagh (Newtown), Henry Slingsby (Portsmouth); E. Cruichshanks, J. Ferris and D. Hayton, 'The House of Commons vote on the transfer of the Crown, 5 February 1689', *B.I.H.R.*, 52 (1979), 45.

[7] William Hanbury, rector of Botley and Edward Worsley, rector of Gatcombe, J. H. Overton, *The Nonjurors: Their Lives, Principles and Writings* (London, 1902), pp. 479, 496.

[8] I.W.C.R.O., 45/16b, p. 256.

[9] *H.C.*, iii. 276–9.

[10] As in Cheshire, but unlike several other shires, the influence of the dominant family was not counteracted by splitting the *custos*-ship from the lieutenancy, Challinor, 'The structure of politics in Cheshire', p. 161; Glassey, *Politics and the Appointment of Justices of the Peace*, pp. 103–7.

[11] H. C. Foxcroft, *The life and letters of Sir George Savile, bart, first Marquis of Halifax, with a new edition of his works* (2 vols., London, 1898), ii. 205, 227, 228, 231, 240, 249.

avail.[12] Other Hampshire Orangists drew a complete blank in the scramble for central office. Thomas Cobbe, former clerk of the peace, wrote bitterly in July 1689 that:

all offices of Advantage being taken up by the best friends of King Jameses; & for w[ha]t I can perceive tis as great a sinn to have done anything for the prince of oringes Interest as if King James weare actually on the throne.[13]

At local level, material grievances were soon undermining the popularity of the Revolution regime. The misconduct and mismanagement of his Irish soldiers had done much to ruin James II's reputation locally. Yet William also made mistakes in this area and so soured attitudes to his regime in the Isle of Wight. Embarrassed by their presence on the mainland, William had ordered 1500 of James' Irish soldiers to be sent to the island on 1 January 1689, until they might be transported to Hamburg to enlist in the emperor's service. The barrack space in the castles could accommodate very few of these and barely 700 could be put up at inns, even if every space in the island were used, so large numbers had to be billeted on private houses.[14] Sir Robert Holmes subsequently made matters worse by forcibly quartering some on his local political opponents such as Sir Robert Dillington (son of the Whig MP) who as a member of the Convention (for Newport) was able to raise the matter in the House. Several other gentlemen also petitioned the government about it.[15]

But for its part the new government in Whitehall not only failed to alleviate the problem, but also compounded it by not providing transports to ship the soldiers away until the spring, and in the meantime, several of the Irish escaped into the interior of the island. They were not finally shipped away until the beginning of May 1689. But far from learning their lesson from this debacle and the bad feeling which it had caused at local level, the king and his ministers continued to use the Isle of Wight as a military camp, sending several more regular regiments down to quarter there in the summer, while failing to provide adequate sums for their pay and quarters. In this situation, even Holmes had to admit that the islanders had a grievance, but nothing was done to relieve it. By August, the magistrates of Newport were refusing to sign the certificates of out-going units on the grounds that their quarters had not been paid for.[16]

People on the mainland did not suffer nearly so badly, but as the war against France got under way, high direct taxation returned, which counter-

[12] M. Goldie, 'The roots of true Whiggism, 1688–94', *The History of Political Thought*, i. (1980), 200, 221, 222, 223, 228.
[13] H.C.R.O., 44M69 E77, Thomas Cobbe to ?, 4 July 1689.
[14] *Hist. MSS Comm. Eleventh Report App. pt V. Dartmouth MSS*, i. 246; P.R.O. (Kew), W.O. 30/48, fols. 72–6.
[15] *C.J.*, x. 112; *Cal.S.P.Dom.*, 1687–9, no. 2139, p. 392.
[16] *Cal.S.P.Dom.*, 1689–90, p. 6; I.W.C.R.O., GW/21, 24, 25, 26, 27 and 28; 45/16b, p. 255.

acted the popularity of developments like the abolition of the hearth tax. Naval impressment was also back in coastal areas. Those who did not share the government's commitment to the struggle against Louis XIV were alienated by these exactions, especially coming as they did after the relatively low demands of the 1680s. By the end of 1689, the government was being openly slandered in Hampshire, and the local authorities did little to prevent it.[17]

Nevertheless, the leaders of moderate Tory opinion in local society gradually rallied to the Revolution. John, lord De la Warr and Bishop Mews of Winchester both supported the ministry in Parliament in 1689–90, though both had opposed the transfer of the crown to William and Mary.[18] Sir John St Barbe (d. 1723), who had initial scruples about swearing allegiance to them was won over by 1691–2 and was posthumously described as 'a friend to the Revolution'.[19] Slowly, a consensus emerged which supported the Revolution.

Nevertheless, Hampshire's gentry continued to be divided by personal political rivalries, which were exacerbated by the annual sessions of Parliament and frequent elections. Competition for seats was intense and personal ambition was to the fore. In the general election in February 1690, Thomas Jervoise junior and Oliver Cromwell (both former Whigs) polled eighty-four freeholders and inhabitants at Lymington to challenge the election of two equally staunch Whigs by the corporation.[20] The attempt was unsuccessful. Next year Jervoise spent nearly £285 for his return in a by-election in the now notoriously corrupt borough of Stockbridge. Its complete disenfranchisement had been mooted back in 1689. But a bill to the same end failed in 1694 because the Hampshire gentry could not agree on where the seats should go; they were divided according to where their interests lay, some favouring Alresford, others Alton or Basingstoke or Romsey for enfranchisement.[21] The political fragmentation remained.

In this book I have attempted to assess the impact of central government upon a particular set of localities over a forty-year period, which was amongst the most turbulent in English history. I hope that several themes have emerged

---

[17] *Cal.S.P.Dom.*, 1689–90, p. 341.
[18] Browning, *Danby*, iii. 174–5; E. Cruickshanks, D. Hayton and C. Jones, 'Divisions in the House of Lords on the transfer of the Crown and other issues, 1689–94: ten new lists', *B.I.H.R.*, 52 (1980), 83, 85.
[19] Urquhart, *Sir John St Barbe Bt of Broadlands*, p. 37.
[20] H.C.R.O., 44M69 F12, indenture of election at Lymington, 24 February 1690; St Barbe, *Lymington*, p. 39.
[21] H.C.R.O., 44M69 06: Thomas Jervoise's election expenses at Stockbridge, 1691; Grey, *Debates in the House of Commons*, ix. 423–5; C.J., xi. 145; G. Holmes, *The Electorate and the National Will in the First Age of Party* (University of Lancaster, 1976), p. 25.

very clearly from this county study. First, there is the striking continuity in government concerns in the localities throughout the period after the watershed of the 1640s. After the Civil War, central government was concerned primarily with defence, internal security and local order defined increasingly in political terms, with harvesting its resources notably the revenues it needed to survive, and with the regulation of provincial religious life in the wake of the divisions of the 1640s.

But though there was continuity in the objectives which regimes pursued, there was considerable variation in performance on the ground. The achievements of successive governments in Hampshire did not conform to the accepted patterns laid down in previous historiography. The traditional image of effective centralizing governments during the Interregnum, freed from the constraints of provincial consent by the omnipresent standing army, enforcing their will upon cowed localities is not supported by the Hampshire evidence. This evidence reveals instead how dependent those in Whitehall were upon the co-operation of office-holders drawn from local social elites to enforce their policies and how little the army altered this situation, even in a county with a large military presence. The lack of consent and co-operation from many in these localities seriously undermined the achievements of successive governments.

The Restoration government was equally dependent on the support of local elites, but proved far more successful in obtaining it than its Interregnum predecessors. It was also able to adjust the power structure at local level in Hampshire in favour of its partisans in a way no government in the 1650s had managed to do. But the Restoration regime was just as involved in the localities in pursuit of its defence, security and fiscal policies and was in several respects more successful than the Commonwealth or Protectorate governments had been. The consent of the gentry in Parliament and in the localities greatly facilitated the establishment and proper functioning of the machinery for raising the militia and collecting revenue in Hampshire. Provincial consent and administrative effectiveness were not apparently alternatives between which the central rulers of England had to choose, rather they went together.

In the light of this re-assessment of the performance of Interregnum and Restoration regimes, the emergence of a stronger, more independent and centralized state after the hiatus of the Exclusion Crisis, though on a narrower, more partisan basis of support (which is well attested in Hampshire) seems less incongruous. Indeed, it seems to conform to an emerging pattern of political instability followed by administrative consolidation from the mid-century onwards, until the combined political upheaval and administrative collapse of the reign of James II. Once again, in the early 1680s, central government was able to intervene decisively in local office-holding to ensure that local government in Hampshire was dominated by loyal men. At the same time, some moves were made towards dealing with the problem which had limited the effectiveness of all governments since the Civil War, as before it, namely the jurisdictional anomalies and administrative complexity which existed below the level of the county. But James II's feckless government failed to follow up these measures.

If the Hampshire evidence is anything to go by, historians have been over-impressed with novel agencies such as standing armies, major-generals and electoral agents, to the neglect of and under-estimation of more traditional institutions such as the lieutenancy. The mere existence of an army did not necessarily render a regime more secure, or more effective in the enforcement of its policies. Nor were armies immune to movement of opinion about government policies. In fact, those regimes which depended totally on an army for their survival, notably those which ruled in the autumn of 1659 and the autumn of 1688 proved to be the weakest of the period and collapsed after relatively small-scale defections from within the military establishments themselves. Even a large army could not defend and police the whole country unaided, even if it were politically reliable. Interregnum governments realized as much and attempted to raise local militias to supplement the army, though their efforts were largely unsuccessful in Hampshire. James II did not realize the limitations of a standing army until too late, and his desperate attempts to salvage the situation in the autumn of 1688 merely added to the growing disarray of his regime.

Reactions to central government in Hampshire between revolutions were influenced by a number of factors, local, material and ideological and it is not easy to disentangle them. High taxation was always unpopular especially when, as during the 1650s, it was levied without real consent. Free quarter too was deeply resented and Hampshire with its constant military presence experienced it more than most counties. But this should not be mistaken for a widespread or deeply felt abhorrence of regular soldiers as such. A wide body of opinion within the county and especially in garrison towns recognized their utility, provided they were paid and controlled properly.

The health of the relationship between Whitehall and the localities of Hampshire depended heavily on the quality of communications between them. One of the most important channels for such communication was Parliament, especially as Hampshire traditionally had a large representation of twenty-six seats. This constituted a means whereby local grievances could be aired, central government kept in touch with local feelings and problems solved by statute. The Hampshire gentry, who had usually dominated the county's representation, could only be alienated by the attacks upon it in the 1650s. Charles II's government worked far more with Parliament than any

Interregnum government had done, which greatly enhanced its popularity, at least with the gentry and made for greater political stability.

Charles II and his court were also more sensitive to local needs and grievances than the governments which preceded them. But as Charles struggled for independence during the 1670s, these qualities were jeopardized and there was a resurgence of opposition in Hampshire, as in other counties, which came to a climax in 1678 and after. But the social elites of Hampshire mostly rallied to Charles II when he dissolved the Oxford Parliament in 1681, and thereafter the king was able to rule without Parliament, while opposition to his rule became increasingly muted. The court and the county were well integrated, through a number of channels during Charles' last years, though this could not prevent some local interests being jeopardized. James II's electioneering, which threatened to turn Parliament into a cipher of royal policy with little scope for the airing of genuine local opinion, was intolerable to most politically aware Protestants in the county and country at large. The achievement of the Revolution of 1688–9 and its aftermath may have been limited, but at least free elections and annual sittings were assured for the future.

But perhaps the greatest complicating factor in the relationship between central government and the localities in this period was religion. The experience of the 1640s had left Hampshire society like the rest of England deeply divided over religion, and throughout succeeding decades, the religious stance of successive regimes was a key element in shaping attitudes towards them in the county. Those who adhered to traditional Anglicanism, who were probably the majority in Hampshire, were offended by the parliamentarian regimes which tried, albeit unsuccessfully, to stamp out their preferred form of worship. There was little chance of conciliation across these divisions, but the restored Rump in 1659, in pandering to the sects, provoked the opposition of a wide cross-section of gentry and other opinion in Hampshire. The divisions within local society remained however, and were not healed by the Restoration, though the vast majority of people did conform to the Anglican church. Ironically, it was the sheer inconsistency and fluidity of his religious policy which helped to save Charles II from provoking a fixed opposition to his government in Hampshire for much of the first ten years of his reign. But thereafter his regime successively alienated intolerant Anglicans and those who favoured toleration by committing itself first to indulgence in 1672 and then to the persecution of dissenters in 1675 and afterwards. The growing association of his regime with Catholicism also alienated a substantial body of opinion in the country, which formed the local wing of the country opposition. Conversely, those amongst the gentry and borough oligarchies who stood for hardline, persecuting Anglicanism rallied to

Charles II's regime when it once again committed itself to an intolerant religious policy in 1681 and after. The Catholicizing policies of James II alienated many in Hampshire, and his attempt to create an alliance committed to broad toleration foundered on the deep-seated anti-Catholicism which existed within local society. The Revolution of 1688–9 brought these policies definitively to an end, even if it did not immediately remove other sources of tension between the centre and the localities.

SELECT BIBLIOGRAPHY

MANUSCRIPT SOURCES

All Souls College, Oxford
MS 223   (Jenkins Papers).
MS 239   (Collection of miscellaneous state and other papers).

Bodleian Library, Oxford
MS Carte 74   Montagu Papers.
MS Carte 216 Ormonde papers.
MSS Clarendon   67, 73, 77, 84, 87 Clarendon State papers.
Dep.C.175   Nalson papers XXII.
MSS Rawlinson
  A 32–3, 35, 56, 58 Thurloe State papers.
  A 136 Copies of orders and examinations concerning the Popish Plot 1678.
  A 139 B Lists of deputy-lieutenants and JPs 1688 (also classified under MS Arch f.c.6).
  A 179, 184 Pepys papers.
  A 227 Copy book of letters written by the Admiralty Committee 1652–3.
  C 179 Council of State Register May–October 1659.
  C 386 Copy book of orders of Committee of Parliament for the Excise, November 1649–May 1652.
  C 984 Compton papers.
  D 666 Jervoise papers.
MSS Tanner
  29, 31, 38, 42 Sancroft papers.
  58 Lenthall papers.
MS Top.Hants e.11 Copy of Richard Ayliffe's account book 1664–7; the original is now in the Hampshire County Record Office, 83M76/PZ3.

British Library
Additional MSS
  5841   Miscellaneous collection of Rev. W. Cole.
  15897   Hyde papers, pensions, Army, Navy etc. 1664–1745.
  18764   Exchequer Accounts 1566–1755.
  18979   Fairfax papers.
  19616   Letter book of the major-generals' registry 1655–6.
  21922   Lieutenancy book of the Nortons of Rotherfield.

237

24860–1 Maijor papers.
24863 Miscellaneous political and other papers 1640–60.
25302 Miscellaneous papers principally copies of the seventeenth century.
26774 Collection of Dr J. Latham for a history of Romsey, Hampshire.
26781 Hampshire correspondence of the lord lieutenant, militia affairs, etc. 1630–43.
28053 Leeds papers.
29319 Sydenham papers.
29975 Pitt official papers: seventeenth century.
33278–33283 Sir F. Madden's collection for a history of Hampshire.
34013 Major-generals' register.
34510–2 MacIntoch's transcripts: Van Citters' letters to the States General 1687–8.
38847 Hodgkin papers.
41803–4 Middleton papers.
41823
46501 Worsley papers.
Additional Charter 32751 Contract for works at Portsmouth, 1679.
Bath–Coventry MSS Microfilm M/863 Coventry papers belonging to the Marquess of Bath at Longleat House, Warminster, Wiltshire.
Egerton MSS
868 Biographical Dictionary of the Mayors of Southampton, 1496–1671 (Delamotte Year Book).
2557 Liber Pacis 1661.
2648 Barrington papers.
Harleian MSS
5121 Excise Survey 1684–5.
7020 fols. 33–48 List of court supporters, c. May 1671.
Lansdowne MS 823 Papers of Henry Cromwell.
Sloane MSS
823 Letter book of Sir Andrew Henley of Bramshill, 1659–69.
873 Sir P. Honeywood's account for Portsmouth fortifications, 1665–7.
3299 Miscellaneous papers, sixteenth and seventeenth centuries.
Stowe MS 577 Liber Pacis 1652.
Verney MSS Microfilm M/636 Papers of the Verney family of Claydon, Bucks.

Cambridge University Library
Dd. 8. 1. Liber Pacis 1653.

Carisbrooke Castle Museum (Isle of Wight)
Serle papers.

Christchurch Civic Offices, Christchurch, Dorset
Old council minute book, 1615–1857.
Volume of sixteenth- and seventeenth-century correspondence relating to elections.

College of Arms, Queen Victoria Street, London
Original of Hampshire visitation, 1686.

Hampshire County Record Office, Winchester

Borough Records
Andover 37M84

4/AC/8	Borough accounts 1656–62.
4/AC/10	1664–5.
4/AC/13	1677–86.
4/AC/14	1687–9.
1/CH/13	Contemporary copy of the charter of Charles II.
13/DI/I, II, III	Bundle of documents relating to the persecution of dissenters
4/EL/1	Privy Council Orders (1679)
2/JC/2	Book of Court Leet and Quarter Sessions 1659–90.
4/MI/1	Town Council Minutes 1641–54.
4/MI/3	1679.
2/QS/4	Copy of writ removing Lord De la Warr, Lord Sandys and others from being JPs at Andover.

Basingstoke 148M71

1/1/2	Copy of Charter of James I with details of mid-seventeenth-century taxation on the back.
1/1/4	Copy of charter of Charles II, 24 June 1671.
1/3	Town council minutes 1641–1700.
2/6/1	Examinations before JPs 1653–63.

Lymington 27M74A

DBC/2	Town book 1616–1715.
DBC/283	Order of Corporation Act commissioners 1662.

Winchester

W/B1/5	Fifth book of ordinances.
W/B1/6	Sixth book of ordinances.
W/B1/7	Seventh book of ordinances.

Winchester city charter, 15 September 1688.
Winchester city charter, 6 November 1688 – re-grant of old charter.

County administration

QI	Quarter Sessions presentment and indictment book 1646–60.
QO2	Quarter Sessions order book (ends 1649).
QO3	1649–58.
QO4	1658–72.
QO5	1672–79.
QO6	1679–91.

Q.S. Files, Declarations against transubstantiation 1679–88.
Q.S. Rolls, Files, nos. 1, 9, 10, 11, 12, 13, 18, 19.
'Quarter Sessions orders 1649–72' summarized by J. S. Finley.

Dissenters

24M54/14	County Quaker Sufferings Book 1655–1799.
24M54/76	Ringwood Sufferings Book 1687–1706.
24M54/151	List of Friends imprisoned at Basingstoke 1667–1832.

Ecclesiastical Records

Diocesan
B/1/A–4.no.36 Abstract of churchwardens presentments 1664.

Churchwardens accounts
25M60 PW1	Fawley.
41M64 PW1	North Waltham.
1M70 PW1	Chawton.
68M70 PW1	Bramley.
72M70 PW1	Easton.
50M73 PW1	Soberton.
88M81W PW2	St John's, Winchester.

Family papers
5M 50 Daly.
4M 53 Borthwick–Norton.
5M53 Wriothesley.
31M57 Chute.
19M61 Kingsmill.
44M69 Herriard
E77	Seventeenth-century correspondence.
F9, 10	Personal papers of Sir Thomas Jervoise (d. 1654).
F11	Personal papers of Thomas Jervoise (d. 1693).
F12	Personal papers of Thomas Jervoise jun.
O6, 7	Parliamentary papers.
O12, 13	Seventeenth century quarter sessions papers.
O21	Taxation papers.
O27XLV 11A	Orders of assessment commissioners.
O29	Militia papers.
Printed:	Herriard/K/pamphlets.

Miscellaneous parochial documents
39M69/PZ7 (Hursley) List of placemen in the House of Commons c. May 1671.

House of Lords Record Office
Main papers, H.L., 13 June 1660, documents relating to Winchester.
3 December 1680, returns of Catholics.

Medina Borough Council Offices, Newport, Isle of Wight
Old 'Leidger' or 'Ligger' Book, 1460–1717.

Isle of Wight County Record Office

Boroughs
45/16a Newport convocation book 1609–59.
45/16b Newport convocation book 1659–1760.
45/59 Newport sessions minute book 1673–1727.
Translation of charter (1661).
Translation of charter (1684).

Family collections
Fitzherbert-Brockholes.
Jerome
    Hall letters (Barrington family).
    Newtown assembly book 1671–96.
    Swainston no. 183.
OG/ Oglander papers.
Ward papers.

Other collections
DOI   papers relating to the defence of the island.
GW10–28   letters of Sir Robert Holmes 1688–9.
Parochial documents
BRX/PR/2   Brightstone parish accounts 1676–1752.
BRX/PR/4   Brightstone poor accounts 1667–88.
Car/D.274   Isle of Wight commission of sewers 1684.
Car/PR/1   Carisbrooke poor rate book 1652–7.
            Carisbrooke parish register no. 5 (1766–1813).
            Northwood parish register 1539–1660.

Portsmouth City Record Office
S3/B/47   Information 21 December 1688.
The documents calendared in *A Calendar of Portsmouth Borough Sessions Papers
    1653–1688*, ed. H. J. Hoad (Portsmouth Record Society, 1971).

Public Record Office (Chancery Lane)

Assize Records
ASSI 23 and 24   Western circuit.

Chancery
C181/6, 7   Crown Office entry books 1653–73.
C193/12, 13   Crown office miscellaneous books, including Libri Pacis.
C220/9/4   Liber Pacis, 1660.
C231/5–8   Crown Office docquet books.

Exchequer
E101/612/72   Muster rolls of Cowes, Portsmouth, Yarmouth, Sandham and
              Carisbrooke, 1686.
E101/67/11B   Treasurers at War, second account, Commonwealth 1649–51.
E112   Bills and answers, box 564 (Hampshire).
E113   Bills and answers of (Interregnum) accountants box 14
              (Hampshire).
E112/218/11   Convictions for illegal sales of liquor in Surrey, Hants and Dorset,
              1671.
E134   Depositions taken under special commissions out of the Exchequer.
E148/8   Informations, Charles II.
E178   Special commissions from the Exchequer.
E179   Lay subsidy rolls.
E351/649–51   Customs Declared Accounts 1648–51.

E351/658　　　　Customs Declared Accounts 1657–8.
E351/296–9　　　Excise Declared Accounts 1650–9.
E360/145　　　　Declared Accounts Hampshire taxation 1660–79.
E360/208　　　　Declared Accounts Hampshire taxation (Interregnum).
E372　　　　　　Pipe rolls.
E377　　　　　　Recusant rolls.
E401　　　　　　Receipt books (Pells).
(Round Room:　　'Exchequer K.R. Decrees Calendar' iii. 16 Chas. II East. – 29 Chas II
　　　　　　　　Trin.).

Privy Council
P.C.2.　Registers.

State Papers
S.P.9/32　　　　Supplementary State Papers.
S.P.18　　　　　State Papers, Interregnum.
S.P.23　　　　　Papers of the Committee for Compounding with delinquents.
S.P.24　　　　　Papers of the Committee for Indemnity.
S.P.25　　　　　State Papers, Interregnum.
S.P.28　　　　　Commonwealth Exchequer Papers.
S.P.29　　　　　State Papers, Charles II.
S.P.30 Case G　Parchments.
S.P.31　　　　　State Papers, James II.
S.P.44　　　　　Entry books, originating in the office of the secretary of state.
S.P.46　　　　　Additional State Papers.

Public Record Office (Kew)

Admiralty
Adm.1/5246　　Copies of orders in Council 1660–88.
Adm.77/1　　　Greenwich newsletters.
Adm.106/343　Navy Board – miscellaneous.

Audit Office
A.O.1 311/1231　Sir Robert Holmes' account for Sandham fort (1662–6).

Treasury
T 51　Lord Treasurer Southampton's General Entry book, no. 1.

War Office
W.O.4/1　　　Secretary at war (Blathwayt) out-letters.
W.O.5/3　　　Marching orders, James II.
W.O.24/5　　　Establishments, 1679.
W.O.30/48　　Survey of Inns, 1686.
W.O.89/1　　　Courts martial, 1666–97.

Southampton City Record Office
SC 2/1/8　　　Assembly book, 1642–79.
SC 2/1/9　　　Town council minute book 1679–1734.
SC 3/1/1　　　Burgess admissions book 1496–1704.

SC 9/1   Sessions rolls.
SC 9/4   Sessions papers.
SC 14/2/18   Assessment book 1647–52.
Town correspondence – miscellaneous.

Staffordshire County Record Office
Dartmouth MSS   D(W) 1778.

Dr Williams' Library, 14 Gordon Square, London
Baxter MSS.

THESES, DISSERTATIONS AND TYPESCRIPT MATERIAL

Barber, N. D., 'Richard Maijor Esq. of Hursley' (Portsmouth Polytechnic Diploma dissertation, 1979).

Carter, D. P., 'The Lancashire Lieutenancy 1660–1688' (Oxford Univ., M.Litt. thesis, 1981): a shortened version of this thesis has appeared in *Seventeenth-Century Lancashire: Essays presented to J. J. Bagley*, ed. J. L. Kermode and C. B. Phillips (Transactions of the Historic Society of Lancashire and Cheshire, lxxxii. 1982).

Challinor, P. J., 'The structure of politics in Cheshire 1660–1715' (Wolverhampton Polytechnic, Ph.D. thesis, 1983).

Davies, E., 'The enforcement of religious uniformity in England 1668–1700, with special reference to the dioceses of Chichester and Worcester' (Oxford Univ., D.Phil. thesis, 1982).

Eames, J. D., 'The poems of Sir William Kingsmill (1613–1661): a critical edition' (Birmingham Univ., Ph.D. thesis, 1982).

Gaunt, P. G. I., 'The Councils of the Protectorate from December 1653 to September 1658' (Exeter Univ., Ph.D. thesis, 1983).

Hammond, W. N., 'The administration of the English Navy 1649–1660' (British Columbia Univ., Ph.D. thesis, 1974).

Jones, J. D., 'The Isle of Wight, 1558–1642' (Southampton Univ. Ph.D. thesis, 1978).

Mildon, W. H., 'Puritanism in Hampshire and the Isle of Wight from the reign of Elizabeth to the Restoration' (London Univ., Ph.D. thesis, 1934).

Nuttall, G. F., 'Early Quaker letters from the Swarthmore MSS to 1660' (typescript calendar, 1952) copy in Bodleian Library.

Pickavance, R. G., 'The English boroughs and the King's government: a study of the Tory reaction, 1681–5' (Oxford Univ., D.Phil. thesis, 1976).

Reece, H. M., 'The military presence in England, 1649–1660' (Oxford Univ., D.Phil. thesis, 1981).

Richmond, B. J., 'The work of the justices of the peace in Hampshire, 1603–1642' (Southampton Univ., M.Phil. thesis, 1969).

Rosen, A. B., 'Economic and social aspects of the history of Winchester, 1520–1670' (Oxford Univ., D.Phil. thesis, 1975): a version of this thesis appeared in the book edited by P. Clark cited below.

Sparkes, H. J., 'The development of Portsmouth as a naval base' (London Univ., M.A. thesis, 1911).

Taylor, J. R., 'Population, disease and family structure in early modern Hampshire, with special reference to the towns' (Southampton Univ., Ph.D. thesis, 1980).

Whiteman, E. A. O., 'The episcopate of Dr Seth Ward, Bishop of Exeter (1662 to

1667) and Salisbury (1667 to 1688/9) with special reference to the ecclesiastical problems of his time' (Oxford Univ., D.Phil. thesis, 1951).

Williams, J. R., 'County and municipal government in Cornwall, Devon, Dorset and Somerset 1649–1660' (Bristol Univ., Ph.D. thesis, 1981).

PRINTED WORKS

Abbott, W. C. (ed.), *The Writings and Speeches of Oliver Cromwell*, 4 vols., Cambridge, Mass., 1937–47.

Airy, O. (ed.), Gilbert Burnett: *History of My Own Time*, 2 vols., Oxford, 1897–1900.

Anderson, H., *A Loyal Tear Dropt on the Vault of the High and Mighty Prince Charles II of Glorious and Happy Memory*, London, 1685.

Aveling, H., *Northern Catholics: The Catholic Recusants of the North Riding of Yorkshire 1558–1790*, London, 1966.

Aylmer, G. E., 'Place bills and the separation of powers: some seventeenth-century origins of the "Non-Political" Civil Service', *T.R.H.S. Fifth Series*, 15 (1965), 45–69.

   The King's Servants: The Civil Service of Charles I 1625–1642, 2nd edn, London, 1974.

   The State's Servants: the Civil Service of the English Republic 1649–1660, London, 1973.

Aylmer, G. E. (ed.), *The Interregnum: The Quest for Settlement 1646–1660*, 1972, revised edn reprint, London, 1979.

Bailey, C. (ed.), *Transcripts from the Municipal Archives of Winchester and other documents elucidating the government, manners and customs of the same city from the thirteenth century to the present*, Winchester, 1856.

Bamford, F., *A Royalist's Note-book: The Commonplace Book of Sir John Oglander*, London, 1936.

Banks, T. C. (ed.), Dugdale, Sir William, *The Antient Usage . . . of Bearing Arms*, London, 1811.

Bate, F., *The Declaration of Indulgence: a study in the rise of organized dissent*, Liverpool, 1908.

Baxter, S. B., *The Development of the Treasury 1660–1702*, London, 1957.

Beales, A. C. G., *Education Under Penalty: English Catholic Education from the Reformation to the Fall of James II 1547–1689*, London, 1963.

Beckett, J. V., 'Local custom and the "New Taxation" in the seventeenth and eighteenth centuries: the example of Cumberland', *Northern History*, 12 (1976), 105–26.

Beddard, R. A., 'The retreat on Toryism: Lionel Ducket, Member for Calne, and the politics of Conservatism', *Wiltshire Archaeological Magazine*, 72–3 (1977–8), 76–104.

Beier, A. L., 'Poor relief in Warwickshire, 1630–1660', *Past and Present*, 35 (1966), 77–100.

Beloff, M., *Public Order and Popular Disturbances 1660–1714*, London, 1938.

Bennett, G. V., 'The Seven Bishops: a reconsideration' in D. Baker (ed.), *Studies in Church History*, 15, Oxford, 1978, 267–86.

Besse, J. (ed.), *A Collection of the Sufferings of the People called Quakers*, 2 vols., London, 1753.

Bingham, C. W. (ed.), *Private Memoirs of John Potenger Esq. Comptroller of the Pipe etc. in the reign of Charles II, James II with a letter to his Grandson going to the University*, London, 1841.

Birch, T. (ed.), *A Collection of State Papers of John Thurloe*, 7 vols., London, 1742.

Black, W. H. (ed.), *Docquets of Letters Patent and other Instruments passed under the Great Seal of Charles I at Oxford in the years 1642, 1643, 1644, 1645, 1646*, 2 vols., 1837.

Boynton, L., 'Billeting: the example of the Isle of Wight', *E.H.R.*, lxxiv (1959), 23–40.

Braithwaite, W. C., *The Beginnings of Quakerism*, 2nd edn, Cambridge, 1955.

Brewer, J. and Styles, J. (eds.), *An Ungovernable People: The English and their law in the seventeenth and eighteenth centuries*, New Brunswick, 1980.

Brooks, C., 'Public finance and political stability: the administration of the Land Tax 1688–1720', *H.J.*, 17 (1974), 281–300.

Browning, A., *Thomas Osborne, Earl of Danby and Duke of Leeds*, 3 vols., Glasgow, 1944–51.

Browning, A. (ed.), *English Historical Documents 1660–1714*, London, 1953.

Browning, A. and Milne, D. J., 'An Exclusion Crisis division list', *B.I.H.R.*, 23 (1950), 205–25.

Brunton, D. and Pennington, D. H., *Members of the Long Parliament*, London, 1954.

Calamy, E., *An Abridgement of Mr Baxter's History of His Life and Times with an Account of the Ministers, Lecturers, Masters and Fellows of Colleges and School-masters who were ejected or silenced after the Restoration in 1660 By or Before the Act of Uniformity*, 2nd edn, 2 vols., London, 1713.

A Continuation of the Account of the Ministers [etc], 2 vols., London, 1727.

Calendar of the Clarendon State Papers, ed. O. Ogle and others, 5 vols., Oxford, 1872–1970.

Calendar of the Committee for the Advance of Money, 1642–1656, ed. M. A. E. Green, 3 vols., London, 1888.

Calendar of the Committee for Compounding, 1643–1660, ed. M. A. E. Green, 5 vols., London, 1889.

Calendar of the State Papers Domestic, 1640–90.

Calendar of the State Papers Venetian, vol. 31, *1657–9* (1931).

Calendar of the Treasury Books, 1660–1689.

Carpenter, E., *The Protestant Bishop*, London, 1956.

Carpenter-Turner, B., *Winchester*, Southampton, 1980.

Cary, H. (ed.), *Memorials of the Great Civil War in England 1646–52*, 2 vols., London, 1842.

Catholic Record Society Miscellany V, Catholic Record Society VI, London, 1909: 'List of Catholic Recusants in the Reign of Charles II', pp. 312–17.

Chandaman, C. D., *The English Public Revenue 1660–1688*, Oxford, 1975.

Childs, J., *The Army of Charles II*, London, 1976.

The Army, James II and the Glorious Revolution, Manchester, 1980.

The Life of Edward, earl of Clarendon being a continuation of the History of the Great Rebellion from the Restoration to his banishment in 1667, 3 vols., Oxford, 1827.

Clark, P. (ed.), *Country Towns in Pre-Industrial England*, Leicester, 1981.

Clark, P., Smith, A. G. R. and Tyacke, N. (eds.), *The English Commonwealth 1547–1640*, London, 1979.

Clarke, J. S., *The Life of James the Second, King of England [etc.] collected out of memoirs writ of his own hand together with The King's Advice to his son and His*

Majesty's Will Published from the original Stuart Manuscripts in Carlton House, 2 vols., London, 1816.

Clay, C., *Public Finance and Private Wealth: The Career of Sir Stephen Fox, 1627–1716*, Oxford, 1978.

Clifton, R., *The Last Popular Rebellion: The Western Rising of 1685*, Hounslow, 1984.

Clode, C. M., *The Military Forces of the Crown: Their Administration and Government*, 2 vols., London, 1869.

Coate, M. (ed.), *The Letter Book of John, Viscount Mordaunt 1658–1660*, Camden Society, Third Series, lxix, 1945.

Coate, W. H. (ed.), *The Journal of Sir Simonds D'Ewes from the First Recess of the Long Parliament to the Withdrawal of King Charles from London*, New Haven, 1942.

Cockburn, J. S. (ed.), *Western Circuit Assize Orders 1629–1648: A Calendar*, Camden Society, Fourth Series, 17, 1976.

Coleby, A. M., 'Military-civilian relations on the Solent 1651–1689', *H.J.*, 29 (1986), 949–61.

Collectanea Topographica et Genealogica, 8 vols., London, 1834–43.

Cruickshanks, E., Ferris, J. and Hayton, D., 'The House of Commons vote on the transfer of the Crown, 5 February 1689', *B.I.H.R.*, 52 (1979), 37–47.

Cruickshanks, E., Hayton, D. and Jones, C., 'Divisions in the House of Lords on the transfer of the Crown and other issues, 1689–94: ten new lists', *B.I.H.R.*, 53 (1980), 56–87.

The Cryes of England to the Parliament for the Continuance of Good Entertainment to the Lord Jesus his Embassadors, London, 1653.

Dalrymple, Sir John, *Memoirs of Great Britain and Ireland*, 3 vols., London and Edinburgh, 1771–88.

Dalton, C. (ed.), *English Army Lists and Commission Registers 1661–1714*, 6 vols., London, 1892–1904.

Davies, J. S., *A History of Southampton*, Southampton, 1883.

Dean, C. G. T., 'Charles II's Garrison Hospital, Portsmouth', *Proceedings of the Hampshire Field Club*, xvi (1947), 280–3.

De Beer, E. S. (ed.), *The Diary of John Evelyn*, single-volume edition, London, 1959.

A Declaration of the Committee for the Safety of the County of Southampton sitting at Winton, 9 June 1648, London, 1648.

The Declaration: together with the petition and Remonstrance of the Lords, Knights, Gentlemen, Ministers and Freeholders of the County of Hampshire, London, 1648.

Delamaine, A. (ed.), *A Volume of Spiritual Epistles being the Copies of several Letters written by the last Prophets and Messengers of God John Reeve and Lodowicke Muggleton*, London, reprint 1820.

Dingley, R., *The Deputation of Angels or the Angell-Guardian*, London, 1654.
    Vox Coeli, London, 1658.

Domestick Intelligence or News from City and Country (1679).

Don Quixote Redivivus Encountering a Barnsdoor [?London, ?1673].

Duckett, G. F. (ed.), *Penal laws and the Test Act: questions touching their repeal propounded in 1687–8 by James II*, 2 vols., London, 1882–3.

Dymond, D., *Portsmouth and the Fall of the Puritan Republic*, Portsmouth, 1971.

East, R. (ed.), *Extracts from Records in the Possession of the Municipal Corporation of the Borough of Portsmouth and from other documents relating thereto*, 2nd edn, Portsmouth, 1891.

Echard, L., *The History of England from the first entrance of Julius Caesar and the Romans to the establishment of King William and Queen Mary upon the throne*, 3 vols., London, 1707–18.

Ellis, G. A. (ed.), *The Ellis Correspondence: Letters written during the years 1686, 1687, 1688, and addressed to John Ellis Esq.*, 2 vols., London, 1829.

Ellis, H., *Pseudochristus: or A true and faithful Relation of the Grand Imposters, Abominable Practices, Horrid Blasphemies, Gross Deceits; lately spread abroad and acted in the County of Southampton, by William Franklin and Mary Gadbury and their Companions*, London, 1650.

England's Standard: To which all the Lovers of A just and speedy Settlement By A safe Parliamentary Authority in City Country and Army are desired to repair or a Remonstrance of the Lovers of the Commonwealth Inhabitants of Hampshire, London, 1659.

The English Currant (1688).

Estcourt, A. H., 'The Ancient Borough of Newtown Alias Franchville, Isle of Wight', *Proceedings of the Hampshire Field Club*, ii (1891), 96–100.

Evans, J. T., *Seventeenth-Century Norwich: Politics Religion and Government 1620–1690*, Oxford, 1979.

Everitt, A. M., *The Community of Kent and the Great Rebellion*, Leicester, 1966.

'Country, county and town: patterns of regional evolution in England', *T.R.H.S.*, *Fifth Series*, 29 (1979), 79–106.

Finlayson, M. G., *Historians, Puritanism and the English Revolution: the Religious Factor in English Politics before and after the Interregnum*, Toronto, 1983.

Firth, C. H., *The Last Years of the Protectorate*, 2 vols., London, 1909.

Furth, C. H. (ed.), *The Clarke Papers*, 4 vols., Camden Society, New Series, 1891–1901.

Ludlow's Memoirs 1625–1672, 2 vols., Oxford, 1894.

Firth, C. H. and Rait, R. S. (eds.), *Acts and Ordinances of the Interregnum 1642–60*, 3 vols., London, 1911.

Fletcher, A., *A County Community in Peace and War: Sussex 1600–1660*, London and New York, 1975.

The Outbreak of the English Civil War, London, 1981.

'The Enforcement of the Conventicle Acts, 1664–1679', in W. Shiels (ed.), *Persecution and Toleration: Studies in Church History*, 21, Oxford, 1984, 235–46.

Reform in the Provinces: The Government of Stuart England, New Haven and London, 1986.

Forster, G. C. F., 'County government in Yorkshire during the Interregnum', *Northern History*, 12 (1976), 84–104.

'Government in provincial England under the later Stuarts', *T.R.H.S.*, *Fifth Series*, 33 (1983), 29–48.

Foxcroft, H. C., *The life and letters of Sir George Savile, bart., first Marquis of Halifax, with a new edition of his works*, 2 vols., London, 1898.

Fraser, P. M., *The Intelligence of the Secretaries of State 1660–1688*, Cambridge, 1956.

Furley, J. S., *Quarter Sessions Government in Hampshire in the Seventeenth Century*, Winchester, 1937.

Gardiner, S. R., *The History of the Commonwealth and Protectorate*, 4 vols., London, 1903.

Gardiner, S. R. (ed.), *The Constitutional Documents of the Puritan Revolution 1625–1660*, 3rd edn, Oxford, revised reprint, 1979.

Gardiner, S. R. and Atkinson, C. T. (eds.), *Letters and Papers Relating to the First Dutch War 1652–4*, 6 vols., Navy Record Society, 1899–1930.

W[illiam] G[earing], *The Arraignment of Ignorance*, London, 1659.

George, R. H., 'The Charters granted to English Parliamentary Corporations in 1688', *E.H.R.*, lv (1940), 47–56.

Glassey, L. K. J., *Politics and the Appointment of Justices of the Peace 1675–1720*, Oxford, 1979.

Godwin, G. N., *The Civil War in Hampshire*, 2nd edn, Southampton and London, 1904.

Goldie, M., 'The roots of true Whiggism, 1688–94', *The History of Political Thought*, i (1980), 195–235.

Green, I. M., *The Re-Establishment of the Church of England 1660–1663*, Oxford, 1978.

Grey, A., *Debates of the House of Commons from the year 1667 to the year 1694*, 10 vols., London, 1763.

The Secret History of the Rye House Plot and Monmouth's Rebellion written by Ford, Lord Grey in 1685, London, 1754.

Gruenfelder, J. K., *Influence in Early Stuart Elections 1604–1640*, Columbus, 1981.

Gutch, J. (ed.), *Collectanea Curiosa*, 2 vols., Oxford, 1781.

Habakkuk, H. J., 'Public finance and the sale of confiscated property during the Interregnum', *Economic History Review 2nd Series*, 15 (1962–3), 70–88.

Haley, K. H. D., *The First Earl of Shaftesbury*, Oxford, 1968.

'Shaftesbury's lists of lay peers and members of the Commons 1677–8', *B.I.H.R.*, 43 (1970), 86–105.

'A List of the English Peers, c. May 1687', *E.H.R.*, lxix (1954), 302–6.

Review of Hutton (see below), *History*, 71 (1986), 155.

Hardacre, P. H., 'Clarendon, Sir Robert Howard, and Chancery office-holding at the Restoration', *Huntingdon Library Quarterly*, xxxviii (1974–5), 207–14.

Hearder, H. and Loyn, H. R. (eds.), *British Government and Administration*, Cardiff, 1974.

Henderson, B. L. K., 'The Commonwealth Charters', *T.R.H.S. Third Series*, vi (1912), 129–61.

Henning, B. D. (ed.), *The Parliamentary Diary of Sir Edward Dering 1670–1673*, New Haven, 1940.

The House of Commons 1660–1690, 3 vols., History of Parliament Trust, London, 1983.

Hibbard, C., *Charles I and the Popish Plot*, Chapel Hill, 1983.

Hill, C., *The World Turned Upside Down*, London, 1972.

Himsworth, S. (compiler) with assistance of Gwyn, P. and Harvey, J., *Winchester College Muniments: a descriptive list*, 3 vols., Chichester, 1976–84.

Historical Manuscripts Commission

Seventh Report Appendix part I.

Eleventh Report Appendix part II Southampton, Kings Lynn MSS.

Eleventh Report Appendix part V Dartmouth MSS i.

Twelfth Report Appendix part VII Le Fleming MSS.

Fifteenth Report Appendix part I Dartmouth MSS iii.

Series 17 House of Lords MSS, 1678–1688.

Series 49 Stopford-Sackville MSS.

Series 51 Leyborne-Popham MSS.

Series 55 Various Collections, ii.

Series 71 Finch MSS ii (1670–1690).

Series 72 Laing MSS.

Hoad, H. J. (ed.), *A Calendar of Portsmouth Borough Sessions Papers 1653–1688*, compiled by A. J. Willis, Portsmouth Record Society, 1971.

Holmes, C., 'The county community in Stuart historiography', *Journal of British Studies*, xix, no. 2 (1980), 54–73.

Seventeenth-Century Lincolnshire, Lincoln, 1980.

Holmes, G., *Augustan England: Professions, State and Society 1680–1730*, London, 1982.

The Electorate and the National Will in the First Age of Party, University of Lancaster, 1976.

To the Honourable the Commons House of England, the Humble Petition and Representation of the Officers and Souldiers of the Garrisons of Portsmouth, Southsea Castle, Southampton, Hurst Castle, Brownsea Castle, Weymouth, The Castles Forts and Forces in the Isle of Wight and the Garrison of Malmesbury, London, 1649.

Hore, J. P., *The History of Newmarket and the Annals of the Turf*, 3 vols., London, 1885–6.

Horwitz, H., 'Protestant reconciliation in the Exclusion Crisis', *Journal of Ecclesiastical History*, xv (1964), 201–17.

Revolution Politicks: The Career of Daniel Finch, second Earl of Nottingham 1647–1730, Cambridge, 1968.

Hosford, D. H., 'The Peerage and the Test Act: a list c. Nov. 1687', *B.I.H.R.*, 42 (1969), 116–20.

Nottingham, Nobles and the North: Aspects of the Revolution of 1688, Hamden, Connecticut, 1976.

Howard, Sir Robert, *The Committee or the Faithful Irishman*, University of Illinois Studies in Languages and Literature, vii, February, 1921.

Howell, T. B. (ed.), *A Complete Collection of State Trials and Proceedings for High Treason and Other Crimes and Misdemeanours from the Earliest period to the present time*, 23 vols., London, 1809–26.

Hughes, A. L., 'Warwickshire on the eve of the Civil War: a county community?', *Midland History*, 7 (1982), 42–72.

Hughes, E., *Studies in Administration and Finance 1558–1825*, Manchester, 1934.

Hughes, J. C., 'Town account of Yarmouth 1646–7', *Proceedings of the Isle of Wight Natural History and Archaeological Society*, i (1928), 580–3.

The Humble Petition of Many Thousands, Gentlemen, Freeholders and others of the county of Worcester, London, 1652 [3].

The Humble Petition of Many Well-Affected Persons of Somerset, Wilts and some part of Devon, Dorset and Hampshire to the Parliament of the Commonwealth of England against Tythes, London, 1659.

The Humble Petition of the Well Affected of the County of Southampton in Behalf of the Ministers of the Gospel and for Continuance of their Maintenance, London, 1653.

The Humble and Thankful Acknowledgement and Declaration of the County of Southampton, London, 1647 [8].

Hutton, R., *The Restoration: A Political and Religious History of England and Wales, 1658–1667*, Oxford, 1985.

'The making of the Secret Treaty of Dover, 1668–70', *H.J.*, 29 (1986), 297–318.

James, E. B., *Letters Archaeological and Historical Relating to the Isle of Wight*, 2 vols., London, 1896.

James, M., *Social Problems and Policy in the Puritan Revolution*, London, 1930.

Jenkins, P., 'Anti-popery on the Welsh Marches in the seventeenth century', *H.J.*, 23 (1980), 275–91.

' "The Old Leaven": the Welsh roundheads after 1660', *H.J.*, 24 (1981), 807–23.

The Making of a Ruling Class: The Glamorgan Gentry 1640–1790, Cambridge, 1983.

Jessopp, P. A. (ed.), *The Lives of Rt. Hon. Francis North, Baron Guilford; the Hon. Sir Dudley North and the Hon. and Rev. Dr John North by Roger North*, 3 vols., London, 1890.

Jones, G. F. T., *Saw-Pit Wharton*, Sydney, 1967.

Jones, G. H., 'The Irish fright of 1688: real violence and imagined massacre', *B.I.H.R.*, 55 (1982), 148–53.

Jones, J. D., 'The Isle of Wight and the Revolution of 1688', *Proceedings of the Isle of Wight Natural History and Archaeological Society*, v (1965), 468–82.

The Royal Prisoner, 2nd edn, Trustees of Carisbrooke Castle Museum, 1974.

Jones, J. R., 'Shaftesbury's "Worthy Men", a Whig view of the Parliament of 1679', *B.I.H.R.*, 30 (1957), 232–41.

'James II's Whig collaborators', *H.J.*, 3 (1960), 65–73.

The First Whigs, London, 1961.

The Revolution of 1688 in England, London, 1972, reprint 1984.

Jones, J. R. (ed.), *The Restored Monarchy*, London, 1979.

Jose, N., *Ideas of the Restoration in English Literature 1660–71*, London, 1984.

The Journals of the House of Lords.

The Journals of the House of Commons.

Keeler, M. F., *The Long Parliament, 1640–1*, Philadelphia, 1954.

Kennett, W., *A Register and Chronicle Ecclesiastical and Civil*, London, 1728.

Kenyon, J. P., *The Popish Plot*, London, 1972.

Kenyon, J. P. (ed.), *The Stuart Constitution 1603–1688*, Cambridge, 1966, reprint 1980.

The Kingdomes Intelligencer (1661).

Lacey, D. R., *Dissent and Parliamentary Politics in England, 1661–89*, New Brunswick, 1969.

Lamont, W. M., *Godly Rule: Politics and Religion 1603–1660*, London, 1969.

Landau, N., *The Justices of the Peace 1679–1760*, Berkeley, 1984.

Latham, R. and Matthews, W. (eds.), *The Diary of Samuel Pepys*, 11 vols., London, 1970–83.

A Letter from a Person of Quality to his Friend in the Country (1675).

A Letter sent from one Mr Parker a Gentleman, dwelling at Upper Wallop in Hampshire, to his friend a Gentleman in London, wherein is related some remarkable passages there, as of a Battell fought between the Inhabitants of the County, and of the Cavaliers about the settlement of the Militia and Commission of Array, London, 1642.

The London Gazette.

Luttrell, N., *A Brief Historical Relation of State Affairs from September 1678 to April 1714*, 6 vols., Oxford, 1857.

Lyon Turner, G. (ed.), *Original Records of Early Nonconformity under Persecution and Indulgence*, 3 vols., London, 1911–14.

Mannyngham, T., *A Sermon at the Funeral of Sir John Norton, bart., lately deceased. Preached in the Parish Church of East Tysted in Hantshire*, London, 1687.

Marsden, R. G., 'The Vice-Admirals of the coast', *E.H.R.*, xxii (1907), 736–57.

Marsh, J., *Memoranda of the Parishes of Hursley and North Baddesley in the County of Southampton*, Winchester, 1808.

Marshall, L. M., 'The levying of the Hearth Tax, 1662–1688', *E.H.R.*, li (1936), 628–46.

Matthews, A. G., *Calamy Revised*, Oxford, 1934.

Walker Revised, Oxford, 1948.

Matthews, W. (ed.), *Charles II's Escape from Worcester: A Collection of Narratives Assembled by Samuel Pepys*, London, 1967.

McGregor, J. F. and Reay, B. (eds.), *Radical Religion in the English Revolution*, Oxford, 1984.

Meekings, C. A. F. (ed.), *Dorset Hearth Tax Assessments 1662–1664*, Dorchester, 1951.

Analysis of Hearth Tax Accounts 1662–5, List and Index Society, vol. 153, 1979.

Analysis of Hearth Tax Accounts 1666–1699, List and Index Society, vol. 163, 1980.

Mercurius Aulicus (1644).

Mercurius Publicus (1660, 1661, 1662).

Mereweather, H. A. and Stephens, A. J., *The History of the Boroughs and Municipal Corporations of the United Kingdom*, 3 vols., 1835: reprinted by Harvester Press, Brighton, 1972.

Miller, J., *Popery and Politics 1660–1688*, Cambridge, 1973.

'The Militia and the Army in the Reign of James II', *H.J.*, 16 (1973), 659–79.

James II, a Study in Kingship, Hove, 1977.

'The Potential for "Absolutism" in Later Stuart England', *History*, 69 (1984), 187–207.

'The Crown and the Borough Charters in the reign of Charles II', *E.H.R.*, c (1985), 53–84.

The Moderate Intelligencer (1646).

Morrill, J. S., *Cheshire 1630–1660, County Government and Society during the English Revolution*, Oxford, 1974.

The Revolt of the Provinces: Conservatives and Radicals in the English Civil War, 1630–1650 (1976), 2nd edn, London, 1980.

Morrill, J. S. (ed.), *Reactions to the English Civil War, 1642–9*, London, 1982.

A Collection of Autograph Letters and Historical Documents formed by Alfred Morrison, printed for private circulation, 3 vols., 1893–8.

Murrell, P. E., 'Bury St Edmunds and the Campaign to pack Parliament, 1687–8', *B.I.H.R.*, 54 (1981), 188–206.

The Names of the Justices of the Peace As they stand in Commission in their several Counties this Michaelmas Terme 1650, London, 1650.

Newman, P. R., *Royalist Officers in England and Wales 1642–60*, New York and London, 1981.

'The Royalist Officer Corps 1642–1660: army command as a reflection of social structure', *H.J.*, 26 (1983), 945–58.

Nickalls, J. L. (ed.), *The Journal of George Fox*, Cambridge, 1952.

Nickolls, J. (ed.), *Original Letters and Papers of State Addressed to Oliver Cromwell concerning the Affairs of Great Britain from the year 1649 to 1658 Found among the Political Collections of Mr John Milton*, London, 1743.

Nuttall, G. F. and Chadwick, O. (eds.), *From Uniformity to Unity 1662–1962*, London, 1962.

Ogg, D., *England in the Reign of Charles II*, 2nd edn, 2 vols., Oxford, 1955.

Oliver, H. J., *Sir Robert Howard (1626–98): A Critical Biography*, Durham, N.C., 1963.

Ollard, R., *Man of War: Sir Robert Holmes and the Restoration Navy*, London, 1969.
   The Image of the King: Charles I and Charles II, London, 1979.

Overton, J. H., *The Nonjurors: Their Lives, Principles and Writings*, London, 1902.

Pares, R. and Taylor, A. J. P. (eds.), *Essays Presented to Sir Lewis Namier*, London, 1956.

The Parliamentary Intelligencer (1660).

To the Parliament of the Commonwealth of England . . . the Humble Petition and Representation of Divers well affected of the County of Southampton, London, 1659.

Penney, N. (ed.), *Extracts from State Papers relating to Friends* (1664–1669) (Supplement to the Journal of the Friends Historical Society, no. 10, 1912).

Pennington, D. H. and Thomas, K. V. (eds.), *Puritans and Revolutionaries*, Oxford, 1978.

Petition of the County of Southampton [that the votes of the popish lords may be taken away, and all papists confined], London, 1641 [2].

Plumb, J. H., *The Growth of Political Stability in England 1675–1725*, London, 1967, reprint 1977.

Pocock, J. G. A. (ed.), *Three British Revolutions, 1641, 1688, 1776*, Princeton, 1980.

Powley, E. B., *The English Navy in the Revolution of 1688*, Cambridge, 1928.

Priestley, E. J., 'The Portsmouth Captains', *Journal of the Society for Army Historical Research*, 55 (1977), 154–64.

A Proclamation For the Better Encouragement of Godly Ministers and others and their enjoying their dues and Liberty according to law, London, 1658.

P.R.O. Lists and Indexes no. ix: Sheriffs of England and Wales to 1831, 1898.

Reay, B., 'The Quakers, 1659, and the Restoration of the Monarchy', *History*, 63 (1978), 193–213.
   'The authorities and Early Restoration Quakerism', *Journal of Ecclesiastical History*, xxxiv (1979), 69–84.
   The Quakers and the English Revolution, London, 1985.

Return, so far as it can be obtained, from the Year 1213 up to the Year 1696, of the Surnames, Christian Names and Titles of all Members of the Lower House of Parliament of England, Scotland and Ireland with the name of the Constituency Represented and Date of Return of each, London, 1878, pt. i.

Reynell, C., *The Fortunate Change: Being a Panegyric to His Sacred Majesty King Charles the Second Immediately on his Coronation, being the 23 of April 1661*, reprinted in *Fugitive Tracts*, 2nd series, 1600–1700, ed. W. C. Hazlitt, privately printed, 1875, no. xxiv.
   The True English Interest, London, 1674.

Robbins, C., 'The Oxford Session of the Long Parliament of Charles II, 9–31 October 1665', *B.I.H.R.*, 21 (1946–8), 214–24.

Roberts, S. K., *Recovery and Restoration in an English County: Devon Local Administration 1646–1670*, Exeter, 1985.

Roots, I. (ed.), *'Into Another Mould': Aspects of the Interregnum*, Exeter, 1981.

Roseveare, H., *The Treasury 1660–1870: The Foundations of Control*, London, 1973.

Rushworth, J. (ed.), *Historical Collections*, 2nd edn, 7 vols., London, 1721.

Russell, Lord John (ed.), *Letters of Rachel, Lady Russell*, London, 1853.

Russell, P. D. D. (ed.), *The Hearth Tax Returns for the Isle of Wight 1664–1674*, Isle of Wight County Record Office, 1981.

Rutt, J. T. (ed.), *The Diary of Thomas Burton*, 4 vols., London, 1828.

Sacret, J. H., 'The Restoration government and municipal corporations', *E.H.R.*, xlv (1930), 232–59.

St Barbe, C. (ed.), *Records of the Corporation of New Lymington*, London, 1848.

Sainty, J. C., *Officials of the Secretaries of State 1660–1782*, London, 1973.

Samuels, A., 'The Itchen navigation: a lawyer's view of the legal issues', *Proceedings of the Hampshire Field Club*, xxxviii (1982), 113–20.

Saunders, A. D., *Hampshire Coastal Defence since the Introduction of Artillery*, Royal Archaeological Institute, 1977.

Scantlebury, R. E. (ed.), *Hampshire Registers*, i, Catholic Record Society, XLII, 1948.

Schoenfeld, M. P., *The Restored House of Lords*, The Hague, 1967.

Schwoerer, L. G., *'No Standing Armies!' The Anti-Army Ideology in Seventeenth-Century England*, Baltimore and London, 1974.

The Declaration of Rights of 1689, Baltimore, 1981.

Shaw, W. A., *A History of the English Church during the Civil Wars and under the Commonwealth*, 2 vols., London, 1900.

Slack, P., *The Impact of Plague in Tudor and Stuart England*, London, 1985.

Smith, N. (ed.), *A Collection of Ranter Writings from the 17th Century*, London, 1983.

Smith, R. M. (ed.), *Land, kinship and life-cycle*, Cambridge, 1985.

Smith, T. S., 'The persecution of Staffordshire Roman Catholic Recusants 1625–60', *Journal of Ecclesiastical History*, xxx (1979), 327–51.

Speck, W. A. and Gray, W. A., 'Computer analysis of poll books: an initial report', *B.I.H.R.*, 43 (1970), 105–12.

Stagg, D. J. (ed.), *A Calendar of New Forest Documents: The Fifteenth to the Seventeenth Centuries*, Hampshire Record Society, 1983.

The Statutes of the Realm, V (1819).

Steele, R., *A Bibliography of royal proclamations of the Tudor and Stuart sovereigns and of others published under authority, 1485–1714*, 2 vols., Oxford, 1910.

Stephens, W. R. W. and Madge, F. T. (eds.), *Documents Relating to the History of the Cathedral Church of Winchester in the Seventeenth Century*, 2 vols., Winchester, 1897.

Styles, P., 'The evolution of the Law of Settlement', *University of Birmingham Historical Journal*, 9 (1963–4), 33–63.

To the Supream Authority The Parliament of the Commonwealth of England The humble Petition of divers well affected Persons Inhabitants of the Town of Portsmouth and Places Adjacent, London, 1659.

Taylor, J., 'Plague in the towns of Hampshire: the epidemic of 1665–6', *Southern History*, 6 (1984), 104–20.

Thirsk, J. (ed.), *The Agrarian History of England and Wales: vol. 4: 1500–1640*, Cambridge, 1967.

Tomlinson, H. C., 'The Ordnance Office and the Navy 1660–1714', *E.H.R.*, xc (1975), 19–36.

Guns and Government, London, 1979.

Tomlinson, H. C. (ed.), *Before the Civil War: Essays on Early Stuart Politics and Government*, London, 1983.

A True Catalogue or An Account of the several places and most eminent persons in the three nations, and elsewhere and by whom Richard Cromwell was proclaimed Lord Protector of the Commonwealth of England, Scotland and Ireland, London, 1659.

Tubbs, C. R., 'The development of the small-holding and cottage stock-keeping economy of the New Forest', *Agricultural History Review*, xiii (1965), 23–39.

Underdown, D., *Royalist Conspiracy in England 1646–1660*, New Haven, 1960.

'Party management in the recruiter elections 1645–8', *E.H.R.*, lxxxiii (1968), 235–64.

Pride's Purge: Politics in the Puritan Revolution, Oxford, 1971.

Somerset in the Civil War and Interregnum, Newton Abbott, 1973.

'The chalk and the cheese: contrasts among the English clubmen', *Past and Present*, 85 (1979), 28–48.

Revel, Riot and Rebellion: Popular Politics and Culture in England 1603–1660, Oxford, 1985.

Urquhart, M., *Sir John St Barbe Bt of Broadlands*, Southampton, 1983.

Verney, F. P. and M. M. (eds.), *Memoirs of the Verney Family during the Civil War, during the Commonwealth and from the Restoration to the Revolution*, 4 vols., London, 1892–9.

Ward, W. R., 'The Office of Taxes, 1665–1798', *B.I.H.R.*, 25 (1952), 204–12.

Warner, G. F. (ed.), *The Nicholas Papers*, 3 vols., Camden Society, New Series, 1887–97.

Webb, J., *The Siege of Portsmouth in the Civil War*, revised edn, Portsmouth, 1977.

Webb, S. S., *The Governors-General: The English Army and the Definition of Empire 1569–1681*, Chapel Hill, 1979.

' "Brave Men and Servants to his Royal Highness": the household of James Stuart in the evolution of English imperialism', *Perspectives in American History*, viii (1974), 55–80.

Welch, E., *Southampton City Charters*, Southampton, 1966.

Western, J. R., *The English Militia in the Eighteenth Century*, London and Toronto, 1965.

Monarchy and Revolution: The English State in the 1680s, London, 1972.

Whetham, C. D. and W. C. D., *A History of the Life of Colonel Nathaniel Whetham*, London, 1907.

[Whitelocke, B.], *Memorials of the English Affairs*, London, 1682.

Whiteman, E. A. O. (ed.) (with assistance of M. Clapinson), *The Compton Census of 1676: a critical edition*, Records of Social and Economic History, New Series, X, published for the British Academy by Oxford Univeirsity Press, 1986.

Whitley, W. T., 'Early Baptists in Hampshire', *Baptist Quarterly: New Series*, i (1923), 223–5.

Woolrych, A., *Penruddock's Rising 1655*, Historical Association Pamphlet, 1973.

Commonwealth to Protectorate, Oxford, 1982.

Worden, A. B., *The Rump Parliament*, Cambridge, 1974.

'Toleration and the Cromwellian Protectorate' in W. Shiels (ed.), *Persecution and Toleration: Studies in Church History*, 21, Oxford, 1984, 199–233.

Worden, A. B. (ed.), *Edmund Ludlow: A Voyce from the Watch Tower: Part Five 1660–1662*, Camden Society, Fourth Series, 21 (1978).

Worsley, Sir R., *The History of the Isle of Wight*, London, 1781.

Wrightson, K., *English Society 1580–1680*, London, 1982.

Young, E., *Two assize sermons preached at Winchester. The first February 26 1694, James Hunt of Popham Esq., being Sheriff of the County of Southampton. The second July 14 1686, Charles Wither of Hall Esq., being Sheriff*, London, 1695.

Yule, G., *Puritans in Politics: Religious Legislation of the Long Parliament 1640–1647*, Sutton Courtenay Press, 1981.

INDEX

257